SCOTLAND'S WINTER MOUNTAINS

The Challenge and the Skills

MARTIN MORAN

DAVID & CHARLES
Newton Abbot   London   North Pomfret (Vt)

For all winter mountaineers
of the future

British Library Cataloguing in Publication Data

Moran, Martin, 1955–
    Scotland's winter mountains: the challenge
and the skills.
    1. Scotland. Mountaineering
    I. Title
    796.5′22′09411

    ISBN 0-7153-9096-1

Text and illustrations © Martin Moran 1988

Typeset by Typesetters (Birmingham) Ltd,
Smethwick, West Midlands
and printed in Great Britain
by Butler & Tanner Limited, Frome and London

for David & Charles Publishers plc
Brunel House   Newton Abbot   Devon

Published in the United States of America
by David & Charles Inc
North Pomfret   Vermont 05053   USA

CONTENTS

PREFACE

In winter, Scotland's mountains form Britain's last stronghold of true wilderness, where the insidious advance of modern civilisation is for once halted and effectively repulsed. The winter mountain domain is both stunningly beautiful and wildly challenging: vast tracts of high snow-bound country, savage cliffs streaked with ice and a thousand secluded corries gripped by frost. Here is an environment which heartens all who seek the path of nature and irresistibly beckons the adventurous spirit.

This book is written essentially as a celebration, firstly of the winter mountains themselves and secondly of the remarkable passion with which humans have pursued their secrets during the past century. It therefore divides conveniently into two parts.

Part I details the building-blocks of the winter environment – the climate, the weather and the many forms of snow and ice. However, the most thorough enumeration and explanation of all these facets still fails to capture the overall appeal of the mountains, for in their winter totality they possess an unfathomable beauty that must lead us to suspect a greater hand in the ordering of the natural world.

Part II examines the wealth and distinct traditions of Scottish winter-mountaineering activities which continue to diversify and grow in popularity. While ski-touring is an important part of this movement, downhill skiing is excluded from coverage. The book is intended for those who raise their sights to the high and wild places, while piste skiing is quite separate in its appeal and environmental impact.

It is to be hoped that the text is revealing and historically informative, instructive without being doctrinaire and above all entertaining. May it assist activists to develop their skills and expand their ambitions, while giving the armchair reader a clue as to why sane and rational human beings should at the darkest season of the year forsake all comforts and throw themselves to the mercy of the mountain storm.

The book may be read sequentially or used as a technical reference source, for which the Subject Index provides a detailed means of access. Throughout the text, the technical content is wholly focused on the winter aspect of the mountaineering skills. Basic methods which are common to all-year-round mountaineering are not discussed in detail, although general climbing terms are defined in the Glossary.

Finally, may I emphasise that winter mountaineering is at all levels a serious pursuit. Everyone who ventures above the snow-line must be aware of the potential hostility of the weather and of the hazards and difficulties even of simple foot travel. As opposed to summer fell-walking and rock-climbing, winter hillgoers must entertain a higher level of risk and discomfort in their excursions. However, the greatest joy of winter mountaineering, whether it be walking, climbing or skiing, lies in developing the skill, experience and judgement to quantify and control the hazards, while penetrating to the heart of Scotland's incomparable natural domain. If this book helps you some way along that path, it will have served its purpose.

Martin Moran
April, 1988

ACKNOWLEDGEMENTS

I should like to express my thanks and appreciation to all those who have lent their time, skill and knowledge to the preparation of this book, especially:
Rab Anderson, Bob Barton, Bill Brooker, Sam Crymble, Arthur Collins, Ken Crocket, Gordon Davison of Berghaus, Mick Fowler, Eric Langmuir, Hamish MacInnes, Jimmy Marshall, Bill Murray, Derek Pyper, Dick Tabony and Tom Weir, and all those who have submitted photographs for use.

In particular, I am indebted to the Scottish Mountaineering Club for permission to use its *Journal* extracts, library facilities and slide collection, without which the text would have been much the poorer in its breadth and quality.

I should like to record my special thanks to Clarrie Pashley for his photographic assistance and expert advice, to Ric Singerton for his excellent illustrations, to my wife Joy for her typing of the manuscript and unstinting support during the writing project, and finally to my contributors, Jim Barton, Helen Charlton, Alan Hunt and Andy Nisbet, whose talent and expertise have amply covered the gaps in my own experience, and who have written so well and with such enthusiasm.

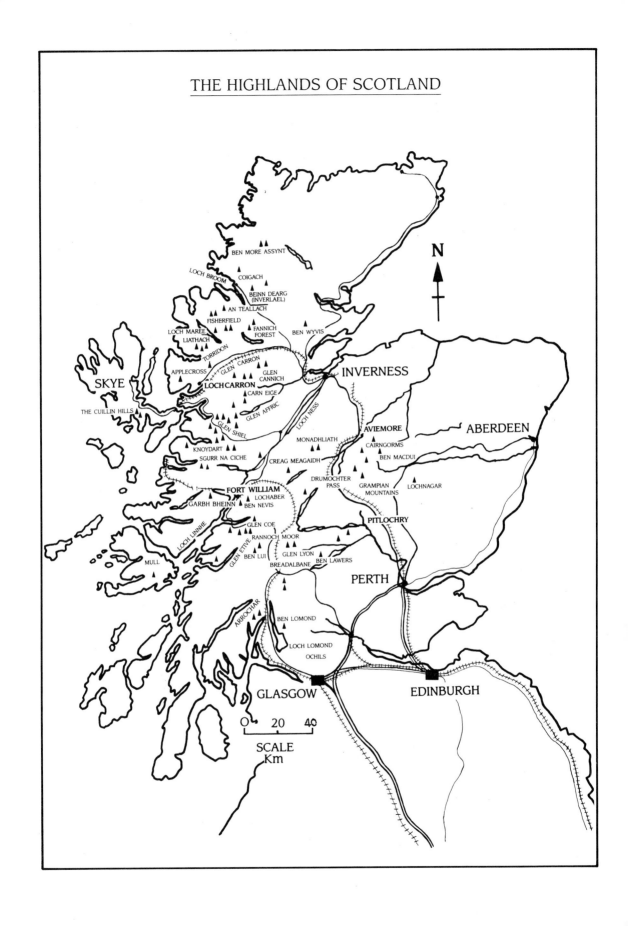

THE HIGHLANDS OF SCOTLAND

N

BEN MORE ASSYNT

LOCH BROOM
COIGACH
BEINN DEARG
(INVERLAEL)
AN TEALLACH
FISHERFIELD
LOCH MAREE
FANNICH
FOREST
BEN WYVIS
LIATHACH
TORRIDON
APPLECROSS
GLEN CARRON
GLEN
CANNICH
INVERNESS
SKYE
LOCHCARRON
CARN EIGE
THE CUILLIN HILLS
GLEN AFFRIC
LOCH NESS
AVIEMORE
ABERDEEN
GLEN SHIEL
MONADHLIATH
CAIRNGORMS
KNOYDART
BEN MACDUI
SGURR NA CICHE
CREAG MEAGAIDH
DRUMOCHTER
PASS
LOCHNAGAR
FORT WILLIAM
GRAMPIAN
MOUNTAINS
GARBH BHEINN
LOCHABER
BEN NEVIS
PITLOCHRY
GLEN COE
LOCH LINNHE
RANNOCH MOOR
GLEN ETIVE
GLEN LYON
BEN LUI
BEN LAWERS
MULL
BREADALBANE
PERTH
ARROCHAR
BEN LOMOND
LOCH LOMOND
OCHILS
GLASGOW
EDINBURGH

O   20   40

SCALE
Km

INTRODUCTION

A Winter on the Hills – Part I

8 October: Winter's First Touch

I am a lucky man. For me the northward drive into the Highlands is a homeward drive. Its beauty and variety never palls, and today it spoke richly of autumnal softness. Fresh sunlight danced on Edinburgh's cobbled streets, playful showers raced across the patchwork fields of central Fife and Dunkeld's textured woodland glowed in a pageant of sylvan colour. Yet on Drumochter Pass I met a wall of lashing rain and only at Inverness emerged from the downpour, blinking in the glaring shafts of light as the evening sun bobbed in and out from the ragged clouds.

Stopping for petrol, I stepped out into a whipping wind that cut straight to the bone. Mellow autumn was forgotten. That wind had the unmistakable bite of winter. In just 240km I had entered another world.

With the car heater on full vent, I sped westwards on the road to Achnasheen. The barren flats of Strath Bran now filled the scene ahead. The roadside heather had faded to a dirty pink and withered fronds of bracken flapped in the wind. Above, a pearly sun sank down behind leaping tongues of livid cloud, which at first obscured all sight of the hills. But then in submission to nature's whim, they tore free and streamed off the tops; and there, up on the boiling pyramid of Sgurr a'Ghlas Leathaid, I spied a speckled coat of white, cut clean at a base of 700m. My heart jumped a beat. The first snows had arrived!

Looking up the strath on the right, the higher ridge of Fionn Bheinn made a clearer smudge of chalky white against the evil sky. So it was lying thick already up there. As sudden as their revelation, the whitened hills were swallowed up once more by the encroaching bank of cloud. A gusty squall blattered on my windscreen and a rough night gathered.

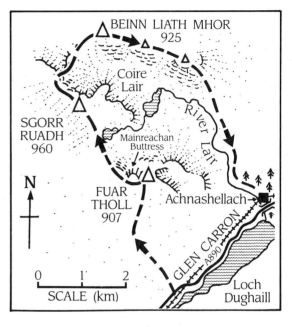

11 October: Coire Lair by Moonlight

On this particular night during winter's first premature visit to the Highlands, the moonbeam cast across the bedroom walls allowed no easy slumber, but instead gave flight to schemes of fancy. At 3am these wakeful dreams were met with the necessary resolve and I left a warm bed, scoured round for clothes, boots, a torch, some hunks of cake and an ice-axe, then made off to the hills and freedom.

A pillow of white cloud hung low in Glen Carron, harbouring a black pond of darkness in the valley floor, while the hillsides above glistened with dew frost under the glare of the full moon. Fuar Tholl is our nearest big hill and gives a fast climb from the Carron road. In an hour, I reached its whitened upper dome. The snow lay deep in the hollows and its surface crust crunched under my feet.

The summit itself was deserted, but reverberated with the bellows of rutting stags, which rose from each and every hollow and entwined into a cacophony of haunting sound. Over on the mountain's central top, I tiptoed out on a snowy ledge to the brink of the Mainreachan Buttress. The corrie beneath was as dark as an inkwell, its tiny lochan discernible as a slightly blacker blotch in the void. So steep is this pillar of ancient sand that one could dive clear and free to join the marauding herds below. The awful thought sent me clambering back onto the gleaming summit snows. I ran across to the western top to thrill at the sight of the profiled buttress edge, which tore the night sky asunder in a single massive slice.

The onward links to Sgorr Ruadh and Beinn Liath Mhor make the circuit of Coire Lair, which is one of Scotland's roughest and finest winter rounds. I now hastened along their snowy crests lest fatigue should regain its ground and recapture my spirit.

Dawn came on the final summit as a burning orange glow over the wild heights of Monar. But as soon as the sun had risen over the horizon, it disappeared behind a blanket of cloud, though still casting the palest emerald glow over the grassy slopes in the lower corrie after it had forsaken the tops. To the north, the moon hazed and faded above the film of cloud and now dropped forgotten towards its daytime sleep behind the Hebrides. Already the frost had lifted. The verglassed sandstone slabs cracked and trickled into life and the crispness of night suddenly vanished from the snow. As the day's lazy embrace stretched up from the glens, my thoughts turned to home and breakfast. It was time to be gone.

7 December: Midwinter on Beinn Eighe
For a week the hills have been stilled and silenced by frost. The dusting of snow on the tops has remained as light and powdery as it fell, while the burns are dried and the springs stifled at source. In its brief daily flight skimming across the southern sky, the sun has barely pierced the mountains' wrap of dense cold air. Dawn comes at eight and the day has ebbed to twilight by the back of three. Through the refrigerated night, only the slow and

graceful orbit of a fully-fledged moon suggests that the universe possesses the least inclination or capacity for change.

This morning the quartzite caps of Beinn Eighe and Liathach shone with a metallic glare under its waning beam. Simon and I crept through the darkened glen between the two, boots crunching the frozen fines of the pebbled track and heels jarring on the hardened peat. The going was fast and we needed the speed for a climb in Coire Mhic Fhearchair in the solstice month is a climb against time.

After the two-hour march, emergence at the corrie lip gives a sudden thrill. A sandstone plinth is breasted and there she is! The Triple Buttress, chiselled and honed into Cyclopean splendour, thrusts high above the corrie's quiet lochan and spears the pale dawn sky. One cannot but feel an intruder in this vault of timeless majesty, yet no mountaineer can ignore the focal challenge of the trident cliff.

The Central Buttress is a classic line of alpine length and quality, complex and committing and with the magic aura of the grade V tag. The crux lies right at the top, to be tackled when the light is short and the stakes are high. Today, the rocks were but lightly sprinkled with snow, save for the final tower which bore a whiter hue that warned of hard conditions. Some routes choose themselves and we were soon embarked on its lower sandstone tier.

At once our total concentration was demanded, for each little step on the lower walls proved deceptively obstinate, requiring any or all of the mixed climbing techniques from bare-fingered rock-climbing, through crampon balancing on verglas smears, to full-blooded axe-hooking on turfs. Only at belay stances could we spare a look at our wider surrounds – a frozen canvas of ice-glazed lochan, plunging cliff and bare brown strath. The scene deserved a more leisurely contemplation than we could afford it. Yet when one's every faculty is engrossed and inspired on a climb such as this, the memory can capture all the atmosphere and grandeur of time and place in the most fleeting glance.

As one moves onto the second tier of the

buttress, there is a sudden change of geology from rounded sandstone to square-cut quartzite, which imparts a unique variety to the climb. Simon led on through the 50m band, levering up on crampon tips and whitened finger joints, stopping only to place protection and shake fresh blood down through the wrists. Within an hour we had breached the barrier and were romping up easy snows and blocks to the base of the final tower.

Its 60m defences are vertical, but looked so well furnished with ledges and cracks that their conquest seemed the merest formality. With the security of over three hours' daylight at our disposal, we allowed ourselves a rest here, but the chill soon began to bite and forced resumption of the climb.

We were wise not to have lingered a minute longer, for the tower flattered to deceive. Hidden ledges materialised as smooth slabs coated in snow, while those friendly cracks turned into verglassed drainpipes quite beyond our powers of adhesion. Several alternative lines of advance were presented, each requiring prolonged scrutiny and struggle before a choice could be made. That precious time began to fly. The pressure was on.

While the leader sweated with effort and tension, the second shivered and stamped as the frost clamped down. 300m below, the shadows quickly darkened the corrie floor. Our concerns switched from the trivial to the serious. No longer bothered that we might miss the summit sunset, we now wondered whether we would be unwilling spectators to tomorrow's sunrise from a bivouac! The whole lower buttress will be long forgotten when the thought of those crucial few feet still raises the hairs down the spine.

A final frost-caked wall barred our exit. Simon entered a groove in its centre, bridged wide and pulled over. A minute later, a yell of relief that was muffled by the frost floated down to my stance. At the stroke of darkness I joined him on the buttress crest. For a minute I steamed with heat before the dry cold attacked, seizing the breath away and stiffening dampened clothes.

As we stumbled and slid down the frozen screes towards the glen, the moon made a shy ascent through pencil-lines of cloud in the east, casting a pale and austere light over the Fisherfield peaks. Once more, the mountain giants were encased in midwinter sleep, unmoved and unblemished by our brief incursion into their domain.

31 December: The Year's Last Tempest
The eastern sky dawned violet, but within an hour its flag of hope was shredded by grasping paws of black cloud, which chased in from the Atlantic. Then a cloak of mist settled over the Glen Shiel hills and nipped daylight in the bud.

For yet another day, the mountains retreated into a gloomy contemplation and we resigned ourselves to a soaking. A fortnight of the like had washed all traces of November's snows from the western peaks and in their place white foaming burns poured down off the heights. Hogmanay was to bring no redemption.

A start at the top of the Cluanie watershed averted an early confrontation with angry waters and gave quick access to the South Shiel Ridge, which sends down a choice of spurs to this point. We took the stalking path onto the slender spur of Maol Chean Dearg.

The warmth of the day made a nonsense of the season. Sheltered from any wind on the ascent, we sweated liberally inside our waterproof shells, thinking more of wet Augusts than sparkling new years. However, on reaching the summit, such comparisons were removed in an instant by a wild southerly gale. A wall of cloud churned volleys of hailstones into our faces and suddenly we were cowering in the blast and scurrying for shelter in the lee of an outcrop.

To have continued would have been grim if not impossible, so we turned our backs and let the wind blow us down to the glen. The storm was rising. No longer was this a dismal rainy day that could be written off the memory by tomorrow's dawn. Great curtains of hail poured onto the north sides of the ridge, turning to stair-rods of icy rain as they swept downhill.

The sluggish waters on the watershed were transformed into bubbling ponds on our return.

The burn we had leapt dry-shod in the morning was now crossed thigh-deep with arms linked for support. A thousand torrents plunged down from the heights. The gale roared up the glen shaking the conifer trees, and the River Shiel thundered headlong down it, only to overspill across the level flats long before the sea. Loch Duich was a raging mass of crested waves. The whole world was in motion, the frost and calm that we hope of winter a dream apart from the overwhelming reality of the present.

4 February: Trapped on the Tombstone
A milky white mist hung around the cliff, deadening all distant sound. Vision was restricted to a two-tone mosaic of black verglassed rock and snow-draped ramps and gangways. Of either the top or the base of this awesome precipice naught could be seen. Occasionally, a downward flurry of spindrift or snowflakes would break the ambient gloom. The only noises to hear were our own vague scufflings and the dull metallic clink of crampon points on rock. We might have inhabited another planet, so isolated was our perch.

Dour, soulless winter weather that gave no warmth or comfort, an unclimbed winter cliff that offered no chink of weakness in its tilted armoury and pale daylight that was fast receding – we were up against the odds, struggling for a toehold of hope.

Simon shuffled and stamped on his tiny stance and pondered the worth of our assorted belays, while I headed diagonally left where the horizon seemed lowest, yearning for an easement of the angle that might herald success. Yet no move could be hurried. Each hold needed careful cleaning and testing before a pull, each crack demanded patient probing until a nut or piton could be placed and after every move a glance at the watch showed that precious day was sliding from our grasp.

A violent heave over one overhang only brought my nose hard up against another. I was forced to traverse left and down a little, leaving runners far behind, clasping snow-caked blocks and hooking bits of grass and heather while my heels hung over space. Having nervously scrabbled onto a suspended ramp of snow, I spied a big cracked block, then above a shallow frosted groove and above again the dusky sky where the angle must surely ease.

Could this be the key? Darkness was 20 minutes away. There was no time for a protection search. I clawed up the bulging block, 15m out from the last runner, and wrapped my last long sling over the top. Only now the shallow groove appeared as a bulging crackless groove. I saw that my stock of gear was running low and remembered that my head-torch lay down in the sack with Simon. Suddenly, I was wavering at the brink of mental control. Beyond and below lay a bottomless abyss. A moment's common sense and the upward drive was halted. I gratefully accepted what security I had, sacrificed the light and belayed from the block.

Simon joined me as the darkness became complete and there we were, two shivering pinpoints of torchlight in the fog, hanging from the same poised block just 9m from success. I gamely probed the frost-furred rocks above, hacked at the rotten ice on the right and scraped at an ice-pearled clump of grass, but it was merely a gesture. The acceptance of defeat was mirrored in my every move.

So we spun down into the black pit below in two long questioning abseils, then crept off sideways on a sneaking ramp to gain the ground we'd left ten hours before. There remained only a cruel haul back over the top of the peak and a silent descent through the soft fresh snow and night mist. The sudden croak of a grouse on the moor and a beam of car headlight weaving up the glen as we dropped out of the cloud, brought us back to the land of the living.

But we remained lost in thoughts, each spinning a cocoon of comfort around jarring knees and tired eyes with dreams of what might have been. Yet, far from feeling humiliation, there was a strange contentment in knowing that, high up on our local hill, there lay one dark forbidding place where we could stretch to our limits of skill and yet still meet our match.

PART I
THE CHALLENGE

Plate 1 'Chiselled and honed into cyclopean splendour' – the Triple Buttress of Coire Mhic Fhearchair, Beinn Eighe

1

HEWN FROM THE ICE

Scotland's Mountain Winter – A Climatic History

The Scottish mountain winter is unique in Britain's natural environment. The Highland winter harbours the last existing remnants of true subarctic conditions in our temperate and maritime climatic regime, and in their winter raiment of snow the mountains are projected in our imaginations a little closer to the glacial past, to the epochs when they were besieged by ice-cap and glacier. For one brief season, we can grasp the hand of time and turn it back to an era whose passing the mountaineer perhaps regrets.

To envisage the Highlands massif at the height of the last major ice advance just twenty thousand years ago is to dream of vast and silent snowfields spanning the high plateaux with only the higher peaks of the Cairngorms poking through; to transform the western glens into ice-choked chasms tumbling off the heights in gigantic séracs and breaking into bergs over the Hebridean seas; to fill the eastern straths with the broad slicks of gently flowing glaciers; to stand in the sea-filled trenches of Lochs Nevis and Hourn and conceive of a 3,000ft (914m) thickness of ice churning and grinding overhead; and to clasp the high corries in perpetual frost and a sheath of everlasting snow. Such visions of nature's awesome power at once rid the notion that the Highlands are changeless hills, and the images seem much more tangible when the mountains are seen today under their winter cloak.

But of course, the mountains were not simply smothered by the ice. Their present variety, complexity and all the more dramatic features of their profiles were in the very process of creation as the moving ice carved and sculpted its pathways. Without its work, our modern scenic legacy would be so much the poorer. The Highlands would comprise a series of plateaux, long-

forgotten relicts from the Caledonian era of mountain-building, their summits a rolling sweep of dip and swell, and their sides dissected gently and predictably into pleasing vales. So it is to the Ice Ages that we owe thrill of the saw-toothed Cuillin peaks, the sudden brink of the Cairngorm corrie, the loch-strewn chaos of Fisherfield and the sheer smoothed cliffs of Ben Nevis and Glencoe. And it is back towards the Ice Age that the winter experience entices the mountaineer.

THE LINGERING SNOWS

From their peak, Scotland's glaciers ebbed and eventually disappeared. Geoff Dutton conjectured as to the time and place of their final demise:

> Our glaciers have gone. The last sulking remnants of the mighty Laggan-Spey glacier died out somewhere above the CIC Hut on a warm September afternoon 9,000 years ago. The half-hardy perennial drifts flowering occasionally since then are no substitute. Our corries are silent and empty; their meltwaters dried and vanished.[1]

However, the retreat was by no means uninterrupted. There were two resurgences of ice before that fatal September afternoon, the second being the Lomond readvance of around ten thousand years ago (Fig 1). In the Lomond phase, the ice was largely confined to the corries, where it pulled and plucked the cliffs into their present delineation and scooped out their hollows and lips, which now hang high above the deeper glens. Only in the major basins were there still confluent glacier systems, and this was the period when great melt-water lakes such as those of Glen Roy

Fig 1 SUCCESSIVE LIMITS OF THE LAST ICE-SHEET IN SCOTLAND with probable dating (*from Sissons, 1967*)[2]

A •—•— A   Aberdeen–Lammermuir readvance (possibly equates to the maximal extent *c*20,000 years ago)

P ————P   Perth readvance (*c*13,000 years ago)

L ⟨---⟩ L   Lomond readvance (10,000–11,000 years ago)

——→   →   Directions of ice movement

were shored up in side valleys by more powerful main valley glaciers.

Nor is it correct to imagine that the climate has continued a progressive warming since the glaciers vanished. Fig 2 shows that the post-glacial maximum of world temperature is thought to have been reached around six thousand years ago and that the current long-term trend is one of renewed cooling. If this is true, it would be more correct to regard Scotland's present semi-permanent snow-beds as harbingers of the next glaciation than the lingering relics of the last Ice Age.

The few dirty patches of near-perennial snow have aroused a volume of research and emotion out of all proportion to their extent or scenic significance. Fig 3 lists the major known sites of these snows together with the assessment of their reliability by those who have watched and recorded their flux from year to year.

The existence of perennial snow is one of the defining characteristics of the subarctic climate which in Britain is now confined to Scotland's higher mountain summits and particularly the Cairngorms whose altitude of 1,200m (3,900ft) and inland location create a climatic environment as close to that of the tundra of northern Scandinavia as is found anywhere in Western Europe. The Cairngorm winter is the hardest and most prolonged of any region of the Highlands and hence there is the greatest likelihood that snowfields will persist in the shaded nooks of their high corries. The top 300m (1,000ft) of Ben Nevis harbours the only comparable climate for snow-patch survival in Britain.

So what determines whether winter's snows will linger through the spring, summer and autumn seasons? Fig 4 itemises the main factors on the accumulation and melting (ablation) of snow-packs. Snowfall volume and low temperatures are obviously important, but do not by themselves guarantee persistence. Wind-packing and avalanche accumulation have an equal influence upon the depth and hardness of the snow-pack that emerges from the winter season. Indeed, it is arguable that the beds in Observatory Gully of Ben Nevis are not true snowfields, being largely comprised of avalanche fall-out, and that only the high open snows of the Cairngorms derive from pure snowfall.

The rate of snow-pack lowering through the summer months on the Ben Macdui drifts was estimated by D. L. Champion as 1cm (0.4in) per day for each degree above freezing point of the daytime temperature. However, Gordon Manley's work on the Nevis beds concluded that there is no necessary relation between absolute temperature

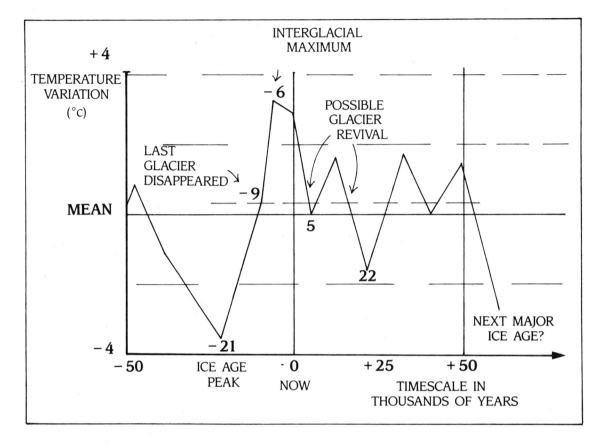

Fig 2 CLIMATIC CHANGE: PAST AND
FUTURE (adapted from Lamb, 1982).[3] Based on
astronomical theory of orbital cycles. Past
pattern agreed to oxygen isotope measurements.
Future projection suggests the possibility of
glacier revival in Scotland in 5,000 or 16,000
years' time

are already small in extent and vulnerable to both
ground and air warmth.

Undoubtedly, these tiny remnants of each past
winter will continue to be watched with close
interest and even the most disciplined scientist
must kindle the fond hope that, within his
lifetime, they will burgeon in size and spawn the
nascent glaciers of the future.

and snow-pack persistence, the abnormally warm
summers of both 1955 and 1960 failing to melt the
snows. The influences of air humidity, wind, the
daily freeze-thaw cycle and the amount of direct
sunlight, must all be considered additionally.

There is a general concurrence that two periods
are crucial to the longevity of the snows. In March
and April, substantial fresh snowfalls are needed –
the volumes of the early winter being of lesser
significance – and the prevailing temperatures of
September and October must be relatively cool to
prevent rapid further shrinkage when the fields

CYCLES AND EXTREMES

An overall rise in mean winter temperature of
some 10–12°C (18–21.6°F) has accompanied
Britain's emergence from the Ice Age. However,
within the shorter span of historical time, a series
of short-term climatic cycles can be discerned
which confuse the general trend. Cycles at intervals of 2,000, 200 and 100 years with temperature
amplitudes between 0.5 and 2.0°C (0.9 and 3.6°F)
have been identified. These temperature variations have had major impacts on both the course

Fig 3 SCOTLAND'S SEMI-PERMANENT SNOWFIELDS

Details compiled for those locations which have been specifically studied or observed. Other semi-perennial sites are likely to exist in the high Cairngorms.

Location	Altitude	Aspect	Reliability
BEN NEVIS Observatory Gully, below apex of Tower and Gardyloo Gullies.	1,160m (3,800ft)	NE	'Snow Book' in CIC Hut maintained from 1933 to 1970 reported its disappearance in 10 out of 38 years; the largest most persistent bed on Nevis.
Observatory Gully, under Observatory Buttress.	1,080m (3,550ft)	NNE	Unlikely to survive after early September.
Observatory Gully, foot of Point Five Gully beside Rubicon Wall.	1,050m (3,450ft)	NE	Unlikely to survive after early September.
Gullies Nos 2–5, Coire na Ciste.	980–1,100m (3,200–3,600ft)	NE	Persistence noted only in abnormally cool or snowy years.
AONACH MOR (LOCHABER) Under summit on E cliffs	1,190m (3,900ft)	E	Not closely observed, but occasional survival has been noted.
BRAERIACH (CAIRNGORMS) Garbh Choire Mor, under Sphinx Ridge	c1,075m (3,500–3,600ft)	NE	'Never known to wholly disappear' – Seton Gordon, 1912. Between 1933 and 1970 it failed to survive in only four years – 1933, 1947, 1959 and 1969. The most likely spot in Britain for glacier regeneration.
BEN MACDUI Garbh Uisge, ½km (0.9 mile) NE of summit; known as the 'snowy corrie'	c1,150m (3,700–4,000ft)	NNE	A true open snowfield rather than a gully bed and therefore exposed to summer sunshine. Not observed over a long period but known to survive through many years.
Feith Buidhe, 2km (1.2 miles) N of summit	1,080m (3,500ft)	E	Easterly aspect and lower altitude makes survival less likely.
CAIRN GORM Ciste Mhearaidh, 1km (0.6 mile) NE of summit	1,080m (3,500ft)	E	Open aspect; persists only in exceptional years.

of human history and the mountain environment. Where, then, does the modern mountain winter stand in this tangle of curves and trends?

The last mini-climatic recession in modern history was the 'Little Ice Age' between 1550 and 1850. At its height in the seventeenth century, observational evidence suggests that temperatures in Scotland were as much as 2°C (3.6°F) below their present level. A Royal Society report of 1675 spoke of:

. . . a little lake in Strathglass at Glencannich in a bottom between the tops of a very high hill . . . This lake never lacks ice on it in the middle even in the hottest summer.[3]

The permanent snowfields were considerably more extensive than now. In 1770, Thomas

Fig 4 THE LIFE OF MOUNTAIN SNOW-BEDS: CONTROLLING FACTORS

RATE OF ACCUMULATION

AMOUNT OF SNOWFALL	Initial depth is a false guide because of the highly variable air content of fresh snow. The *density* of the initial snow-cover is the crucial determinant of the eventual snow-pack depth.
WIND DRIFTING AND PACKING	In Scotland, the role of the wind is essential in the building of deep permanent beds. Without wind redeposition, the snow-cover remains thin and evenly distributed.
AVALANCHE DEBRIS	Localised accumulations of densely packed ice-blocks in high corrie and gully-bed sites.

RATE OF ABLATION ie, both the melting and removal of the snow

WINTER THAWS	Rapid melting of fresh snow which has not had time to compact and harden under a freeze/thaw cycle. Timing of thaws is therefore important.
WARMTH OF SUMMER	The *average* warmth of summer is the main overall control over the rate of ablation; lowering rate of around 1cm (0.4in) per day per degree C (1.8°F) of daytime temperature above zero (32°F) observed on Scottish beds.
DAILY TEMPERATURE RANGE	A night/day routine of freeze/thaw in the spring months greatly hardens the snow-pack and raises its resistance to all forms of ablation.
DIRECT SUNLIGHT (INSOLATION)	Although fresh snow reflects as much as 85 per cent of incoming solar radiation, direct sun deeply penetrates the pack, especially if it is initially soft, creating slush which is quickly lost by evaporation. Therefore, the semi-perennial beds have minimal exposure to the sun.
AIR HUMIDITY	Rate of evaporation from snow-cover falls as the humidity rises due to increased atmospheric vapour pressure. Therefore, a warm moist spell will thaw the pack, but its moisture will be retained unless it runs off as liquid.
CLOUD COVER	High humidity but also an insulating effect, keeping the snow warm and soft. A night-time cloud-cover is especially significant in preventing any freeze-hardening of the snow-pack.
RAINWASH	Surface and basal erosion of snowfields, but only important if snow is initially soft.
WIND	Warm air-flow convection at the snow surface increases the rate of evaporation from the pack during summer months by continually resupplying drier air. Any wind also raises the *rate* at which the snow temperature adjusts to that of the atmosphere, accelerating or retarding the thawing process.

Pennant noted perennial snow on Ben Wyvis north of Inverness, which at 1,046m (3,431ft) is considerably lower in altitude than the higher haunts of the Cairngorm corries, which themselves were observed as holding sizeable summer snowfields by several eighteenth-century travellers.

So perhaps there was less exaggeration than might be thought in the comment of an eighteenth-century English army officer quartered in the Highlands who wrote to a friend in London bemoaning that: 'as for the climate, there are nine months of winter, three months of spring and there is no summer at all'.[4]

It is, however, open to debate whether these snows were sufficient to compact into ice and form glaciers. A 2°C (3.6°F) diminution in average temperature is theoretically sufficient to sustain glaciers in Scotland, and David Sugden's work on lichen dating on the moraine debris in the Garbh Choire of Braeriach has suggested that a tiny ephemeral corrie glacier may have subsisted there as late as 1810. He also found similar evidence for six other glacier sites in the Cairngorms at around 1740.

However, thermometer readings for central England for the seventeenth to eighteenth centuries averaged only 0.5–1.0°C (0.9–1.8°F) below today's levels. How, then, could Scotland's temperatures have been so much lower during these centuries? Certainly, Gordon Manley was sceptical that glaciers could have existed so recently:

> Undoubtedly there were groups of cool years in the 17th, 18th and early 19th centuries . . . but their duration appears insufficient to lead to revival in Scotland.[5]

By contrast, in the period from 1900 to 1960, the Highland winters were, on average, warmer than during any comparable period since the early Middle Ages, yet these sixty years were an era of remarkable activity and advances in snow- and ice-climbing and skiing. However, reading between the lines of great winter deeds during the harder seasons of this period, one can find regular complaints of prevailing wet, warm and windy weather. Of a February visit to the Western Highlands in 1905, S. A. Gillon lamented:

> . . . the climate is becoming less continental and more maritime or insular, or whatever is the term for dampness, unseasonable mildness and more than feminine changeableness.[6]

A local native Scot would have compressed this description into a single word – 'dreich'. Unfortunately, it still remains essential to the vocabulary of the winter mountaineer. Some winter months in the first half of this century deserve the term 'drenching' rather than 'dreich', especially on the west where the maritime Atlantic influence is so much stronger. The rain gauge near Kinlochquoich in the wildlands between Glen Garry and Knoydart collected 111cm (44in) in January 1916 and another 127cm (50in) in March 1938, which is approximately half of their average annual totals and double the annual average rainfall for eastern England. Within these exceptional months are contained single 24-hour storms of 10–12cm (4–5in), an intensity that could only be matched by the tropical monsoon. Variously dreich and drenched, Kinlochquoich suffered a wholly appropriate fate, for it was finally drowned by the extension of Loch Quoich for hydro-electricity generation in the 1950s.

Mild snowless winters were also experienced further east in the Cairngorms. The great naturalist Seton Gordon remembered the remarkable sight of stags grazing on the snow-free summit of Braeriach in mid-January. He also recalled the confusion that warm winters caused to the bird populations. Miscalculating the seasons, they would make for their spring nesting haunts on the high moors, and the 'wild vibrating whistle' of the curlew, so evocative of spring, might be heard on the hills in the dark depths of January.

While little further warming would have been needed to wipe out the season of dependable snow-and-ice mountaineering as we know it, in fact over the last twenty-five years the winters in Scotland have become progressively cooler and, thankfully, preserved our sport. Recent winters have also been notable in producing more diverse extremes of weather than hitherto reported. Dramatic news headlines of the format 'the worst blizzard' or 'the biggest freeze for XX years' are becoming tiresome to the public, but they do have substance – for example:

1978–9 The severest winter and lowest temperatures recorded in two hundred years over much of northern Europe.

1981–2 4–14 January: a prolonged freeze. The temperature at Braemar plunged to a UK record minimum of −27.2°C (−17°F) on the 10th, and sea lochs surrounding the Cuillin of Skye were partially iced up during this period.

1983–4 Winds of over 161kmph (100mph) and blizzards on 21 January produced the worst Highland storm in living memory.

1986–7 10–20 January: another severe continental freeze, temperatures in Eastern Europe fell to new record minima; the lowest daytime temperatures of the century in England and Wales were recorded; Cairngorm summit recorded −16.5°C (2.3°F) on the 12th, the lowest in ten years of automatic readings.

Interspersed between these seasons of prolonged refrigeration, there were still some remarkably mild winters, notably in the early 1970s. The *Scottish Mountaineering Club Journal* of 1971 reported several sightings of the dreaded 'midge' on the Allt a'Mhulinn track to the cliffs of Ben Nevis during February and 1974–5 was the mildest winter on English records since 1834. 1980–1 was another warm and snow-free season, with mean temperatures 1.2°C (2.1°F) above normal and Lochnagar's great cliffs were almost entirely bare of snow in the last days of January.

The greater volatility and cold of recent winters is undoubted, has added new excitement as well as hazard to winter mountaineering and stimulated great debate as to what is happening to our climate. The greater cold is clearly related to the increasing incidence of Scandinavian and continental anticyclones over the country which

effectively block the ingress of moister Atlantic air and are so stable as to persist unbroken for several weeks at a time. Conversely, the exceptional mild winters have been dominated by Atlantic weather systems and barely a peep has been allowed to the continental 'highs'. Between the two, there seems no longer to be a happy medium. An 'average' winter simply does not exist.

WHAT AND WHEN IS THE MOUNTAIN WINTER?

While the 'calendar winter' is strictly defined between the 21 December solstice and the 21 March equinox, the 'mountain winter' falls into no convenient mould. To many hillgoers, winter is the period during which a snow- and ice-cover will be encountered during the greater part of a mountain excursion, and it is patently true that the calendar and mountain winters are rarely coincident. Remarkable and frustrating mild spells can intervene at any time within the calendar span, and there is an equal probability that full snow and ice conditions will suddenly develop outside it.

For instance, the 1984–5 calendar season when I was engaged on the ascent of all the Munros, was abnormally snowless. Cold but dry weather persisted through most of January and February in the North-West Highlands. The lying snows were shallow and discontinuous and so were rapidly removed by a spring-like heatwave between 22 and 28 February, plus the rain-wash of an extremely wet and windy spell in early March. The hills emerged completely bare and seemingly ready for springtime's greening, yet successive snowfalls in the last week of March regenerated winter conditions that persisted into April, a fatal avalanche accident occurring on Ben Wyvis on 31 March. The spring of 1986 repeated this pattern. On 25 April, I climbed Tower Ridge on Ben Nevis as a pristine flute of fresh-fallen

Plate 2 Haunt of the Permanent Snows – Garbh Choire Mor Braeriach in Winter (*Brian Findlay*), and on 1 October 1984, with sizeable perennial drifts (*Andrew Nisbet*)

snow from bottom to top. In every year the summer visitor must remember that blizzards are regularly encountered on the high Cairngorms in May and June.

Equally probable is an early autumnal freeze-up. On an early ascent of the Tower Ridge in September 1896, W. Inglis Clark and J. A. Parker found the last 180m (600ft) of the cliffs plastered with snow and before commencing the climb were obliged to borrow an ice-axe from the then-staffed summit observatory whose doorway was found barred with 1m (3ft) long icicles. Although a true winter climb in September is but a freak, a sustained spell of snow and ice conditions can be anticipated with certainty at some stage between mid-October and early December.

Fig 5 summarises the incidence of snow falling on the summit of Ben Nevis in the period 1895–1904 as recorded by the observatory staff. While there is but minimal chance of a snow-storm in July and August, in any of the other ten months of the year, an appreciable proportion of precipitation comes as snow. The 'extreme maximum' curves proves that the 'mountain winter' may begin as early as September and end as late as June, while the 'minimum' trace shows that it may all but disappear in a mild January when 60 per cent of precipitation can be rain and this on Scotland's highest acre of ground.

Winter conditions are not only determined by snow falling, but also by the amount of snow lying on the tops. The accumulation of snow on the high summits tends to be progressive after mid-January, periods of thaw lowering the snow level only briefly before further falls pile up. Thus, the maximum depth of snow-cover lags considerably after the big midwinter blizzards. Fig 6 lists the Ben Nevis Observatory records of maximum snow depths on the summit together with the dates attained between 1884 and 1903. The greatest depths vary widely, from 137cm (54in) in the leanest to 361cm (142in) in the snowiest years, and in only four of these twenty years was the maximum reached within the calendar season, a date in mid-April more usually marking the

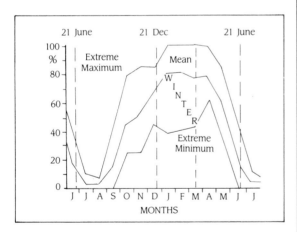

Fig 5 THE PERCENTAGE OF MONTHLY PRECIPITATION FALLING AS SNOW ON BEN NEVIS SUMMIT (1,344m/4,406ft), 1895–1904 (from the observatory records as summarised by A. S. Thom, 1974).[7] Extreme maxima and minima are the individual months with the highest and lowest percentages within the nine-year period of observation

Fig 6 BEN NEVIS SUMMIT: MAXIMUM SNOW DEPTHS RECORDED, 1884–1903 *From summit observatory records, Buchan et al 1905*[8]		
Year	Depth	Date of Max Depth
1884	358cm (141in)	28 May
1885	360cm (142in)	10 April
1886	312cm (123in)	10 April
1887	175cm (69in)	28 April
1888	195cm (77in)	6 May
1889	144cm (57in)	24 April
1890	243cm (96in)	25 April
1891	142cm (56in)	4 May
1892	188cm (74in)	9 March
1893	167cm (66in)	17 March
1894	322cm (127in)	13 March
1895	137cm (54in)	13 April
1896	193cm (76in)	28 March
1897	203cm (80in)	7 May
1898	195cm (77in)	1 March & 15 May
1899	170cm (67in)	19 April
1900	226cm (89in)	15 April
1901	231cm (91in)	16 April
1902	157cm (62in)	3 April
1903	317cm (125in)	18 May
20-year mean: 221cm (87in); mean date: 15 April		

Fig 7 SNOW-COVER AND ALTITUDE Observations of Annual Number of Days Snow Lying at Three Scottish Mountain Locations *(From Manley 1971)*[9]						
Altitude	457m (1,500ft)	610m (2,000ft)	762m (2,500ft)	914m (3,000ft)	1,066m (3,500ft)	1,220m (4,000ft)
GLEN LYON (Ben Lawers range) (24 seasons, 1946-7 to 1969-70)	75	100	125	150	—	—
BEN NEVIS (11 seasons, 1950-1 to 1960-1)	66	103	139	167	202	220
BEN NEVIS (Summit Observatory) (1883-1904 approx)	—	—	—	—	—	230
CAIRNGORMS (13 seasons, 1955-6 to 1967-8) (figures to end of May only)	79	116	153	178	191	200

turning point when the rate of melt exceeds that of accumulation.

At lower altitudes, the snow-cover is increasingly transient. Fig 7 gives observations of the total number of days of snow lying on average each year in three Highland locations. At a height of 450m (1,500ft) the expectancy is just 70 days per year compared to over 200 on the 1,220m (4,000ft) summits. Furthermore, the date of maximum depth usually occurs much earlier at lower levels, where melting is predominant from the start of March onwards. Thus, in early spring conditions become strongly polarised to the higher slopes and the sheltered corries, where the snows lie at their thickest, while the lower slopes might be completely bare. Indeed, much of the early pioneering of winter climbing was accomplished during April, when the most continuous cover for ski-touring on the high tops of the Cairngorms can be generally guaranteed.

Therefore, a definition of 'winter' solely by snow-cover would include the first half of the calendar spring, but would ignore other factors intrinsic to the challenge of the mountains. The darkness of the December solstice, coupled with the prevalent storminess of those bleak harsh months on its either side, make strong claim on the mountaineer's conscience. One cannot pretend that to ski shirt-sleeved over the Cairngorm plateau in April, under the sun's full glare and with the assurance of its company for a full twelve hours, equates to the late-December battle with the oncoming storm and night, however much more snow there might be underfoot.

The 'mountain winter' is therefore a complex and elusive hybrid. Fickle in nature, it can arrive unannounced at any time twixt October and May and vanish again without trace. However, if the probabilities of snow-cover, low temperatures, icing and blizzard are combined with the known allowances of daylight, then the four true months of maximum elemental hostility are surely those from December to March, and within this period the real mountain winter might most likely be found and challenged.

WHITHER NOW?

But looking to the future, will our 'mountain winter' extend, intensify or disappear within the coming generations? The air is rife with rumours. Trends have been projected forward and the profound events of recent years interpreted in several different ways.

And is there a likelihood that the hidden crevasses of resurgent glaciers will menace the steps of the winter mountaineer within the foreseeable future? Gordon Manley postulated that

the creation of a moving glacier required the accumulation and compaction of firn snow (perennial beds) into an ice layer approaching 45m (150ft) in depth. His work on the snow-beds of Ben Nevis led him to conclude that it would take a continuous succession of fifteen summers with a mean temperature 2°C (3.6°F) below its present norm to produce such a condition. The change required seems nominally small and the prospect of seeing an 'Observatory Glacier' on Ben Nevis within our lifetime is tantalising, but Manley firmly squashed such optimism:

Nothing in our knowledge of the behaviour of the atmosphere from past instrument records allows us to contemplate such a continuous succession.

The long-term projection of the cooling of world temperature based on orbital variables in Fig 2 (see p 14) indicates that the temperature threshold for glacier revival will not be passed until either five thousand or sixteen thousand years hence, but even this expectation is highly doubtful. Scotland's climatic patterns may be quite different from average global trends. Furthermore, glacier revival depends not just on temperature but on the supply of snow. If the cooler climate is also drier, then glacier development may be further delayed.

However, some experts dispute the impression of smooth, unhurried change which is given by the trace of a graph. They argue that climatic flux is a rapid process, a sudden destabilisation triggered when certain environmental thresholds are exceeded. By this theory, long static periods are separated by short phases of violent and momentous change, of which the current period of climatic turbulence could be an example. One research group concluded that the swing between warm and glacial epochs can occur within the space of three hundred years. One threshold thought to be crucial is the stability of the antarctic ice-cap, which, if undermined by pro-

longed melting, may suddenly surge forward to exert a new cooling effect on the world's oceans. Cooling could also be accelerated by the increasing reflectivity of the earth's surface if the areal extent of snow- and ice-cover expands. Random environmental disturbances, such as cooling produced by volcanic-dust veils in the atmosphere, may also lead to these thresholds.

Man's own activities are currently posing a major threat to the natural climate, chiefly through carbon dioxide (CO_2) air pollution from the burning of fossil fuels. CO_2 release raises the capacity of the lower atmosphere to absorb infrared radiation emitted from the earth's surface and could produce a 'greenhouse effect' on our climate. On current trends of fossil-fuel usage, atmospheric CO_2 will reach double its pre-industrial level by 2050, which it has been estimated would raise average surface temperatures by 1.9°C (3.4°F). On this basis, Scotland's mountain winter would be but a fond memory in a hundred years' time. The current cooling of our winters disputes these prophecies of doom, but the 'greenhouse effect' might indeed be protecting the climate from an even greater cooling than has already been detected. Other scientists question the greenhouse theory. As well as preventing the earth's heat getting out, the excess CO_2 in causing extra cloud-cover might be preventing the sun's radiation from getting in.

There is no simple answer to these conflicting theories. The current cooling could be a twenty-year cycle, fickle and short-lived, or else the precursor of profound climatic change on the geological time-scale. Meanwhile, we watch with interest, but must revert to our dreams to project the future Highland winter.

Will the ice once more be chipping at the Cuillin pinnacles, tumbling the quartzite piles of the Torridon peaks into oblivion, and gouging the glens of the west still deeper? Or will the winter season be a brief release from stifling heat and subtropical humidity, the hills once more swathed in trees, the cliffs carpeted with moss and slime, never again to feel the pinch of frost or the peck of crampons and ice-axe? In the greater book of time, Scotland's present mountain winter is but the briefest clause.

Plate 3 Heavy snows on the Forcan Ridge of The Saddle, Glen Shiel, in April

2

STORM-LASHED OR FROST-BOUND

Winter Weather on the Mountains*

From the booming tempests to the wonderful days of silent frost, the Highlands' winter weather is a compendium of fear, fascination and utter delight to the mountaineer. To select its most distinctive features one would be wrong to focus upon its extremes of temperature. Although notable by the norms of lowland Britain, the Highlands do not match the severities of the high altitude or continental ranges and, while the winter winds are certainly remarkable on hills of such small stature, it does not uniquely mark them out from other mountains of the world.

Rather, it is the unpredictability and the variability of the winter weather that gives the Scottish mountains a singular stamp of quality, an infinite range of colours and moods and a scenic impact out of all proportion to their modest height. Grim and cloud-swathed one day, gleaming and sparkling white the next, our hills have a lure and mystique that alpine ranges thrice the height cannot surpass. Some may complain of our mountain weather as unkempt and fickle, but this very variety equally inspires awe and yearning in all who look to the winter hills.

The mixture of weather conditions and their rapid changes also poses both challenge and hazard to the winter hillgoer. The alpine and continental winter climate generally divides into prolonged spells when one type of weather is predominant, and the conditions, however severe, can be predicted with some accuracy.

By contrast, a single mountain day in Scotland may start with a calm frost of −10°C (14°F) and a

good forecast, yet end with a blizzard of wet sleet, which catches the climber unprepared. Stable periods do occur in each season, but changeability is more the norm. Rarely can our weather be wholly trusted. Furthermore, our maritime mountain climate frequently produces wet, windy and cool conditions that are more difficult to survive than the extreme dry cold typical of the greater ranges.

WEATHER RECORDS ON THE MOUNTAIN-TOPS

Our knowledge of the weather conditions on the Scottish summits derives partly from the personal observations and descriptions of mountaineers themselves, but more importantly from the records of mountain meteorological stations. Without some data from the summits we would be forced into subjective guesswork as to the actual temperatures, wind speeds and precipitation experienced on the tops.

Thus, we are lucky in Scotland to have the legacy of twenty years of complete weather records from the Ben Nevis summit observatory which operated from October 1883 to October 1904. Given the great cost and the enormous physical difficulties of taking weather readings throughout the year at an altitude of 1,344m (4,400ft), the observatory was a remarkable accomplishment, a monument to Victorian philanthropy and scientific zeal. Its data forms the most comprehensive British record of all weather elements in such an environment.

The observatory scheme was instigated by the Scottish Meteorological Society but its building

*For the theory and detailed data of Scotland's mountain weather, please read this chapter in conjunction with Appendices IV and V.

cost of £5,000 was funded by public appeal together with the larger part of its annual maintenance of £1,000. Constructed and operational within a year of conception, the observatory was manned continuously. In winter, its staff had to endure both isolation and privation as their quarters were pounded by the weather. Theirs was man's first-ever prolonged experience of the hostility of winter on the Scottish summits.

One of the observers, W. T. Kilgour, remembered the storm of 22 November 1898 as the most gruelling of all, a wind of over 161kmph (100mph) coupled with a driving blizzard. Despite barring every door and window 'fully a ton of snow sifted inside into the lobby and passages'. The average indoor temperature fell to −3°C (26.6°F) and just 2m (6ft) away from the kitchen fire the thermometer could struggle no higher than −1°C (30.2°F).[1] The severity of the conditions outside can be left to the imagination. Taking readings in bad weather exposed the staff to considerable danger as well as hardship, for the cliffs of Nevis's north face were only yards away. At the height of one February gale, John Begg noted:

At 4pm the notebook for the observation was torn in two and blown away . . . At 6, 7 and 8pm the observers went out at the tower door on a long rope, and had to be hauled back.[2]

The observatory was finally closed through lack of funds. From 1905 to 1978 mountain-weather statistics are highly fragmentary and such records as were obtained are owed to the dedicated work of a few individuals. Most notably, a small station was sited close to the summit of Ben Macdui by Pat Baird during 1956. Over 182kg (400lb) of instruments and equipment were man-hauled to the site and erected during that most hostile period of late December and January. Thereafter, weekly visits, mostly by Baird himself, were made to recalibrate the graphs, rewind clocks, reink pens and measure snow-depth changes. In winter, these stints were a prolonged battle against the cold. Baird remembered one particular occasion when:

. . . determined to have warm feet while standing for eight hours on site, I foolishly went up in felt-lined sealskin boots. On the gentle hard snow-slope covering the Etchachan path I could get no grip, and while carrying a delicate instrument couldn't afford to slip. I was forced to cut steps with a snow shovel but fortunately no other climber was around to witness this feat.[3]

On 23 March he found the anemometer encased in a solid pillar of ice 2.4m (8ft) high with a rime crystal nearly 1.2m (4ft) in length growing out from the windward side of the screen. Keeping a station running in these conditions required as strong a love for the mountains as the cause of science.

Modern technology has fortunately overcome the need for such heroics. Since March 1977, an automatic weather station (AWS) has operated with little interruption on the summit of Cairn Gorm at an altitude of 1,245m (4,084ft) (Plate 4). The details of its functional design and its summarised winter records are given in Appendix IV. Automatic operation is enabled by the housing of the sensors and instruments within a thermostatically heated unit, from which they are deployed outside at half-hourly intervals to sample the weather. This prevents icing up and wind damage. Readings are broadcast direct via VHF transmission so that visits to the station are required only once every six weeks for routine maintenance.

Together, the Ben Nevis archives and the Cairn Gorm records provide an objective picture of mountain weather through the winter, against which mountaineers can match and compare their personal experiences.

TEMPERATURES

The November to March average and record minimum temperatures for the Ben Nevis and Cairn Gorm stations are as follows:

	Ben Nevis (1884–1903)	Cairn Gorm (1978–9–1986–7)
Average	−3.8°C (25.1°F)	−3.0°C (26.6°F)
Record Minimum	−17.4°C (0°F)	−16.5°C (2.3°F)
	(6 Jan 1894)	(12 Jan 1987)

Plate 4 The Automatic Weather Station (AWS) on the summit of Cairn Gorm (1,245m). Note the rime icing on the instrumentation (*by courtesy of Heriot-Watt University*)

While −3°C (26.6°F) is sufficiently low to present a slight risk of frost-bite and at −10°C (14°F) bare skin will stick to a metal surface, these figures are not inhuman by worldwide standards. −20°C (−4°F) is a normal winter temperature on the high Alps or the Scandinavian tundra plateaux.

Nor do the extremes of summit temperatures match the depths of frosts which are experienced in the adjacent glens when inversion conditions are present (Fig 8). The sinking of cold dense air into valley floor 'reservoirs' occurs during stable anticyclonic spells when there is no wind to mix the air. Thus, when Braemar experienced Britain's record known minimum temperature of −27.2°C (−16.9°F) on 10 January 1982, Cairn Gorm's summit was 'basking' in a mere −12.6°C (9.3°F).

February is generally the coldest month both on the summits and in the glens. Braemar's average daily minimum from 1951 to 1980 was −3.1°C (26.4°F) in February and that on Cairn Gorm from 1978 to 1987 was −6.0°C (21.2°F) while the longest continuous frost recorded on Cairn Gorm, when the temperature never rose above zero night

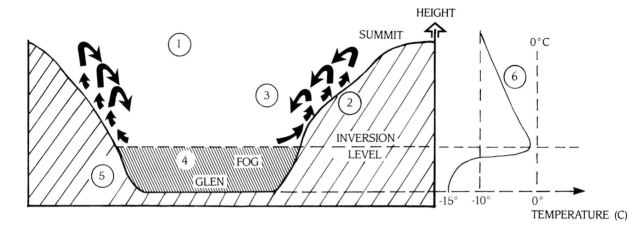

Fig 8 THE VALLEY TEMPERATURE INVERSION:

1 Calm, clear, stable upper atmosphere
2 Intense night-time cooling of mountain slopes by outward radiation from the snow surface
3 Cooled surface air layers are colder, denser and therefore more heavy than the outer atmosphere. Thus they tend to sink and displace any warmer valley air-pockets
4 Cold air reservoir formed glen bottoms often condensing into thick fog – temperature typically −15°C (5°F)
5 U-shape of glacial glens traps the cold air
6 Normal atmospheric lapse above the inversion to −10°C (14°F) at summits

or day, was thirty-six days between 27 January and 3 March in the superb winter of 1986.

The feature of temperature of most importance to the mountaineer in determining both snow conditions and personal comfort is its range and variability over varying time-scales:

Diurnal (ie, night:day): The daily range is greatest in clear stable weather when the daytime receipt of sunshine (insolation) and night-time heat loss by radiational cooling are maximised. These effects are more pronounced on south-facing slopes and in the valleys than on the summits where cooling breezes are prevalent even in a settled anticyclonic spell. The diurnal range is much reduced in windy or overcast weather when radiational heat exchanges are small. On 12 January 1987 when Cairn Gorm recorded its record minimum of −16.5°C (2.3°F) the maximum temperature attained during the same 24 hours was just 1.5°C (2.7°F) higher at −15.0°C (5°F) thanks to a continuous south-east wind and the cover of blowing snow on the summit. A diurnal movement across freezing point 0°C (32°F) produces a daily freeze/thaw cycle which consolidates the snow and ice into a safe enjoyable condition for walking and climbing.

Systematic (ie, day to day): Here the main control on temperature is the prevailing local weather system. During changeable phases dominated by Atlantic depressions, the mountain temperatures may oscillate between −5 and +10°C (23 and 50°F) as warm and cold air sectors succeed one another during frontal passage. A day-to-day range around the freezing point promotes consolidation of the existing snow-pack. Less desirable is an airstream which varies between south and west and whose range might be typically +2 to +6°C (35.6 to 42.8°F) at 914m (3,000ft), thus causing the sustained thaws which frustrate the climber's plans.

Periodic (ie, weekly and longer): Anticyclonic conditions produce sustained spells of low temperatures upon which only the diurnal range makes significant impact. These may last up to a month, as in February 1986, but more normally in Scotland are displaced after a week or a fortnight at most. The changeover from a settled cold phase to a stormy maritime spell often produces a huge temperature change. Over 27–28 January 1985, Braemar's thermometer rocketed from −17.9°C to +5.7°C (0–42°F) as frontal systems advanced across the country. Even more remarkably, a rise of 4°C (7.2°F) was recorded in the space of thirty minutes on my local summit of Fuar Tholl as a warm front arrived on 5 March 1988.

The variation of temperature with altitude (the lapse rate) is of equal interest to the hillgoer. In dry air the average lapse with height is 1.0°C (1.8°F) every 100m (328ft), but this falls to 0.65°C (1.10°F) per 100m (328ft) in air at saturation point. With these rates in mind, one can translate valley temperatures to those on the summits before commencing the day. The freezing level is all important to the snow conditions. Supposing on a cloudy morning the sea-level reading is +6.5°C (43.7°F), then the freezing level will be around 1,000m (3,300ft) and one would be better advised to climb on Ben Nevis than to make a futile search for a frost on the lower hills of Glencoe. The normal fall of temperature with height is reversed in inversion conditions, but then the prevailing air-mass is usually so cold as to guarantee a frost at all levels (see graph on Fig 8).

Finally, there are two regular confusions among mountaineers which should be clarified:

Wind chill: Having read the statement that our mountain temperatures are not particularly extreme, many will have exclaimed: 'But what about wind chill? Doesn't a strong wind reduce −10°C to −30°C?' This is a popular misconception which any unscrupulous retailer of cold-weather clothing might wish to perpetuate in order to sell the more expensive '−30' duvet jacket. In fact, the ambient temperature can never fall below the still-air thermometer reading. The wind merely serves to accelerate the rate at which the exposed body cools towards that level. Put another way, a strong wind at an air temperature of −10°C (14°F) produces a net rate of bodily heat loss equivalent to that on a calm day at −30°C (−22°F). Extra insulation is an expensive and ultimately futile solution to the wind. It is windproof garments that are required (see Chapter 8).

Air and ground temperature: The *air* temperature is used almost universally in meteorological recording, but the *ground* temperature (ie, of the snow surface) behaves rather differently, particularly in clear, calm weather when radiation is the dominant agent of heating and cooling. The earth's surface (and this includes snow) is far more

Fig 9 CAIRN GORM SUMMIT: ANNUAL WIND EXTREMES, 1979–87										
(Wind speeds given in kmph (mph in brackets))										
Year	1979	1980	1981	1982	1983	1984	1985	1986	1987	1979–87
MAXIMUM MONTHLY MEAN	55.8	72.7	73.2	64.5	88.3	62.7	57.6	68.8	56.6	88.3
	(34.7)	(45.2)	(45.5)	(40.1)	(54.9)	(39.0)	(35.8)	(42.8)	(35.2)	(54.9)
Month	Nov	Dec	Jan	Nov	Jan	Dec	Feb	Nov	Mar	Jan 83
MAXIMUM DAILY MEAN	93	109	112	122	135	143	128	125	146	146
	(58)	(68)	(70)	(76)	(84)	(89)	(80)	(78)	(91)	(91)
Average direction	SW	W	NW	W	W	SE	SE	S	SE	SE
Date	4 Dec	18 Apr	6 Feb	19 Nov	5 Mar	23 Mar	9 Feb	15 Mar	7 Mar	7 Mar 87
MAXIMUM 3-SECOND GUST	177	202	194	188	235	235	196	275	207	275
	(110)	(126)	(121)	(117)	(146)	(146)	(122)	(171)	(129)	(171)
Direction	SW	W	S	SW	W	SE	W	SE	SE	SE
Date	4 Dec	29 Dec	13 Dec	12 Feb	25 Oct	24 Mar	31 Jan	20 Mar	7 Mar	20 Mar 86
Note total dominance of winter and late autumn dates even though these statistics are for the whole year.										

responsive to radiational heating and cooling than the overlying air. Therefore, in sunshine the surface snow will absorb more heat and thus melt more rapidly than the air temperature might suggest. Conversely, on a clear night, radiational heat loss from the surface may cause freezing and hardening even though the air temperature stays above zero. A prediction of the state of the snow should therefore not depend solely upon the forecast air temperature.

THE WIND AND THE WUTHERING

The mountain wind can on successive days be the mountaineer's implacable foe and then his inspiration:

2 January 1892: The summit of Cairn Gorm:
Simultaneous with the discovery of the cairn came a terrific blast of wind before which we were glad to throw ourselves face downwards on the ground and remain in that position till its violence had subsided. (*W. Brown*)[4]

3 January 1892: Ben Cruachan and Taynuilt Peak:
Two white peaks, soaring out of the mist appeared on either side in all their spotless sublimity; struck with a gleam of sunshine, throwing light and shade on their gleaming pinnacles, with wind-blasts howling round them like a legion of 'storm fiends' shrieking their notes of wailing. (*W. Douglas*)[5]

The autumn and winter vie for supremacy as the windiest seasons in the Scottish mountains, but in terms of extreme gusts and severe individual storms, winter has the upper hand. In all nine years between 1979 and 1987 (Fig 9) the windiest month of the year at Cairn Gorm summit was between November and March. The highest individual monthly average was a remarkable 88kmph (55mph) (gale force 9) in January 1983. Over the same period, the highest recorded single three-second gust came between December and March in eight out of the nine years. Fig 10 gives the rather disturbing information that a gale can be expected on Cairn Gorm summit for 30 per cent of the duration of the calendar winter

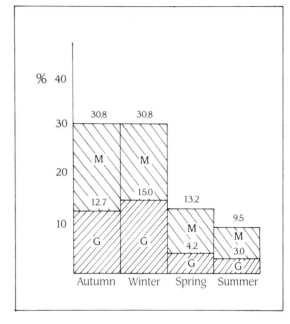

Fig 10 SEASONAL FREQUENCY OF GALES ON CAIRN GORM SUMMIT, 1979–82
M: percentage of hours in which a *mean* wind speed above gale force (61kmph/38mph) was recorded
G: percentage of hours in which a *single gust* above storm force (109kmph/68mph) was recorded

compared to only 9 per cent of the summer season.

Why, then, is the winter so much more windy? The answer largely lies in the behaviour of the global air-masses. The polar zone of cold air greatly intensifies and expands during the winter, whereas the temperature of air-masses nearer to the equator is little affected by the seasonal change. Thus, the boundary between the drier polar air and the maritime subtropical zone shifts south and becomes more pronounced in terms of both temperature and pressure difference. This boundary, the polar front, is less stable than in summer as a result, breeding more active depressions and shorn by higher winds due to the pressure gradient. The average winter position of the polar front lies east-west across Britain's latitudes. Therefore, our mountains lie directly in its storm-tracks, and as the first line of defence to the 4,800km (3,000 mile) expanse of the Atlantic Ocean, the Western Highlands receive the full blast of the roaring westerlies. Many are the dark December nights when the very ground itself reverberates with their power.

A secondary cause of winter's windiness is the greater intensity and stability of anticyclones over continental Europe. As the Atlantic depressions track eastwards, they frequently become blocked against these huge high-pressure masses which produce persistent and bitterly cold gales typically from the south-east.

The mountains themselves produce further intensification of winter's vigorous air-flows. Winds blow faster at higher altitudes anyway due to the absence of surface friction. Over Britain, the 'free air' wind speeds at 1,000m (3,300ft) are 50 per cent higher than at sea level. Therefore, a

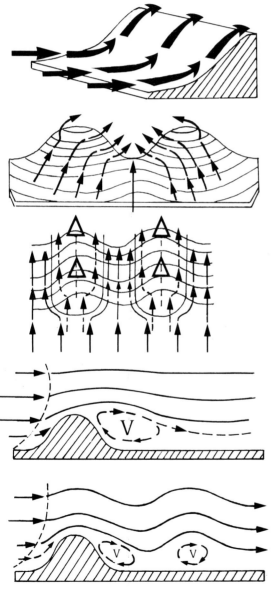

Fig 11 MOUNTAIN EFFECTS ON WIND-FLOW

a Forced uplift and compression: unbroken mountain barrier; concave windward slope; wind-flow perpendicular

b Diversion and channelling: linked rounded hills; convex windward slope; wind-flow perpendicular

c Up-valley channelling: wind-flow parallel to the main relief ridges

d Lee slope turbulence – standing eddy: moderate wind speeds; weak reverse flow and updraught

e Lee slope turbulence – waves and rotors: strong winds over 40kmph (25mph); rotor vortex (v) in lee depression; standing rotor (v) under waves; turbulent reverse flow and updraught

64kmph (40mph) (force 8) gale in the valleys will blow at 96kmph (60mph) on the higher summits. In addition to this, mountain topography creates remarkable local effects on both the wind's speed and its dynamic behaviour. For example, on Goat Fell, Arran, an astounding wind phenomenon was observed and reported by W. Inglis Clark during the SMC's 1923 New Year meet:

> . . . a series of wind vortices swept down the slopes, tossing members here and there. Owing to the slight sprinkling of snow, the passage of these cyclones was made visible, each circle of wind raising a margin of snow like a wall some feet in height. Each large circle, revolving, say at 40 miles per hour, had on its margin five vortices, where the velocity seemed more like 100mph, and at each of these a pyramid of snow was raised to a height of perhaps 30 feet. The whole circle with its satellites had a rapid movement down the mountain face . . . when in the secondary vortex, the writer was thrown certainly more than 20 feet in a fraction of a second.[6]

And yet, while such a gale can be devastating one side of a hill, perfect calm may reign over a brow just a few metres distant. It is as if the wind gods have chosen one small patch on which to vent their anger and left the rest unscathed. Walking around the northern end of Beinn Eighe one day in February 1986, we enjoyed a pleasant breeze and warming sunshine until the entrance gates of Coire Mhic Fhearchair were reached. Suddenly, we were plunged into a whirling gale. Stinging blasts of spindrift whipped into our faces. It became too painful to look ahead. We scrabbled to the shelter of some boulders and struggled into full storm clothing, but as soon as we breached the corrie's lip and entered its inner bowl, the blizzard cleared and the wind fell light.

Tom Weir remembers a real howler of a south-easterly on Maoile Lunndaidh above Loch Monar in 1946. When he and his companion reached the dome-shaped summit plateau, they were suddenly gripped by the wind and forced onto hands and knees. Despite crawling and clinging to ice-axes, they felt powerless to prevent the wind sliding them inexorably across the ice-bound top towards the brink of the mountain's northern cliffs. With great effort, they managed to impose enough control over their direction to reach the summit cairn, where, amazingly, they staggered into a near calm. This could only have been the centre of the vortex of the hurricane which was sucking the air to either side of the topmost point.

These orographic wind effects make a fascinating study and their intrigue is all the greater for the impossibility of predicting such localised occurrences. There are three fundamental controls on wind-flow over mountains:

1 The shape of the mountains.
2 The direction of the wind in relation to the mountain relief.
3 The general stability of atmospheric conditions.

Fig 11 schematically illustrates the general effects of factors 1 and 2. If the wind blows perpendicularly to the alignment of relief as in (a), the air is forced upwards and over the summits, the uplift being accentuated where the windward slopes are uniform and concave in shape, so that the maximum winds are experienced on the tops themselves. A convex windward slope tends to deflect the air sideways, until it finds a suitable gap through which to escape (b). This channelling effect produces extreme winds on the intervening bealachs between rounded and convex hills, while the summits themselves escape the worst blast. Where the wind blows parallel to the main mountain ranges (c), as a westerly may blow across the west-east alignments of the Western Highlands, a similar channelling will occur with a gale roaring through the glens like a high-speed express. Isolated summits, for example the peaks of Sutherland, although fully exposed in all directions, do not have as strong a compressing or channelling effect since the air-flow can easily divert into the surrounding free air-space.

A particular feature of the wind in the mountains is its gustiness. On Cairn Gorm, single gusts are on average 25 per cent greater than the mean wind speed, but in winter, storm gusts can be double the average velocity. A gusting wind is the

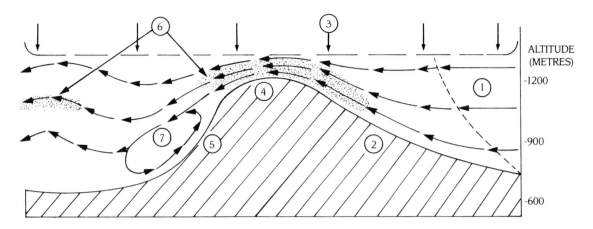

ALTITUDE
(METRES)

-1200

-900

-600

most difficult to handle on the hills for it is impossible to predict its timing and so take the appropriate guard. It is frustrating and exhausting when the wind 'plays with you' in this fashion. On occasions, I have experienced isolated gusts which arrive with no warning and leave no trace. One afternoon we were sitting in Coire Ardair on Creag Meagaidh in a near calm, relaxing over a snack after a climb. Unannounced, a blast of wind funnelled down from the cliffs and sent lunch-boxes, balaclavas, camera cases and other accoutrements flying onto the frozen surface of the lochan, some of which were retrieved on its far side.

Gusting is a sure sign of turbulence in the air-flows, Figs 11 (d) and (e) show how uplift and compression of the wind over a mountain massif creates an oscillating wave motion on the lee side. If the wind is strong, the release of pressure on the lee slopes and the associated down-rush of air may create standing eddies or even a series of rotor vortices in which the air-flow may be reversed or sent upwards. Violent updraughts are regularly experienced on the corrie head-walls by climbers, who then have to suffer a spindrift blast from below and above at the same time and can reasonably complain of unfair treatment from the weather. Much of the gustiness in the hills is caused by these complex and ever-changing forms of turbulence.

The Cairngorm plateau and its northern corries provide a model example where all these oro-graphic effects can act in devastating combination if there is a strong south-east air-flow, particularly

Fig 12 THE NOTORIOUS CAIRNGORM WINTER WIND-STORMS
The factors:
1 Strong south-east air-flow blowing perpendicularly to the massif
2 Smooth concave south-east slopes forcing uplift
3 Stable upper atmosphere at high pressure and therefore with a tendency to sink; restricts vertical uplift
4 Severe compression and acceleration of wind at summit level (112–161kmph/70–100mph)
5 Steep corrie head-walls on the north-west side cause a sudden release and down-rush into free air-space
6 Layer clouds often formed over plateau summit and in lee wave crests where saturation levels are reached
7 Vortex and eddies and corrie bowls: calm air-space, updraughts and random gusting

1 (right) The chisel-topped summit of Beinn Alligin, Torridon, with the turreted Horns in front, as seen from the neighbouring Beinn Dearg

2 (overleaf) The lonely majesty of the Torridon hills in winter. The western end of Beinn Eighe viewed from Beinn Dearg, with Ruadh Stac Mor (left) and Sail Mhor (right) guarding the entrance to Coire Mhic Fhearchair

Plate 5 The Coire Cas wind-bowl. A bitingly cold March day on the Cairn Gorm ski slopes, with the notorious storm shroud hanging over the summit plateau, and a strong south-easterly in flow

3 (*left, above*) The great corries of Beinn Bhan, Applecross. The awesome 'Giant's Wall' of Coire an Fhamair is profiled, with the 'pot' of Coire na Poite to its right (*Clarrie Pashley*)

4 (*below*) Looking south from the frost-caked summit of Cairn Gorm. The cliff tops of Stacan Dubha and Carn Etchachan rise beyond the Loch Avon basin, with Ben Macdui to the right and the Deeside hills on the horizon (*Andrew Nisbet*)

in association with a stable subsiding upper atmosphere (Fig 12). The resultant wind storms can hold sway for many days during every winter, but are so highly localised that an innocent observer enjoying sunshine and a light breeze down in Aviemore would not credit their severity. However, on taking a drive up to the ski car park at 610m (2,000ft) he will step out into a searing gale and a billowing cloud of spindrift (Plate 5) which will soon persuade him that this is not a day for the pistes (nor any other mountain activity). Similar local winds may be experienced in other areas of the Highlands when the juxtaposition of air-flow and relief so favours, although the Cairngorm case is undoubtedly the most notorious.

There is no strongly prevailing wind direction in winter. The wind comes from all directions with substantial frequency, although there is a slightly greater incidence from the west to south-west quarter. Severe gales can be experienced from all directions, although more rarely from the north and north-east (see the maxima for the Cairn Gorm AWS on Fig 9). Indeed, a gale can veer from south-east to north-west during the twenty-four-hour passage of a single depression over Scotland.

To be on the hills on a day of buffeting winds is an exhilarating, if exhausting, experience. There can be no half measures. Pitched into the teeth of a gale, one must give one's all or else be beaten. Traversing the Mamores Ridge on such a wild day during my winter Munros round in 1985 gave excitement and atmosphere that no tranquil day of sun and calm could ever match. The mountains are alive and bellowing with an unbridled and untameable strength.

However, beyond certain limits the wind becomes not just intolerable but inimical to human survival. Man is presumptuous to think otherwise, but he does. Witness the disbelief and anger which lowland storms such as devastated southern England on 16 October 1987 arouse in the general population. Immediately, the weathermen are made scapegoats for failing not just to have predicted, but also to somehow have averted, the catastrophe. He who seeks the winter hills is quickly rid of such cant. It is soon clear who is the 'boss'! The sights of waterfalls blowing vertically upwards or of great plumes of snow streaming off the summits are some of the most impressive and awesome granted to the mountaineer and are a sure sign that these thresholds have been exceeded. Fig 13 gives a practical translation of the main wind-speed scales into the sphere of human experience.

When caught in a big wind on the hills, one's tactics are crucial to a successful extrication. If the dynamics of the wind can be roughly interpreted, then one can vary the route in search of shelter. A more fundamental decision is whether to escape or retreat. Retreat may not be so easy if the wind is at your tail. As the great south-east gale of 21 January 1984 gathered force, three ski-tourers were heading north-west across the Monadhliath plateau, intending to stay overnight at the remote Findhorn bothy. On reaching the tops near Carn Balloch, they were blown over 'like skittles'. With the gale at their backs, it was tempting to have continued in search of the bothy. Such a decision might have served short-term convenience but could have proved disastrous given the severity of the ensuing blizzard. Wisely, they turned back. After a desperate hour, they emerged on civilisation's side of the mountain and reached Newtonmore that night.[7]

Shielding the people behind, tacking against a head-wind, clawing with the ice-axe, crawling and even jumping – these are all techniques of progress which have been applied in a gale. It is important in all such situations to remove protruding impedimenta. Skis are the greatest nuisance, for they cannot be worn in a severe gale, but conversely produce an effect of a windmill if removed and strapped to the rucksack.

In March 1980, I was descending Coire Leis on Ben Nevis after a climb on the Minus Face, fully decorated with ropes and hardware, despite a raging southerly wind. Caught off-balance on hard névé snow-slopes, I was suddenly cartwheeled head-over-heels, my rotational momentum many times increased by the orbit of my iceaxe and hammer which were still attached to my harness. I was, however, glad to be wearing a helmet as I crashed into a field of boulders 30m (100ft) lower. Thereafter, all slings and every other piece of projecting armoury save for the axe were removed and stuffed safely into my sack before I continued.

Undoubtedly, Scotland's mountains experience their fair share of atmospheric disturbance. We might be thankful, therefore, that our winter winds do not nearly compare with those of Antarctica, Patagonia or the Himalaya, nor indeed with Mt Washington which sits directly across the Atlantic in New Hampshire, USA. Its 1,830m (6,000ft) summit has a mean velocity of 83kmph (51½mph) in winter and a record gust of 372kmph (231mph). With their winter mean a mere 56kmph (35mph), the winds on Cairn Gorm summit are quite sufficient for most tastes.

RAIN, RIME AND SNOWFALL

For all the interest of temperature and wind, it is the complex behaviour of moisture in the atmosphere that gives mountain weather its greatest fascination. This is especially so in Scotland's maritime climate, and particularly in winter when the moisture translates into snowfall over the high

Fig 13 WIND SPEEDS: A PRACTICAL CONVERSION GUIDE

Beaufort Scale		Kmph/Mph	Visual Indicators	Travel Problems on the Hill
0	CALM	0		
1–3	LIGHT	2–20 (1–12)	Surface drift of loose snow	
4	MODERATE	21–29 (13–18)		
5	FRESH	30–39 (19–24)	Tree branches in motion	
6	STRONG	40–50 (25–31)	Wavelets on loch surfaces	Severe windchill-rate of cooling at 0°C (32°F) equivalent to −10°C (−18°F).
7	STRONG	51–61 (32–38)	Cairn Gorm's winter average; snow/rain falls 'horizontally'	Risk of frost-nip on exposed flesh if temperature is below zero (32°F).
8	GALE	62–74 (39–46)	Shroud of blowing snow on hills up to 50m (165ft) thick	Leaning into wind – energy output doubled.
9	SEVERE GALE	75–87 (47–54)	Streams blown back; large trees in motion	Trailing ropes will blow outwards horizontally.
10	STORM FORCE	88–100 (55–63)	Raised whirlwinds of blowing snow on crests; plumes and streamers	Buckled against the wind; walking difficult – effort trebled.
11	SEVERE STORM FORCE	101–116 (64–72)	Storm shroud of suspended spindrift 100m (330ft) thick	Extreme windchill (−20°C/−36°F) exposed flesh freezes below 0°C (32°F).
12	HURRICANE	over 117 (over 73)	Extensive structural damage	Crawling at 125kmph+ (80mph+); breathing difficult facing wind; humans can be blown off the ground for short distances at c160kmph (c100mph).

NB: Wind speeds indicated at valley level should be increased by at least 50 per cent to give a prudent estimate of the wind on 900m (3,000ft) summits.

NB: Knots and metres per second are also used to describe wind speeds in some sources. The unit conversions are:

1m per second = 3.6kmph (2.24mph)

1 knot = 1.85kmph (1.15mph)

ground. Snowfall exhibits an unfathomable complexity of form and process and, of course, produces a marvellously varied scenic effect. The wild grandeur of a blowing blizzard, the silent grace of drifting flakes, the delicate tracery of hoar from a long deep frost – these are some of nature's most wondrous sights and are all the more appreciated for their rarity of occurrence in Britain's temperate climate.

But before fancies fly away to a surreal world of unbroken snowscapes, it is only proper to remind ourselves of the bad tidings. Moisture means cloud and of this the Scottish hills have more than their just share in every season, while heavy winter rain is a well-known and long-cursed phenomenon. In sheets and stair-rods, drizzle or deluge – it comes with appreciable frequency and intensity at all altitudes. As Fig 14 shows, the total precipitation of the winter months is greater than in any other season except autumn, the four months December to March giving 168cm (61½in) which is 41 per cent of Ben Nevis's

Fig 14 BEN NEVIS SUMMIT: AVERAGE MONTHLY PRECIPITATION TOTALS, 1885–1903 (from the observatory records, Kilgour, 1905)[8]

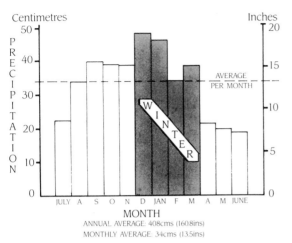

ANNUAL AVERAGE: 408cms (160.8ins)
MONTHLY AVERAGE: 34cms (13.5ins)

Plate 6 Valley temperature inversion: morning fog blankets Benmore Glen by Crianlarich. On this day in December 1984 the valley floor temperature was −8°C, but on climbing to 200m we emerged into dry air and warm sunshine

annual total, and of this, on average 25 per cent falls as rain. On lower summits the proportion of rain to snowfall is considerably higher, reaching 50 per cent at an altitude of 750m (2,460ft). If prolonged, the rain simply washes away the lying snow and because it typically falls at temperatures less than +6°C (43°F), creates the wetting chilly conditions that are so difficult to survive.

Records of cloud cover from the Nevis observatory concluded that, on average, in winter only 10 per cent of the possible hours of sunshine were enjoyed and the summit itself was clear of fog for only 21 per cent of the time between November and March. Ben Nevis is, of course, the highest ground. Independent observations from sea level over the winter of 1901–2 estimated the proportions of cloud cover as 67 per cent at the summit, 1,344m (4,400ft), 50 per cent at 1,000m (3,300ft) and 20 per cent at 700m (2,300ft). You will obviously see a good deal more if you climb on the lower hills.

These averages ignore the happy fact that settled spells of anticyclonic weather break through the gloom of every winter to give an atmospheric clarity unequalled in any other season. During such periods, remarkably low relative humidities of under 20 per cent (70–80

per cent is normal) were measured on Ben Nevis. In a dry winter air, free from heat haze, one can perch on the Cuillin crest and pick the teeth of every range of mainland hills from Sutherland down to Ben More on Mull.

Under an anticyclone, the only cloud encountered is likely to be the valley fog of the night-time temperature inversion, when sinking air condenses its water vapour as it cools. Alternatively, a warmer slick of moist Atlantic air attempts to creep under the high-pressure belt, cooling and condensing as it rises to meet the stable overlying layer. In February 1983, we awoke in a camp by the Allt a'Mhuilinn to a dreich morning, so dank and mild as to guarantee a rapid thaw of the snow and ice on Nevis. Nevertheless, we decided to climb high in vain search for a freezing level. The

450m (1,500ft) trudge up Observatory Gully in moist heavy snow acquires special purgatorial powers when you don't expect the reward of an ice-climb at its top. So picture our excitement when, at the foot of Gardyloo Buttress at 1,220m (4,000ft), our heads poked through the cloud into a brilliant blue sky and a keen frost. Ben Nevis's summit skull was the only piece of sunlit ground in the Highlands. We got our climb and stood on top above an unbroken sea of cotton-wool cloud which reflected the sun with a dazzling white glare.

Fig 15 classifies the main forms of precipitation experienced in Scotland in winter, the list being ordered in a decreasing sequence of air temperature. Nearly all winter rainfall commences its life as snow crystals which melt during descent. The crucial temperature threshold where snow turns to rain at ground level is +2 to +3°C (35.6–

37.4°F). The prevalence of temperatures within the −5 to +5°C (23–41°F) range produces a greater variety of precipitation and frost deposits on our hills than might be encountered in a colder, less changeable climate. Attempts to recognise and identify these types both in the air and on the ground can add a new dimension of interest to a winter day on the mountains.

A complete understanding of the physical processes underlying the forms of precipitation is currently beyond our scientific grasp, yet possessed of a few basic ideas, weekend mountaineers can combine identification with explanation to their infinitely greater satisfaction. Four main processes are at work in the production of winter's raindrops and snowflakes:

Supercooling: Water droplets can exist in the atmosphere even though the temperature is below

Fig 15 THE MAJOR FORMS OF WINTER PRECIPITATION			
Type	Description	Size in mm (diameter)	Mode of Formation
RAIN	Aggregates of water droplets of variable size.	0.5–5	Winter rain is usually derived from ice crystals which melt and coalesce during descent.
SLEET	Partially melted snowflakes or a mix of rain/snow.	0.5–5	
FREEZING RAIN (GLAZED FROST) (SILVER THAW)	Rain deposited as ice on impact with frozen ground.	0.5–5	Air temperature: 2–5°C (35–40°F); ground temperature: below 0°C (32°F); raindrops coalesce, then freeze to form a sheet-ice surface.
RIME ICE	Ice accumulations on windward sides of exposed objects; feathery fir-cone growths.		Cloud droplets freeze on contact with frozen ground; typically formed by uplift of warm moist air over frozen hills; best formed in fog and moderate wind.
SURFACE HOAR (WHITE FROST)	Deposits of water vapour on ground surface; white feathery flakes with no cohesion.		Deposition from vapour to solid state on contact with colder ground; air and ground temperature will be both below 0°C (32°F) for thick hoar to develop.
SNOWFLAKES	Aggregates of snow crystals interlocked and of low density.	2–20	Coagulation of grains/pellets during descent; growth is promoted in moist warm air (temperature: −4–0°C/25–32°F); interlock of stellar crystals produces biggest size. *continued overleaf*

Fig 15 THE MAJOR FORMS OF WINTER PRECIPITATION continued

Type	Description	Size in mm (diameter)	Mode of Formation
ICE PELLETS	Frozen raindrops or melted and refrozen snowflakes.	Less than 5	Formed in turbulent air where strong vertical updraught causes secondary uplift and recooling of raindrops; not easily differentiated from hail.
SMALL HAIL	Translucent, spherical; snow pellets encased in ice.	Less than 5	Originating as rimed pellets but coated with ice as water droplets collide, condense, coalesce and freeze during descent; will form when liquid content of air is high.
LARGE HAIL	Spherical ice-balls; usually showing layering of opaque and clear ice layers.	5–50	Forms as for small hail (ie, in moist air, temperature close to 0°C (32°F)), but with turbulence causing repeated uplift and cooling, so causing aggregation.
SNOW PELLETS (RIMED CRYSTALS)	White opaque low-density ice growths showing roughly round, conical or irregular shape.	2–5	Formed by riming onto freezing nuclei (supercooled water droplets condensing onto ice particles); growth is gradual compared to hail; lower frequency and speed of impact; moist rising air.
BROKEN GRAINS	Tiny granular grains of high density.	0.1–0.5	Pulverisation of crystals by wind; collision in air and on ground impact.
SNOW GRAINS (SNOW CRYSTALS)	Crystalline opaque ice grains (columns, plates, needles or stellar shapes); infinite variety of growths.	0.5–1	Deposition of water vapour onto freezing nuclei; form of growth depends on air temperature and degree of supersaturation of air with respect to an ice surface; growth maximised at air temperatures −12 to −16°C (10–3°F).

NB: Snow pellets and grains are not independent types; riming and crystalline growth can occur simultaneously or else grains are rimed during descent.

freezing point, and in this condition they are termed 'supercooled'. For droplets to freeze, there must be tiny impurities active in the air, called freezing nuclei, onto which the droplets freeze. As the temperature drops, the numbers of active nuclei increase, but only at −40°C (−40°F) do all droplets in the atmosphere freeze spontaneously. Therefore, a parcel of saturated air at −15°C will contain a mixture of supercooled liquid droplets and frozen ice particles. This is the usual state in Scotland where temperatures in the lower atmosphere are rarely lower than −20°C (−4°F).

Supersaturation: The amount of water vapour present in the air decreases as it cools, any excess condensing into droplets at its saturation point to form clouds. In subzero temperatures, some of the droplets will freeze to form ice particles. As the temperature falls further, as, say, when an air-mass is forced to rise over the mountains, the air becomes supersaturated and more vapour must be shed. However, the saturation point of vapour with respect to an ice surface is reached at a higher temperature than its saturation point with respect to a water surface. Therefore, there is a range of temperature where vapour is supersaturated over ice but as yet unsaturated over water, and the suspended ice particles will attract the vapour at the expense of the water droplets. Thus, a snow crystal is born.

Deposition and vapour transport (see Fig 16): The excess vapour is deposited directly onto the ice particles. It therefore passes from a gaseous to solid state without going through the liquid phase. While this is happening, the water droplets may be evaporating because the vapour remains un-saturated relative to their water surface. This supplies further vapour which is deposited onto the crystals. This process of vapour transport is therefore self-sustaining until the crystals grow to such a size that they fall out of the atmosphere as snow grains or new snow.

Riming: The ice particles may also grow by their collision with suspended water droplets which freeze on impact. This is riming (Fig 16) and becomes predominant over deposition when the air is saturated with respect to both water and ice (so that vapour transport no longer occurs), or else when crystals are falling down through moist air layers. In these situations, snow pellets are formed.

The varieties of pure crystals (or grains) and their modified rimed forms are literally infinite. Over six thousand different kinds of snow crystal were identified and photographed by an American, Wilson Bentley, in a life-long study between 1885 and 1931. Crystal development depends on two main controls:

1 Air temperature – which determines the direction of growth as between plate-like and columnar structures.
2 The degree of supersaturation to ice – which at high levels enables branching and elabora-tion into stellar forms.

Fig 17 illustrates some basic types of crystal and how they might be modified by riming, tempera-ture change and wind action.

In Scotland, atmospheric depositions of surface hoar and rime ice on the ground surface are of particular prominence, due to the regular influx and uplift of moist Atlantic air. Although created

Fig 16 THE GENESIS OF SNOW: VAPOUR TRANSPORT AND RIMING (*from* Avalanche Handbook, *1976*)[9]

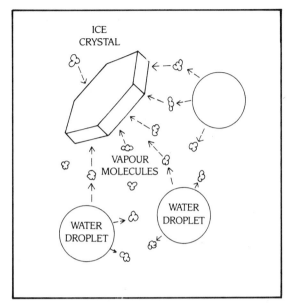

Vapour transport and deposition: water molecules evaporate from the droplets and are then deposited onto the ice crystal

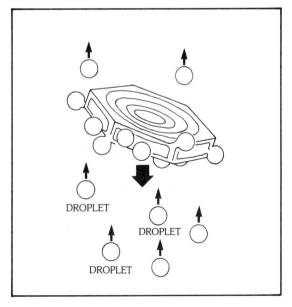

Riming: water droplets collide with the ice crystal and freeze on impact

Fig 17 SNOW: some basic crystals and their possible modifications

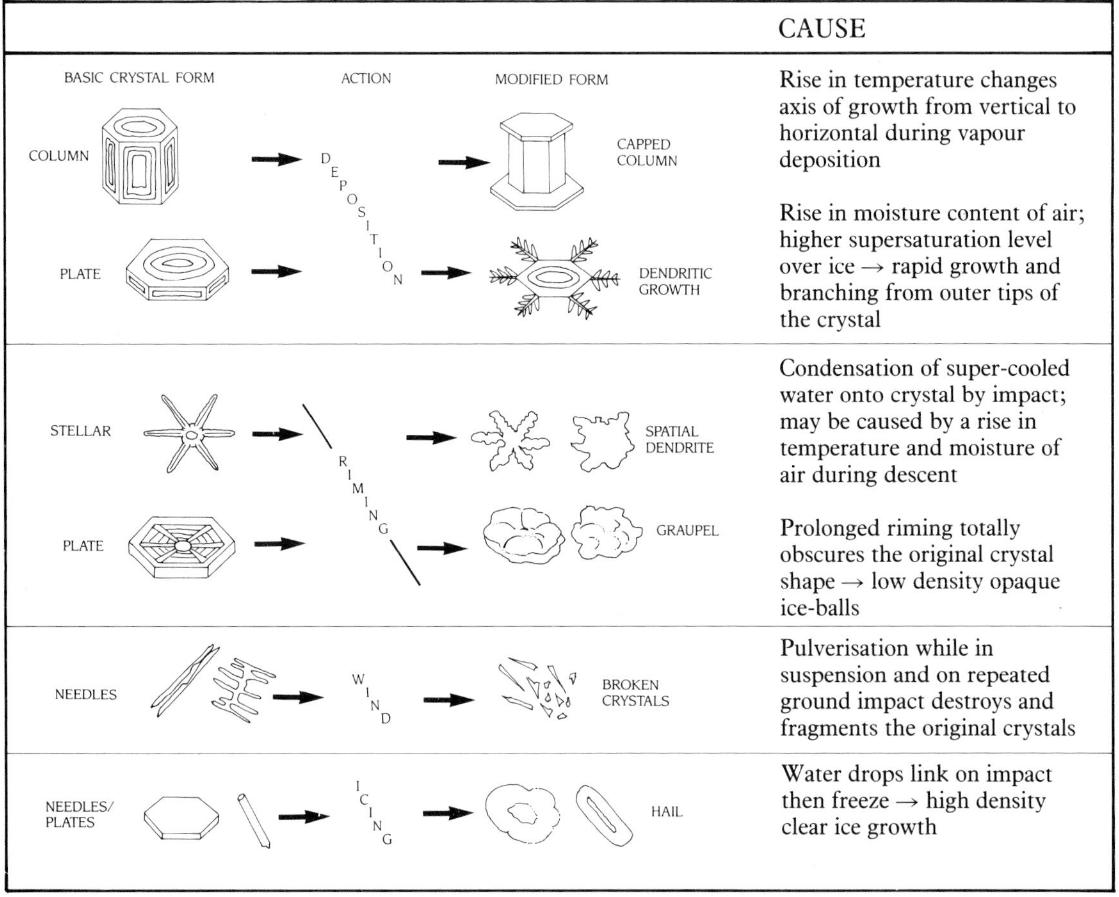

			CAUSE
BASIC CRYSTAL FORM	ACTION	MODIFIED FORM	
COLUMN	DEPOSITION	CAPPED COLUMN	Rise in temperature changes axis of growth from vertical to horizontal during vapour deposition
PLATE		DENDRITIC GROWTH	Rise in moisture content of air; higher supersaturation level over ice → rapid growth and branching from outer tips of the crystal
STELLAR	RIMING	SPATIAL DENDRITE	Condensation of super-cooled water onto crystal by impact; may be caused by a rise in temperature and moisture of air during descent
PLATE		GRAUPEL	Prolonged riming totally obscures the original crystal shape → low density opaque ice-balls
NEEDLES	WIND	BROKEN CRYSTALS	Pulverisation while in suspension and on repeated ground impact destroys and fragments the original crystals
NEEDLES/ PLATES	ICING	HAIL	Water drops link on impact then freeze → high density clear ice growth

purely by the impact freezing of cloud droplets onto exposed objects, the Ben Nevis observers witnessed the growth of rime at an incredible rate of 30cm (1ft) per day. Surface hoaring may likewise be remarkably intense, producing aerated and cohesionless layers of crystals of ankle, or even calf, depth in clear cold weather when the diurnal temperature range is large. Daytime heating/evaporation loads the surface air layers with moisture that is deposited as thick frost in the ensuing night.

Snowfall quantities are notoriously difficult to measure and compare because of their varying density. For example, a 10cm (4in) fall of light snow crystals may equate to 0.5cm (¼in) of rain, whereas the same depth of heavy wet snowflakes might give a water equivalent of 2.5cm (1in). The volume of snow on the ground is therefore wholly misleading as an indicator of water quantity. The heaviest falls in water content indeed occur when the temperature is close to zero and the air is able to hold more moisture, which is carried up and over the hills where it is shed as snow.

While the winter weather of the Scottish mountains can indeed be wild and turbulent, never should it be regarded as uniformly hostile. Headlines and memories may tend to dwell on the blizzards and storms, but it should not be forgotten that there are an equal number of days of stunning clarity and scenic magnificence when the trials of endurance are replaced by the thrills of pure enjoyment.

This said, it is vitally important that the mountaineer can predict with reasonable accuracy how, when and where the one extreme or the other, or any of the shades between, will occur, and it is into the realm of forecasting that we move in Chapter 3.

Plate 7 Heavy riming on the rocks of the Cairngorm plateau (*Roger Stonebridge*)

3

WINTER WEATHER WATCHING

Weather Prediction and Patterns

Weather forecasts produce diverse and radical reactions among hillgoers and mountaineers. Three typical responses can be identified:

Those who seek a world of scientific certainty will adopt the attitude of blind trust in whatever the weatherman says. This cosy self-deception rarely lasts longer than a few days. As the forecasts repeatedly go awry, they are to be found alternately sheltering in the glens on the most invigorating of days and gritting their teeth on the tops in the unexpected storm. Their mood changes by degrees from absolute faith to total disillusion and eventually matures as an ingrained cynicism. They become the embattled but cheery types so often met in the hills, who continually invoke 'Sod's Law' to explain their every misfortune and are convinced that the malevolence of the weather gods is intended for them alone. Yet they dutifully continue to obey the broadcast prediction to its last word and seek no other aid in planning their mountain days.

Next come the cautious or indolent types who view every omen with a morbid pessimism. No matter how bright is tomorrow's weather picture, or reassuring the forecaster's smile, they will pick out the least blot on the immediate horizon or else some minor cloud in the long-term outlook and, with a feat born of hopeful presentiment and imaginative conjecture, convert this blemish into an imminent storm, whereupon plans are curtailed or abandoned. At least they never waste effort on the chance of good weather and keep out of trouble on the hills, but their sole achievement is a 100 per cent safety record.

Finally, and in complete contrast, are the swaggering and usually youthful individuals who treat the forecast with downright contempt. It is going to take more than a bit of bad weather to stop them getting where they want to go. Forecasts are dismissed as unreliable and therefore go unheeded, their warnings shrugged off with a comment such as 'the mountains create their own weather anyway'. With such energy, self-confidence and determination, one can predict an exciting and eventful future for these characters – indeed, a guaranteed succession of epics and avalanches. If they survive long enough to acquire a proper respect for the winter weather, they often mature into excellent mountaineers.

All three attitudes possess an element of truth. Indeed, one should never ignore the general forecast and at the same time one should always be wary of a sudden unheralded change in the weather, yet without personal ambition and the preparedness to go out and try in marginal conditions, little is ever achieved nor are the mountains fully experienced. Planning for the weather is a problem of juggling with a host of probabilities. Its success requires a balanced assessment and an intelligent judgement somewhere between these three extremes if the best of the Highland winter is to be gained.

However, the simple national forecasts scarcely give the mountaineer an adequate basis to make a sound judgement. General predictions first need to be translated and adapted to estimate conditions on the high mountains. Then it helps greatly to have some understanding of the underlying meteorological systems (ie, the synoptic situation) which provide the wider context in which to assess the potential range of likely weather. Finally, one's own visual awareness of the local weather can provide direct personal evidence upon which to predict the coming events.

THE TRANSLATION PROBLEM

Prior to the 1980s, hillgoers had to make their own interpretation of the general weather forecasts, but with the increasing popularity of skiing and winter mountaineering, specialised mountain forecasts are now issued both on radio and recorded telephone message. The latest such service is 'Mountaincall', which breaks the Highlands up into its main component regions – Skye and Torridon, Cairngorms and the Eastern Highlands, Lochaber and Argyll and the Southern Highlands – and gives a prediction for each with a detail that a national forecast could never achieve. No longer does the climber have to make his own translations in order to uplift the general sea-level forecast. 'Mountaincall' gives the experts' prediction of the cloud base, freezing level, and the 610 and 1,220m (2,000 and 4,000ft) mean wind speeds, gust velocities and temperatures, as well as providing a general synopsis and outlook, and it is updated twice daily. The source data is almost wholly derived from low-level weather stations. Only the Cairn Gorm AWS with its on-line transmission link-up provides direct input from a mountain summit, and 'Mountaincall' reports its most recent readings to convince those sceptics who refuse to believe how bad it is on the hill.

It is wise to maintain some margin of doubt even in the specialised forecast, for the translation problem is not merely a case of raising the sea-level weather by 915m (3,000ft), but rather of assessing the effects of the mountains themselves on cloud, wind and precipitation, a problem which understandably is often beyond the powers of the Meteorological Office experts. A mountain massif as broad and as continuous as the Highlands may also deflect or retard approaching weather systems so that the expected weather is delayed or diverted, or else the windward slopes trap and intensify the bad weather while the lee sides of the relief are spared.

Realising this great complexity, one should forgive the mountain forecaster the occasional lapse of judgement and rather be glad that the specialised forecast exists and is improving in accuracy. While it is wrong to say that our

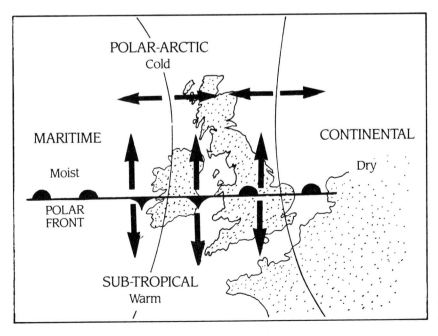

Fig 18 THE WINTER BATTLEGROUND

Fig 19 AIR-MASS
INFLUENCES ON
SCOTLAND'S
WINTER WEATHER

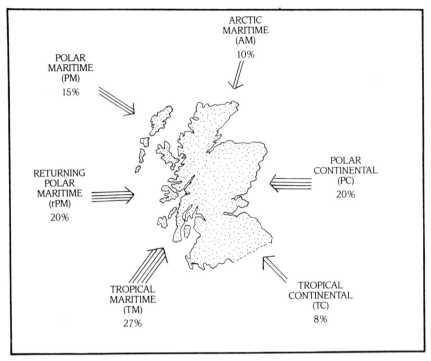

relatively small mountains create their own
weather as do the Alps and Himalayas, they can
modify the existing meteorological pattern almost
beyond recognition.

WINTER AIR-MASSES AND AIR-FLOWS

In winter, there are two main controlling dimen-
sions to our weather (Fig 18):

1 The East-West division between moist maritime air over the Atlantic Ocean and the dry
   stable air-masses which are prevalent over the
   continental interiors of Europe and Asia.
2 The North-South boundary between cold
   arctic airstreams and the warm subtropical
   air over the mid-Atlantic – the 'polar front'.

Since Britain lies at the approximate meeting
point of these two global boundaries, any slight
shift in one or the other may cause a completely
different airstream to cover the country – hence
the variability of our general weather. Five major
air-flows affect our winter weather and these are
detailed in Figs 19 and 20. Each airstream is in its
character the product of its 'source region' – the

area in which it originated – and the modifications
which it undergoes during its passage towards this
country. Britain is not itself a typical source
region, so our weather is largely determined by
far-travelled and highly modified air-flows.

Air-masses may be modified, but they remain
as separate entities. There is little mixing at the
boundaries, which therefore maintain their temperature and moisture differences and so become
zones of instability. It is along the polar front that
depressions are spawned and it is on meeting the
continental air-mass that they often intensify.

As depressions evolve, various constituent air-
masses are drawn into the system and form
distinct sectors of air which are divided by the
warm and cold fronts. Thus, each air-flow
remains identifiable. In a typical frontal sequence,
one might experience Polar Continental (PC) air
replaced by Tropical Maritime (TM) at the warm
front and in turn by returning Polar Maritime
(rPM) at the cold front – all within the space of
twenty-four hours. On the mountains, this may
mean a hard frost succeeded by wet snowfall
turning to rain, and then by high winds and hail
squalls. The feeling of being 'weatherbeaten' will
be fully understood after experiencing such a day.

Conversely, when an anticyclonic air-mass commands our weather, the air-flow may remain unchanged for more than a fortnight. In 1987, PC air remained unchallenged from 23 November to 15 December, a period of sustained frost in which the mountain environment seemed all but fossilised, so unchanging was the regime.

As Fig 19 indicates, the winter mountaineer must accept an appreciable probability that the prevailing airstream will be of the warm moist TM variety or the cool and showery rPM – neither of which alone will produce heavy snow accumulations or hard frosts on the hills. Indeed, almost 50 per cent of winter air-flow over the mountains comes from the quarter from south to west. This

unwelcome news accepted, it must be said that an occasional dash of TM or rPM within a pattern of PM or PC air-flow does naught but good for the snow conditions. It is the sequence that is all-important.

With this basic knowledge of the weather influences and an outline idea of pressure patterns and frontal systems as is given by Appendix 5, one is unshackled from a total reliance on the broadcast forecasts and can make one's own interpretation of a synoptic weather-chart.

Condensed verbal forecasts and simplistic maps liberally dotted with sun, cloud and rain symbols imply exactitude. This is patently not justified by the ever-changing mass of air-waves and currents

---

Fig 20 WINTER AIR-FLOWS AND MOUNTAIN WEATHER

Typical Synoptic situation

POLAR MARITIME (PM)
Generally north-west

Source region:	Polar regions of North America – therefore very cold and dry.
Modification:	Gradual warming and rapid moistening during south-east track over North Atlantic.
Mountain weather:	Cold and unstable: −5 to 0°C (23–32°F) on summits; warm moist lower air layers rising quickly over hills; heavy snow showers; strong blustery winds.
Typical occurrence:	Cold air-mass following cold front passage; low to north of country.

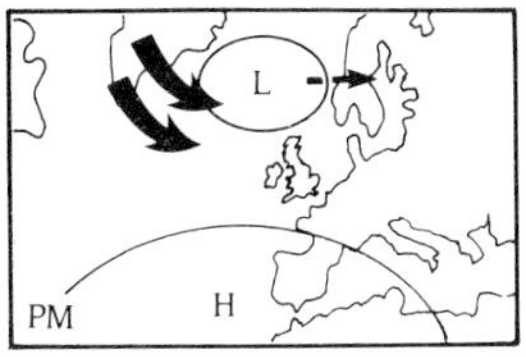

RETURNING POLAR MARITIME (rPM)
Generally west

Source region:	Same as PM.
Modification:	Forced into a more southerly track when a low lies to west of country; warmer and moister than PM, but slightly more stable.
Mountain weather:	Cool and showery: −2 to +2°C on tops; snow, hail or sleet; windy.

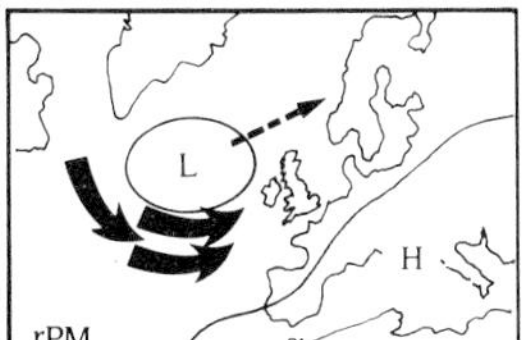

ARCTIC MARITIME (AM)
North to north-easterly

Source region:	Arctic Sea; very cold.
Modification:	Slightly warmed but quickly moistened beyond saturation point during southward passage to Britain.
Mountain weather:	Very cold and snowy: −15 to −5°C (5–23°F) on tops; heavy falls as air is uplifted over northern hills; winds bitingly cold.

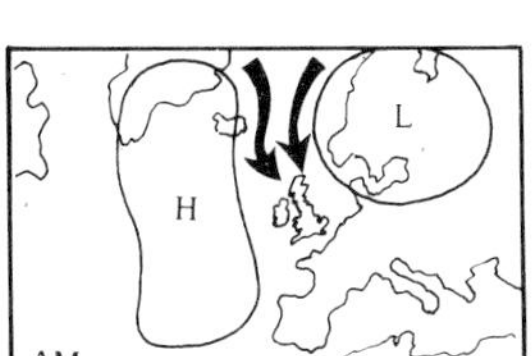

continued overleaf

Fig 20 WINTER AIR-FLOWS AND MOUNTAIN WEATHER continued

Typical Synoptic situation

POLAR CONTINENTAL (PC)
East to south-easterly

Source region: Scandinavian and Siberian continental interiors; very cold and dry.

Modification: Brief warming and moistening as air passes over North Sea.

Mountain weather: Very cold and stable: −15 to −5°C (5–23°F) on tops; snow showers on east coasts and hills; clear and fine further west; any wind is bitter and persistent; gales over mountains if pressure gradient is high.

TROPICAL CONTINENTAL (TC)
South-east to south-easterly

Source region: Central and southern continental Europe; dry and can be warm.

Modification: Cooled during passage over western Europe; moistened slightly by North Sea.

Mountain weather: Rarely affects Scotland; weather is similar to PC but warmer; dry; wind speed depends on pressure patterns.

TROPICAL MARITIME (TM)
South to south-westerly

Source region: Mid-Atlantic, sub-equatorial; very warm and moist.

Modification: Progressive cooling and stabilisation during north-east track towards Britain.

Mountain weather: 'Dreich' conditions; warm and moist; 0 to +8°C (32–46°F) on tops; thick low cloud over mountains; light or steady drizzle; rapid thaw; wind may be strong if associated with a deep low.

Typical occurrence: The warm air sector behind the warm front of an Atlantic low.

Key to maps:
H : High-pressure system (anti-cyclone);
    air-flow clockwise.

L : Low-pressure system (depression);
    air-flow anti-clockwise.
→ : Likely direction of movement of depression.

which comprise meteorological reality. By comparison, the synoptic map gives a better 'feel' for general trend and range of the weather, the timing of its changes and its regional variation. Knowing the range of possible conditions, a mountain tour can be planned with closer regard and preparedness for all likely eventualities. Knowing the weather's future trend, one can save a great deal of time and money on futile journeys north to the Highlands which would otherwise founder in the thaws and storms.

UNRAVELLING THE WEATHER MAP

The synoptic chart is itself a projection. Most usually, it gives the estimated pressure and frontal patterns for noon on the forthcoming day. To assess the immediate weather prospects, look for four features on the map:

1 General air-flow direction – the temperature and moistness of the prevailing airstream. Arrows are often used to indicate the movement of the major air-masses.
2 Frontal systems – warm, cold or occluded. Frontal systems indicate the degree of atmospheric instability and the type and intensity of cloud and precipitation.
3 Pressure gradients – as shown by the spacing of isobars, indicating wind speeds.
4 Local wind directions – often shown symbolically but easily inferred from the pressure pattern (clockwise with respect to 'highs', anti-clockwise around 'lows').

To gauge the longer-term outlook from today's map requires a more practised eye. Three crucial determining factors can be identified:

1 Boundary zones between distinctly differing air-mass types which will be sources of future instability.
2 Specific points of 'frontogenesis' (ie, minor disturbances along the boundaries from which future depressions are likely to evolve).
3 The positioning and relative strengths of anti-cyclones which may block or divert approaching weather systems.

Two case studies will illustrate these influences, comparing the differing mountain-weather patterns which may arise first when Atlantic airstreams are dominant and secondly when continental air takes command.

New Year 1984: In the Polar Storm-tracks (Fig 21)

Even through a stormy Hogmanay one expects the weather to have the decency to offer one quiet day between each tempest. However, 1984 was heralded by a continuous succession of Atlantic storms. The wind blew hard throughout with a raw moist cold that turns the flesh blue and gnaws the bones. Each night a blanket of wet snow was laid down on the moors. The higher tops remained swathed in cumulus cloud-masses that piled up and spilled over the crests in streaming plumes, ever fuelled by the moistened air that roared down from the polar seas.

We ended 1983 with a storm-thwarted sortie into the Fannichs and then a day pinned indoors by a mighty gale and lashing rain, which sent the klondykers' factory ships scuttling for shelter to the head of Loch Broom,

Fig 21 1–2 JANUARY 1984

Warm/cold/occluded front

940 Air pressure in millibars

P–P Polar front pronounced and unbroken across the North Atlantic and South Britain; cold polar low (L) to the north, warm stable high (H) to the south

① Minor wave on the front on the 1st becomes a major depression and frontal system bringing new storms on the 2nd

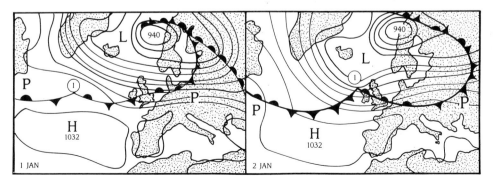

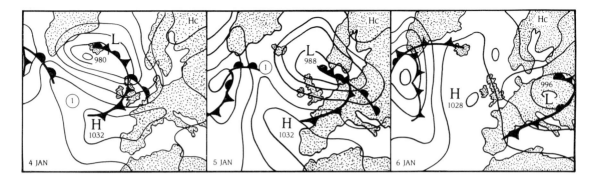

Fig 22 4–6 JANUARY 1987

On the left side:

yet where they continued to spin on their anchors in the wind. The fond hope of first-footing Beinn Dearg sent us up Glen Sguaib on New Year's morning despite a leaden pall of cloud and a restrengthening wind that presaged a blizzard.

In the upper glen, squalls of stinging pellets blasted our backs, but on top the snow fell drier and blew up into a real maelstrom. Due to the white-out we dared go no further than the angle in the wall 200m from the summit, and turned back into the glen, faces bared to a bitter nor'wester. Ice-crusted and battered we reached the safety of Lael Forest as a wild night gathered.

On the 2nd we escaped the Highlands just before the next big depression [Fig 21b] swept unchallenged towards the continent, sending further gales and snow over Scotland in its wake. Thenceforth, for a further fortnight, the polar maritime storms continued without respite, producing awe-inspiring weather that leaves no doubt as to the frailty of humanity.

4–6 January 1987: Tumult to Tranquillity (Fig 22)

The sequence started innocuously enough – a low over Iceland trailing its fronts down over the Highlands without especial energy. Sunday the 4th gave a moist muggy morning typical of the warm air sector, then a refreshing swing to cooler conditions as the cold front passed.

On Monday God made the fullest amends for his Sabbath slumber. Those brave enough to venture on the hills were treated to a fireworks display of lightning bolts accompanied by

On the right side:

Fig 22 4–6 JANUARY 1987

① Polar front is broken in the mid-Atlantic allowing a high (H) to build and form a stable ridge by the 6th

Hc Scandinavian high squeezes low (L), forcing it south-east to produce the storms of the 5th

---

echoing thunder as a series of violent squalls swept down from the north-west. Each was a miniature whirlwind raining a mixture of hailstones and pulverised snow pellets with the intensity of an inch (2.5cm) in five minutes, and the consistency of iron filings. This was polar maritime air at its most turbulent. The best policy was to sit through them, enjoying the spectacle to the full, and moving in the lulls, but three hours on the gentler heights were quite sufficient to satisfy the inner urge.

Yet overnight the storm unwound, and in its lee came a softening northerly breeze, signalling a truce, and which itself fell light by Tuesday night. The hills emerged, their snows scoured by the storm but unbowed. A deepening frost banished all memories of yesterday and once more the climber could hatch his plans in the surety of a fine day to come.

Such a remarkable clearance heartens the spirit, but how did it happen, whereas in 1984 the storms continued unabated? There are two crucial differences in the weather maps. In 1984, the polar front was an unbroken chain across the Atlantic, spawning an endless series of lows, while in 1987 it left a gap ((1) in Fig 22) in which a ridge of high pressure could build and stabilise. By 5 Jan, despite the squalls then lashing the mountains, the onset of a settled phase could be predicted with some certainty.

The second contrast is the absence of any blocking effect of continental air-masses in 1984 which allowed the depressions to rush through to Scandinavia without deflection, whereas in 1987 the high (Hc in Fig 22) squeezed the low into a south-eastward track which produced the stormy day of the 5th. The difference is not obvious, but it can be spotted on the respective charts and it played an important role in the subsequent weather. Five days later, this anticyclone (Hc) had strengthened to produce the memorable 'big freeze' of 1987 (see below).

The Continental Influence

21 January 1984: Blizzard (Fig 23a)

When continental air asserts its strength and moves westwards, Britain can become the battleground where Atlantic fronts are emphatically blocked. The sou'easters then sweep the hills with bitter persistence, but why was this storm so much more extreme than others of its ilk?

Notice first the pressure drop of 60mb between Denmark and the Hebrides and you have the guarantee of storm-force winds. Then

follow the air-flows through the pressure block. They have a moist southerly influence and then stream up the full length of the North Sea to produce heavier snowfall than might normally be borne on polar continental air. Thirdly, see the rapid occlusion of the Atlantic front over Britain. The ingredients were all there for an evil brew of weather, but not even the forecasters gauged its full severity.

The headlines and anecdotes amply retell the resultant havoc: 6m drifts on the Grampian roads, two hundred skiers trapped overnight at the Lecht, a hundred cars stranded on Rannoch Moor, climbers arriving down on the Glencoe road still roped together, a genuine time of six hours to get *down* from the CIC Hut to Fort William, Glenmore Lodge survival courses forced to snow-hole in the Coire na Ciste ski carpark, and tragically but not surprisingly, five lives lost on the hills – the climax to a month of chequered weather.

12 January 1987: Freeze (Fig 23b)

A Siberian high of exceptional stability can even push the fronts back out to sea and force them to seek a southward course across the Mediterranean. No longer is Britain in the blocking zone, but it is now exposed to the full blast of undiluted PC air. The 'big freeze' of 1987 emanated from the high of 1,048mb which plunged the temperatures in Russia to a record −40°C and on Cairn Gorm summit to −16.5°C. While the high was intense, lows of 984 were

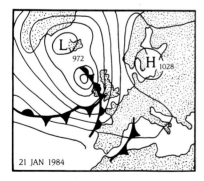

Fig 23a Blizzard: depression and occluded front blocked just west of Britain

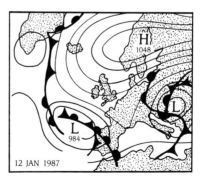

Fig 23b Freeze: burgeoning high forces Atlantic lows to the south

lying just offshore in the Atlantic. This pressure gradient brought strong winds, and the air was so cold that any moisture picked off the North Sea brought saturation and was immediately shed as snow down eastern Britain.

The result was chaos in Fife, East Anglia and Kent, while the Highlands escaped with a bitterly cold but settled week, the snowfalls and cloud cover decreasing westwards, so that the Cuillin enjoyed a rare phase of sun and frost. The snow was hard, the ice copious and the weather manageable if one wrapped up well. It was a rare stroke of irony that many climbers willing to make the journey were snow-bound in the east and south, so that a winter raid on the misty isle remained as elusive as ever.

11 March 1987: Magic (Fig 23c)

Let a continental anticyclone fill out over Britain, and watch for the polar front resetting itself well to our north-west to leave the mid-Atlantic slack and quiet. Then the formula is right for a day of such splendour that one suspects it was especially ordained in the service of human delight. It was our luck to climb on Creag Meagaidh such a magical day in March when the air was utterly still, and its clarity unblemished save for the lazy trails of valley fog. The Highlands were arrayed with serene grace on our every side, and sunset's glow lingered long into the night. Yet the most romantic sight was on the homeward drive over

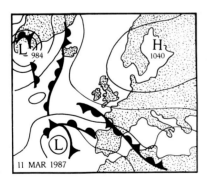

Fig 23c Magic: polar front lying far to the north-west of Britain: stable high, light winds

Cluanie where the dark and silhouetted hillsides on either side were girdled with great rings of dancing red flame. Never is the heather in a drier state for burning than during a winter drought. This strange and beautiful vision tugged us still deeper into the land of dreams, the capping to a perfect day, and the sure promise of another to come.

Witnessing three days of such total contrast, it is hard to credit that the weather of each was dominated by the same type of continental anticyclone. The differences lay first in the specific positioning of the high and secondly in the pressure pattern on its margins. The 1984 blizzard might never have occurred had the high pressure edged just 300km (200 miles) further to the west and blocked the front out over the Atlantic. The severity of 1987's freeze could be guessed on tracing the Siberian origin of the anticyclone and noting its remarkable intensity, while those days of perfection can be imagined on a glance at a chart so devoid of conflict and incident as that of 11 March. The weather map foretold the likely story of all three: it can be an invaluable tool to the mountaineer.

AN EYE TO THE WEATHER

With regular trips into the hills, it is surprising how one develops an instinctive visual and sensual awareness of changes in the weather. Native hill-dwellers even claim to be able to 'sniff' a coming storm. Whatever the confidence and quality of the forecast, it is most reassuring to be able to make an 'on the spot' prognosis of the coming weather and, if committed to a multi-day expedition in the hills, personal observation is the sole means of prediction.

But omens of the 'red sky at night' variety have three drawbacks. They are by no means infallible, are sometimes ambiguous and they err strongly on the side of caution. Many times I have curtailed an itinerary or hurried nervously through a day due to the sight of a wall of cloud in the west, only for the expected front to falter or fail, or else to materialise as a harmless sea-haze rather than the imagined storm. Furthermore, it is much easier to spot possible symptoms of bad weather than to foresee the change to good simply because in the latter case vision is likely to be limited to 20m (22yd) by the prevailing storm. Therefore, weather pessimists tend to make great play of the visual signs, for they can always offer the 'better safe than sorry' excuse if they prove groundless.

It is particularly hard to estimate the timing and the intensity of bad weather from the sight of distant cloud banks. However, with experience, a better discretion can be developed in their judgement. Cloud forms and sequences (Fig 24) provide the best evidence of the pending weather, but there are other general signs – the sudden awareness of the temperature rise and the flatness of the light as high pressure is displaced by an advancing low, or else the drier chill in the air as an easterly breeze takes hold and repels the maritime weather. A common ploy is to gauge the position of low-pressure areas from the wind direction. Applying the law of anti-clockwise airflow, if you stand on a summit with your back to the wind, then the depression is on your left. With this information, one can piece together the approximate synoptic pattern even when on the hills. Regular climbers soon acquire a 'feel' for the weather. It is an integral part of a mountain education.

THE REGIONAL PATTERN

An area 325 × 240km (200 × 150 miles) in maximum extent as is the Highlands is bound to exhibit significant local variations of weather and these may crucially influence where one should choose to climb.

Regional contrasts may be briefly manifested when a slow-moving depression crosses directly over Scotland, the differences lying in the timing rather than the substance of the associated weather. With practice, they can be effectively exploited. For example, if the depression or front has a northward track, it will bear easterly winds to its north and moist westerlies to its south. By keeping to the Northern Highlands, as much as twelve hours of cold, hard conditions can be snatched before the centre passes and the thaw sets in. So, living near Torridon, I never abandon

hope for the day if the depression is encroaching from the south. 'Beating the weather' is the most smugly satisfying of all mountain pastimes. The pleasure of supping tea by the fireside with the rain drumming outside, yet having just enjoyed a hard dry traverse of Liathach is incomparable, but its achievement often demands an early start and a spurt of speed.

The mountains also exert a barrier effect on the weather which produces a more persistent regional effect, usually between east and west. Regularly and at any time of year, Atlantic fronts lie over the west coast, yet either fail to penetrate or else expend their moisture before reaching inland. The western hills are dreich and clouded, sweating in the tropical maritime air, while the east remains dry and even frosty.

The greater cold and dryness of the rain-shadowed east is, of course, generally known. Less widely appreciated is the winter phenomenon of the 'snow-shadowed' west, when continental air-flow brings cloud and snow off the North Sea over the Grampians and Cairngorms. The case of the 'big freeze' of January 1987 (Fig 23b) is a perfect illustration, but it is not an isolated instance. West-coasters secretly enjoy long periods of winter sun that are denied elsewhere when the easterlies blow, and the further west the better.

THE SEASONAL PATTERN – WHEN TO GO

The variability of winter weather is not entirely random. There are distinguishable patterns through the season that deserve close scrutiny when you plan a winter mountain holiday. These patterns might best be defined as singularities – periods in which one type of weather tends to be dominant. The timing of the phases is flexible and there is no certainty that they will occur at all, yet the tendencies became apparent to the regular hillgoer.

The least fortunate yet most persistent of these regularities is the mild and stormy period which centres on Christmas, the one period when people can get to the hills en masse for a week's holiday. The end of 1987 gave a particularly sustained deluge, tropical maritime air sweeping the whole

Fig 24 A HEAD IN THE CLOUDS: WEATHER OMENS

Cloud Forms		
LAYERED (STRATIFORM) Uniform layer above summits, eg fish-scale pattern.		Stable air; usually an inversion lies above; quiet weather with anticyclonic conditions.
Multi-layered; thickening and lowering in distance.		Imminent approach of warm (or occluded) front; prolonged steady precipitation likely; accompanying warmth.
HIGH LEVEL CIRRUS 'White mares' tails', wisps.		Indication of moisture in upper atmosphere and an early sign of a frontal system 12–24 hours away.
HALOES/ATMOSPHERIC HAZE Watery sky-haloed sun.		General moisture in upper air; more reliable sign of the approach of fronts; layering sequence of cloud will follow.
CUMULIFORM Vertical development; 'cotton wool'/ 'cauliflower' shapes.		Instability and uplift in atmosphere; typical of a cold-front passage; air cooling; general weather likely to improve; snow showers.
CUMULONIMBUS Towering cumulus forms; thunder clouds.		Extreme instability; violent uplift and cooling; squalls of hail and ice; frequent in winter under strong NW air-flow.
Anvil-shaped CuNimbus.		The forward edge to the lee of the wind indicates a rapid rise of wind speed with height; gales on the tops.
LENTICULAR/WAVE FORMS Regular waves or lens-shaped clouds in lee of summits.		Uplift over mountains causing condensation; wave forms suggest an inversion against stable upper air; weather possibly windy but usually settled.
Summit cappings/shrouds.		Often indicates severe wind on the tops, but not a reliable sign of a coming storm as is often thought.
FOGS AND LOW-LEVEL INVERSIONS Smoke/mist rises vertically, then spreads at distinct level.		Stable sinking air; anticyclonic conditions; light wind.
CLOUD MOVEMENTS		
DIRECTION Cloud layers veer with height often from SW-NW.		Indicates the pattern of wind-shear typical of warm fronts.
Cloud layers back with height often from NW–SW.		Opposing wind directions indicate cold-front conditions.
SPEED Judged against hill-sides.		An obvious indication of wind speed, especially if clouds are individually distinct.

country in a series of fronts originating from lows 'standing off' in the Atlantic and leaving hardly a patch of snow anywhere by New Year's Day. The tremendous spate made waterfall visits obligatory, but rendered every river-crossing highly hazardous. Capitulation to the temptations of alcohol at Hogmanay can be excused after such a spell.

Yet early January often sees a complete swing to

Plate 8 Cirrus cloud wisps – often the first harbingers of an approaching frontal system– high above the Lancet Edge in the Ben Alder Forest (*Jim Barton*)

polar air and heavy snowfall, although the weather may remain stormy. Later in the season, conditions typically settle down. The odds greatly

Plate 9 A thickening sequence of stratiform clouds threatens the Braeriach plateau in the Cairngorms – a sure sign of approaching frontal weather

favour a dry anticyclonic spell in mid-February, the hope of which, coupled with school half-term vacations, attracts greater numbers to the hills than any other period of the season. However, for the first year in five, 1988 failed to offer a single settled spell through February's span.

It is easily forgotten in our preoccupation with the dramatic and the extreme that there are also long periods of what is best described as 'quiet' weather, when the pressure patterns are slack and the fronts indecisive, the sky thinly overcast and the breeze light and chill. They might not be wildly inspiring but are ideal for getting things done on the mountains and are regularly encountered late in the season – but you should watch out for a final cold snap around Easter-time when a sequence of polar maritime storms often brings heavy fresh snowfall.

The phasing of weather through the winter is determined by the pressure pattern in the middle and upper layers of the troposphere. Large-scale pressure ridges and troughs at an altitude of around 5km (16,000ft) essentially control the sequence of weather types, but the mechanisms of change are highly complex. The seasonal pattern is also influenced by the annual heat budget of the earth's surface. While the receipt of sunshine reaches its minimum on the shortest day, the cooling of the earth is lagged so that the minimum temperatures at the surface are reached long after 21 December. The delayed response is especially marked in our maritime climate because of the sea's greater heat-retention capacity (specific heat). Thus, February is the coldest month of the year. Thereafter, the re-emergent sun produces a progressive heating back towards the summer.

So this is our winter mountain weather. It challenges, baffles and inspires, and it still remains far beyond our complete understanding. The hillgoer can gain immeasurable practical benefit from its study, but is never its master. And indeed, much of the particular fun of being in the Scottish hills in winter derives from planning in the face of its uncertainty. So we climb in the surety that the weather will continue to spring its surprises. Whatever our abilities, nature will on occasion assert an insuperable power and leave us humbled, yet strangely content . . .

AN IMPOSSIBLE STORM

20 March 1986 on the Cairngorm Plateau

On the night of Wednesday 19 March, three groups from Glenmore Lodge occupied snow-holes at 1,050m in the valley of the Garbh Uisge Beag between Cairn Gorm and Ben Macdui. Their leaders were Sam Crymble, Mark Diggins ('Digger') and Willie Todd, and the students were undergoing their Winter Mountain Leadership Assessment, which involves a two-night expedition with intensive navigation exercises.

While they lay sound and snug in the holes, insulated from the world outside, a depression and its associated fronts were tracking steadily eastwards over the Atlantic. At first the weathermen saw no particular evil in this approaching system, but as the night progressed it was squeezed into a north-east trajectory as a huge zone of high pressure built to its south. Then, quite suddenly, its further advance was barred by an equally strong anticyclone sitting over continental Europe [see Fig 25]. With nowhere to escape, the depression could only deepen, and it deepened fast. At half-past midnight, as its fronts occluded and swept into Britain, the anemometer on Cairn Gorm's summit recorded a southerly gale averaging 162kmph (101mph) and rising to an incredible gust of 275kmph (171mph) – Britain's highest-ever measured wind speed. All hell was breaking loose.

Thursday morning's weather forecast was still a step behind the reality. When the groups radioed to the Lodge at 9am, they were told to expect 110kmph (70mph) winds gusting to 160kmph (100mph). Now 70mph is difficult

Fig 25a: AN IMPOSSIBLE STORM
The forecast chart for 12 noon on 20 March 1986. Pressure in millibars

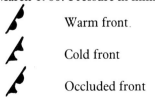

Warm front.

Cold front

Occluded front

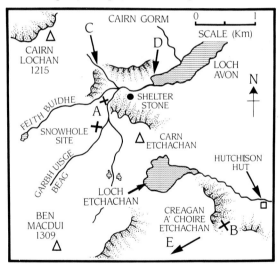

b: THE DRAMA ON THE PLATEAU

A: Crymble's avalanche
B: Diggins' fall and avalanche
C: Barton/Peter rescue route
D: Fyffe/Walker rescue route
E: Escape to Glen Derry/Braemar – Diggins' team

and 100mph means crawling, but Lodge instructors are hardened to severe winds, for these speeds are by no means exceptional in winter on the high Cairngorms. Provided they were no worse, they could cope, and so at 9.30 the teams dug themselves out of the holes and separately embarked on a day of navigational tests.

The wind indeed had dropped, and for a brief half-hour fell below gale force, but the storm was far from spent. The depression centre was just crossing northwards over the Cairngorms massif, a vortex of calm within a tightening funnel of plunging pressure. Aviemore met office staff had watched their barometer drop at the alarming rate of 10mb every three hours to a minimum of 974mb at the centre. Now the occluded front pushed through, causing the wind to veer sharply to the WNW and commence a rapid reacceleration, but by this time the parties were far from the holes.

Crymble took his three students north to Cairn Lochan, Todd went over to Loch Etchachan and Diggins further south on the upper slopes of Macdui. At 11.20, the wind was averaging 85mph and gusting 115. By 12.50, it averaged 97 and gusted to 141. The 100mph threshold of control was quickly exceeded, and with the frontal passage there came frequent blizzards to add to the furious clouds of spindrift. Diggins describes the havoc caused by the sudden rise of wind as his team were crossing a col south of Loch Etchachan:

After 500m, the wind seemed to increase tenfold. The leading student was hardly able to stay on the ground at this point, being blown across the surface for 50–60ft (15–18m) before braking with his axe. The wind would subside and we would slowly crawl to regroup, swinging our axes ahead of us and then hauling ourselves along with them. Sometimes the wind was so strong that we had great difficulty holding onto our axes while lying on the ground . . . Communication was also extremely difficult. It was largely done by gesticulating, for a shouted sentence could not be heard from more than 2in (5cm) away from an ear.

Any pretence at training was quickly abandoned. They *had* to get some shelter. For Diggins' party the Hutchison Hut in Coire Etchachan was the nearest sanctuary, and luckily their route lay with the wind, but was snared by steep cliffs and bluffs at the corrie rim. Digger therefore took the lead but as he neared the edge was caught in an especially vicious squall. Moments later he was airborne. He had walked straight over a cornice and landed 15m lower, minus axe but unhurt with his party now stranded above. He tried vainly to climb back up but the cornice edge was overhung and as soon as he tried to descend, the whole slope avalanched. With a desperate scramble, he climbed up and off the moving slab and braked to a halt with fingers clawed in the underlying snow.

There was no choice but to descend to the hut and hope against hope that his students had avoided the edge and could somehow find a route to safety. In the clearances he went out to search, but there was no sign. On one sortie the wind blew him into the air and he landed only after a complete backward somersault. Nor could he make any radio contact with the Lodge, and after a couple of hours decided to attempt to crawl the 2km over to Loch Avon and thence regain the snow-holes.

Meanwhile, Crymble had been close to the Feith Buidhe when the hurricane rose, and made straight back for the holes which were only a kilometre distant. He navigated solely by instinct and his intimate knowledge of the terrain, for compasswork was quite impossible. As he neared the site, he turned to check his team and was horror-struck to discover that one man was missing: 'I could only assume that he had been blown away, onto and down the steep ground to the east.'

With the remaining two students, he sweep-searched the area without success before crawling back to the holes, which were reached at 2.30 as the gale reached its climax with a 180kmph (112mph) mean and a 243kmph (151mph) gust. No sooner had he radioed the loss to the Lodge, than his radio, like Digger's, packed up.

Down in Glenmore, a major rescue operation was mounted. Within an hour, instructors Barton and Peter, and Fyffe and Walker were battling up onto the Cairngorm plateau in 100mph crosswinds and the Police, the RAF and local rescue teams were all on alert.

Despite the extreme weather and avalanche risk, Crymble's team had to face the fearful prospect of going back out to search for their man as soon as the wind had abated slightly. They were spread out 5m apart on the steepening ground NE of the holes when the wind-slab released. All were carried off, but Crymble went the furthest. He was spat out of the avalanche minus axe and gloves in a pile of debris 90m lower, alive but with a suspected broken ankle. Rejoined by his students who were unhurt, it was to be a long slow crawl back to the holes . . .

5.20, and just two hours of daylight remained. Still the wind gusted over 100 and in the north-west air-flow the temperature had dropped to −5°C. At the Lodge, the air was fraught with tension. There had been no radio contact with any of the teams, Todd's included, for nearly three hours. In desperation, the RAF were even asked whether they could raise a Nimrod jet to provide an airborne radio relay aerial above the plateau. There were eighteen people on the hill, one known to be missing and thirteen unaccounted for. Then miraculously things began to happen:

5.45: Braemar police ring to report Mark Diggins' four students safe. With great courage, they had retraced their steps from the cornice edge and found an alternative route down to Glen Derry. In Digger's later words, it was 'a true display of their ability'.

At base, however, anxieties for Diggins were immediately redoubled. One could only fear for the worst, but as the wind ebbed to 80mph, some semblance of control could be regained by the men on the hill:

5.46: Barton and Peter radio to report they have reached the Garbh Uisge Beag and are searching for the holes.

5.47: Tim Walker radios; nothing heard except ' . . . Digger!? . . .'

6.11: Walker radios again from Shelter Stone. By pure chance they have found Diggins safe and well.

6.30: Crymble reaches the holes just before Barton and Peter arrive. To his incredible relief, the missing student is there. For nearly an hour he had remained where he had lost contact and then found his own way back to the holes, probably passing just metres away from Crymble's ill-fated search team. Using Bob Barton's radio, the good news is broadcast.

6.32: Walker, Fyffe and Diggins are climbing the avalanche-loaded slopes beneath the Garbh Uisge. Relaying messages via base, Barton guides them to the holes, using bearings and estimated distances from a boulder landmark.

6.50: The three reach the holes.

Of Willie Todd's group there had been neither sight nor sign. Then, at 7.25, as if by magic, they walked through the front door of the Lodge, having evacuated by a 16km hike over the Saddle and down Strath Nethy when radio contact was lost at Loch Avon.

All were safe thanks to exceptional skill, resource and courage in the face of impossible conditions, though the element of luck cannot be denied. It was just fortunate that none less experienced were on the high tops that day. A helicopter evacuation of the injured Crymble was arranged for the morning, and at the Garbh Uisge Beag, nine exhausted men recovered and repaired their wits.

No sooner was the drama over than the storm declined, almost in admission of its defeat. Having wreaked merciless fury for twenty-four hours and put those caught in its path to the ultimate survival test, the cyclone unwound, passing away north into oblivion somewhere over Scandinavia. By 10pm, Cairn Gorm's anemometer was spinning merrily at a mere 65kmph (40mph), just gale force 8 on the Beaufort scale and a playful breeze by the standards of the day.

4

THE INFERNAL CONDITIONS

Snow and Ice on the Scottish Hills

No topic arouses more discussion in Highland bothies and bar-rooms on winter nights than the state of the snow and ice. Our obsession with the conditions is understandable, for they largely determine both the safety and enjoyment of all the winter mountain activities. Since they are dependent upon the weather regime, they exhibit its same capricious temperament. During the typical Scottish winter, the conditions can be eternally damned and immortally praised by the same climber on successive days without his feeling the least inconsistency of opinion.

THE SUPPLY OF SNOW

'Conditions' are the product of what is laid down as precipitation and its subsequent alteration on the ground. The mechanics of snowfall have already been discussed in Chapter 2 (p41). There are four typical weather situations when significant snowfall is produced over the mountains:

1 **Polar maritime (PM)** air-flow in depressions gives frequent and often heavy showers of hail and rimed pellets, usually accompanied by wind. The snowfall is widespread, but is most concentrated on the west and north-west coastal mountains. Returning PM air from a westerly quarter tends to produce wetter, heavier snow turning to sleet or rain low down (ie, snowflake aggregates). The duration and intensity is much increased by associated frontal activity.

2 **Polar continental (PC)** air-flow over the North Sea gives snow showers, which are strongly localised on the east of the country. The snow is usually drier and exhibits less rime icing. If the easterly or south-easterly air-flow is intensified by approaching depressions, the snowfall may spread inland as blizzards over the Cairngorms.

3 **Depression tracks over southern Britain** often produce winter's greatest blizzards, especially when a deep low moves north-eastwards across England and southern Scotland, and entrains an easterly airstream over the Highlands, which is more moist than the pure PC air of 2 above, but is cooled sufficiently to give heavy widespread snow at all levels.

4 **Northerly arctic maritime** air-flow (AM) produces localised falls on exposed coastal hills, usually as showers, but occasionally intensifying into gentle steady snowfall of a dry crystalline type over the whole country. When a depression is sitting in the North Sea, the resultant northerly flow may bring particularly heavy snowfall over the Cairngorms and Northern Highlands.

CHANGES ON THE GROUND

Settling: As fresh snow piles up, it becomes compressed by its own overlying weight. The new grains may be considerably deformed and the density of the snow cover increased. Typically, the air content of fresh snow which has fallen without wind is 90–95 per cent. Settling may on its own reduce this to 70 per cent in twenty-four hours.

Equitemperature metamorphism (ET met) (Fig 26): Simultaneous with settling, there occurs a process of vapour transport within the lying snow-pack which produces first a rounding of grain shapes (Fig 26a) and then their joining together by

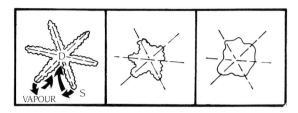

S: Moisture sublimates from crystal tips into vapour

D: Vapour deposited at centre of crystal

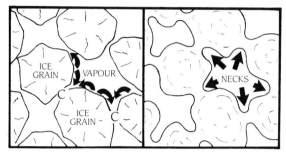

C: Vapour is deposited at the contact points between the grains

Fig 26 EQUITEMPERATURE METAMORPHISM:
a) Of a single stellar crystal
b) At the contact points within the snow-pack
(*from* Avalanche Handbook, *1976*)

the formation of necks at the contact points (Fig 26b). During the first stage, there is a temporary loss of stability as the interlocked crystals are modified, but once bonding begins, a progressive stabilisation of the snow-pack is promoted.

Vapour transport and deposition have already been explained in Chapter 2 (p43) in relation to snow crystal formation. Within the snow-pack, the similar process occurs because there is a lower vapour saturation pressure with respect to concave than convex ice surfaces. Thus, there is a progressive migration of vapour from the crystal tips to their concave interstices. ET met is accelerated at temperatures of just below zero, and has a more pronounced effect on elaborately branched crystal forms, whereas rounded pellets and hail may lie unaltered in loose piles for long periods. If uninterrupted, it will, over many days, produce

hard stable firn snow with about 35 per cent air content. Note that the process does not involve any melting of the snow. It proceeds wholly at subzero temperatures. In the Scottish climate, however, the gradual progress of ET met is usually eclipsed either by wind action or a thaw.

Melt-freeze metamorphism (MF met): Thawing and refreezing within the pack is the more usual stabilising agent of Scottish snow. Snowfall may be subject to immediate melting on contact with a ground surface with temperature above freezing point. Alternatively, a lying snow-cover will melt from its surface downwards when a warm air-mass encroaches overhead and initiates a thaw. Melting creates 'free water' within the snow which clings by surface tension to the larger remaining snow grains. On refreezing, whether due to night cooling or on arrival of a colder airstream, the grains are enlarged and bonded. A strong uniform snow-pack is produced with as little as 20 per cent air content.

However, if MF met proceeds through many successive cycles, grain sizes enlarge to a point where free water can percolate down through the snow during the melt phase. No longer do the grains bond on refreezing and loose granular snow is produced which is roundly cursed as 'sugar' or 'corn' by mountaineers, but more correctly termed 'spring snow'.

Wind transport and alteration: At the higher altitudes, wind is a guaranteed accompaniment to nearly every snowfall, lifting and pulverising the grains into tiny broken particles (typically a tenth of their original size) which are then packed into drifts in sheltered lee slopes. As Fig 27 shows, the mode and volume of transport varies with the wind speed. Wind-deposited snow may be three times denser than new loose snow, with an air content around 35 per cent and a uniform grain size. It has a dull chalky appearance because rounded grains are not reflective of light as is unaltered crystalline snow.

Water infiltration: This is highly significant in Scotland's warm climate and occurs in three ways:

1 Direct rainfall penetrating the surface of the snow and percolating downwards as 'free water'.

2 Surface drainage channelled from above, seeping between the snow layers or else draining along the ground base of the snow – important in gullies or beneath cliffs.

3 Ground-water drainage from joints or spring lines, which is significant in initiating ice development.

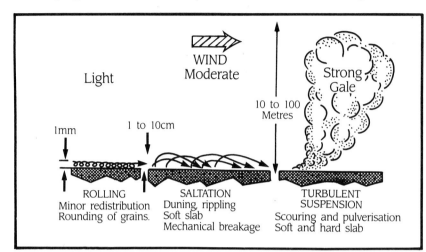

Fig 27 FORMS AND EFFECTS OF WIND ACTION ON SNOW (*from* Avalanche Handbook, *1976*)

Plate 10 Snow in motion. Spindrift clouds on Sgurr Dubh, Torridon (*Clarrie Pashley*)

Fig 28 FORMS OF WATER ACTION ON THE SNOW-PACK

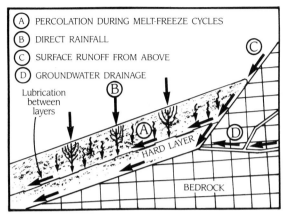

(A) PERCOLATION DURING MELT-FREEZE CYCLES
(B) DIRECT RAINFALL
(C) SURFACE RUNOFF FROM ABOVE
(D) GROUNDWATER DRAINAGE

Lubrication between layers

HARD LAYER

BEDROCK

In its liquid form, external water lubricates and destabilises the snow, but if it freezes within the pack, it causes immediate bonding and hardening to produce what British climbers call 'névé', with an air content of 20 per cent or less.

Surface crusting and hoaring: MF met may be confined to the surface layers during a temporary rise in air temperatures and will produce an icy top to the snow-pack. However, crusts and hoar crystals also form readily in subzero conditions, given a regime of daytime insolation (radiational heating by the sun) and night-time radiational cooling. This will occur in clear, settled weather when the flux of surface temperature is far greater than that of the overlying air (as explained in Chapter 2, p44).

Convection and evaporation: A dry wind at a temperature of above zero rapidly accelerates the removal of snow, by evaporation of melted water on the surface and by direct sublimation of the snow grains into vapour. A block of snow may be reduced in volume by 20 per cent due to direct evaporation if exposed for just 1½ hours to a dry wind of 32kmph (20mph). Accompanying this shrinkage is a disintegration of the bonds between the snow grains to produce a granular texture. Convection therefore accelerates the development of rotten spring snow (see melt-freeze metamorphism, above). Conversely, when a fall in temperature to below zero is accompanied by a wind,

Fig 29 CHANGES WITHIN THE SNOW-PACK. At any stage a sustained thaw can completely melt the pack. In Scotland, routes 1 and 2 usually overtake the central route (3)

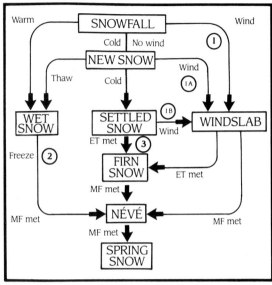

freezing and hardening of a wet snow-pack is almost instantaneous.

Several of these processes may operate concurrently and they may be complicated by further snowfall, but they do link into regular sequences of snow and ice development, the major of which can be traced in Fig 29.

THE RESULTANT SNOWSCAPE

The layered profile: The progressive deposition and modification of snow during the season produces a multi-layered pack in the major accumulation areas – ie, the corries, gullies and sheltered concavities.

If a trench is dug to expose a multi-layered profile, a visual history of the snow is obtained and potential avalanche danger is often revealed in the form of weak layers, sharp discontinuities or water lubrication. By visual inspection of the snow type and 'rule-of-thumb' tests of snow hardness and moisture content (Fig 30), each stratum can be classified and the composite profile

Fig 31 FOUR TYPICAL SCOTTISH SNOW PROFILES:

a EARLY SEASON DANGER

Weather: see Chapter 3, for detailed reconstruction; turbulent polar airstream → hail, followed by northerly wind (strong at first) → slab

Conditions: in sheltered gullies and lee hollows wind-slab is deposited on loose hail, an unstable weak layer → avalanche risk

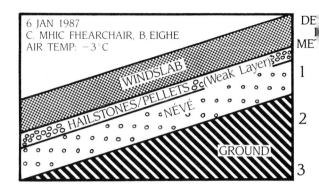

b HEAVY ACCUMULATION

Weather: slow-moving front giving prolonged steady snowfall. Wind light, then rising to fresh → very soft slab laid on top of loose grains.

Conditions: deep 'bottomless' snow in corries; danger of collapse due to overloading of loose snow and growing avalanche risk as wind-slabs thicken on top. Awful climbing conditions

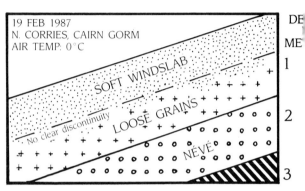

c A QUICK FREEZE

Weather: heavy rain on the previous day; a cold-front passage bringing an overnight frost; light snow showers.

Conditions: rainwater penetration of the top 30cm (12in) enabled a rapid freeze to give an excellent stable crust. Superb snow-climbing conditions were created overnight. No avalanche risk because water flowing through the profile has now refrozen and stabilised the layers

d SPRING CONDITIONS

Weather: successive snowfalls over the last four days were separated by sunny spells; frost during the previous night

Conditions: four layers of moist slab and frozen crust were identified, directly reflecting the sequence of the weather. Surface sun-crust was supportive early in the day, but insolation quickly melted the top layers producing slush by early afternoon. Possible wet-slab avalanche risk due to water lubrication later in the day. Best to make an early start

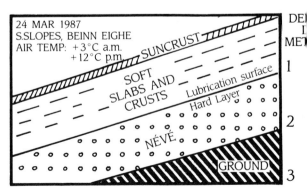

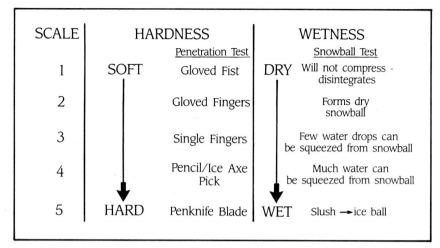

SCALE	HARDNESS		WETNESS	
		Penetration Test		Snowball Test
1	SOFT	Gloved Fist	DRY	Will not compress - disintegrates
2		Gloved Fingers		Forms dry snowball
3		Single Fingers		Few water drops can be squeezed from snowball
4		Pencil/Ice Axe Pick		Much water can be squeezed from snowball
5	HARD	Penknife Blade	WET	Slush → ice ball

Fig 30 EXAMINING THE SNOW PROFILE: THE RULE-OF-THUMB SCALES. NB: Sharp differences in hardness or moisture between adjacent layers indicate instability and avalanche risk

assessed. Fig 31 examines four profiles that were encountered during the winter of 1986–7, each reflecting a different weather history and offering wholly different climbing and walking conditions.

Wind-slab: Most prominent and notorious of all layered forms of snow in Scotland is the wind-slab. Wind-blown snow is deposited as an independent layer of broken grains which has little or no physical anchorage with the larger grains and crystals of the underlying layers (see Fig 31a), yet is internally cohesive due to its uniformity of texture and dense packing. The texture of different slabs varies greatly, but it is normal to apply a single division between 'soft' and 'hard', depending on whether their surface will bear the weight of the human boot. The factors determining the hardness of slabs are:

1 Wind speed: The degree of pulverisation varies directly with the speed of wind, and the finer are the resultant grains the denser is the slab.
2 Distance of transport: The degree of mechanical breakage also must vary with the duration of transit. Therefore, if grains are moved only a short distance, they will retain both size and shape and so form a less dense 'soft' slab when they are deposited.
3 ET met and settling within a slab after it has been deposited will promote its progressive hardening.

4 Air temperature and humidity must also be of significance in the form of mechanical damage and the subsequent slab-packing, but their exact role has not yet been studied in detail.

Slabs remain weakly anchored to the slope beneath until metamorphism creates some bonding. This can be achieved by prolonged ET met, but in Scotland a melt-freeze cycle more normally intervenes, the melting destroying the definition of the slab and the refreezing bonding the snow into an amorphous profile.

Cornices: The tearing wind that blasts the wearied climber and lays down the hidden trap of the wind-slab is also responsible for creating the most elegant snow sculptures of which the cornice is pre-eminent. Gerald Seligman described the contrast thus:

Curling over the crest of a ridge, the shrieking storm whirls the snow grains with it, and deposits them with a gentle care fantastic for so wild an agent, gradually fashioning the most perfectly moulded cornice coverings to the ridge, every curve a delight to the eye – surely one of the most extraordinary paradoxes of beauty arising from evil.[1]

The typical cornice shape and features are shown in Fig 32 and Plate 11. Cornice and wind-slab

Fig 32 THE CORNICE: FEATURES AND FORMATION

1 Outward growth by surface deposition and interlocking
2 Scoop and overhang enlarged by lee vortex and updraught

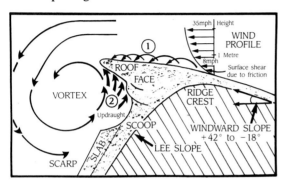

formation is closely associated, the corniced crest usually harbouring a wind-slab in its lee scarp. The wind is the cause of both, but how exactly does it produce an overhang of snow?

The question has long intrigued snow scientists. Traditional theories invoked the dynamic action of wind-flow over ridge crests (as described in Chapter 2, p30) in creating a standing vortex with associated updraught on the immediate lee side (Fig 32(2)). The up-draught could conceivably erode snow from the scarp and redeposit the grains on the underside of the roof, so extending the overhang. However, this process requires the prior existence of a roof on which to build.

A possible key to the problem lies in the observation that cornices develop within the wind-speed range of 24–72kmph (15–45mph), above which they tend to be scoured and destroyed. Thus, a fresh cornice has the texture of soft wind-slab. Due to surface friction, a free air speed of 56kmph (35mph) is reduced to 11–13kmph (7–8mph) at ground level. At this speed, snow grains could easily be deposited on the top of the crest and interlock with existing snow to give a surface strength that resists further wind removal (Fig 32(1)). This is especially plausible since at moderate wind speeds, the degree of pulverisation is limited, so that grains retain their tips and thus their ability to hook and interlock. In this way, an initial canopy could be built out over the lee slope.

During a thaw, a wetted snow-pack tends to sag and slump at a break of slope, producing a meringue-shaped roll over the edge. This could also provide the initial canopy for subsequent extension by vortex updraught.

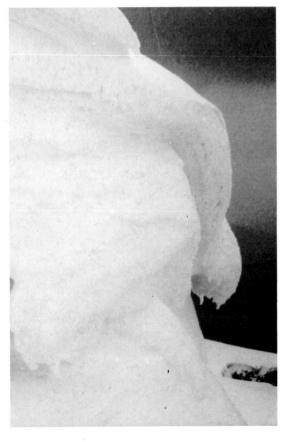

Plate 11 'Beauty arising from evil' – cornice at the top of Tower Ridge, Ben Nevis

5 (*right, above*) Cloud window through the head of the Allt Daim valley between Aonach Beag and Carn Mor Dearg as viewed from the upper slopes of Aonach Mor, Lochaber (*Helen Charlton*)

7 (*below*) Climbers descending from the Saddle under a cumulus-filled sky on Easter Sunday 1988, against a backdrop of Ladhar Bheinn (left), Eigg and Rhum (right)

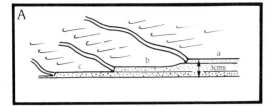

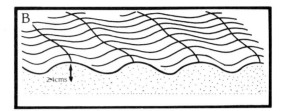

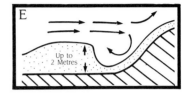

Fig 33 SNOW SCULPTURES

A Surface striations: a, b, c – laminae of different grain sizes sorted by wind (largest on bottom), then exposed by differential wind erosion

B Wind ripples: wind sorting in to ridge and furrows possibly by bombardment of surface grains (saltation). NB: wind-slabs are never rippled

C Wind ridges/dunes: continuous saltation of grains by light winds

D Barchans: horseshoe dunes formed by eddy in lee of dune crests

E Wind scoops: eddy action at base of obstacle

Whatever the validity of these conjectures, the enormous size of cornices deserves our respect. The Garbh Choire of Braeriach develops some of Scotland's biggest cornices due to its altitude and the vast snow supply area of the Great Moss to its windward. Horizontal projections of over 6m (20ft) are normal late in the season. Cornices harden and stabilise in the same ways as any other snow, and an alternating cycle of fresh snowfall and melt-freeze enables the progressive construction of these huge multi-layered features.

Double cornices projecting on either side of the same ridge are the nightmare of climbers in the

6 (left) Climbing into the winter domain. Spindrift and snow devils dance on the cliffs of the south-east corrie of Fuar Tholl

Andes and Alaska and are not unknown in Scotland. Hamish Brown has been repulsed by double lips on modestly inclined ridge crests of Sgurr nan Ceathreamhnan above Glen Affric, and Bob Barton and Dave Morris were greatly hindered by them in an attempt on the Cuillin Ridge traverse in January 1982. They may form in a disjointed fashion by changes in wind direction, or else simultaneously by the side-streaming of a wind-flowing parallel along a ridge crest.

Other wind forms: In its more tender guise, the wind creates a variety of small-scale snow forms, each the product of differential rates of erosion and deposition, and which are closely akin to desert sand features. When in a dry loose state, snow behaves mechanically in similar fashion to sand. For example, dry snow of varying crystal content can be sieved and sorted by a light wind, then deposited as a series of laminates of equal grain size to produce a striated surface (Fig 33a) evocative of desert scenery. Likewise, the scoops, dunes, ripples and barchans depicted in Fig 33 are all formed by surface drift under gentle wind action, a constant flow and sifting of grains close to the ground which produces a mesmeric and disorientating visual effect. Together they produce a winter landscape of soft and lonely beauty on our high moors.

Sadly, light winds and low temperatures are rarely sustained for long in Scotland and these delicate features will often be destroyed by a gale or else collapse during a thaw. More commonly encountered are sastrugi which are erosion forms carved by stronger winds. Typically, they are initiated by the selective penetration of a surface crust which allows the wind to dig out pockets and troughs in the loose snow beneath. The resultant ridge and furrow pattern is a delight to behold but a bane to enjoyable ski-ing. The sight of sastrugi should also arouse the sneaking concern that the eroded snow is likely to have been deposited as wind-slab on the lee slopes.

The scoured summits: Wind is the predominant agent in the construction of Scotland's snow-scapes, but its action also leaves the exposed parts

Plate 12a Wind carving. Duning and ripples on the crest of Aonach Meadhoin, Glen Shiel

Plate 12b Wind erosion. Sastrugi ridges on Ben Wyvis on 23 January 1985. Picture taken minutes before our avalanche during the winter Munros round. The bare grass between the ridges indicates severe wind scouring of the lying snow

of our mountains relatively bare for most of the season. It is rare for a snow profile to develop beyond a single layer plus surface crust on windward convexities and summit plateaux. Regularly the summits are ice-glazed or coated with rime and hoar deposits to give a suitably wintry appearance, but hold no lying snow as such.

ICE FORMATION

A liberal smearing of ice on the hills adds a spectacular splendour to the winter scenery, while a satisfactory ice development is crucial to the climber's sport. It is, therefore, unfortunate that we have very little knowledge of the laws of its formation upon which to base our climbing plans. All too often we are fooled by the ice conditions or lack of them, and even living in the mountains, I remain perplexed how, when all conditions seem to lie in their favour, the cliffs remain quite bare. Here is a subject worthy of a PhD thesis by a mountaineering academic, but in its absence let us try to connect some basic ideas of processes and forms.

There are five possible water sources from which ice can develop:

1 Direct rainfall: typically freezing rain which ices on impact or percolates through the snow.
2 Ground-water drainage: the seepage of stored water from joint-lines in the rock.
3 Surface drainage in gullies and stream-lines.
4 Water circulation within the snow-pack from melt-freeze cycles.
5 Melt-water draining out of the snow-pack above.

Looking at these supplies, it is clear that copious quantities of ice will not develop during a prolonged spell of intensely cold and dry weather. A winter drought merely stifles all the forms of water flow. Any pre-existing surface water will, of course, freeze at its onset, but there can be no progressive development thereafter. A series of melt-freeze cycles would thus seem to be essential, each phase releasing a flow of free water which

thickens and extends the ice on its subsequent refreezing.

Superficially, the idea of cyclical development sounds logical, but on closer thought, how can ice grow when it must surely melt itself and drain off during the thaw phases?

The answer lies in the greater density (or specific gravity) of ice than snow (85–90 per cent compared to 10–60 per cent). This means that snow is far more vulnerable to thawing because of its higher air content. An influx of warm air therefore melts the snow by contact conduction far more rapidly than it penetrates the ice. Thus, as can be observed on icicles, an air thaw produces water from snow melt which trickles down over the ice. Some of this drainage will freeze on contact with the ice. The remainder drips incessantly (often down the unfortunate climber's neck) until the air temperature begins to fall. The rate of melting is at once reduced and as the flow of water over the ice decreases, it is more likely to freeze, particularly the small drops at the bottom of the ice. Thus the ice is extended as well as thickened. The cycle of melt-freeze may be diurnal (night:day) or systematic (ie, controlled by the weather system).

On slopes and cliffs exposed to insolation (direct sunlight), radiational heat exchanges may produce a MF cycle irrespective of the air temperature and thus promote ice formation. This is particularly important where the snow lies thinly over rocks. A dark rock surface is a far better absorber of radiant heat than a reflective white snow-cover and rocks will conduct their absorbed heat to melt the overlying snow. This releases a water supply which will form ice on refreezing. Thus, the edges of snowfields which are in close contact with the ground become very icy and treacherous during a period of insolational melt-freeze, while the deeper snows in the centre remain little altered.

Neither of these thaw processes – an air temperature thaw or radiational melting – must be so intense as to destroy the ice. South-facing cliffs like Hell's Lum in the Cairngorms can be wiped bare by a couple of days of strong sun after mid-season. In fact, the whole cyclical development must be finely calibrated within a limited range of temperatures and durations.

With this framework, we can explain many observations on the mountains. For instance, when a prolonged thaw follows a freeze-up, it is always the ice patches that are the last to melt. Water ice persists on the tracks for two or three days after the snow has disappeared due to its greater density. It is also often seen in very cold, clear weather that the only ice encountered is on south-facing cliffs where an insolational melt-freeze cycle can operate, while north- and east-facing crags remain dry and bare.

One can differentiate several types of ice, depending on their water source and formation process:

White ice: The further hardening of névé snow by MF met and rainfall infiltration which increases the ice content of the pack; absolutely stable and yielding; the climber's dream, but it rarely forms above 70° in angle.

Blue ice: More dense and watery, therefore less reflective and so blue or even green in hue; develops from water drainage combined with direct snowfall (or spindrift fall) which 'sticks' to the ice, augmenting its volume and giving it a plasticity of texture; may thicken progressively to 50cm (20in) plus; forms at any angle; safe and dependable.

Water ice: Pure icicle development from external water flow with no crystalline content and therefore transparent; lacks plasticity and so is hard and brittle; often thin and hollow; may exhibit organ-pipe development or else is layered and 'dinner plates' on being struck; hard and scary to climb.

Verglas: Surface skin of water ice, firmly stuck onto ground surface; formed by impact freezing of rain (ice-glaze) or melt-freeze of surface trickles over rocks; tough and glue-like, less than 25mm (1in) thick, and a hazard to walkers and climbers alike.

Ice crust: Overlies loose snow; a film of ice may initially form by melt-freeze at the surface; it is developed by water trickling from above which freezes over the top of the initial film; highly brittle, false appearance of stability.

Eggshell ice: Bloated ice crust with air gap beneath, which may develop under daily sunshine cycle, the transparent surface film exerting a greenhouse effect on the underlying snow which is evaporated; highly disturbing when encountered on a climb.

IDEAL CONDITIONS

The definition of ideal conditions depends entirely on the sport. The mountaineering all-rounder who can switch between walking, climbing and skiing can exploit a wide range of prevailing conditions, while the specialist becomes frustrated. This is illustrated by briefly comparing the requirements of each winter activity:

Walking: A hard fast surface – either bare frozen ground or névé snow; wind action clears the tops and improves the ridge-walking conditions.

Snow-climbing: Large accumulations of snow (ie, a good 'banking'); stable firn or névé or a melt-freeze crust (see Fig 31c); recent wind action is unfavourable since it produces soft drifts, cornices and wind-slabs.

Ice-climbing: Prolonged melt-freeze cycle; a steady water supply and regular small snowfalls to build up blue or white ice; sustained thaws disastrous.

Mixed climbing: Melt-freeze to consolidate snow on the rocks, then a good frost to freeze vegetation; heavy snowfall swamps the cliffs; wind action may favourably clear them; good conditions can evolve from naught within three days.

Ski-touring: Continuity of cover is paramount, plus a good depth or solid base, light consistent surface texture (ie, powder) is better than hard névé; surface icing or crusting makes skiing very difficult; strong wind action is therefore highly detrimental.

Snow and ice conditions have certain seasonal tendencies which favour one activity over another. December and January may be excellent for walking or buttress climbing. They can give the hard frosts and light snow-cover ideal for either, but rarely develop the volume, continuity or

Fig 34 1985–6: THE BEST WINTER EVER?		
Period	Weather Pattern	Snow and Ice Conditions
THE BUILD-UP 1–25 Dec	Continual TM and rPM air from south and west; lows in mid-Atlantic; mild and wet throughout.	Good snow-cover at end of November completely washed away; Ben Nevis bare of snow by the 14th; large ground-water stocks for future ice development.
26–9 Dec	AM air-flow as a polar high extends south; very cold saturated north to north-east airstream.	Heavy widespread snowfall under light winds; good snow base laid for further accumulation.
30 Dec–9 Jan	Mixture of east and north-west air-flow as lows are pushed down across southern Britain by polar high.	Alternation of snowfalls and brief thaws; varying conditions; consolidation promoted at lower levels.
10–28 Jan	Lows tracking to north of Britain; PM and rPM air dominant; unsettled, windy, snow showers.	Melt-freeze cycles without hiatus; accumulation consolidation and ice development excellent low down, but deep powder over Nevis and Cairngorms slower to consolidate.
THE PROLONGED FRUITION 29 Jan–11 Feb	Atlantic and Scandinavian highs build at same time and join together, cutting the depression tracks and immobilising lows over Greenland and southern Europe; sustained cold PC air-flow from the east.	Conditions stabilised especially in the west; continuous frost; excellent climbing conditions including Ben Nevis; low-level waterfalls freeze all over country.
12–16 Feb	Atlantic high recedes – the spell could be ending, but new lows are blocked by continental high; very windy with snow in the east.	No change in the west, but Cairngorms snowed up.
17–27 Feb	High rebuilds over North Atlantic; the expected break in weather fails; lows pushed south; superb sparkling conditions with light winds.	Conditions unchanged except for occasional snow shower and insolation on southern slopes; snow base rose just 200m all month due to sunburn; no further development; existing snow/ice fossilised.
28 Feb–2 March	The storms regather; frontal activity in arctic pushes high south-west down the Atlantic; weather unchanged but final break now inevitable.	Frantic final burst of climbing activity from Sutherland down to Argyll; hard new ice routes climbed even in the Cuillin.
THE EMPHATIC BREAK 3 March	Sudden change as first front arrives, heralding three weeks of stormy Atlantic weather.	Conditions ruined within two days, but Nevis and Cairngorms retain enough snow and ice to come good again at the season's end.

stability of cover needed to give a good skiing surface or else to fill the gullies. Heavy snowfall early in the winter tends to remain unconsolidated or wind-slabbed (see Fig 31b).

Later in the season, progressive accumulation and more pronounced melt-freeze metamorphism gives the stability needed for snow-climbing and there is a more continuous base for skiing. However, pure ice-climbing becomes highly vulnerable to the incidence of strong sunlight by mid-March. The sustained and intense insolation that can occur in the longer days of late season also produces wet slushy snow on the ridges and southern slopes (Fig 31d) which is inimical to pleasurable walking. Repeated MF met ánd wind-drying can render the gullies full of sugary 'spring snow' by April. Thus, through an average Scottish winter only the prolonged and unmitigated thaw will keep the all-rounder at bay, and even then there is always bothying or river-crossing for amusement.

Occasionally, however, the weather pattern contrives to create superb conditions for every mountain activity. The winter of 1985–6 provides the perfect model of their evolution (Fig 34) and gives a practical basis on which to predict a future repetition. The ordering of each link in the sequence was essential to the development. Had the anticyclonic spell arrived earlier, the required accumulation and consolidation would not have been present. While the conditions during the build-up phase were variously wet, unpleasant or murderous, their final effect was 'the best winter ever' as proclaimed by *Mountain* magazine.

Four features of the sequence can be picked out for future reference:

A wet December is in no way indicative of a poor coming season.
Heavy snowfall over New Year provides a solid starting base for snow/ice development.
A prolonged subsequent spell of cool changeable weather enables a progressive build-up and stabilisation of snow and ice.
A period of settled easterly weather is hard to unseat, but the five-week spell of February 1986 astonished even the natives.

AN AVALANCHE AWARENESS

'Dangerous avalanches are not likely to be encountered in Scotland.' (*W. Naismith, 1893*)[2]

'We have practically no avalanches . . . and no fear of ice cornices.' (*Prof G. Ramsay (1st President of the SMC), 1896*)[3]

'Fresh powder snow lying on old hard snow, which is so frequently the precursor of avalanches in the Alps, is not often encountered in Scotland.' (*Graham Macphee (author Ben Nevis guidebook), 1936*)[4]

To our modern generation which is accustomed to regular news reports of avalanche accidents and is educated by a growing technical literature on the subject, the comments of these early notables of winter mountaineering seem astounding in their complacency. The neglect of the avalanche hazard was due to several reasons. First, Scotland does not produce the large-scale destructive avalanches which in the Alps can overwhelm valley habitations. By comparison, our avalanches are minor localised snow-slides, easily ignored although no less deadly to climbers caught up in them. Secondly, there were only tiny numbers of mountaineers on the hills in winter prior to 1945 compared with today, and even fewer who climbed on steeper snow and in gullies. Therefore, those incidents that did occur were regarded as isolated mischances and did not arouse suspicion of a general hazard. Thirdly, most early snow-climbing was done late in the season around Easter, when the dry wind-slab hazard is less likely to be present and the main danger is the more obvious wet-snow avalanche or cornice collapse during thaw.

Indeed, the first recorded incident involving climbers in Scotland was a cornice collapse and wet-snow avalanche which snubbed a presumptuous attempt on Creag Meagaidh's Centre Post in April 1896. Only two wind-slab avalanches were reported prior to 1914, neither fatal but both on Ben More, Crianlarich, which is still a notorious site.

Only with a series of gully avalanches in the

Plate 13 A windslab fracture in Coire an Lochain, Cairn Gorm, 30 March 1975. The crownwall is 1.5m in vertical height. Contrary to initial impression, it is fairly safe to examine the fracture. Once the slab has released, there is but minimal residual avalanche risk (*courtesy of Bob Barton and Glenmore Lodge*)

1950s, several of which were fatal, was a proper awareness stimulated, although the misconception that open slopes of medium angle (25–45°) were relatively safe still prevailed until corrected by events.

The categorisation, explanation and prediction of important avalanche types in Scotland is the fruition of observation, research and bitter experiences. Five main types demand close attention:

Dry wind-slabs on open slopes: The slab may be 'hard' or 'soft' and threatens climbers, walkers and skiers alike. The avalanche on Ben Wyvis which so nearly ended my designs on a winter Munros traverse in 1985 was of the latter type, fracturing across an open corrie head-wall of a 30–35° angle over a distance of at least 200m (650ft) and leaving the characteristic crown-wall at the fracture line, a fine example being shown in Plate 13. The Wyvis avalanche was full depth down to the ground surface of matted frozen grass which provided the ideal sliding surface. Considering that the slab was released solely by the combined weight of two people, its extent was remarkable but not unusual. Wind-slabs hang by a hair-trigger, waiting for a false move.

Dry wind-slab in gullies and fresh cornice collapse: These often occur together owing to the typical formation of cornice plus wind-slabbed scarp on cliff head-walls overlying old névé (see Fig 32). A cornice collapse will almost always trigger the slab beneath. Both cornice and slab are usually of the 'soft' variety and the hazard can develop literally within minutes of the onset of a blizzard. These avalanches are as likely to be triggered naturally by overloading of the slab as by the weight of unwary climbers. However, the risk may persist for long after the cessation of wind action and is often confined to the final metres of a gully climb with no prior warning signs lower on the slopes.

Large-scale cornice collapses give spectacular results if the debris falls out over a big cliff face. A visit to the corries of Beinn Bhan, Applecross, in January 1986 was rewarded by the sight of a continuous series of airborne powder avalanches, some of which came rather close for comfort (see Plate 14). It was not snowing at the time, but a south-westerly gale was blowing such vast quantities of loose snow onto the corrie head-walls that each gully was avalanching every 20 minutes. Although impressive in appearance and sufficient to have dislodged any climbing party unwise enough to have been on the cliffs, they were feeble in substance and pale imitations of the devastating airborne avalanches that are common in the world's greater ranges. Scotland's hills lack both the height and snowfall volume to produce such

Plate 14 Airborne powder avalanche in Coire na Feola, Beinn Bhan, 17 January 1986 – impressive in sight but feeble in substance (we were merely deluged in fine needles!). Nevertheless, these powder clouds were caused by cornice and windslab fractures on the cliff headwall and indicated deadly climbing conditions

hurricane blasts, although a cornice collapse may be greatly augmented in volume by the scouring of all loose powder snow on the cliffs below.

Overloading during snowfall: Loose slides are common on cliff-faces and in gullies during heavy prolonged snowfall. They do not have great destructive power, but are quite sufficient to dislodge climbers. A greater number of Scottish avalanche casualties are injured during the subsequent fall than by burial.

Wet slab: Given a sudden thaw, water percolation at the slab base (see Fig 28) may so weaken its anchorage as to trigger an avalanche. During spring, the drainage of running water at the base of the snow-pack may cause a full-depth dislocation, especially over rock slabs. The Great Slab of Coire an Lochain in the Cairngorms is the prime example of this type.

Wet-snow slides and cornice collapse: These may be associated with either a widespread thaw or localised insolation on sunny slopes. The snowslide is quite different in nature from the slab, commencing at a single point and accumulating in width and volume downslope. Typically, a 'snowball' rolling off a sun-warmed rock-face will trigger the slide which is slow-moving and usually small in scale. However, the spring cornice collapse may produce far greater slides which possess considerable destructive power. Wet-snow avalanches are more easily predictable than the dry-slab varieties. Given an intense thaw, there is no excuse for any climber wandering across threatened slopes or attempting gully climbs. Wet snow has a minimal air content and the chances of survival in burial are very slim.

Other avalanche types should not be discounted, but their occurrence is rare or not proven. With a constant awareness of the main avalanche types as summarised above and a recognition of their causatory mechanisms, the mountaineer should be able to steer a safe course in Scotland's hills – always following the pattern of weather and conditions, always watching for the visual signs of wind action and wind deposition, and always prepared to retreat or change plans if the hazard is perceived.

The wind-slab avalanche particularly is a hidden menace. It may linger for many days after a storm or be re-created at random by wind redeposition. The oft-quoted rule that one should not climb in the twenty-four hours following a major snowfall is sound in substance, but implies that it is safe to do so thereafter, a presumption which is patently untrue. Any concession to complacency in avalanche matters is an open temptation to fate.

WHERE TO CLIMB –
THE REGIONAL PATTERNS

The regional contrasts in winter weather that were discussed in Chapter 3 are greatly amplified in the resultant snow and ice conditions. The major areas each have their own regime and often come into good 'nick' at quite different times and through wholly different circumstances. By drawing out the specific qualities of each region an aide-mémoire can be offered in the prediction and planning of trips. It is rare that there is nowhere in the Highlands which can offer good winter sport. By keeping a flexibility in arrangements and developing a keen awareness of the likely conditions, one can usually put both journey and effort to good profit:

Cairngorms and Eastern Highlands: Owing to their greater average altitude and protection from the warming maritime influence of the Atlantic, there is a greater chance of finding a freezing level on the eastern mountains than in any other area. I have enjoyed frozen snow and good ice in the Cairngorms on days when the Western Highlands have been deluged by rain. It is undoubtedly wise to travel east when Atlantic weather systems have commanded the weather over recent weeks.

The eastern plateaux also receive a greater volume of snowfall, a polar continental air-flow often producing local blizzards which do not spread elsewhere. Because of their lower temperatures, they maintain their accumulations for longer, thus producing good conditions in late March and April when other areas are cradled in springtime warmth. The greater continuity of snow-cover gives much the most reliable conditions for ski-touring in Scotland. Invariably, a good spell of climbing conditions is enjoyed in late autumn in the Cairngorms when a local snowfall is followed by a freeze/thaw cycle. Undoubtedly, the potential span of the winter season is greater than elsewhere in the Highlands.

However, the cold and relatively low humidity of the eastern hills is disadvantageous both to consolidation processes within the snow-pack and the formation of ice. Particularly early in the season when the sun is low and frosts are sustained at all levels, the snows may lie loose and unaltered (save for a slow ET met), and the climber might scrape away this drape of powder over the cliffs to find not a single smear of decent ice beneath. Without some degree of water lubrication, hard stable conditions are very slow to develop. Indeed, only the Cairngorms remained aloof from the wonderful conditions of February 1986, being muffled by large volumes of powder snow to nobody's satisfaction except the skier's, but which consolidated during March to give prime climbing conditions late in the season.

The West – Argyll, Glencoe, Torridon: Here the maritime influence plays a decisive and often disruptive role. Conditions may be the mirror image of those in the east, developing very rapidly by melt-freeze (viz, Fig 31c) and water percolation after a single initial snowfall, but disappearing overnight in a major thaw. The relatively low altitude of many of the cliffs and corries accentuates the volatility of the conditions. The progressive accumulation of a solid snow base may not occur at all in a winter of widely fluctuating temperatures.

Ice formation is accelerated by humidity and moisture supply. Water ice predominates at low levels, developing initially from ground-water seepage lines. The Torridonian geology particularly favours ice-fall development. Water drains through the permeable quartzite cappings of the peaks, but is channelled outwards on meeting the impervious sandstone bands beneath to produce distinct spring lines, which can propagate copious ice within a week, given a continuous melt/freeze routine.

Walkers can more often enjoy harder snow and

ice conditions on the ridges in the west, and are usually spared the labour of trail-breaking in deep powder. However, for long periods of nearly every season, the western hills are all but bare of snow. Good conditions like those of February 1986 must be grabbed with the fullest embrace.

The Central Highlands – Perthshire, Ben Alder Forest, Creag Meagaidh, Easter Ross: These intermediate regions offer a mixture of both the east and west, and often avoid their unhelpful extremes of conditions. They are ideal locations for the man who likes to 'hedge his bets' and are excellent fall-backs if a long drive to the north-west proves fruitless.

Ben Nevis: Offering an extra 300m (1,000ft) of height over all other mountains of the western seaboard, the Ben produces heavy snowfall in a humid environment, and so develops the most reliable snow- and ice-climbing conditions of anywhere in Scotland, fully deserving its reputation as the king of the winter playgrounds. Indeed, the calibre of its ice conditions is unique. Blue and white ice can choke the gullies and, coupled with a good banking of snow, gives magnificent and relatively 'easy' climbing, while a thick ice-plating that is rarely seen elsewhere develops on the higher faces. The plating process is a particular product of the humid environment. Thick riming of the rocks coupled with slight thaws offers an ideal sticking surface for spindrift and snowflakes. A prolonged alternation of riming, melt-freeze and snow sticking forms an ice layer up to several inches thick, which has spawned a distinctive style of pure ice-climbing on the faces. However, like the Cairngorms, good conditions may be slow to evolve, and, after heavy fresh snow, a high avalanche risk can persist long after the lower climbing venues have consolidated. Yet, once established in the mid-season, the conditions are hard to shift – an ice ascent of Orion Face Direct has been recorded as late as 1 May.

The Cuillin of Skye: Although hardly in the mainstream of Scottish winter mountaineering, the Cuillin deserve a separate niche, for they epitomise all the frustration of a maritime environment and yet can occasionally form a necklace of white pearls that has no comparison in the British Isles. Opinion among the experts has varied widely on the rarity of winter conditions on the ridge. Naismith was dismissive of the chance as long ago as 1890:

> Indeed considering their sharpness and their exposure to wind and sun (to say nothing of the Gulf Stream) it is doubtful, I think, whether much snow is ever likely to be found on them.[5]

And, after an abortive attempt on the Main Ridge traverse (defeated because the wind had blown the crest completely bare of snow, which ironically lay knee-deep and blocked the roads at sea level), Tom Patey lamented:

> I doubt whether satisfactory conditions for the Main Ridge ever obtain. By the time new snow consolidates, the principal rock features should have lost their winter garb.[6]

However, he caught his elusive bird in full winter plumage three years later in 1965, when the first traverse under full snow- and ice-cover was achieved. Others had more faith, knowing that if an anticyclone and an east wind are established following snowfall, the Cuillin may give more than a week of settled conditions. Tom Weir spent his winter army leaves at Glen Brittle in the 1940s on this chance and recalls a traverse from Sgurr Dearg to Sgurr a' Mhadaidh thus:

> . . . that was one of the most perfect things I have ever done in my life, a day of absolute bliss. You couldn't have had better conditions if you'd prayed for them.

If it is unfortunately true that the search for good winter conditions in Skye, or indeed elsewhere in Scotland, often requires a great deal of prayer, then they are savoured with immeasurably greater appreciation when they are found. And in the meantime we can always dream and yearn for those days of bliss when the Scottish conditions could hardly be bettered anywhere in the world.

PART II
THE
SKILLS

Early pioneers on the winter hills, with long axe
and alpenstocks (*SMC Collection*)

5

BREAKING THE TRAIL

Winter Hillwalking – Tradition and Techniques

BEGINNINGS

Winter hill-outings have been undertaken of necessity ever since man inhabited the Highlands. Prior to the clearances and accompanying migrations of the late eighteenth and nineteenth centuries, the high glens were densely peopled, in contrast to their desolation today. Cattle-droving, shepherding, hunting and soldiering for either clan or country involved movement across the hills in every season.

The hazards of the winter mountains were therefore well known and viewed with fear and mystical significance. A famous Cairngorm landmark is the Clach nan Taillear (Tailors' Stone) in the Lairig Ghru where three tailors are reputed to have succumbed to a Hogmanay blizzard. Legend holds that the pretext for this excursion was a wager that they would dance a reel on the same night in both Rothiemurchus and Braemar. In January 1805, five privates of the Inverness militia perished in a snow-storm on the neighbouring Lairig an Laoigh route. On 4 January in 1800, Scotland's first fatal avalanche was recorded – the Gaick tragedy. Five hunters were overwhelmed as they slept in a small cottage near the present site of Gaick Lodge in the central Grampians. This freak incident remains to date the only occasion when a human habitation has been destroyed by avalanche in Scotland. Understandably, winter was not 'appreciated' by the native Highlander in the manner of the mountaineer of today.

The seeking of the hills for recreational challenge, even in summer, awaited the Victorian era of industrialisation and urbanisation, which spawned a disaffection with city life and, by the light of stark contrast, an awareness of the beauty of natural mountain scenery. However, while summer tourism and mountain exploration developed in popularity, the hills were largely left alone in winter until very late in the nineteenth century, being still regarded with awe and trepidation and as offering little by way of beauty or fine weather.

The first two recorded winter conquests of Ben Lomond, for example, inspired only a fearful respect for the wild natural elements. After his ascent on 12 November 1812, Colonel Hawker recounted:

> To get to the most elevated point of the shoulder we found impossible, as the last 50 yards was a solid sheet of ice, and indeed for the last half-mile we travelled in perfect misery and imminent danger. We were literally obliged to take knives and to cut footsteps in the frozen snow, and of course obliged to crawl all the way on our hands, knees and toes, all of which were benumbed with cold . . .[1]

On their ascent in April 1822, William and Mary Howitt were caught in a snow squall: '. . . we were obliged to hold each other's hand, and in this manner endeavoured to retrace our steps until we could get below the cloud.'[2]

Indeed, the aesthetic qualities of the mountains in winter remained largely ignored until small groups largely of professional gentlemen formed the Cairngorm Club (CC) and Scottish Mountaineering Club (SMC) in 1887 and 1889 respectively. At its inception, one of the avowed purposes of the SMC was the encouragement of winter ascents, and to these earliest pioneers the winter hills were something of a revelation, their enhanced scale under snow making it 'difficult to realise that the ordnance surveyors have not been mistaken by some few thousands of feet' (*Sir Hugh*

Munro, 1891);[3] the clear mountain air 'like a draught of champagne, with no gout or headache at the bottom' (*Hely Almond, 1893)*;[4] and the sheer enjoyment of winter walking on the tops 'after a big fall of snow, followed by a severe frost, I know of no excursion more pleasant . . .' (*A. I. McConnochie, 1890).*[5]

The most remarkable feature of early winter rovings when viewed against the norms of a century later is the prodigious distances that were covered. Living in a generation when a 24km (15-mile) hillwalk in snowy conditions is considered exceptional, it is a shock to read of McConnochie walking the 42km (26 miles) from Derry Lodge to Ballater in heavily drifted roads the day after a failure to climb Ben Macdui and thinking nothing of the effort; and few would be fain to emulate Munro's three-day round in the Eastern Grampians in January 1890 (Fig 35):

1 Jan: Milton of Clova; Broad Cairn; Lochnagar; Glen Callater; Braemar: 40km (25 miles) with 1,280m (4,200ft) of ascent.
2 Jan: Morrone; Glen Ey; Beinn Iutharn Mhor; Glas Tulaichean; Glenshee: 34km (21

Fig 35 A RESPECTABLE WINTER ROUND IN 1890

miles) with 1,370m (4,500ft) of ascent.
3 Jan: Walked home to Lindertis near Kirriemuir; 35km (22 miles) on roads in 10cm (4in) of new snow.

Such a march must have required a military pace and discipline and displays fitness and fortitude that shames our modern standards.

These performances were, of course, a product of the pre-motorised era when walking was the natural and traditional mode of country travel, especially in winter when snow rendered roads impassable to horse and carriage and when mountain excursions perforce had to start and end at the rail-heads or widely spaced inns and hotels. Thus, Boat of Garten and Ballater became the starting points for trips into the Cairngorms from Speyside and Deeside respectively, necessitating approach treks of the order of 16km (10 miles) just to reach the base of the mountains.

Nevertheless, there was also a sporting spirit which stimulated these great treks. Although no rivalry is ever declared or implied, one can sense an element of competitive pride in the formal reports of early winter expeditions. Perhaps the epitome of such exploits was Naismith and Thomson's novel means of getting to the Easter meet of the SMC at Inveroran near Bridge of Orchy in 1892. Taking the night train to Dalwhinnie, they reached Bridge of Orchy via Loch Ericht, the summit of Ben Alder and the whole expanse of Rannoch Moor, a distance of 66km (41 miles) which took seventeen hours. Here was no deed of necessity, but a piece of pure mountain madness, and next day both were out on the hills with the rest of the gathered club. No doubt the trip gave Naismith a thorough test of his immortal rule of 3mph plus 30 minutes for every 1,000ft of ascent.

THE ICE-AXE

Whatever the extent of his ambition, the winter hillgoer has to acquire basic proficiencies in the use of the ice-axe and crampons, and develop his balance and climbing techniques far beyond the simplicities of a summer fell-walk. Winter walking is comparatively a serious game and its safe enjoyment is duly dependent on this appreciation.

The use of the ice-axe is paramount. Crampons are highly effective on a winter walk, but they must still be regarded as an accessory to the essential tool. The issue was put into its plainest perspective by Mick Tighe on the ice-bound summit of Stob Coire nan Lochan, Glencoe, during an instructional course: 'If you were dropped here by helicopter stark naked and with no rucksack or equipment what single item would you need to survive and get off the mountain safely?', he demanded. There was a chill wind blowing at the time and no little fear among the students that Mick might intend to put their answers to the immediate test, so responses were slow in coming. Woollen underwear was suggested first for both warmth and decency. Another more ingenious idea was a polythene bivouac bag which would enable survival and/or a rapid slide down to the valley, but this was rejected on safety grounds. Indeed, the correct answer – an ice-axe – took a long time to dawn, yet was obvious when considered. Not only could the axe be used to fashion an igloo or snow-hole for survival, but it is also indispensable to safely negotiate hard snow or icy ground both to cut steps and arrest oneself in event of a slip.

It was a lesson quickly learnt by the early pioneers. Colin Phillip was one of several who ventured forth in winter without an axe and relied instead upon an alpenstock, which is simply a spiked walking-stick. In 1890, without a proper implement to cut steps, he was stranded on the north-east slope of Sgor na h-Ulaidh, south of Glencoe, unable to chip more than the most exiguous nicks on the sheet-ice surface which curved down and away over the brink of the mountain's northern precipices. Without larger steps he could not retreat and it took a highly fraught 90 minutes to edge and balance up a slope of just 107m (350ft) and no greater than 35° in angle. He vowed never again to venture on the hills in winter without an axe, despite the mild ridicule the implement attracted when it was seen at low levels on sunny days.

Alexander McConnochie was another rapid convert to the use of the ice-axe, learning that without the implement a mountaineer has no effective brake. On a traverse of Ben Macdui in 1889, he slipped several hundred feet down the Loch Avon head-wall, probably in the vicinity of the Feith Buidhe. With the greatest of difficulty he stopped himself with his alpenstock and was only able to quit the slope by facing in and clawing his finger ends into the hard snow surface. Even more alarmingly, his companion who was watching from above thought his hurried descent was voluntary and an easy way of getting down. So, with gay abandon, he too plunged into the fray, coming to a rest 61m (200ft) lower. Both were lucky to escape injury.

Never to forget the ice-axe was therefore quickly enshrined as an unwritten law of the mountain winter that still holds good whether you are on the jagged western ridges or the rolling eastern plateaux. Yet the sin of omission is inevitably committed on occasions. In early May, I have been embarrassed on Bruach na Frithe on the Cuillin Ridge. Late snow from a heavy Easter fall still lay thick on the ridge crests and its prolonged exposure to daily sun and night freezing had rendered it treacherously icy at its fringes where it was lying very thinly over the rocks. The ascent of the easiest walking route in the range was a trial of nerves and plans to traverse to Sgurr nan Gillean had to be abandoned. So the rule not to forget your ice-axe holds good for much of the spring as well as for the calendar winter.

To the experienced winter walker, the ice-axe becomes so trusted a friend that it seems like an extra limb. Many hillgoers always use a safety wrist-loop when they hold the axe, but this becomes a nuisance on the typical zig-zag ascent of medium-angle slopes, for at every turn the loop must be swopped as the axe is transferred to the uphill hand. With regular experience, one gains the self-assurance to dispense with its encumbrance. True lovers of their axe will even carry it in their hands throughout the approach to the snow-line, enjoying the feel of its smooth swing and fine balance, so allaying some of the tedium of the march. I must admit to such devotional behaviour, but could never pretend to the practice suggested by Harold Raeburn, who in 1920 prescribed that in order to feel for balance and

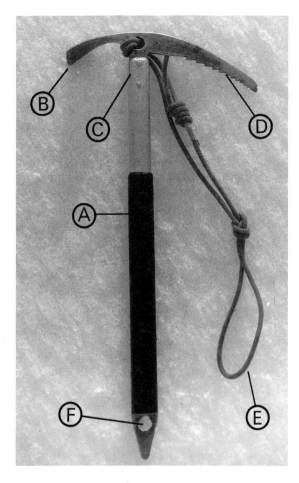

Plate 16 The ice-axe for winter mountain walking

Ⓐ Shaft normally alloy metal with rubber sleeve, 50–70cm in length, depending on height

Ⓑ Adze: wide adzes are better for step cutting and give good grip when pulled down in soft snow

Ⓒ Headmounting countersunk and bolted; look for two bolts for greater strength

Ⓓ Pick preferably slightly curved for traction, should be longer than 14cm and its width at least 4mm thick (2cm from the tip) for effective braking performance; teeth on underside improve grip in hard snow or ice

Ⓔ Wristloop: knotted to give tight fit to a gloved hand and adjusted to the length of the shaft for good swinging action

Ⓕ Spike (or ferrule): for use as a stick or as a prop across the body

an ice-axe for general walking and mountaineering use. There are plenty of points to consider when you purchase one, but the eventual choice of model should be one of personal preference. An axe of comfortable weight and length, and which gives a smooth effortless swing, will be appropriate to your individual arm length and wrist strength. If in addition it is of good quality, it will give a lifetime of pleasurable service in the hills.

SELF-ARREST AND GLISSADING

To mountain pedestrians, it may be a shock to be told that, quite apart from using an axe as a walking-stick, they should be capable of hurling themselves down a 35° slope of frozen snow and, with the sole assistance of the axe, be able to brake and stop. However, the vulnerability of those who climb the hills in winter without the ability to self-arrest is akin to that of the ocean yachtsman who cannot swim.

train for co-ordination:

> . . . the axe may be thrown in the air, caused to revolve a determined number of times and caught on the descent, in either hand, as a good step-cutter should be ambidextrous. This is done while running down a steep slope without stopping.[6]

Considering that the hickory or ash-shafted axe of his era was 1m (40in) in length and 1.35kg (3lb) in weight, the feat clearly required strength and nerve as well as remarkable dexterity.

Modern convention now sees a rather shorter axe for winter walking, while lightweight alloy and fibre shafts give a weight of less than 900g (2lb). Plate 16 summarises the design features of

Plate 17 Ice-axe self-arrest: the braking position. Axe held across the body, one hand over the head, the other round the bottom of the shaft. Chest over the axe to provide braking force. Legs well apart for stability, and heels raised to avoid catching points if crampons are worn. When practising, crampons should NOT be worn, but wear a helmet if possible

Plate 18 Ice-axe self-arrest: falling head-first on chest.
1 Take hold of bottom of shaft with free hand
2 Plant axe pick in snow horizontally to the side
3 Body will then automatically pivot round the axe (to its right in the photo) and into the braking position as above

Plate 19 Ice-axe self-arrest: Falling head-first on back.
1 & 2 As above
3 As the body pivots, twist the trunk to roll onto the front and into the braking position

It is tempting for less adventurous walkers to presume that they will never encounter inclines and exposures steep enough to require application of the technique. The fallacy of this argument was amply demonstrated by McConnochie's plunge from the rolling gradients of the Macdui–Cairngorm plateau a century ago. Even on the level Grampian moorlands, steeply incised valleys and channels are encountered, while the convex swells of their gentler summits may also pose a hazard when ice-glazed, a slip accelerating into a serious fall over the unseen steepening. A hard snow-cover renders the most innocuous slopes worthy of respect. Summer's 'hills' become winter's 'mountains'.

Of all skills, self-arrest is not one that can be learnt and revised from a textbook and then reproduced with perfection in a life-or-death situation. Plate 17, therefore, is informational rather than instructive. Repeated practice out on the hills is the only route to competence. All angles of slope from 20 to 50° and all types of snow from slush to névé should be tried, and the falling position varied from front to back and feet-first to head-first (Plates 18 and 19). Experts enjoy making an initial somersault before arresting, but such gymnastics would be dangerous to the majority. Personally, I find ice-axe braking unnerving, especially on steep slopes where one attains a velocity of 30kmph (20mph) in a few metres. However, initial fear is all the more reason to practise for, once self-arrest is mastered, it is remarkable how one's confidence is boosted when negotiating frozen and exposed snows.

In Britain, the 'across-the-body' method of arrest is now universal. It requires that the axe is always held with the pick pointing to the rear of the holder and in the uphill hand (Plate 20). From this initial stance, the braking position is easily and safely attained whatever the type of fall. The 'pick back' position becomes instinctive with habit.

While one should practise braking simulated falls at considerable speed, in a real situation it is vital to check a slip before it accelerates into a fall, either by thrusting the shaft of the axe into the slope as balance is lost or else by an immediate across-the-body arrest. Fast reactions will prevent

a dangerous slide. The chances of successful arrest decline as rapidly as speed is gained.

The across-the-body technique has, through trial and practice become universally accepted since 1945. It is best handled with a 55–65cm (22–6in) axe and becomes awkward and unwieldy above 70cm (28in). To attempt it with a shaft of nearly a metre (1yd) would be akin to grappling with a self-propelled broomstick. Therefore, pre-war Scottish mountaineers used a different method which was closely equated with the control of glissading. Here the climber faces out and uses the axe as a rudder and brake at his side where the longer shaft is no hindrance. In this

Plate 20 On steeper snow. Axe held on uphill side, hand over the head with fingers and thumb twisted round top of shaft, and with the pick pointing back; body in sideways stance to slope, uphill foot toe-kicking, lower foot edged horizontally. From this stance the self-arrest braking position is gained immediately by gripping the axe shaft with the free hand

position, either the pick or spike might be used for control and braking, the spike giving a smoother control of speed and direction.

Indeed, the one notable deficiency of the modern self-arrest is the pick's inherent design function as an anchor rather than a brake. Instead of giving a gradual braking force, the pick tends to grip the surface and thus jerk out of the climber's control on hard snow or irregular terrain. Of course, it is vital that the axe is not lost in a fall. It is well to remember that successful self-arrests don't just happen by lamely adopting a textbook pose. They require every ounce of strength and energy and in particular the grimmest effort to keep a firm hold on the axe.

Now glissading itself is a delicate topic to discuss in an instructional text. On the one hand, to quote Raeburn, a great enthusiast of the glissade: 'Within the letters of this word are contained some of the most subtle and fascinating joys of the snow-climber.'[7] Yet on the other, reckless glissading has caused repeated accidents in the hills in recent decades. Modern hillgoers tend to forget that glissading is a skill as well as being great fun. Indeed, it may be compared to skiing without skis, and this requires balance, knee strength, deft body-weighting and good judgement of the condition of the snow. Few people nowadays perform the more demanding standing glissade where the body's weight is wholly borne and controlled by the heels and soles. Instead, one sees an inelegant sitting posture with the legs flopping uselessly in front, a position which gives no control over direction or speed and is guaranteed to choke every cranny of one's nether garments with snow. Many of the accidents have also been caused by the inopportune choice of slopes. Blind convexities or boulder-strewn and icy inclines are strictly to be avoided and clearly it is much safer to glissade a slope that one knows from climbing earlier in the day.

As to the delights of the glissade, the early mountaineers enthused as greatly over their rapid descents as their summit conquests. We read of a 'terrific glissade of 2,100 feet on Cairn Toul' and even a claim to a record continuous descent of 2,500 feet on Ben More by Crianlarich in 1898.

Others made speed the criterion of performance. In 1928, an average velocity of 40kmph (25mph) was calculated for a descent off the east end of Beinn Eighe.

If the art is well practised and combined with absolute confidence in axe arrest, then glissading might even be cautiously recommended. It adds a unique excitement as well as saving vital time on a winter day in the Scottish hills. However, if, like me, your knee-joints creak and groan in the throes of premature arthritis, then maybe their strength and longevity is better preserved for the real work of climbing the hills!

Step-cutting is historically the most essential function of the ice-axe, but nowadays is neglected because mountaineers use crampons. It is hard, slow work, particularly if, through inexperience, you lack the subtle action of arm swing and wrist action which enables the adze to slash a step with the minimum of muscular effort. Since most walkers never bother to learn the craft, they find it all the more strenuous when forced to chop steps in situations of real need, which arise more frequently than might be anticipated. A dozen steps cut across a frozen watercourse can save all the fuss and time of putting on crampons (and taking them off again half a minute later). On many winter days, the snow-cover is soft, intermittent or powdery and, given the facility to cut steps across such icy or steep sections as do occur, one's crampons can happily remain in the rucksack throughout. Even when you wear crampons, the security offered by the occasional step should not be spurned, for it can steady your balance and nerves, particularly when you change direction on a steep zig-zag ascent or descent, or in crossing patches of water ice.

CRAMPONS IN WINTER WALKING

The use of crampons for winter walking was hardly considered in the days of nailed boots. A nailed-boot edge could grip almost as well as crampons on snow and ice, and in combination

Plate 21 Standing glissade, with axe shaft used as brake and rudder

with step-cutting, sufficed to handle nearly every situation encountered on the Scottish hills. Furthermore, when one compares the total weight of the modern vibram-soled boot plus crampon combination with that of the nailed boot, the difference is insignificant.

However, once vibram soles were adopted for year-round mountain walking after 1945, crampons were gradually accepted as a necessary accessory for winter excursions. At first, many rejected their use, relying on vibrams alone and cutting steps on hard ground, but this proved to be a risky style since vibram soles lack both friction and edge grip. The speed and convenience

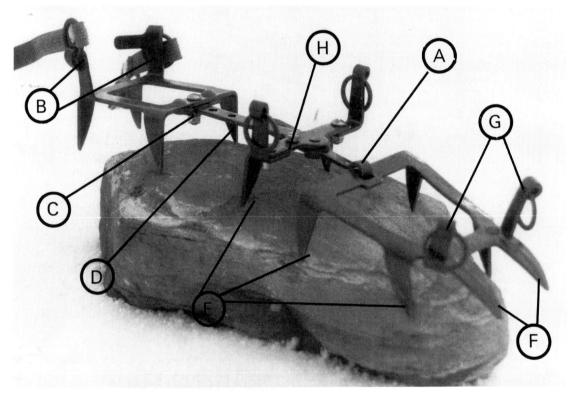

Plate 22 Crampons for winter mountain walking

(A) Hinged instep enables crampon to flex with the semi-stiff boot sole

(B) Heel retaining posts: the longer the better for fit

(C) Length adjustment: clamps and screws or a locking nut arrangement; spanner/ screwdriver/spares should be carried to enable adjustment and repair on the hill

(D) Hinge bar: wise to carry a spare in case of breakage

(E) Sole points: 2 to 2½cm in length when new; sharpening with a file improves the grip but rapidly wears the crampon

(F) Frontpoints: not strictly needed for simple walking, but are now standard on most models and greatly improve performance on steeper ground. Points should protrude 1½– 2cm from toe of boot and be 2½–3cm apart in width

(G) Toe posts and rings for straps: posts can be slightly bent in with pliers to improve fit

(H) Midsole width adjustment

of crampons on icy terrain also became clear, so that by the 1970s their usage was general and they are now rightly recommended as essential for safe winter travel.

Hinged eight- or ten-point crampons will suffice for walking, but four-point instep models are quite inadequate. However, nearly all models available today have the additional front points to make twelve in total (Plate 22). These are of little disadvantage to the walker and can be used for steeper climbing.

Before one enjoys the ease of cramponned walking, it is wise to be fully aware of their disadvantages and indeed their danger in conditions of 'balling up', when moist snow clogs on the heels on descent. Wet snow is, unfortunately, the norm on south-facing slopes and during thaws, particularly late in the day. Even fresh powder, given a few minutes' warming by the sun, is sufficiently moistened to compress and cling to the points. In such conditions one has three options, none of them wholly satisfactory:

To slow the pace by a half and carefully tap the boot every few steps to remove the accumulated mass of snow.

To face in to the slope and descend backwards, kicking the front points of the crampons, with the axe ready for an immediate arrest in event of a slip – much the safest method on exposed slopes but also much the slowest.

To take off the crampons and trust your weight to the dubious grip of vibram-boot heels – this is fine on deep soft snow, but unsafe if there is a hard or icy underlayer.

Plastic-sole plates which shed snow are widely available on the continent of Europe, but have rarely been adopted in Britain. They certainly reduce the balling problem, but their fitment is, of course, just one more fussy job that can spoil the flow of the day.

'Balling up' is the most frequent cause of a slip when descending. My own left calf bears a permanent black pockmark which was sustained when I was descending wet snow on An Teallach and was unwisely positioned directly beneath cramponned companions. With no warning other than a sudden 'sloosh' from behind, my leg was impaled and suddenly spouting a stream of thick red blood. At least this effectively arrested my friend's slip.

The time wasted in the fitment of crampons is quickly apparent to the novice. The delay is much reduced for those who purchase models with 'step-in' bindings, but for the majority with strap bindings, 10 minutes is normal for newcomers, while even the most experienced must endure 3 or 4 minutes of bare-fingered fumbling sitting bent double in the snow, which is sufficient to make you painfully chilled.

It is not generally appreciated that crampons slow one's pace by 10–15 per cent on most types of snow (or alternatively require an extra energy output to maintain one's speed). This becomes obvious when one considers the drag effect of ten sole points each at least 25mm (1in) in length. 'If in doubt, put them on' is a safe motto whenever steep or icy ground is encountered, but on soft, gentle slopes, travel is faster and neater without them.

Beginners understandably find walking in crampons awkward and clumsy, and fear an accidental trip. Even with the straps properly tied with buckles on the outside, one can easily catch a point on gaiters or breeches. While it may be amusing to be spread-eagled on level ground in this way in spite of torn garments, on steeper ground the consequences are more serious. The wearing of crampons is a potential hazard in attempting self-arrest. If the points catch on the ground surface, especially in irregular or frozen snow, then the result is an immediate somersault. Thus, an essential feature of the ice-axe arrest position is to keep the heels raised. For the same reason, crampons must never be worn when glissading.

Crampons are therefore by no means an unmitigated blessing, but in certain conditions they are a godsend, and of course it is only when you don't have them that this is realised. I can remember how a personal misjudgement came close to ruining a Cairngorm weekend in January 1983:

For the second successive weekend, Joy and I chanced a 600km drive up north, the previous trip having been a wind-blown disaster. This time, however, we arrived at Linn of Dee under a canopy of stars, and after four hours' sleep in the reclining seats, we rose with a temperate degree of enthusiasm and set off at seven into a clear chill dawn bound for Macdui.

The hills appearing largely clear of snow, we decided to save a few ounces from our two-day packs. I took just one crampon while Joy used 4-point instep models which are very useful for old ladies on icy garden paths! Up at 750m we met wind-hardened snowfields and a fierce southerly gale, which in combination made our trifling concessions to lightness seem more than a trifle ridiculous. Negotiating the narrow and icy link from Carn a'Mhaim to Macdui, we were on perpetual tenterhooks, being forced to crouch and cling to our axes in the gusts. Joy in her insteps fared the better of us. Ostrich-like hopping would best describe my own advance across the ice, the vibram sole giving no grip whatsoever for the other foot.

On Macdui's summit plateau, sheet-ice predominated. I attempted to weave a safe course by linking patches of protruding rocks, but inevitably was forced to skid across the intervening ice-rinks. The hardness and extent of the ice precluded any thought of cutting steps. That one crampon which now idled in the car-boot down in Glen Derry would have rendered the day passive and pleasant. Instead, I progressed by involuntary lurches and bone-crunching falls, wasting precious time in the process. The crossing of the frozen outlet of Loch Etchachan provided the final excitement of the day. Here it was essential to hew proper steps in the bloated water-ice.

That night, we camped peacefully in the Lairig an Laoigh. Traversing over Beinn a'Bhuird and Ben Avon on the morrow, our embarrassment continued, especially on the steep descent of Beinn a'Bhuird to The Sneck where the exposure warranted our cutting a ladder of steps. However, not even the 21km walk out from Avon to the Linn of Dee could dampen our exuberance over such a grand trip. Yet, oh how different it might have been had the wind risen stronger and the storm clouds

gathered when we were skating about on those icy plateaux.

It is particularly in those relatively dry and snow-free periods of winter, when the view from the glen tempts one to discard the essentials, that bare ice of this nature is encountered and where (two) crampons are most needed. Even the old nailed boots could not have handled these conditions. A strong thaw or a mild spell with rainfall at all altitudes predisposes the plateaux to sheet icing on the first subsequent clear night. Freezing rain can also produce this sudden glazing – conditions which will guarantee a complete conversion to crampon usage on every winter hill day.

Fig 36 summarises the techniques of cramponnage on various types of snow- and ice-cover. Two principles guide the basic style: the conservation of energy and one's strength of grip. While short-term speed often seems best served by a reliance on the toe points alone, this soon exhausts the strength of the calves and offers the least security of grip. The splayed foot ('duck' walk) style or else a sideways stance to the slope is much to be preferred on both counts. Contrary to the edging techniques which one uses with boots on snow, one's grip is doubled with crampons by flexing the ankles, as in Plates 23 and 24, so that the full sole of the boot strikes the snow, giving ten points of contact instead of five. The ankle flexions involved seem initially unnatural and strain the ligaments, but as well as improving grip on frozen snow, the technique distributes the weight over the full sole area and can prevent one breaking through a crusted surface.

Crampons have greatly added to the facility and assurance of winter mountain walking. However, because of their unquestioned modern acceptance, their limitations are tending to be overlooked and traditional step-cutting skills are being neglected.

BOOTS

Boots for winter walking have evolved a long way from the traditional nailed style, and the proliferation of new materials and designs in the last decade has created a major problem of choice.

Fig 36 CRAMPONS: PERFORMANCE AND TECHNIQUES

Snow Conditions	Suitability for Crampons	Techniques
CLIMBING ON HARD SNOW Frozen spring snow Névé	Excellent grip and fast movement.	Body-weight and balance kept over the feet. Sideways stance, ankles flexed out, zig-zags *pieds à trois'* (see Plate 23) on steep ground.
CLIMBING ON SOFT SNOW Sun-softened Thawing	Progress is markedly slowed; hazard of 'balling up'; better without crampons.	Step-kicking with or without crampons.
PURE ICE Glazed plateaux Frozen watercourses	Crampons essential.	Stamping action needed for points to grip; axe spike used as prop; cut steps if ground is steep.
ICED ROCKS Verglas Heavy riming	Crampons needed under heavy icing, but are cumbersome on bare rock.	Neat and careful footwork.
THIN SNOW OVER FROZEN GROUND	On steeper ground, crampons give excellent hold on frozen turf/fine scree.	Crampon techniques same as for hard snow.
PATCHY SNOW/ICE-COVER 50 per cent or less	Constant removal wastes time, constant use quickly wears down points and is slower/cumbersome; best to avoid using if possible.	If worn, vary route to keep on snowfields; if not worn, cut steps when required.
CRUSTED SNOW	Unless crust is hard and icy, crampon points tend to break through; better not used.	Plant full sole to distribute weight; light nimble steps help prevent breaking through.
DESCENDING HARD SNOW	Crampons offer much greater security; small extra risk of an outward trip.	Gentle slopes; face out, toes pointing down, feet well apart and flexed forward (see Plate 24). Medium angles; sideways stance, outer foot flexed downhill, zig-zag descent. Steep ground; always face in, slow but safe.
DESCENDING SOFT SNOW	'Balling up' renders crampons dangerous.	Kick good steps; face in if steep.
SOFT SURFACE WITH ICY UNDERLAYER	An unpleasant combination; crampons ball on surface, but if removed, soles skid on the ice; better to keep crampons on.	Steeper slopes best avoided, especially on descents; cut steps in ice as a last resort.

Leather versus plastic uppers, vibram versus skywalk soles, and semi-stiffened versus fully-stiffened shanks are the three main decisions confronting the bewildered purchaser. Fig 37 examines three main styles of boot on the criteria of comfort and mobility, warmth and water resistance, performance with and without crampons, and durability. One must place personal loadings against each factor and choose accordingly.

Prevention of snow and water entry at the boot ankles is crucial to comfort and warmth, so gaiters

Plate 23 Crampon technique on steeper snow. Lower foot sideways and flexed outwards to give full sole grip, upper foot toe kicking with front points. This style is termed *pieds à trois* in France, and will handle slopes between 30 and 45°

Plate 24 Crampon technique on descents. Facing out with ankles flexed downslope to give full sole grip; knees bent and hips held low; axe for support at side. This style suits slopes up to 35°. Above this, it is more secure to adopt a sideways stance or else face in to the slope

are an essential accessory to winter footwear. The 'yeti' style overgaiter is ideal for use on snow, offering complete waterproofing and extra insulation. Otherwise, cheaper knee-length alpine gaiters should be used.

The selection of boots is interdependent with that of crampons. As they form an integral unit, their compatibility is vital. In terms of stiffening, the 'performance flex' midsole (injection moulded nylon) of the heavier Trionic models or the half-length steel shank of the traditional leather mountain boot, give the minimum acceptable for use with crampons. A fully-flexible walking boot will work loose on many models of crampon and gives

inadequate edging grip on snow when crampons are not worn.

Crampons with long retaining posts, especially at the heels, and width adjustment at toe, midsole and heel give the best fit. The Salewa Everest, although more expensive than the traditionally popular classic model, offers these features and can be adjusted to any type of boot. I have even seen them used successfully on running shoes, although this is not a recommendation to try.

Nothing is more wasteful of winter's precious hours of light, nor more infuriating, than an ill-fitting crampon which springs loose at every tricky juncture of a mountain day. Having bought

Fig 37 BOOTS FOR THE WINTER HILLS			
	'TRIONIC' LEATHER	TRADITIONAL WELT-STITCHED LEATHER	PLASTIC-SHELLED
	1 Outer leather 2 Cambrelle lining 3 Blake stitching 4 Foot-bed cushion 5 Moulded nylon midsole 6 Bonded 'Skywalk' sole	1 Leather outer and lining 2 Leather insole 3 Double welt stitching 4 Half-length steel shank 5 Leather/rubber throughsoles 6 Bonded vibram sole	1 Moulded PU outer shell 2 Fibre insole 3 Vibram sole bonded to shell 4 Inner boot; PU/loden
COMFORT/ MOBILITY	Light, comfortable and neat; easily walked-in; weight 1.6kg (3½lb) per pair.	Longer walking-in period; less pliable and heavier, 2.1kg (4½lb).	Stiff shells so boots do not walk-in; initial comfort depends on careful lacing; weight 2kg (4⅓lb) cumbersome for fast walking.
WARMTH/WATER-RESISTANCE	Excellent with 'yeti' overgaiter; warm fast-drying lining, but less sole insulation.	Satisfactory, but improved by 'yeti' overgaiter.	Excellent insulation; 100 per cent watertight.
PERFORMANCE Without crampons	Adequate; lack of toe and edge stiffness on hard snow, but stepped heel grips well.	Good reliable grip and edging on both snow and rock.	Clumsy on rocks but good edging on snow.
With crampons	Wholly satisfactory for walking if crampons are well-fitted.	Good all-round performance.	Excellent; good for steeper climbing; step-in bindings can be used.
DURABILITY	Resoleable; stiffness gradually reduces with use; uppers last longer if made of anfibio rather than calf leather.	Resoleable; permanent flex in sole with age; vibram slightly harder wearing than trionic sole; welt protects the uppers.	Resoleable; inners wear quickly, and lace hooks suspect, but shells highly durable.

a good crampon-boot combination, there is no excuse for such an occurrence. Prior adjustment of the crampon so that it cannot be shaken off the boot before the straps are tied and careful fitment on the hill will ensure trouble-free travel. Careful fitment means that the crampon chassis should be pressed proud against the boot sole at all points, but especially the toe and heel where any gap creates potential for independent movement. The subsequent strapping of the crampon should be regarded merely as an accessory attachment to the main fit.

Winter mountain walking involves much more than the axe and crampon skills, although they are fundamental. Less tangible is the psychological commitment of a winter excursion – the knowledge that you are likely to be alone and self-dependent. Here is where navigation, fitness and survival play their vital roles. I suspect that it is largely because of this commitment that there is currently an upsurge in the pastime of winter hill-climbing.

The numbers on the hills in winter have roughly quadrupled in the last twenty years according to the observations of local climbers and rescue teams. On a busy weekend, over two hundred cars and vans may be parked along the 13km (8-mile) length of Glencoe, which gives an estimated thousand people on the surrounding hills.

Yet despite the multiplying numbers of devotees, the extent of the Highlands is such that, once you are away from the isolated honeypots of Glencoe, Nevis and the northern Cairngorms, you are indeed likely to find yourself 'breaking the trail' when you take a winter walk. In contrast to the galloping erosion of summer paths, this is a trail that happily leaves no scar. A set of snow-tracks will soon melt or be covered and the mountain left unblemished. For this reason if none other, the winter experience is to be lauded.

And this detailed examination of tools and techniques for winter mountaineering should not obscure' their eventual purpose, for they are the means to enable you to break that trail quickly and safely over the whitened braes and crests. In their competence, the 48km (30-mile) days of Munro

and his generation can be attained by the ambitious, while a 8km (5-mile) stroll to the tops is rendered still more perfect in enjoyment, given the harmony of mind, body and mountain beauty that is thus achieved.

From Hell to Heaven on the North Shiel Ridge
'Sheer bloody murder,' said Dave.
'Purgatory!' exclaimed Ray.
'Horrendous! You couldn't even ski up this,' moaned Simon from the front.
'Well, at least it's good for the soul,' I encouraged from behind.
We were ploughing thigh-deep in powder snow up the flank of Meall a'Charra, already enveloped in cloud and frantically searching a rationale for the toil. Sheer desperation was one strong motive, for this was the final day of a week of vicious weather when the depressions had spun over Scotland from every angle. We'd had blizzards from the north and south-east, gales and sleet from the west and torrential rain from the south. To cap all this, a gentle north-west breeze laden with moisture had now deposited over a foot of powder from sea to summit and, from the present look of the cloud, we were imminently due a few inches more.

To wallow helplessly in drifts of snow on slopes that you could jog up in summer even for a few minutes is apt to bring tears of frustration. To persist in the folly for three hours in pursuit of one Munro summit – in this case Sgurr a'Bhealaich Dheirg, the highest of the three Brothers of Kintail – is guaranteed to engender

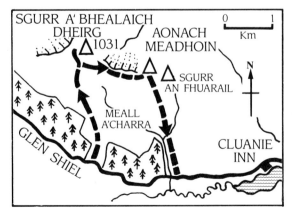

intense fatigue coupled with a salty dehydration that only a litre of tea could cure.

It was not a time to advocate the joys of winter walking. True to expectations, the snow commenced soon after, blotting out the glen and whitewashing the onward view. There was a naughty wind behind the squall, and it blew head on from the north-west, so we proceeded in a bowed line, one crusted eye on the compass dial, the other blinking into the blizzard for a glimpse of the cornice that must surely lie over the summit ridge.

When we found ourselves tripping in the drifts we knew the ground had levelled, and so turned right to gain the narrow promontory which holds the vital summit cairn.

On top we could squat low beneath the crowning plinth, and with our backs to the storm, achieve a semblance of control over our flasks and lunch-packs.

'Well, at least all we have to do is stagger back down our tracks now,' mused my companions and I could sense their urgency to be off homewards. Yet, having expended a monumental effort to get here, it seemed to be crazy not to stay just a little while in the faintest flicker of hope that the storm might cease.

So we lingered until the cold began to pinch and even an eternal optimist was forced to admit the negative, but when we had gone just a hundred metres down the ridge the snow stopped, a smudge of blue raced overhead and a sun began to refract through the cloud with a brilliant glare. Had it happened five minutes later or had we bolted straight down for home, we would have burnt our boats and been plunging down to the glen.

In a few seconds, the clouds parted and peeled away off the summits. We greeted a brilliant new world of pristine whiteness and steely blue sky. The residual breeze raised dancing waves of snow grains which scurried over our ridge and raised a narrow fringe of spindrift above its corniced edge. Looking out across the glen, the pattern was repeated on every crenellation of the Cluanie chain, creating a visual symphony of flowing grace. We glanced behind and there was The Saddle majestically framing the mouth of Glen Shiel. We looked ahead to an unbroken curving edge of wind-carved snow, which beckoned our steps towards the adjoining top of Aonach Meadhoin. In the hushed coombes on our either side, the drifting snow had sifted and sorted into an infinite patchwork quilt of alternately smoothed and rippled surface textures. The only mark of human presence on this perfect snowscape was our own heart-breaking trail of steps.

The transformation left us lost for either words or action. From thinking of a warm car, a steaming cup of tea or the chocolate bar left over from lunch, the mind is forced to switch in an instant to an altogether higher plane of thought. The world is seen afresh with a spiritual vision and sentiment. So we downed sacks and for ten minutes wandered to and fro in spell-bound admiration.

In winters past, all four of us had probably witnessed similar revelations in the mountains, but a scene of such utter perfection can never fade in impact by repetition. It lent us new legs for the climb to Meadhoin, but an hour later the vision had passed. New cloud banks clogged the distant view and the sun had already burnished the snow surface. What for brief minutes was sublime receded to the merely pleasant, but we descended to Glen Shiel in the after-glow of ecstasy, the memories stocked full, comment now superfluous. One fine hour in a week of hell – it was enough to explain every toil and hardship of winter mountain walking, and to think we had nearly forgotten the reason why. No other season could have given an experience the like.

6

ON THE EDGES

The Classic Winter Ridge Traverses

A turreted snow-furled crest suspended in an ice-blue sky – Liathach in winter's clutch is the possessor of a true majesty. Screes and grasses, tracks and terraces, that coarse-grained spread of summer shades – all are whitewashed crystal clean. A brilliant gloss gleams in the midday sun down the southern flank, while a muted chalky mat hushes the ever-shadowed northern cirques. These two sides soar to meet in the glittering apex of the summit ridge. Only the sheer cliff bands of ancient sand break the icy glare, thrusting bold and black against the hazy western seas.

To straddle this winter crest is to perch atop a cathedral roof whose polished eaves plunge down both left and right to unseen voids. The most hardened heart can quiver with the thrill, for here is a geometry and symmetry of stunning simplicity, drawing eye and mind into grand designs. Here is the mountain shape that a child might sketch, a rare instance where reality meets the ideals of youth. And here, too, is found a mountaineering which combines classical purity with technical intrigue.

The great Scottish ridges! How they fire the passions of those whose sights are drawn to the snowy tops. Liathach is but one – albeit one of the finest – of a score of scything edges which chequer the Highland mountain scene. All are pleasing if modest summer scrambles with a spice of exposure and a wealth of views. All are quite transformed by snow and ice. To embark on their winter traverse is to engage a graded climbing expedition of I or II in standard, and some are harder in the worst conditions. For now, the exposures are real rather than perceived. They can menace as well as delight; and our gentle rocky clamber requires varied and even devious climbing on every conceivable type of winter terrain, where speed is of the essence and no elaboration of modern gear can by itself ensure safe passage.

So, while the winter lustre of an Aonach Eagach or an An Teallach must surely entice the dedicated walker, there is seemingly a quantum jump of skill and experience needed for the task. On many occasions, I have encountered parties on the ridges who are uncertain, confused and sometimes utterly bemused as to the best means of tackling their routes. Rope is usually conspicuous either by its over-abundance or total absence, but in both events progress is slow and halting.

Unfortunately, the answers are not readily to be found either in instructional textbooks nor, indeed, in practical teaching. Both have tended to draw a convenient barrier between the walker and the technical climber. The crucial intermediate ground is left unturned, perhaps understandably, for the roped ridge traverse cannot be reduced to a set of unvarying rules and procedures. There is rarely a single means of solving any particular problem en route and no two problems are ever quite the same.

Might the ensuing discussion help redress the neglect of this topic, for one should not and need not be deterred from the challenge of the ridges for want of knowledge. The skills to be sought are merely those of traditional Alpinism whose natural simplicity is the very antithesis of the modern climbing technicality. Equipment needs are not onerous. Good fitness, steady balance and technique, a clear knowledge of the purpose and effective application of basic ropework when

Plate 25 'A magic crest . . . wrapped in a silken mist'. The Devil's Ridge of Sgurr a' Mhaim on the Ring of Steall

Fig 38 THE WINTER RIDGE TRAVERSES: A SELECTION

Southern Highlands	Technical Difficulties
THE NE CORRIE OF BEN LUI: Tyndrum Ascent via S Rib and SE Ridge; descent by Stob Garbh ridge. A classic mountaineering round requiring frozen conditions. The descent is optional. Access from Tyndrum or Glen Lochy.	Grade I on good snow; S Rib steep and mixed at bottom, mainly snow thereon; S Garbh descent is straightforward.
Glencoe and Lochaber	
AONACH EAGACH: N side Glencoe Usually done E–W, Scotland's most popular winter ridge; compact and magnificently positioned. Rapid access from glen but inescapable to S once started. Final descent tricky (Clachaig Gully the main trap).	Grade II in full conditions; intricate weaving on pinnacled crest with steep pitches both up and down.
SRON NA LAIRIG – BEINN FHADA: S side Glencoe A fine route, less intimidating than A Eagach and rarely as crowded. Quick access up Lairig Eilde; the Sron is easily quitted at top to the SE, but continuation over S. C. Sgreamhach and B. Fhada recommended.	Grade I/II; steep initial buttress, then exposed knife-edge and snow head-wall to finish.
CURVED RIDGE: Buachaille Etive Mor, Glencoe Ridge and face route exploring superb cliff scenery. Fast approach but inescapable once engaged; descent from Buachaille down Coire na Tulaich is treacherous and hard to locate in severe conditions.	Lower ridge can be grade II/III if taken direct, otherwise grade I; varied climbing, interesting route-finding.
RING OF STEALL: Mamores Forest Airy circuit of five Munros. Best start via Nevis gorge to An Gearanach. Escapable at cols but Steall Fall bars lower exit of Coire a'Mhail.	Devil's Ridge and An Garbhanach arêtes rate mild grade I.
CARN MOR DEARG ARÊTE: Ben Nevis Finest approach to the Ben with stupendous views of NE face; very popular but a hard round from lower Glen Nevis in heavy snow. Arête escapable at its end (easily to S but steeply to N into Coire Leis).	Exposed rock edge; a straightforward grade I usually but problematic given verglas, thick powder, or high wind.
Western Highlands	
LADHAR BHEINN, ROUND OF COIRE DHORRCAIL: Knoydart Ascent via Stob a'Choire Odhair, descent over Stob a'Chearcaill. A great round and very remote (base at Barrisdale bothy).	Grade I; S. C. Odhair a knife-edge with a steep snow exit; full conditions rare.
FORCAN RIDGE: The Saddle, Glen Shiel Direct access from Glen Shiel on good path. As fine an arête as any on the mainland. Fast descent from summit to SE, but the W ridge makes a grand (though easier) continuation, finishing at Shiel Bridge.	Grade I/II; rocky buttress to Sgurr na Forcan, tricky descent, then an exposed razor-edge and easier slopes to summit.
MULLACH FRAOCH-CHOIRE, S. RIDGE: Cluanie – Glen Affric A fine gendarmed ridge. Remotely situated with a long approach over A'Chralaig, but difficulties are short. Descent via N ridge to Affric.	Grade I; broken rocks, winding descents and traverses; dangerous in soft snow.

Fig 38 THE WINTER RIDGE TRAVERSES: A SELECTION continued

North-west Highlands	Technical Difficulties
BEINN ALLIGIN TRAVERSE: Torridon Best done E–W starting with the Horns. Fast tracked access from Coire Mhic Nobuil. Not escapable from 1st Horn to main summit; thereafter down W flanks. Scenically magnificent and not technically demanding.	Grade I; difficulties concentrated on Horns (exposed rocky drops off 1st and 3rd); avoiding traverses not advised.
LIATHACH, MAIN RIDGE TRAVERSE: Torridon The mainland's most serious peak in winter; a worthy challenge. Short but brutally steep access from Glen Torridon. No escapes on pinnacles and retreat from main summit complex. Normally done E–W.	Pinnacles are sustained and grade II if taken direct; avoiding traverses often too dangerous in loose or soft snow.
THE BLACK CARLS OF BEINN EIGHE: Torridon The first link in the B. Eighe traverse. Approach from Kinlochewe. Exciting but short and escapable at either end.	Mild grade I; weaving route around the carls with one steep pitch to finish.
AN TEALLACH TRAVERSE: Dundonnell–Fisherfield Forests The queen of the ridges usually done W–E with a long arduous approach over the main summits. Pinnacled section escapable only to S and with difficulty. Easiest descent at end down SE ridge of Sail Liath.	Grade II but less serious than Liathach, all types of terrain and exposed; crux is finding best way off Corrag Bhuidhe.
STAC POLLY: Coigach Intricate and exhilarating little route when in its rare winter state. Quick approach. Escapable via steep gullies between the pinnacles.	Grade II; rock gendarmes and arêtes; hard moves at short steep steps.
Isle of Skye	
BRUACH NA FRITHE – AM BASTEIR: Northern Cuillin Approach over Sgurr a'Bhaster, descent via Coire a'Bhaster. Easily escapable to Fionn Choire. Basteir Tooth avoided on LHS and Am Basteir climbed up E ridge. A good introduction to the winter Cuillin.	Sensational knife-edges, grade I; firm snow conditions essential; Sgurr a'Fionn Choire gives a taste of mixed climbing.
SGURR NAN GILLEAN TRAVERSE: Northern Cuillin Up W Ridge, down SE Ridge (Tourist Route). A good mixed outing which added to that above gives a magnificent long day. Route-finding on descent will be problematic in mist and thick snow.	Chimney pitch on W Ridge is a steep grade II; otherwise sustained at grade I and exposed throughout.
MHADAIDH – GHREADAIDH – BANACHDICH: Central Cuillin Approach from Glen Brittle over Sgurr Thuilm. A sustained and demanding expedition. Only easy escape is at An Dorus, but final descent down W ridge of Banachdich is easy. Good snow is rare but essential.	Sustained at grade II with razor crests, long descents and steep pitches.
COIRE LAGAN ROUND: (excluding In Pinn and An Stac buttress) The technical limit of the classic mountain traverses. Start up W ridge of Sgurr Dearg; descent by Bad Step (abseil) or Great Stone Shoot of Sgurr Alasdair. Inescapable between Mhic Choinnich and Thearlaich.	Grade II/III; crux is descent of Sgurr Mhic Choinnich – King's Chimney (long abseil) or Collie's Ledge (sensational).
CLACH GLAS – BLAVEN TRAVERSE: Eastern Cuillin Together with the Lagan circuit a step above the other ridges in technical difficulty, but a tremendous route when in condition. Start from Loch Slapin over Sgurr nan Each. Escapable at Blaven – C. Glas col.	Grade II/III with the descent of Clach Glas the crux (weaving line, abseils); sustained and varied mixed climbing.

moving together, coupled with a keen instinct (or failing this a proper patience) in route-finding – with these alone the winter ridges may be tackled in a flowing joyous rhythm and they are open to those whose ambitions make no pretence to broach the domain of technical climbing.

THE SCOPE AND THE PLEASURE

It would be an unmanageable as well as an invidious task either to specify exactly the relative quality and difficulty of Scotland's great ridge traverses, or to compile a comprehensive gazetteer of the routes. Their charm and challenge depend crucially on the uncertainty and variability of their winter condition, while a spirit of adventure can still prevail in seeking out obscure or hitherto unknown gems on the far-flung hills.

Fig 38 therefore attempts no more than to list the most famous together with a selection of lesser known expeditions, giving but an indication of their technical difficulty, length, remoteness and escapability. The basis for inclusion is that, whatever their summer character, they attain a difficulty of at least grade I in average winter conditions, but are also recognised summer scrambles up or over the major summits.

The greatest ridge of all, the Black Cuillin, cannot be omitted, but is split into those easier sections that may be tackled by those whose interests lie within our present ambit, while its complete traverse *integrale* demands ·a wholly separate niche, for it is a sustained grade III/IV expedition of super-Alpine length.

The Ring of Steall around the heart of the Mamores Forest exemplifies the quality of the longer easier circuits and, enhanced by an approach via the Nevis gorge, is an expedition as fine as any on the mainland. I took a party there from Lochcarron in February 1987 when the clouds rolled back from a two-day snowfall:

Jangled by the alarm at 5.30, pitched out into the deathly cold of late night, then struck with terror by a 50mph wobble on sheet black ice as I steered the curve at Auchtertyre hill – today's start was ruder than most, leaving the nerve ends raw and visions of graceful Mamores quite askew.

But we drove out from under the sheet black clouds that haunted Wester Ross, and by Spean Bridge the pinks of dawn were flush and a brilliant day was soon to flower. A trace of frost hugged the shady chasm of the Nevis, but the waters of Steall still flowed and spouted down to the glen. Aloft, the new snow thickly daubed the massive shanks of An Gearanach and Sgurr a'Mhaim, the sentinels of the Ring. Hard work lay ahead, but our spirits were at last awake and in that ascendant mood when all things can be done.

And, as so often after a windless snowfall, all things had to be done to reach the heights. First I led a breathless battle up the vertical birchwood to escape the gorge, squirming in seeping grooves, hauling over heathered ribs, grasping snapping twigs and boughs, and clawing the snow with sore bare hands. Freedom was tasted 400m up on the north-east spur of Sgurr a'Mhaim, but from here to the top, thick powder showed no mercy. At least we were five and trail-breaking could be shared on the knobbled ridge, but as we flogged and flailed up collapsing steps, team morale was at that crucial stretch where the legs quiver and convictions waver.

But a magic crest was gained at last, wrapped in a silken mist and suffused with a golden midday sun whose rays shone close above. Now wearing crampons, we picked up speed and strength on a burnished edge which some slight breeze had feathered clean, and all but floated along the Devil's Ridge.

No rope was needed for the footing was good both on the crisp névé and in the light dry drifts that clung in the hollows. We forged our tracks around the ring in certain anticipation that the mist would clear. From Iubhair to Am Bodach was a broad-backed stroll, but then the onward link was barred by an icy face which slips, then swoops in deceiving convexity for 300m to

8 (*right*) **Winter camp beneath the Tower Ridge of Ben Nevis**

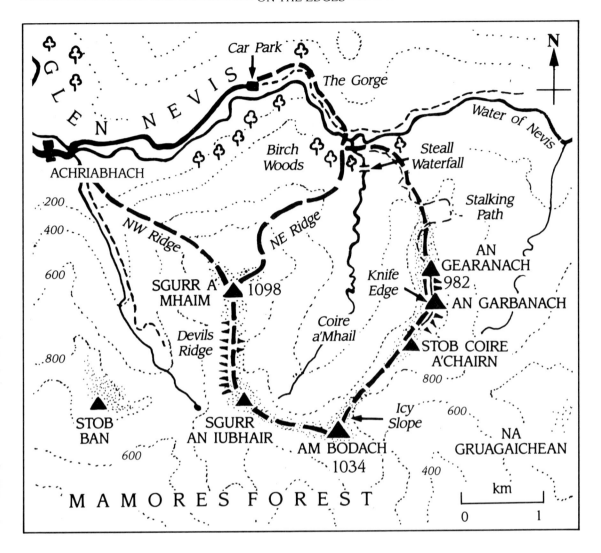

either side. Again we trusted to ourselves and the rope stayed coiled. With precise crampon style, a secure sideways stance and the ultimate insurance of the ice-axe brake, this 40° slope need cause no fears when the surface is firm.

The sun had slowly burnt through the summit mists, but now the colder valley air boiled skywards in towering cumulus masses which framed the silvery pate of Bodach. Time

and again we turned our eyes to the sight as we climbed the continuing ridge. Yet through all this spectacle of atmospheric convolution, not the softest breath of wind had stirred to deflect our gaze.

The newborn clarity of the afternoon distilled the pleasure of the final link over An Gearanach, much the trickiest section of the Ring with exposures both on left and right that can bite deep into one's composure. We weaved, edged and balanced along the bare-boned spine until at the highest point its defences parted and a sweep of open slopes unfolded to offer a romping descent to Steall.

9 (*left*) As sharp as an arrowhead. The main summit of Liathach, Spidean a'Choire Leith after fresh snow

After just a few hours of filtered winter sun the lower snows were wholly altered, now slumped and heavy, balling on our crampons and cloying our patience in contrast to their fine-grained aeration of morning.

We forded the Nevis in the valley twilight, while the summits above still proudly burned in the glory of the waning day.

So much for this cameo of frost and calm. Such days are seldom granted and only rarely will a winter edge yield with such serenity. Searching for the contrast is not a problem. I go straight to Beinn Alligin, whose traverse is of comparable calibre to the Ring of Steall. But it is 1986 and January's storms were loath to leave the western hills. Our party of three made no further than the Second Horn on an attempted anti-clockwise round.

What was a bracing breeze down in Coire Mhic Nobuil rose to a flapping hurricane on the ridge. The rope was needed at the first hint of icy

Plate 26 'The silvery pate' of Am Bodach as it was revealed on our traverse of the Ring of Steall

exposed rock, its security especially welcome on the open névé slope under the second horn whose fall-line curls deceptively into the jaws of Deep South Gully. Here a tight short line was vital to keep in touch and give fair chance to stop a slide should Paul or Jack have been blown over.

After a crouching lunch in the lee of the final rampart beneath the horn, we gladly beat a retreat. A fiercesome blast down at the gap swiped Paul's contact lens clean out of his eyeball. We crawled and squinted back over the first horn in fits and starts, then unroped and thankfully staggered off the ridge as soon as the steep stuff ended. Our account of this little epic failed to convince two Sunday strollers on the corrie track below, yet had they looked hard, they might have discerned the rising waves of spiculae still scurrying over the ridge in the throes of the gale.

ROPEWORK ON THE RIDGES

Rope technique on the ridges is beset by the eternal paradox of trying to ensure speed as well as security of progress. Taken to their extremes, one is the diametric opposite of the other. To tackle the length of the Aonach Eagach by a series of fixed belays with only one man moving at a time invites a certain bivouac. Yet for a novice to do it unroped courts disaster unless you have near-perfect snow or the temperament of a budding Patey. The solution is an ever-varying compromise between the two, and in choosing the best compromise at each junction of a route lies the key to success.

The idea of moving together on a rope is distrusted by the majority of novices who see its inevitable result as 'one off – all off'. Nor is this scepticism easily dispelled, for first attempts to use the rope usually cause irritation and disharmony in an untried party.

Individuals must adjust their pace to that of the whole team. It is of no effect for a quick leader to drag the party to exhaustion, and it is dangerous that a fit tail-ender should be continually catching up, for this creates slack in the rope and thus the potential to accelerate in the event of a slip. Meanwhile, the middlemen are always getting the rope twisted around their backs each time the party changes direction, unaware that, by stepping over the rope behind at each turn, such tangles can easily be avoided. The end result is a dishevelled, ill-tempered group. The rope is a hindrance and even a danger, and everybody yearns for that moment of freedom when the accursed thing can be taken off.

Figs 39, 40 and 41 offer some guidance as to the alternative modes of roped travel – continuous movement without belays on open slopes, the use of both natural and inserted running belays and fixed belaying on more technical or steeper sections. This gives the range of speed versus

Plate 27a Short rope technique on steep snow. Rope held tight with no hand coils, and no more than 3m between each climber

Fig 39 TACKLING THE WINTER RIDGES: ROPEWORK GUIDELINES

Assume a party of three. Gear carried: One 45 or 50m rope, 9 or 11mm diameter,
waist-belts and screw-gate karabiners, minimum of 4 long and two short slings,
6–8 wired nuts and larger hexentric chocks, 6–8 karabiners,
2 prusik cords per person, spare 13mm – (½in) abseil tape, figure-of-eight for abseils.

	Terrain	Example	Method	Pros and Cons
A	**OPEN SLOPE** Ascent, descent and traverse	Liathach, traverse round the south side of pinnacles.	Short tight rope; 2m maximum spacing; no belays; continuous moving together.	Fast travel over long sections. *Security highly dependent on immediate arrest of a slip.*
B	**LEVEL ARÊTE** Rock or snow	Carn Mor Dearg arête; Forcan Ridge, Saddle.	5–10m spacing; continuous moving together; hand coils optional.	Fast travel. *Counterweight arrest is sole security (jumping to other side).*
C	**GENDARMED RIDGE** (Grade I) Undulating and twisting	Sgurr nan Gillean, Tourist Route.	5–10m spacing; rope threaded over *natural* belays (ie, spikes, flakes) and woven side to side; continuous movement at same rate (no slack).	Fast rhythm of progress. Good security on broken rocky ground (friction and counterweight). *Rope abrasion (11mm better) and risk of jamming.*
D	**GENDARMED RIDGE** (Grade II) and **STEEP TRAVERSES** Exposed	Aonach Eagach pinnacles.	5–15m spacing; rope clipped into *placed* runners; last man collects gear; always at least 1 runner on rope; continuous movement as in C.	Smoother running than C. Placed anchors more reliable. *Party must regroup to exchange gear. Delays for placing/ removing runners. Rope abrasion (11mm better).*

continued

security compromises that a party may strike on a climb. A day of prior practice or instruction on rock outcrops to gain a basic confidence in belaying and abseiling is recommended before these methods are applied on a high ridge.

General principles of rope management apply to each and all, and might help prevent the mess outlined above. Most people's idea of moving together derives from old pictures of Alpine arêtes where the climbers strike a dramatic pose with an indeterminate length of slack between them and a long loose bunch of coils in one person's hands. Modern thinking strongly disfavours such practice. With two minor exceptions, all the methods represented in Fig 39 require a tight rope between the climbers and no hand coils. Having

gauged how much rope the party needs for each main section of a route, the lead man should coil any surplus around his shoulders, then tie his dead coils off at the waist. This spare is an accessible reserve should the live lengths have been misjudged or an emergency arise.

Even without a belay, a climber can effectively stop a slip in the party behind on steep snow by bracing the body, digging in the feet and thrusting the axe shaft into the slope. However, if there is slack in the rope and the slip has become a slide before the strain is felt, the chances of arrest are much reduced. If hand coils are held by the person falling, they are usually dropped in the panic, creating the very slack that invites disaster, while if coils are held by the leader, they tighten

	Terrain	Example	Method	Pros and Cons
	Fig 39 TACKLING THE WINTER RIDGES: ROPEWORK GUIDELINES continued			
E	**SHORT STEEP STEPS** Easy pitches up to 5m (16ft)	The Horns of Beinn Alligin.	5–8m spacing; party moves one at time from ledge to ledge; leader gives body belays at each stance; rock anchors used only if quickly accessible.	Delays for belaying are minimised. Seconds get a tight top rope. *Leader has no protection, and must not fall. Stances must be good and rope kept taut.*
F	**STEEP PITCHES** 10–15m (33–49ft)	Sron na Lairig, lower section.	Both leader and seconds belayed and anchored; Italian hitch belay used, direct on anchor by leader, indirect waist belay by seconds; seconds climb together 2m apart.	Fastest method of belaying. Anchors must be solid if direct belay used. *Italian hitch jams on frozen rope. Potential double load on top belay.*
			As above but seconds tie in 15m apart and climb one at a time.	More secure, seconds can't pull each other off, *but much slower.*
			As above, but leader ties on middle of rope; seconds tie one on each end and climb together for speed.	Leader has double rope protection. *Problem of belaying two ropes at once (Sticht plate needed). Party has to retie if reverting to any other method.*

like a vice around the wrist under the strain, completely immobilising the holding arm and so preventing further efforts to arrest. It is wise to do your own practice testing with simulated falls on safe ground, after which I am sure you will come to these conclusions.

Hand coils are a positive aid to safety only on a level snow arête where belays are wholly absent and the *human counterweight* method must be applied in event of a fall. If the terror-struck 'counterweight' has a few spare coils to cast away, he gives himself vital seconds before he or she must leap down the other side of the ridge to stop the plunge. The trick has worked on many occasions.

Hand coils might only otherwise be gathered as an aid to speed on ground of uneven difficulty where rear-guard members can pick up their coils on easy ground and catch up the leader who might be momentarily delayed on a tricky step.

The relative positions and stances of the party members need constant attention and adjustment. If all are precariously perched on a pinnacle crest or when all are insecurely placed on the same side of the ridge, then there should be some running belays between the party. On steeper exposed rocks the leader should always have a solid stance and the party will move in short pitches, placing belays whenever available.

The leader's role in the system is especially crucial here. Confident leaders climbing well within their margins of safety require little extra protection and enable their parties to climb with much greater speed. Perhaps on the steepest ground the leader will require a waist belay (or an Italian hitch from the waist) from the person behind, and will place sufficient runners to avert a serious fall. A party of equal ability can share the

Fig 40 ROPEWORK GUIDELINES FOR STEEP DESCENTS

Method	Typical Example	Pros and Cons
DOWN-CLIMBING Moving together as in Fig 39(D) placing running belays.	An Teallach, descent from Corrag Bhuidhe pinnacles.	Fast, with reliable placed anchors. *Leader easily pulled off if second slips.*
TOP-ROPING Seconds climb down on direct belay placing runners to protect leader and fixing belay at bottom of pitch, ie the reverse of Fig 41(F).	Aonach Eagach, descent of chimney off Am Bodach.	Much more secure especially for leader. *Time-consuming. Relies on seconds being able to fix good protection and belay anchors.*
LOWERING As for Top-roping except seconds are lowered on direct belay with an *Italian* hitch one at a time.		Quick and smooth unless ropes frozen. Saves energies of seconds. *More difficult for seconds to clear and prepare route for leader. Italian hitch can kink rope under load.*
ABSEILING Using a figure-of-8, karabiner brake or Italian hitch on rope, back-up anchor at top for first people down; safety prusiks advised (ie, sliding autoblock on abseil rope tied to waist).	All the dyke lines cutting the Cuillin Ridge, eg An Dorus, tops of Bidean Druim nan Ramh; mainland ridge descents in bad conditions.	Only possible method on snowed-up vertical ground. Leader relieved of strain of down-climbs. *Rope retrieval/anchor strength critical. Rope has to be doubled, so 20–5m is maximum drop for each abseil. Much slower in a big party.*

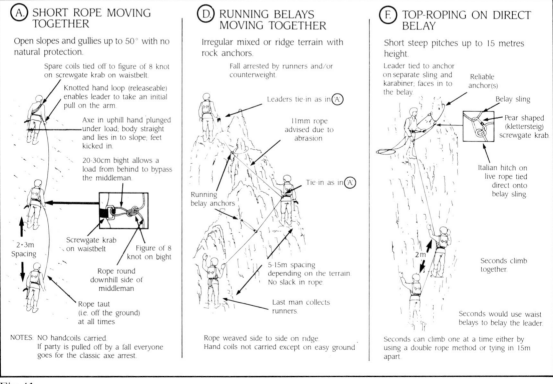

(A) SHORT ROPE MOVING TOGETHER

Open slopes and gullies up to 50° with no natural protection.

Spare coils tied off to figure of 8 knot on screwgate krab on waistbelt.

Knotted hand loop (releaseable) enables leader to take an initial pull on the arm.

Axe in uphill hand plunged under load; body straight and lies in to slope; feet kicked in.

20-30cm bight allows a load from behind to bypass the middleman.

2·3m Spacing

Screwgate krab on waistbelt
Figure of 8 knot on bight

Rope round downhill side of middleman

Rope taut (i.e. off the ground) at all times

NOTES: NO handcoils carried. If party is pulled off by a fall everyone goes for the classic axe arrest.

(D) RUNNING BELAYS MOVING TOGETHER

Irregular mixed or ridge terrain with rock anchors.

Fall arrested by runners and/or counterweight.

Leaders tie-in as in (A)

11mm rope advised due to abrasion

Tie-in as in (A)

Running belay anchors

5-15m spacing depending on the terrain. No slack in rope.

Last man collects runners.

Rope weaved side to side on ridge. Hand coils not carried except on easy ground.

(F) TOP-ROPING ON DIRECT BELAY

Short steep pitches up to 15 metres height.

Leader tied to anchor on separate sling and karabiner; faces in to the belay.

Reliable anchor(s)

Belay sling

Pear shaped (klettersteig) screwgate krab.

Italian hitch on live rope tied direct onto belay sling

2m

Seconds climb together.

Seconds would use waist belays to belay the leader.

Seconds can climb one at a time either by using a double rope method or tying in 15m apart.

Fig 41

Plate 27b A tricky crossing on the Sron na Lairig, Glencoe. For this exposed arête, the second has taken a fixed stance to belay the leader

leading in order to spread the mental strain of going ahead. The leader has to select and organise the roping system, as well as find the route, and of course is the ultimate backstop to a fall anywhere down the rope. A long day out guiding a party on a grade II ridge leaves me as mentally worn as a grade V ice climb.

A day on Liathach in early January 1987 left me and two of my students in particular need of a night in a cool dark room or a week in a fireside chair. However, for those who still mistrust the

rope techniques proposed above, our story should convince that these are not just fanciful designs. They do work!

We were couched on the main summit just before noon on a clear fine day, with ample time to traverse the Fasarinen pinnacles to Mullach an Rathain. My team of four were fit and well drilled from five days out on every sort of grade I and II terrain. The conditions today seemed generally good, though the tough old névé that

Plate 28 On Liathach, approaching the main summit with Beinn Eighe in the background on the left; our eventful traverse of the Fasarinen pinnacles yet to come!

had lain since Christmas week was partially covered with more recent drifts that had not yet hardened to a reliable skin. These might pose problems on the steeper ground and could prevent a flanking traverse of the major obstacles.

As soon as we had roped up at the first notch before the pinnacles, this difficulty became apparent. Moistened by the sun, the fresh snow was distinctly slabby and sufficiently liquid to cling tenaciously to our crampons. Furthermore, it was a virgin cover. There were no lines of tracks to guide our passage. We would have to take the ridge direct. I went ahead as a rope of three with Glaswegian

brothers Peter and Paul following close behind on a separate rope, but using and collecting any runners which I had placed up front. The system seemed a fair solution to give us sufficient speed without abandoning my responsibility for the party. It also paid due respect to the brothers' ability, for they had shown care and craft throughout the week.

5m gaps between each man enabled us to weave a secure thread over the initial gendarmes where one is suddenly exposed to the sensational drop over Coire na Caime to the north. Few would deny a quiver of tension on these first delicate edges, but after a kilometre of the same, most are revelling in the 'crow's nest' situations and are only sad that the pinnacles end so soon!

Now the ridge drops steeply for over 100m to its lowest col and we were forced onto the soggy snows of its southern flank, descending a shallow chimney facing in, then turning out and shuffling rightwards along the base of the

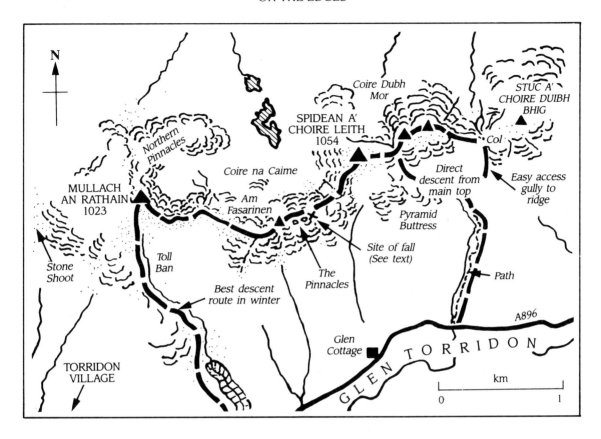

buttress. We hugged the rocks, handling its flanks and edges wherever we could, for the snow was soft and lay only thinly over matted clumps of grass.

Not until 10m beyond the chimney was I able to place a sling for a running belay. The unprotected traverse was unfortunate but unavoidable, so on I went, trusting the lads behind to take extra care as they bridged the gap.

But a yelp and then a piercing shriek said otherwise. Peter was in front down and along the traverse, and Paul just turning out at the bottom of the chimney when he tripped and shot off downwards.

'Brake!' I yelled instinctively, but Paul was completely out of control from the moment he slipped. Below him lay a gully starting at 40° and steepening down left and out of sight to I knew not where. The bump of a rock outcrop turned him upside down, and he was accelerating beyond the speed where self-arrest

is of any avail. My eyeballs bulged with horror, riveted to his fall.

Then, in an instant, he swung in an arc on a tautening rope and came to a stop. Looking straight back up, there was Peter rolled over his axe, in the classic braking pose and absolutely still. He had made a magnificent arrest, digging his pick mightily into the underlying turf and no doubt saying a momentary prayer before the rope came tight. To stop a 5m fall from above and to the side without any belay was testimony not just to Peter's skill but equally to the crucial worth of the linking rope.

Paul picked himself up with no worse than a bruised knee and a shell-shocked gaze. They joined our rope forthwith and I pressed ahead before the impact of the fall sunk home, keeping moving without a pause for an hour and a half until the pinnacles were behind.

Tensions mellowed on the sweeping slopes that curve up towards Mullach an Rathain:

'Practise your ice-axe brakes somewhere else next time, lads,' I quipped, knowing full well how close they had been.

Much the most problematic parts of every ridge traverse are the descents (Fig 40). The chimney pitch of Am Bodach on the Aonach Eagach, the eastern face of the Corrag Bhuidhe pinnacles on An Teallach and the weaving descent of Clach Glas en route to Blaven on Skye are three notorious obstacles. The simplest line of route is hard to spot from above, the exposure is more acutely felt when facing out and scanning the space beneath one's feet, and blind downward moves require a deft balance and a measure of faith in the footing below.

The winter descent of Sgurr nan Gillean's South-East Ridge (the Tourist Route) at a mild grade I has taken my party just as long as the preceding ascent of the grade II West Ridge. The greatest cause of trouble is in failing to allow the extra time and spare mental energy necessary to make a safe descent.

Decisive ropework is bedevilled by the uncertainties of descent. At every potential impasse, parties are usually tempted into abseiling in preference to down-climbing. Abseiling relieves the tension of down-climbing, but it invariably takes much longer, especially in a big party, and the consequences of a rope jam during retrieval are serious.

In April 1986, when I was traversing the Pinnacle Ridge (III) on Gillean in heavy spring snow, I encountered a full-length 9mm rope hopelessly jammed around a huge rock bollard on the descent from the Fourth Pinnacle. Luckily for its owners, the abseil reached to the col from which a broad snow-chute offered an easy escape into Coire Basteir. The same occurrence higher on the Pinnacle, particularly in the execrable snow conditions against which we were battling, would likely have left them stranded to await a rescue. By the simple means of putting a sling over the bollard and rethreading the rope, we enabled its smooth retrieval. One could imagine that on a stressful descent, the original party had panicked into abseiling direct from the biggest fang in the vicinity and in so doing had sacrificed their rope.

The moral of this story is always to have a goodly length of spare tape for abseil anchors stowed in your sack.

With improving personal skill and developing experience, the confusions and inhibitions of ropework disappear and the ridges can be traversed with both speed and security. In the Scottish mountain winter, speed is itself your ultimate guarantee – beating the storm, pre-empting the thaw and chasing the setting sun. It keeps you in clear and confident command of your mission and in joyful harmony with the hills.

If through the hesitance of inexperience the mountain is allowed to take the upper hand, it may show no mercy to the victim in its clutch. Yet equally the great ridges can merely tease when they seem to threaten and, if so inclined, will yield up their treasures in a sudden flush on days when all seems lost. On An Teallach in February 1986 we were granted just such a reward:

A month of frost and sun had reached its zenith of perfection. To Fisherfield we were bound with plans of a 'grande entrée' by the An Teallach traverse. This meant carrying overnight loads of some 12kg for a sojourn at Shenavall bothy. The mountain beckoned strong in a brilliant morning sun. There was not a single blemish in its coat of recently laid snow. Just beyond the lovely fall where the Allt a'Glas Thuill burn joins the Allt Coir' a'Ghuibhsachain, we hit thick drifts and were soon persuaded to aim direct for the spur of Glas Mheall Liath instead of wallowing into the inner corrie. Out of a dawn of −10°C, a midday heatwave now simmered and we spluttered and sweated up the interminable lower slopes roundly cursing our packs and thick long-johns. A refrigerated oven would best describe the conditions.

Glyn at 55 was no longer endowed with the youthful power to swim up powder drifts that slid as they melted on the ice beneath. But he battled gamely, graciously accepting my helping hand here and there. Admittedly, his incentive was strong. His final Munro, Ruadh Stac Mor, lay awaiting for tomorrow.

Plate 29 'The mountain beckoned strong in a brilliant morning sun'. An Teallach – Sgurr Fiona (R) and the Corrag Bhuidhe pinnacles (L) from Glas Mheall Liath

Meanwhile, Gordon at 17 exhibited an all-conquering energy, but with a youngster you can never be sure of the stamina reserve.

The spur offered a respite of clean névé, but at around 900m we met an eggshell crust of sugared snow. This fragile skin was probably the product of strong daytime insolation and deep night-frost. It demanded some murderous trail-breaking and once more our pace was slowed.

We were all visibly wilting when we flopped down on Bidein a'Ghlas Thuill at 1pm. The whole of the mighty ridge gleamed and bristled from across the Toll an Lochain, teasing our desire while taunting our fatigue. With weighty sacks and with such snow on the pinnacles, it looked unlikely we could make the far end in four hours of remaining light, my experience knowing just how much more difficult things could get, especially in this burning sun. In

such magnificent weather, to contemplate defeat seemed a trifle ridiculous and the sight of Gordon reading yesterday's *Times* (brought to kindle our bothy fire) nonchalantly perched on the summit trig seemed only to emphasise our pending humiliation!

The top of Sguurr Fiona is the final escape point before the grade II pinnacles. From there we could drop steeply but direct to Loch na Sealga and still make Shenavall by night; and that was our agreed intent until we picked up a trail of crampon prints on the intervening bealach.

Lo and behold, the tracks had destroyed the dreadful crust. No longer did powder drifts mask the underlying ice, and right on the same cue we were all infused with a spurt of energy that could be traced in part to the lunch we'd devoured on Bidein. In a moment, we clean hurdled the gates to the full traverse.

Up to Fiona and on with the rope; then creeping out to Lord Berkeley's Seat, taking turns to lean on stomachs over the brink of the mainland's most stupendous drop; belaying carefully down its farther edge, then on together over the triple-headed Corrag Bhuidhe

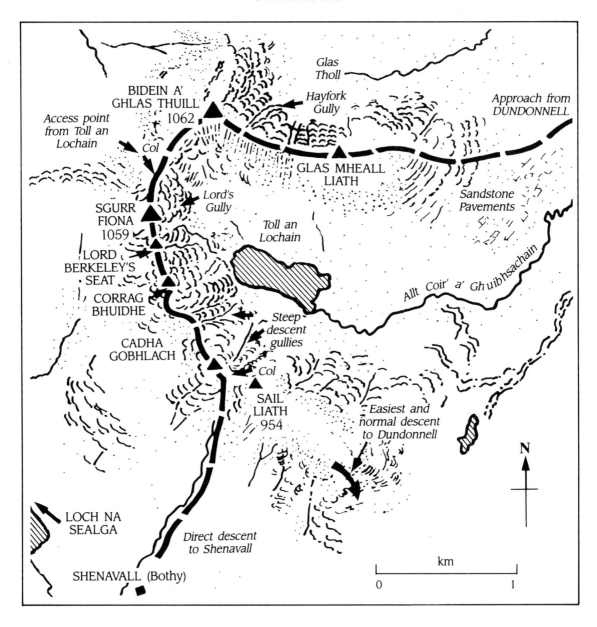

- we relished every twist and turret and disdained the avoiding traverses that sneaked along on our right.

Only where the terminal buttress of Corrag Bhuidhe barred the ridge did we turn off the crest, dropping 100m in a series of little pitches down a gully cleft on the sun-soaked southern flank. From its hoary crispness on the top, the snow now sank to an unleavened dough, clogging our crampons and calling for the

greatest of care in footwork. Again, the tracks were a godsend, compressing the surface and proudly showing the way along the airy gangway which regains the ridge on easy ground.

With a stiff pull over Cadha Gobhlach and a scramble down its other side, we gained the Sail Liath col at just 4pm. Time had stood still for us since Fiona, for the masterly traverse had held our spirits captive. Its joy was all the keener in

Plate 30 On the crest of An Teallach. Glyn contemplates the day's destiny. (L to R) Corrog Bhuidhe, Lord Berkeley's Seat, Sgurr Fiona

the surprise of our success.

Shenavall was plumb beneath this final col and already wrapped in the frigid evening shade. In less than an hour we were at its door. I can gladly report that Gordon warmed us with his fire that night, while Glyn notched up that last Munro on the following day – a tear in his eye and a pang of regret at the end of a ten-year campaign. Yet I know that out of two unforgettable days, those heady hours on An Teallach's crest will be held most dear in all three hearts.

7

NAVIGATIONAL NIGHTMARES

The Problems of Winter Route-finding

227° for 200m, then hold dead steady to 296 for just over 1km . . . or for absolute precision, split the second leg into 288° for 500m, then 308 until broad slopes sweep safely down and into the realm of vision . . .

This is the most-often used piece of navigation in every Scottish winter and for many climbers is the only piece they will ever remember – the crucial bearings to locate the Red Burn track from the summit of Ben Nevis (Fig 42). How simple they sound, yet within these figures lurk the countless

ghosts of navigational nightmares past and present; of hours creeping on the corniced brink of the North-East face, or dicing with fate in the exit chutes of the Glen Nevis gullies. A thousand or more ice-plated heart-stopping battles in the storm and dark have been fought on Britain's highest and most hallowed mountain-top, tales that would be worth the telling but are rarely put to print, for it takes a mighty pen to capture the Ben in merciless mood.

Those whose sole experience of Ben Nevis is of following the cairns and candyfloss of the Tourist Path in summer would find such tales quite incomprehensible. The contrast between summer and winter navigation is astonishing when it is first experienced. Basic methods of route-finding are similar, but there is a huge gulf in practice. In summer, the ground is always visible to guide the route. Even in the thickest fog there is a boulder or a clump of grass to give scale to the scene and fix the line of travel, while the general rise and fall of the land can always be judged. Compare the winter white-out, when cloud and snow form a blank monotone blotting every nearby landmark. Then one's sense of scale, direction and slope is not just distorted, but on occasion can be wholly eliminated. Recognition of a path or some friendly feature of the terrain will often correct an errant summer trail, but no such comfort is granted on a snow-covered summit when the mist gathers. Most of the extra techniques and ploys in winter navigation are attempts to compensate for the visual loss of the terrain.

Winter conditions also conjure up other more

Plate 31 Setting map and compass by the Ben Nevis summit shelter

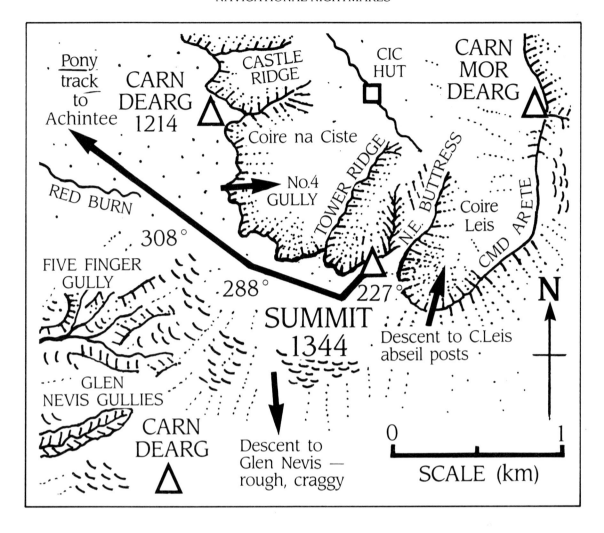

Fig 42 BEN NEVIS: THE SUMMIT AREA.
Bearings for the normal Red Burn descent and
lines of more difficult routes off marked

specific route-finding challenges, the avoidance of
corniced edges, avalanche hazard, the threat and
arrival of darkness, and the particular severity of
blizzard conditions when wind and snow are
unleashed together.

Above all, winter navigation is an intensely
personal skill. Map and compass methods, well
learnt and practised in summer climes, must be
played with greater patience, precision and
discipline on the winter hills. And in winter,
however many are the days that pass without

major incident, there will at some time come that
hour of dire need, perhaps not on the Nevis
plateau but on some other remote and hostile top,
when the odds are stacked and the clouds are
down. Then it is one's human worth that bears the
test – the ability to hold to a course with absolute
conviction, a self-belief in each decision and
calculation, unrelenting logic even though the
mind is befuddled by cold and fatigue, and of
course the strength and will to see the issue
through and get home safely.

PLOTTING THE COURSE

In deciding the detailed line of a winter route, one
must be keenly aware of the likely absence of

identifiable terrain. Paths, minor streams and small lochans may all be lost under the snow and quite invisible, even in clear weather. So a winter route must link those few features which can be identified with reasonable certainty in any conditions.

The intervening featureless sections can only be bridged by techniques of distance, estimation and assumed positioning. To navigate in bad visibility for long distances without any help from the terrain requires great self-confidence and rigorous accuracy in calculations and assumptions. A minor initial error can compound beyond recall over a long stretch. For instance, a 10° error in a compass bearing produces a 50m (55yd) deviation over a 300m (328yd) section, but this multiplies to 500m (547yd) if the leg is 3km (1¾ miles) in length. Therefore, the length of each link in the overall route must be kept as short as possible. It is worth making deliberate detours from the shortest line of travel in order to prove one's position at obvious features.

Summit cairns and bothy doors are particularly difficult to find in mist. Although they are obvious once found, they are pinpoints in the wilderness that will be missed if there is any error in the line of attack during a white-out. Yet they often are the crucial points in the achievement and safety of a winter outing. Bothies are also prone to burial under large accumulations of drift. The Lochan Buidhe shelter on the Cairn Gorm–Ben Macdui plateau was regularly completely buried through late winter and early spring before its removal on safety grounds in 1976, while discovery of the lower level Garbh Choire (Braeriach) and Fords of Avon refuges in a blizzard requires a big slice of luck, so low and squat they crouch in their respective valley bottoms.

Well-defined tops are found easily, simply by climbing the fall line directly uphill, but the level plateaux of the Eastern Highlands pose major problems to the summit-bagger. Their cairns usually stand proud of the snow when the wind has been working, but are the devils to find in white-out. Most Munros have big summit piles, but Aonach Beag (1,236m/4,000ft) in Lochaber is a notable exception. A tiny cairn is rumoured to exist, but is quickly masked by rime and wind-crust in the winter. Many lower or subsidiary tops do not possess any marker.

Wherever possible, one should try to navigate to linear features that will forgive a reasonable margin of error in the line of approach. Fences are the only safe linear features that might be encountered on the tops, but are not marked on the OS 1:50000 maps. In some areas, there is a good argument for the use of the 1:25000 maps on which fences are shown. Here one thinks of the Grampians, Monadhliath and much of the Southern Highlands, whose rolling tops possess a network of fences and are otherwise well-nigh impossible to define. However, one must beware that fences can quickly become derelict and only the odd post may remain. Other suitable linear features are forest edges, longitudinally shaped lochs and pronounced stream channels. They are difficult to miss provided a transverse (ie, approximately perpendicular) line of attack is taken. One should always employ the *aiming off* technique of bearing towards the centre of a linear feature rather than its edges.

If one is searching for a pinpoint feature, such as a top or a bothy, then any nearby linear features can be used to attain an identifiable position in its vicinity (Fig 43a).

Once in its near locality, a set procedure should be adopted for finding a desired point. Deliberate *overshooting and backtracking* is one method, which seeks some clear terrain indication that the point has been passed – a downward break of slope beyond a top (though not a cliff), a loch or river beyond a bothy or, as in Fig 43a, a wall beyond the summit. However, overshooting is hardly practicable on featureless moorland expanses, for example the heights to the east of Drumochter where you could walk a kilometre past the cairn without an inkling of downward incline.

In these situations, or where backtracking from an overshoot still fails to bring success, a *block search* should be mounted from the point of presumed location, covering the nearby ground completely and methodically in a series of squares (Fig 43b). Alternatively, a *sweep search* can be tried with the party spread across the zone but keeping within visual contact.

Fig 43 THE CRUCIAL SUMMIT CAIRN
METHODS OF POINT LOCATION

a Aiming off and overshooting (approaching Beinn Dearg from the south-west)

Ⓐ Direct bearing to the cairn: any eastward deviation brushes the cliffs to the east or misses the summit completely

Ⓑ Deliberate aiming off west of summit and overshooting to hit the wall; then follow the wall to the corner and backtrack 200m (600ft) to the cairn (requires the use of OS 1:25000 map)

b Block search on a featureless top

Ⓐ Point of presumed location based on timing/pacing estimation. Search starts here
1, 2, 3: searcher walks to edge of each square, always keeping visual contact with the rest of the party at A
NB: If one block fails, then the whole party moves to a new starting point on one of the outer corners of the grid

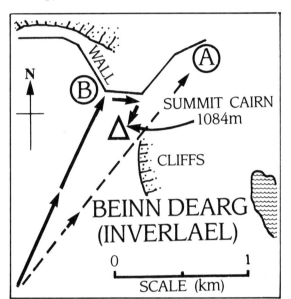

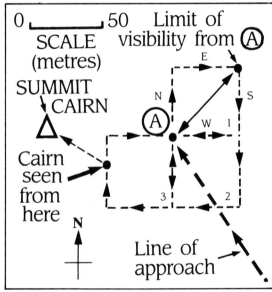

An Elusive Snow-hole

At the beginning of February 1987 four of us were dwelling in the snow-hole 'city' that is constructed by Glenmore Lodge parties in Coire Domhain on Cairn Lochan each season. Our occupancy was uncontested as the Lodge was on a week's vacation, and it was grand to have a ready-made 'bed and board' less than a kilometre from the top of our routes on Hell's Lum Crag instead of the torturing walk out to the ski-road. However, convenience tempted laziness. We slept long in the hole and left late next day for Garbh Uisge cliff, not arriving below its central gully until well after midday. The gully's four pitches so wholly absorbed our energies that the glowering sky and whirling spindrift on the plateau top received no more than a cursory glance through the afternoon.

So the sudden blast of a south-west gale on our reaching the cornice rim arrived as a rude surprise. Hell's Lum Crag was a rapidly dimming blur in the dusk and our sanctuary no longer seemed so close to hand. We strode briskly down over ice-clad boulderfields to escape the wind under the Feith Buidhe headwall. If we could pick up the base of the Lum cliff before total blackout it would be feasible to retrace this morning's approach. To our fortune, as soon as the open slabs of the lower cliff were located in the murk, we picked up lines of tracks – possibly our own. The problem was solved or so we thought, until emerging

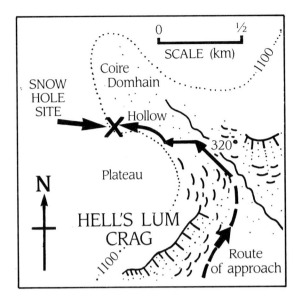

over the lip of Coire Domhain all footprints vanished under a sheet of new drift.

Strangely, there was little wind, but a dank and silent mist choked this upland coombe. Our shelter, food and sleeping-bags lay a kilometre away. With a deft turn of the compass dial we'd be there . . .

Ploughing up the valley bottom, its incline barely perceptible; 320° for 210 double strides, torches throwing searching shafts that rebounded on the wall of fog at 40m, now turning left to meet the corrie side-wall; then contouring the bank until it curved west into the little fold that harboured the holes – all checked and double-checked; as the terrain complied with each command and our goal drew near, our confidence mounted into absolute certainty.

But to our utter dismay, not the faintest smudge of snow-hole debris appeared. As the contours bent out of the fold and back to a northward pitch, the first nervous tingles went coursing down our spines. Was there another fold, were we too high on the bank, or were we too low, had we paced the right distance, or was the map disguising the truth? Yet our many musings missed the crucial clue even though we wallowed knee-deep in it. An afternoon of spindrift had not just covered tracks, but in the

sheltered fold had buried four large holes with new-blown snow – recessed tunnels, metre-high walls and debris fans – the lot! Not a trace was left to behold! So complete was the process, it wholly escaped our credence that we might have been standing right on top of them.

Meanwhile, we had formed a sweep search to scour the area. Four bobbing lights of flickering hope strung out across the slope 30m apart – first north two hundred strides, then doubling back south and over the fold again until we met the rush of wind and the stones of the plateau top, so back again into the fold, east a hundred steps, then west again . . . Panic rose. How could we possibly be lost? But then a shout came from Dave.

'It's the shovel.'

The orange plastic tip and 150mm of its wooden shaft, no more no less, stood proud of the drift. A stronger wind or an hour longer and it might have disappeared. We suppressed the thought and just thanked the heavens that we'd left a marker.

It remained to probe and dig for an hour and a half until the entrance door was found and cleared, and at half past eight the soothing purr of stove and pan announced us safely lodged.

CLIFFS AND CORNICES

Because of their cornice hazard, the most obvious mountain-top features of all, the cliff edges, are out of bounds as an aid to positioning. Paradoxically, one must do the utmost to steer away from the very places that might tell you where you are, and W. Naismith's 'method' of finding the summit of Ben Nevis in 1880 certainly should not be taken literally:

With appalling suddenness we found ourselves upon the brink of a yawning gulf walking straight for it. The black rocks were capped by heavy folds of snow many feet thick which overhung the abyss in a grand cornice festooned with colossal icicles. This episode enabled us to rectify our bearings and thence to the top no difficulty was experienced.[1]

Naismith clearly had the canny ability to convey his misadventures in a most kindly light. The plot of a route for bad visibility should ideally avoid any close contact with cliffs, especially a direct approach. The theory is admirable but cannot always be followed – for example, the return journey from the head of Loch Avon over the Cairn Lochan–Cairn Gorm plateau to Coire Cas inevitably involves shaving close to the head-wall of Coire an t-Sneachda. In the 1960s, Hamish MacInnes and Jack Thomson were returning by this route in a white-out from a rescue search with dogs around the Shelter Stone. Their dog saved them. Sniffing a few metres ahead, he suddenly disappeared over a void that was later decided as the top of Aladdin's Couloir. Happily, the dog landed well in steep but soft wind-slab and was able to climb back up the funnel without triggering an avalanche. Thereupon, MacInnes and Thomson too were able to rectify their bearings.

The more conventional means of reducing cliff-top danger is to rope up, and this is one good reason why a winter walking-party should carry a safety rope (eg, 7mm diameter) for the high tops. By roping up, cornice fears can be greatly reduced, at least for the rear members of the party who will tie close together on one end of the rope, while the unfortunate leader ties to the other and runs out its length towards the sus-pected edge. With a spacing of around 30m (100ft) of rope, there is minimal chance of the rest of the party being dragged over should the leader fall over the lip.

Even with a rope, one should avoid the cliff-tops if at all possible. It is the wise climber who abandons any ideas of finding the No 4 Gully descent on Ben Nevis in bad visibility and heads for the safety of the Tourist Path, even though this may greatly lengthen a walk back to the CIC Hut, and likewise the wise walker who heads south to Glen Etive from the summit of Buachaille Etive Mor rather than looking for Coire na Tulaich's narrow corniced exit.

For the most graphic illustration of the dangers of dicing with a cliff edge, witness the fearful minutes spent by the late Mick Geddes on the notorious brink of the Post Face on Creag Meagaidh in 1971 (Fig 44). As if a solo ascent of

the grade IV/V North Post was not sufficient adventure, he emerged onto a misted plateau at nightfall with the realisation that he had forgotten a torch. Instead of chancing the longer route over towards the Window notch, he took the bigger gamble of skirting the cliff edge in the hope of quickly finding the Easy Gully descent into Coire Ardair, failing which, a southward march would take him down the less fearsome slopes of Moy Corrie and off the mountain, albeit with a 13km (8-mile) trek back to his base at the corrie's howff:

> Soon the white-out, or black-out, became complete. My feet were lost from view and the angle of the ground became difficult to judge. I thought I felt the short steepening before the bowl of the gully top, and the timing seemed about right, so I turned left, but after a few yards I lost my balance as the ground steepened alarmingly. The feeling of total disorientation was harrowing. I groped back until I was on the plateau again (perhaps), followed the bearing a bit more, and turned off left again. This time I

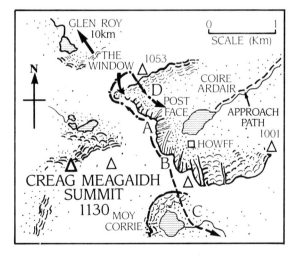

Fig 44 CREAG MEAGAIDH: TWO NAVIGATIONAL NIGHTMARES
A: Top of North Post
B: Top of Easy Gully
C: Geddes' approximate route of escape to Loch Laggan (1971)
D: Approximate route of Bonington's party in 1965

backed down on all fours so that, with luck, I could follow the steepening over the crest and into an uncorniced Easy Gully. Then my feet went from under me again, leaving me clinging to my axe and hammer.

That was enough. You'd better stop fooling about, I told myself, and cramponned up the way. I headed south, thankful for the fluorescent dots on my compass . . .[2]

The Moy Corrie route took him below the cloud, leaving a long but safe march home.

Avalanche risk goes hand in hand with cornice danger, as was amply illustrated by my own navigational indiscretion on Ben Wyvis during the winter Munros round of 1984–5. Veering off the line of our bearing, we fell through a small cornice and triggered a massive wind-slab fracture on the slope beneath. This experience was a forcible reminder that a lethal combination of cornice and wind-slab can form on grass slopes no steeper than 35°. The vertical cliffs are not the only places of which to be wary in the winter storm. Cornices regularly form at a break in angle of a downward slope and one must be prepared for their likely existence in such locations.

A winter route-plan should take account of any prevailing avalanche danger, assessing the aspect and location of loaded slopes and steering well clear of such high-risk areas. Taking the example of the route from the Cairn Gorm ski car-park to Ben Macdui, such an evaluation will often counsel a high-level route up the Fiacaill a' Choire Chais and over the plateau rather than the more sheltered and direct approach via Coire an t-Sneachda and the avalanche-prone Goat Track head-wall.

The plotting of a safe winter route for bad visibility is as much a matter of deciding which areas to avoid as of linking those few features which can be identified. The resultant route line may therefore look very different from that of summer.

GAUGING THE DISTANCE

Improvisations of positioning and distancing are therefore essential to follow a course over a featureless snowscape. The bearings off Ben Nevis are a good example where you walk towards nowhere for so many metres, then change direction and repeat the process, never able to prove your location with exactitude, but hopefully getting there in the end. In this situation, the accuracy of gauging the distance travelled is equally crucial to that of direction.

Two methods of judging distance are available. *Timing* is the better known, thanks to Naismith's Rule, and is used habitually to fix an overall route duration. However, over smaller distances en route, it does not have the same precision as *pace counting*. Provided one has prior knowledge of one's length of stride on various types of ground, pacing can be applied on the hill to within a 10 per cent error margin. Pace length does, of course, alter slightly with conditions, especially the depth of snow, wind speed, fitness and fatigue, but these variations can be allowed in the calculations, and they are insignificant compared to the wild fluctuations which conditions can produce in one's speed of travel.

Naismith's Rule of 5kmph (3mph) plus 10 minutes per 100m (½hr per 1,000ft) of ascent is a spanking pace in rough pathless country and rather optimistic for most people's fitness levels. It also ignores the extra time taken on steep descents. Very often the final descent from the last summit of the day is sorely underestimated. If the average slope is 30°, then the horizontal distance as measured on the map can be increased by 10 per cent to give the actual distance travelled on the ground. More significantly, direct descending is highly strenuous. The extra effort translates into extra time. Alternatively, one zig-zags downhill, which greatly increases the actual distance walked. Therefore, it is advisable to add 5 minutes for every 100m (300ft) of steep descent on top of Naismith's formula.

One can make various such adjustments to the basic rule which will improve the accuracy of overall journey timing, but it is often impossible to apply an average speed of travel in the timing of short individual sections. For example, on hard wind-blown névé, a speed of 6kmph (4mph) is quite feasible, for the ground is as firm and even as a metalled road. By contrast, in deep powder drift 2kmph (1¼mph) may be the maximum, and indeed I have recorded a genuine 1kmph (approx ½mph) floundering across the bottom of a corrie filled with freshly fallen snow. The strength of head or tail-wind on the tops can produce the same range of speeds, and of course a pre-calculated speed of travel makes no allowance for halts which can be many and prolonged when the compass is in use.

The length of stride varies relatively little with the terrain or wind. One tends to take slower rather than shorter steps when the going gets tough. Pacing does, however, require a basic numeracy and a total concentration on the count. Beyond 1,000 (ie, a distance of around 1½km (1 mile) in average double strides) the risk of losing the tally becomes so great that a reversion to timing is advised or else the navigation legs should be shortened. Counter devices (tachometers) can be purchased to fit onto the compass and ease the problem, although I am not convinced as to how a numbed and double-mittened hand can be trusted to work the dial.

Even if pacing is used as the prime gauge of distance, a timing estimate should always be set in reserve to provide supportive proof. All this plus compass work will sorely tax the solo mountaineer, whereas a big team can divide and double-check the tasks.

The calculation of total time and paces for a forthcoming section is a tricky task in severe conditions. Those who wish to avoid such high-stress (and high-risk) arithmetic will take a memory card such as Fig 45. This gives the range of speeds and pacings for my personal use on the hills, which I have tested to an acceptable reliability through repeated practice over fixed distances. With the table tucked into the map case, one simply has to convert the map scale to the ground distance and then read off the appropriate column against the particular slope/terrain of the section. On a storm-bound mountain, the

Fig 45 MEMORY CARDS FOR TIMING OR PACING THE MAP DISTANCE TRAVELLED
(my personal guidelines are noted in the left-hand columns)

a) TIMINGS BASED ON VARYING SPEEDS OF TRAVEL (IN MINUTES)

Speed (kmph) and Terrain	Distance Travelled (metres)											
	100	200	300	400	500	600	700	800	900	1,000	2,000	3,000
2 Deep snowdrifts, severe head-wind	3	6	9	12	15	18	21	24	27	30	60	90
3 Soft snow, strong head-wind	2	4	6	8	10	12	14	16	18	20	40	60
4 Variable rough terrain	1½	3	4½	6	7½	9	10½	12	13½	15	30	45
5 Hard level surface	1.2	2.4	3.6	4.8	6	7.2	8.4	9.6	10.8	12	24	36

Add: 10 minutes for every 100m of ascent
5 minutes for every 100m of steep descent

b) TOTAL NUMBERS OF DOUBLE PACES BASED ON VARYING LENGTHS OF STRIDE

Nos of double paces	Distance Travelled (metres)									
	100	200	300	400	500	600	700	800	900	1,000
Hard surface, level or gentle descent	50	100	150	200	250	300	350	400	450	500
Average on a firm surface	60	120	180	240	300	360	420	480	540	600
Rough undulating ground	70	140	210	280	350	420	490	560	630	700
Steep climbs, heavy drifts	80	160	240	320	400	480	560	640	720	800

card acquires all the wizardry of a home computer. Each person must work out individual pacing rates, for they can be highly variable.

HOLDING THE COURSE

To maintain a compass bearing on snowy terrain necessitates some devious tricks. The normal method in summer is to walk between objects within the field of vision such as boulders lying in the line of travel. In a winter white-out other members of the party or even footprint trails are used to check the course. The accuracy of these methods is highly subject to interference from wind and snowfall.

A blizzard may render intricate methods of route-finding difficult or else wholly impracticable. In a bad storm, the rule is to keep things simple. For instance, roping up may seem a good idea in a white-out and will be of help in keeping the party in line and together with a steady force 6 in flow. However, in a gusting force 10, roped movement will be abandoned as impossible what-

ever may be the cornice hazard.

This was well illustrated when we were coming off Beinn Bhan in Applecross in the wild sou' wester on 2 March 1986. We thought it prudent to stay roped about 3m (10ft) apart at the top of our climb. What followed was probably the best music-hall impression of three drunks at closing time that never made the stage. No sooner were we all upright than a gust would catch someone off balance and he would drag the others to the ground, writhing helplessly in the crampon-tangled rope. So we tried crawling yet with only a marginal improvement in stability. Meanwhile, the compass needle was gaily pirouetting round the dial, anywhere but its required 161°. Indeed, in our total disorientation we began to feel light-headed but also very frightened. All memory of our intended direction had been immediately erased and we could easily have been moving back

Fig 46 HOLDING THE COURSE ON SNOW-COVERED TERRAIN

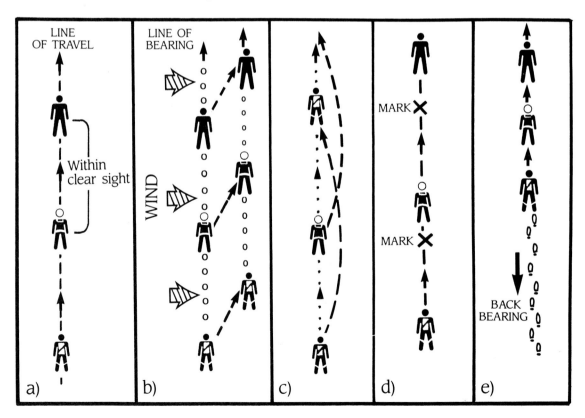

towards the cliff edge. As soon as we thought to untie and stuff the rope away, a semblance of order was restored, although we were now unsure of our exact position. Luckily, a chance encounter with a long-frozen set of crampon tracks confirmed the route down the ridge to Kishorn.

It is all too easy to theorise a method of travel for every set of conditions, but when a storm is raging you cut out the niceties, stick grimly to the compass and trust your instinct of terrain – for instance, pace counting will be of little help if you find yourself crawling off the tops.

Nevertheless, one should have the theories lodged somewhere in the memory ready for use as and when the conditions allow. Fig 46 summarises the main methods that are available for following a bearing without the aid of terrain. If, as in Fig 46a, a party lines its bearings ahead and behind to moving members, there is a high risk of veering off-course in a strong crosswind. Fig 46b shows how the veering process is imperceptible within the line at any one instant, but were the Big Grey Man of Macdui lurking behind, he would see a gradual accumulative deviation in the party from the intended line.

Possible corrective measures are given in Figs 46c–e. Leap-frogging fixes the ground position by one member being stationary at any time, but is far too slow for a situation where frost-bite, hypothermia or darkness threatens. Marking the snow ingeniously enables more constant progress to be maintained, although it is not possible on an icy surface. The back-bearing down one's line of tracks is the salvation for the lone walker, provided one has at least 30m (100ft) of visibility. All the lining-up methods require clear methods of communication within the party. In a roaring wind, a simple semaphore system is vital for their efficient operation.

Veering can also occur when one traverses a slope in bad visibility, especially when a surface drift of snow produces the mesmeric effect of shifting quicksand across the line of travel. Although one can try hard to make deliberate compensation, natural human laziness dictates that there will always be a degree of down-slope slippage in the party. Long contouring sections are therefore to be avoided if possible on a winter route. A much clearer awareness of terrain is maintained by tackling slopes directly up or down their fall-lines.

GAUGING HEIGHT: THE ALTIMETER

In the necessary event of a long traverse, an altimeter can provide a constant check that height is being maintained. While the high expense will deter most walkers and climbers from its purchase, the mountain skier will find the device invaluable for two reasons. First, on skis and particularly on downhills one has no gauge of speed of travel nor any means of pacing, so that a knowledge of altitude becomes an essential aid to positioning. Secondly, the skier will often (and on Alpine equipment nearly always) seek to traverse around intermediate relief on a ridge in order to save both effort and the constant delay of taking skins on and off.

To the walker or climber, an altimeter can introduce an unnecessary extra complexity into his navigational arsenal – as if timing, pacing, map-reading and compass-watching are not sufficient additions to the problem of looking where you are putting your feet. While it is good practice to use several independent threads of evidence to prove one's course, every truism has its limits and I personally baulk from the use of an altimeter when I am climbing on the Scottish hills, having job enough to keep a hold on the map and compass. An exception would be on the Cuillin Ridge where not only is the compass magnetically distorted by up to 40° on the crest, but the OS maps are an indecipherable mass of cliff, gully and screes. With an altimeter plus a guidebook list of the tops and bealach heights, the ridge traverse can be navigated with much greater certainty, for in mist the Cuillin is a weird and frightening switchback.

The altimeter is not an infallible device, for its readings rise and fall with the prevailing air pressure to produce small but sometimes crucial errors over the course of a day. Unless one remembers to reset the height on known landmarks, a pressure drop of 6 millibars, which is quite normal over three hours in frontal weather as a depression approaches, can produce an apparent height gain on the meter of 50m (160ft).

Nick Parks was once tricked by such an occurrence during a winter guides' assessment. During the six hours of an ascent on Hell's Lum Crag, the pressure had dropped sharply and in the hurry of gathering darkness, Nick omitted to reset his meter at the top of the cliff, then chose to take the contouring route around the southern slopes of the plateau to the head of Coire Cas. In a misty dusk, this meant a high dependence on altimeter accuracy and its error caused him to pass below the top of the Fiacaill a' Coire Chais. Because his attention was focused on the meter rather than on the compass, he had walked 300m (300yd) south around the flank of Cairn Gorm before he realised his mistake. Even with an altimeter, traversing is a risky navigation ploy.

NIGHT MOVES, ROUTE TIMES AND ROUTE-CARDS

Strictly, one should never go into the winter hills without a rough idea of the overall duration of the expedition. Some computation using Naismith's Rule or a modification thereof needs to be made, and if one is unsure of the conditions on the hills, then the most pessimistic estimates of speed of travel should be applied. Additionally, one should provide generous allowances for halts for rest, for changing gear, especially crampons, and for the map and compass work itself.

If a night finish is predicted, then one must have the wherewithal to handle the difficulties of navigating in the dark, and these cannot be imagined until they are experienced. Any night sections on the tops should be timed at half one's normal daytime pace. Those who wish to avoid nocturnal gropings should set routes with a safe margin of daylight or else which will get down onto easy ground by nightfall. A late finish can be more acceptably entertained if the well-tracked length of a Glen Tilt or Derry comprises the homeward trek. An early start is the best means of averting navigational epics when one is exhausted at the end of the day, and is indeed to be admired. The morning sloth of the Scottish winter climber has evolved from a tradition into something of an institution.

Plate 32 Heads down and into the blizzard. A party line on the tangled moorland approach to An Ruadh Stac from Glen Carron

If one is caught out on rough ground after dark, the value of torches is well appreciated. In the care-free days of the 1930s, many parties never took torches on winter expeditions. Alastair Borthwick recalled the amusing consequences of such an oversight when he was trying to locate Forest Lodge by Loch Tulla after battling over Stob Ghabhar in a blizzard with Hamish Hamilton and Mary Stewart. While lacking torches, they did have matches, although these had been brought for lighting cigarettes rather than for illumination. Now the three huddled together, each holding different sections of the

thanks to the car headlamps of their waiting friend, which provided a guiding beacon.

Route timing necessarily beckons a discussion of the desirability of route-cards. For the less experienced, or if one is venturing into new country, the preparation of a detailed card for personal use can be invaluable. Each main section can then be measured and timed to give a yardstick of progress upon which either to prolong or else to abort the expedition. While seasoned hillgoers can pluck a close time estimate from the most cursory glances at map, weather and snow conditions, they are wise to make prior note of all the critical bearings and distances on the higher level parts of the route. These can then be assessed immediately they are required in the heat of the battle without any of the fumbling needed to set a flapping compass against plastic-coated map in the storm. Particularly in winter, a route plan must allow for escape or curtailment, with alternatives evaluated and assessed, and 'points of no return' identified.

But is there an obligation to deposit route-cards at base, with police or in car windows, for safety reasons? This is a vexed question.

It has always struck me as both an infringement of our mountaineering liberty and almost an admission of one's lack of ability to survive and evacuate successfully, which to me is the essence of our winter sport. The obligation raised by the card can lead to the intemperate attitude of getting down at all costs when it might be safer to bivouac if one has been caught by darkness, or else take a wholly different route back. Equally, one may be afflicted with the glorious impulse to prolong a stay on high when the weather is fine and the sky alive with stars, but were a card left, such a course would be likely to have the rescue teams out and the sky alive with flares, especially if those at base are seized by premature alarm. The choice is yours, but I feel strongly that we all should be allowed that choice.

Plate 32a 'Stick grimly to the compass and trust your instinct of terrain'. White-out conditions with a SE gale gusting to 80mph on The Great Moss above Glen Feshie, Cairngorms

map and one the compass. There were ten matches left. As each was struck, a gust of wind would extinguish the spark. After seven matches had been wasted, tensions and tempers were rising, but the eighth burst into flame, giving five or ten seconds of flickering light in which to read the map, fix the mountaineers' location and set the compass. Even with a rough estimate of the direction of the Lodge, the compasses of the 1930s were of little use in the dark, lacking the luminous markings of modern Silva models. Borthwick's party did eventually find Forest Lodge, but only

ADAPTING TO THE TERRAIN

Good winter navigation is highly responsive to the subtleties and nuances of geology and relief, both in one's instinctive awareness of terrain and in the

Plate 33 On the approach to Coire Ardair, Creag Meagaidh – scene of many a navigational epic. The Post Face with its prominent vertical gully lines is in the sunlit centre of the corrie, with Easy Gully to its left, and The Window notch to the right of the cliffs. It all looks beguilingly simple on a perfect clear morning!

methods used. Scotland's mountain scenery is infinitely varied, from Grampian moorland to the jagged Cuillin. These differences are accentuated in winter. Fig 47 classifies the main types of navigational terrain encountered in the Highlands, the distinctive route-finding problems and the specific methods used to handle them.

Those who enjoy map-reading as they would read a book, develop an invaluable ability to interpret the map symbols into the ground terrain they depict. At a glance of previously unseen map

sheets of the Western Highlands, the experienced map-reader will differentiate the roughs of Knoydart from the sweeps of Affric and the plateaux of Easter Ross. With such an awareness, the navigational problems of each type of land can be assessed and predicted. This prior 'feel' for the terrain enormously helps one's confidence on the hills.

Although they are not widely used, the 1:25000 Ordnance Survey maps give a better overall impression of terrain than the larger scale 1:50000 series. Screes, outcrops and cliffs are drawn in great detail to give a more immediate visual impact than the smoother lines of the 1:50000 sheets, although their crowded symbols and faint contours can make the detailed map work more difficult. However, if you intend to climb regularly in an area, it is recommended that you buy the relevant 1:25000 maps. Happily, special Outdoor Leisure 1:25000 editions are available for

Fig 47 TERRAIN INFLUENCES ON WINTER NAVIGATION

Terrain Type	Route-finding Problems	Methods and Adaptations
MOORLAND Cairn Mairg Glen Tilt-Shee hills Drumochter hills Monadhliath	1 Absence of features; long sections without landmarks. 2 Prone to heavy drifting; slow and arduous progress. 3 Slope definition poor and difficult to judge. 4 Long traverses along contour lines often necessary.	1 Use of channelling relief (ie, stream valleys, passes) aids terrain awareness; fences often indispensable. 2 Vary route to seek firm ground (ie, névé on windward slopes rather than powder drifts on lee sides). 3 Distance travelled must be accurately known, so pacing and timing crucial. 4 Bearings difficult to follow; 'lining-up' methods must be applied.
GLACIATED PLATEAUX Cairngorms Ben Alder Creag Meagaidh Beinn Dearg (Inverlael)	1 Featureless tundra terrain. 2 Remote, high and exposed. 3 Major cliffs, cornice risk. 4 Discordant drainage (eg, river capture, overflow channels).	1 Pacing accuracy paramount; long improvised sections. 2 Safe margins needed in route time and/or confidence in night navigation. 3 Roping up in vicinity of edges; 'aim-off' away from cliffs; avoid descents through cliffed terrain. 4 Terrain instinct confused; total trust in compass and ignore conflicting impulses – it is never wrong.
REGULAR RIDGES Mamores Forest South Glencoe Glen Shiel/Affric	1 Main danger is complacency on well-defined terrain. 2 Ridge definition is sometimes lost in broad convexities. 3 Distance hard to gauge on steep ridge ground. 4 Cornice risk on crests	1 Errors at ridge junctions (and three-way cols) are critical; compass checks, close map-reading, keep on crests. 2 Prime example is gaining the CMD arête from Ben Nevis; compass check essential; risk of complacency. 3 Pacing inaccurate; timing works on ascents but allow extra on steep descents; count ups and downs. 4 Roping up in white-out (provided wind is not severe).
CONTORTED RIDGES Knoydart, Sgurr na Ciche Fisherfield Forest Black Cuillin Ridge	1 Irregular twists not shown on map (ie, as geology changes); ridge junctions confused; direction constantly changing. 2 Detours and delays at obstacles. 3 Escape is often difficult.	1 Terrain awareness and close map-reading essential; prior guide-book scrutiny helpful; judgement of height important, altimeter useful; counting ups and downs or tops and cols. 2 Allow extra time; keep direction of party lined to course; keeping to crests helps. 3 Careful route-planning; 'points of no return' and all escapes clearly noted.

the Cairngorm, Torridon and Cuillin tops, which cover the crucial areas at a lower cost than the individual sheets. Snow- and ice-climbers will find the 1:25000 maps of special use in locating the bottoms of routes on the cliffs, which is no easy task in bad visibility. So clear is the crag detail of the 1:25000s that major gully and buttress lines can be identified with precision. Some climbing routes are even named on the maps.

Of all the terrain types, the glacially discordant territory of the Cairngorm and Central Highland plateau is perhaps the most difficult and certainly the most nerve-racking to navigate, and is epitomised by the summit zone of Creag Meagaidh (see Fig 44). The land is high and barren, and so is cruelly exposed to the wind. The corries have eaten great random chunks out of the plateau, disrupting the pre-existing drainage network. Their cliffs are immense and rambling. Meltwater channels cut the main ridge, obscuring the line of the true watershed, while to the north, the plateau sweeps for 6km (4 miles) away into the featureless outback of the Monadhliath.

For the walker or skier traversing the plateau eastwards, the location of the Window notch, a typical overflow channel, can be extremely difficult, for it is deeply incised and rimmed with crags to the east. Yet its definition is completely lost once the plateau is reached. Not only is it a crucial turning point on the traverse, but it is also the sole escape route from the 3km (2 miles) stretch of the top.

On my first visit, its location eluded us in a dreich December mist. We steered a bearing a safe distance to the west of its furthest indentation, but in so doing passed it unawares. Having retraced our steps, I remember sitting down in some perplexity, sensing wet clothing and a near-empty rucksack, and pondering the rigours of the northward trek into the wild reaches of upper Glen Roy. A fortuitous clearance of the cloud saved further distress on this occasion, for the Window's exit snick was suddenly revealed, coyly . abutting the plateau top.

The problem of discovering the Window in a January blizzard in 1965 made a deep impression upon Chris Bonington. Tom Patey's irrepressible enthusiasm had persuaded him and four other experts into an impulsive and woefully late assault on Meagaidh's cliffs. Topping out from their gully at nightfall, Bonington's rope of four found that Patey, the local expert on whom they relied for route-finding, had deserted them, having climbed the route in front. His footprints were quickly covered over and the team was thrown back on its own resources. A check on the equipment revealed that these resources were rather scanty – they had, in fact, no maps and only one compass. Yet, in Bonington's words:

It was a strange elating feeling – the situation

was undoubtedly serious for a bitterly cold and gusting wind was playing across the surface of the plateau. We had no bivouac equipment, very little food and only one torch which we couldn't expect to last for more than a couple of hours' continuous use.[3]

Bonington recounted the ensuing epic as on a par with any of his Alpine or Himalayan encounters. The Window's location proved elusive and only when they were certain that they had overshot its exit and therefore were clear of major cliffs, was a blind southwards descent attempted. More by luck than design, they landed back in Coire Ardair at midnight, respects for Meagaidh immeasurably increased. The hardened winter climber is often the most culpable of blithely ignoring the basic rules and equipment for navigation.

From all my own experience of Scotland's winter mountains I would conclude that route-finding is the most crucial and demanding skill of all, more than any of the individual techniques of steep climbing. In contrast to the cavalier attitude of some climbers, mountain walkers tend to realise its importance and place navigation at the forefront of their learning and practice on the hills. It may lack glamour and excitement, but there is an equal mastery to win over map and compass as over any of the other tools of the mountaineer's trade, and a quiet pleasure to be gained both in its acquisition and effective application.

But if all this is known ground and merely preaches what you already practise, please don't be smug. Perhaps one day you will be alone on the Cairngorm plateau, ploughing through shifting drifts in a milky white-out. You're simultaneously watching the compass and tripping and falling on hidden rocks. After an especially bruising crash, you stagger up and go on a hundred steps until the compass needs a check. It has been conveniently dangling on a cord from your anorak zip, so you gather it up, and where dial and needle are supposed to lie, you view a one-inch hole gaping through a broken plastic base. Well, it happened to me, and someday, just when you think you know it all, it may happen to you!

8

COMBATING THE COLD

Clothing, Nutrition and Training

To the critical but uninitiated reader, a snow bath may appear to be an extreme of asceticism or bravado . . . In fact it is neither . . . It is far less of a shock to roll about in deep powdery snow on a calm sunny afternoon than to dive into ice-cold water, and enormously less than the revolting chill of the domestic cold bath . . . In any case, whoever indulges in a snow bath on a mountain crest will continue his progress along the ridges with renewed zest and vigour. (*Dr J. H. Bell*)[1]

Before embarking on a discussion of winter survival, it is well to take heart from the bare-fleshed cheek of Doctor Bell. The cold need not always be our enemy and on occasion it can be a source of bodily refreshment, if one has the courage to take the plunge. However, for the majority of thin-blooded lily-livered mountaineers, the 'cold' of winter is more usually to be stoically endured. The seasoned hillgoer comes to memorise and minutely differentiate its every degree and variety, and in the Scottish climate these are many.

There is the creeping cold of the deep night-frost that enters at the soles and stealthily ascends the lower limbs as you linger on the tops at sundown. Then comes the searing dry cold of the easterly gale that cuts straight through every garment and sucks away your heat without mercy. More gradual, but no less penetrating, is the insidious wet cold of the westerly storm of sleet and moist snow. As the clothes slowly saturate, an eruption of goose-pimples gives way to a tingling chill, then a chattering of teeth and finally a convulsive shivering.

Most painful, though, is surely the cold that attacks only the extremities. Fingers and toes turn to veinous blue, then deathly white. An unpleasant and distressing numbness is sensed, and somehow the nerves are activated, ready to inflict a throbbing torture when the circulation finally returns. The 'hot aches' or 'freezing hots' as they are variously known, are so exquisite as to bring tears to the eyes of the toughest countenance. The agony subsides only once the blood-vessels are fully flushed. Then one can savour the pleasure of a glowing warmth and safe relief from the risk of frost-bite.

Undoubtedly, the most dangerous form of cold is that which gives no pain. If the body is sufficiently cooled, the nervous system is suppressed and will fail to sense the chill. Frost-bite or hypothermia can then make a stealthy attack without alerting the potential victim. Alastair Borthwick's intimate analysis of this condition could not be bettered. After standing motionless for 2½ hours in Stob Ghabhar's Upper Couloir belaying his leader during a storm-whipped ascent of the 1930s, he was well qualified to comment:

Intense cold has a strange numbing effect on the brain as well as the body, and both reach their limits of endurance before very long. Thereafter those parts of the brain which register pain and fear hibernate. A body is cold and miserable, but it is not, somehow, quite one's own body. The brain has retired into a protective casing, from which the circumstances glance off, leaving no mark. He who is cold lives in a passionless and almost painless world. That is why death by exposure must be, contrary to popular opinion, one of the more pleasant routes to Paradise.[2]

MAINTAINING THE HEAT

A winter mountaineer has two overriding pre-occupations: the successful completion of the expedition if at all possible and the maintenance of an acceptable degree of personal comfort. In scientific terms, personal comfort means keeping the inner body temperature close to its norm of 37.5°C (99.5°F). In reality, the first goal is hardly feasible without a proper regard to the second.

Man is a warm-blooded animal. His survival and physiology are geared to his sustaining constant core temperature. Faced by the cold, there are three automatic mechanisms by which the body protects its vital organs: the accelerated breakdown of fats to provide extra heat, the cutting off of the blood supply to the extremities, termed vasoconstriction, and involuntary shivering. If these are not sufficient, then the body progressively cools and Borthwick's 'passionless world' of incipient exposure will be entered as the core temperature dips below 34.5°C (94.1°F). At around 32°C (89.6°F), the brain becomes helpless to resist the onset of severe hypothermia, which will prove fatal without treatment.

Apart from these natural reactions, the climber has a threefold armoury with which to wilfully combat the cold: clothing, nutrition and fitness. Yet, however good are the mountaineer's clothing, nutrition and fitness, they must be accompanied by a determined mentality when he is on the hill. The cold is a constant threat that demands constant vigilance. In severe conditions, it must not just be endured but fought tooth and nail by making every possible adjustment to personal comfort and pitching a measured physical effort in its path.

Once confronted, cold is far more easily contained and withstood. Even the brazened behaviour of Bell in his snow-bath should be seen more as a psychological ploy than as a display of eccentricity. By giving in or even briefly dropping the guard, one can easily find oneself treading perilously close to that exposure threshold and suffering all the more for the self-neglect.

So, as we explore the demands of clothing, nutrition and fitness made by the Scottish winter, it should not be forgotten that the ultimate battle cannot be won without the right psychology, regardless of preparation. Hardiness, toughness or wily experience – call it what you will; the quality is quickly cultivated during a career in winter mountaineering.

CLOTHING: QUALITY NOT QUANTITY

The prime function of clothing is the prevention of heat loss from the body, but many people who climb in Scotland for the first time make the error of equating personal warmth with the maximum thickness and bulk of insulation. In fact, the key to keeping warm in the Scottish climate requires rather different and more specific qualities of one's clothing system:

Waterproofing The insulation value of one's clothing is derived not from the material fibres themselves but from the volume of air which those fibres trap, both within each garment and between the garment layers. This is because the thermal conductivity of air is many times less than that of a solid material. In other words, still air is far more resistant to heat transfer. A good insulating material therefore is typically composed of 10–20 per cent by volume of fibre and 80–90 per cent of air.

Wetting eliminates the air spaces that are trapped by the material fibres. In other words, they lose their loft. The greater weight of wet garments causes their compression which eliminates the air layers between each garment. Water has a conductivity some 240 times greater than air. Therefore, the insulation value of any clothing system is rather more than halved, even when it is only partially saturated. It is, therefore, essential to keep one's clothing dry in the wet cold typical of Scotland's winter climate. A waterproof shell is literally worth four times its weight of absorbent insulation material.

Manufacturers make much play of the relative performances of different insulation materials when they are wetted, but this obscures the crucial point that no material – feather down, fibre pile or wool – is adequate to withstand the winter chill if it is wet. Keeping dry is therefore the key to keeping warm.

Windproofing Effective insulation requires that there should be minimum movement of the trapped air within one's clothing. A wind causes continual displacement of trapped air by colder air from outside, so that the body is unable to create and maintain a cocoon of warmth. This 'convective loss' of heat is hugely accelerated by the wind. The rate of cooling of bare skin is trebled in a wind of 64kmph (40mph). All other forms of heat loss, radiation, evaporation and still-air conduction, are of minor relative significance when the wind blows.

All clothing offers some degree of protection from this effect, but a steady wind will penetrate all but the most closely woven materials in order to displace the trapped air right down to the skin surface.

It is essential, therefore, to have an outer shell which is windproof as well as water-resistant. Happily, wind- and waterproofing are achieved by the same type of garment. While an impermeable shell is of paramount importance, it also helps to have closely woven undergarments which offer some additional wind protection. The mechanics and problems of wind chill are more fully explored later in the chapter.

Moisture transmission As well as providing external insulation in a cool moist environment, winter clothing should be able to dissipate effectively the internal moisture that is produced by bodily perspiration. The high work rates involved in winter mountaineering are often underestimated. Despite subzero temperatures, a clothed body walking or skiing uphill with a pack can produce a sweat volume of more than 600ml (1pt) per hour.

Fig 48 THE CLOTHING SHELL: A COMPARISON OF MATERIALS		
Material	Construction	Winter Performance
VENTILE COTTON	Tightly woven cotton yarn which swells on wetting (see Fig 49); the traditional anorak material from 1940s to 60s but still available.	Showerproof and fairly windproof; breathable when dry but not when the material is wetted; a wet jacket can freeze to form a stiff but totally windproof 'armour shell'; very durable.
PROOFED NYLON	Polyurethane or neoprene-coated nylon; introduced in 1960s and a major development in weather protection; cheap and therefore still popular.	Wind and waterproof but not breathable; 'sweat-box' effect when working hard; light in weight and not wettable when new; durability depends on thickness of nylon used.
GORE-TEX	Breathable laminate (two or three layers); a microporous membrane with water-repellent outer face (see Fig 49); first used in 1977 and still the field leader.	Wind and waterproof and can transmit at least half of body vapour even when working hard; not wettable when new; three-layer GORE-TEX is highly resistant to abrasion.
Other Breathables		
MICROPOROUS PROOFED NYLON	Coating process produces vapour-permeable pores (ENTRANT/CYCLONE).	Field tests have found these inferior to GORE-TEX on all counts but much better than the simple coatings.
HYDROPHILIC PROOFED NYLON	Solid coating but with molecular modification to allow vapour transmission (AQUATION).	Field tests have found these inferior to GORE–TEX on all counts but much better than the simple coatings.
HYDROPHILIC LAMINATE	Solid polyester membrane with breathable molecular structure (SYMPATEX).	Still awaiting full field-testing but a potential long-term competitor to GORE-TEX.

Fig 49 SHELL MATERIAL CONSTRUCTION

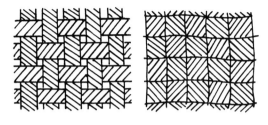

DRY: water vapour escapes through spaces between the yarns

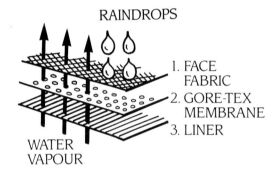

RAINDROPS

1. FACE FABRIC
2. GORE-TEX MEMBRANE
3. LINER

WATER VAPOUR

WET: yarns swell and seal up the spaces, preventing the entry of water droplets
1 Water-repellent outer
2 Vapour permeable, waterproof membrane (pores 20,000 times smaller than water droplet, 700 times larger than a vapour molecule)
3 Lining

If this moisture is unable to escape through the clothing, the skin surface becomes saturated so that the body is unable to disperse its heat by further sweating. Paradoxically, overheating then results, and at the same time the clothing becomes damp. A 15 per cent saturation level is quickly reached in absorbent undergarments, which reduces their insulation value by approximately one half. Therefore, overheating on an initial climb may lead to serious chilling on the summits when the perspiration rate falls but the cold is more severe.

In the absence of wind or rain/snow, the problem is easily containable. Inner garments are effective in 'wicking' moisture and transmitting vapour away from the skin. However, when one is forced to wear the outer shell for external protection, it is almost impossible to achieve a satisfactory heat and moisture balance unless the shell material is 'vapour permeable' in some way. Therefore, for winter use, it is strongly recommended that you invest in a breathable shell garment, which can transmit a high proportion of the internal vapour created by perspiration while remaining absolutely resistant to external liquid moisture.

GORE-TEX® (the registered trade mark of W. L. Gore & Associates, Inc) (Fig 49) is currently the field leader in such fabric. It is compared with the other available shell materials in Fig 48. Non-breathable waterproofs such as simple polyurethane or neoprene-coated nylon produce a 'Turkish bath' effect during prolonged exertion, which cannot be tolerated in winter. The extra cost of GORE-TEX should not be spurned. Of all clothing items, the outer shell is by far the most important. Its quality should not be spared even if one is forced to wear a set of patched-up rags underneath.

Layering The absolute insulation demands of the Scottish winter are not great and it is a big mistake to wear thick integrated garments such as down duvets, synthetic fibre-filled jackets or fur-lined parkas. These are designed primarily for the extremes of a polar or Himalayan climate where a temperature of −20°C (−4°F) is considered mild. They provide beautiful warmth when one is stationary at a camp or bivouac, but cause desperate overheating when one is on the move in all but the worst Scottish weather. Yet if a single garment forms 90 per cent of one's insulation it cannot be removed without causing severe chilling.

10 (*right*) The knife-edged crest of the Forcan Ridge of the Saddle, looking up Glen Shiel

11 (*overleaf*) The great cliffs of Lochnagar under a heavy coating of hoar frost (*Andrew Nisbet*)

Plate 34 Traditional winter clothing. Tweed jackets, plus fours, puttee gaiters, wool balaclavas plus a liberal coating of snow! (*SMC collection*)

A layering of clothing is therefore essential to provide a flexible response to the wide range of Scottish temperature and changes in one's work rate. During a weekend in the hills, one can

12 (*left, above*) Romping up the easy snows at the top of The Alley (II/III), An Teallach

13 (*below*) Modern mixed climbing. Andy Cunningham smiling and torquing his way up Bloodhound Buttress (V), Coire an Dubh Lochain, Beinn a'Bhuird (*Andrew Nisbet*)

experience any combination of the following: a range of −15 to +10°C (5–50°F) in the glens depending on the weather system, a lapse of −6°C from valley to summit, a wind chill of up to −20°C and an additional insolation (radiational) effect of +7°C in strong sunlight.

The layered system should preferably be easily interchangeable to enable quick adjustment as the wind rises or the sun begins to burn, but this is not feasible with regard to one's choice of thermal underwear. Long-johns tend to go on at the start of the day and stay on, or else are not worn at all. Yet the delay and temporary discomfort of changing layers when one is on the hill is fully repaid in terms of comfort and warmth. There is little point in having a flexible system if one is too lazy to make the necessary adjustments. Especially in severe conditions, discipline is needed to stop and remove outer layers in order to top up one's inner insulation. It therefore helps to anticipate changes in clothing demands. Extra layers can be donned with ease and comfort in the lee of a summit. One then emerges into the gale on the crest well-wrapped and fully prepared for the blast. This is preferable to grappling with flapping sleeves and cords on the summit itself, when valuable body heat is lost and discarded clothes and gloves can be blown away during the changing operation.

The clothing needs of the Scottish winter are therefore simple but specific: a top-quality weatherproof shell backed by a series of under-layers to enable balanced insulation over a 40° range of sensed temperature. There are four supplementary considerations to the main requirements: the suppleness of clothing for ease of movement, its weight, durability and its speed of drying.

Fig 50 (opposite) examines three clothing assemblies on all criteria, the traditional woollen clothing of the early winter mountaineers: an integrated system highly dependent on a single-lined jacket, and the flexible combination that represents the best that is offered by modern technology and knowledge.

Prior to 1960, very little attention was paid to the particular needs of our winter climate in clothing style and fabrics. British mountaineers were thus forced to use garments that were primarily designed for alpine or expedition use. Inner clothing was bulky and inflexible, and the most popular outer material, ventile cotton (Fig 49), while superbly durable and resistant to wind and dry snow, was not fully water-resistant. The advent of nylon waterproofs in the 1960s was therefore heralded as a major development in clothing performance, even though the GORE-TEX 'revolution' was still a decade ahead. In terms of function, design and comfort, winter clothing has advanced beyond all recognition within a generation.

The clothing requirements of walking, skiing and climbing are, of course, slightly different. Ski-touring involves a higher rate of energy expenditure than either walking or climbing, and therefore demands thin garments which are especially effective in transmitting moisture and

are quick to dry, such as polypropylene or polyester underwear. As the skier's speed of travel is so much greater, outer windproofing is particularly important. Thus a skier might be ideally clothed by thermal underwear plus a light cotton wind-suit, with any thicker insulation and water-proofs stowed spare in the rucksack, whereas a walker would wear thicker layers since his work rate is lower but his exposure to the elements is liable to be more prolonged.

The climber has the insoluble problem of reconciling long periods of immobility on belay stances with sudden surges of maximal energy on the pitches, plus an inability to change layers due to the impediment of harness, rope and helmet. My own preference lies towards ensuring a sufficient warmth during the waits. A certain muscular warmth is essential to embark on the gymnastics of technical climbing, while a short-term overheating can usually be tolerated higher on a pitch. Slow technical climbing may therefore be one situation where the wearing of an integrated lined jacket is warranted.

While this discussion has focused on what is actually worn while one is moving on the hills, it is essential to provide also for the chance of enforced immobility by taking one spare garment over and above the maximum mobile requirements plus a bivouac bag. Like the outer shell, every serious winter hillgoer should spare no expense in purchasing a top-quality GORE-TEX material survival bag. Cheap orange polythene sacks may suffice for a short emergency, but they are condensation traps and so will wholly saturate one's clothing over a few hours. They also display a disturbing propensity to slide off downhill, with the victim inside. In 1981, one unfortunate climber forced to bivouac at the top of Hell's Lum in the Cairngorms after an accident made a nocturnal ski jump down the full 130m (400ft) height of the cliff inside his polythene bag. He was discovered in the morning, alive and still cocooned, a further 150m (500ft) down-slope by his rescuers.

Having experienced the remarkable recuperative effect of a few hours inside a GORE-TEX bag after lurching about on the brink of exposure, I am immensely reassured to know that it always is in my sack, adding only about ½kg (a pound) of

Fig 50 CLOTHING SYSTEMS FOR THE SCOTTISH WINTER			
	Traditional (pre-1914)	Modern (Integrated)	Modern (Multi-layered)
THE LAYERS	Wool vest	Long-sleeved wool vest	Light breathable vest (eg, polypropylene)
	Wool long-johns	–	Light breathable long-johns (eg, polypropylene)
	Wool shirt	Fine cotton shirt	Fibrepile blouse (eg, Polarplus)
	Wool jerseys (2 or 3)	–	Fibrepile jacket (eg, Polarplus)
	Tweed breeches	Full-weight salopettes (helenca or fibrepile)	Light stretch salopettes/ track-suit bottoms
	Tweed jacket (proofed with alum solution)	Integrated 'wadded' jacket (GORE-TEX outer with feather-down or polyester fibre filling)	GORE-TEX fabric shell jacket
	–	Nylon/GORE-TEX overtrousers	Nylon/GORE-TEX overtrousers
MAXIMUM INSULATION: DRY	Fibrous wool has good loft TOG value★ 5–6	Very warm down to −20°C (−4°F) TOG value★ 6–8	High volume of air trapped between layers TOG value★ 5–6
INSULATION: WET	c50 per cent when saturated	c20 per cent for a feather-down filled jacket.	c35 per cent for fibrepile when saturated.
WATERPROOFING	Showerproof only	Excellent	Excellent
WINDPROOFING	Poor, except when jacket freezes solid	Excellent	Excellent
BREATHABILITY	Very poor if sweating; wool absorbs moisture readily.	Jacket lining tends to soak up moisture reducing transmission to GORE-TEX outer.	Undergarments transmit vapour and moisture readily, excellent breathability.
SPEED OF DRYING	Very slow due to high absorbence of wool.	Slow, especially feather down and cotton.	Fast drying due to low moisture capacity.
FLEXIBILITY	Extra jerseys easily added or removed.	Poor: jacket and thick salopettes give 'all-or-nothing' insulation.	Excellent: four layers on upper body, three layers on legs.
SUPPLENESS	Cumbersome; stiff when frozen; shrinks when wet.	Bulky and restrictive of movement.	All garments except shell stretch; excellent flexibility.
WEIGHT	Heavy (may be trebled when saturated)	Medium	Light
CONCLUSION	Have pity but the greatest admiration for the pioneers.	Fine for camp or bivouac but a potential sweat-box when on the move.	Perhaps the ideal combination for Scotland's winter climate.

★TOG value: The standard measure of insulation (thermal resistance) – the estimated total TOG rating for clothing system plus trapped air is given extra weight on every winter outing. This confidence enables me to prune my clothing down to the essential minimum for the journey and thus save weight.

PROTECTING THE EXTREMITIES

The feet and hands require particular thermal care in winter. They are the most remote as well as the most exposed parts of the blood circulation, hence their vulnerability to frost-bite, while the retention of a basic manipulative capacity in the hands is essential to one's operational functioning on the hill. The muscular efficiency of the arms and legs is also dependent on their maintaining an adequate warmth. The skin temperature of limbs may be halved from their norm of 20–25°C (68–77°F) during exercise in wet, cool and windy conditions without adequate weatherproofing. At such reduced levels, severe muscular impairment may be experienced. Speed of progress falls, the journey is prolonged and a spiral of further cooling can occur. Loss of physical co-ordination is indeed one of the warning signs of pending hypothermia. Finally, the discomfort of cold in the extremities has already been graphically described and this is sufficient reason in itself for keeping them as warm as possible.

Yet even taking the greatest of care, I frequently find myself hard-pressed to turn the key in the car door at the end of a mountain day. One simply has to acknowledge that on occasions the hands and feet will refuse to maintain an acceptable level of warmth despite constant attention. Tall and thinly built people have a particular problem, since the blood has further to travel to reach the extremities, nor does it enjoy the protection of a thick casing of fat and muscle en route.

So what can be done to protect one's hands and feet? Most importantly, one must keep the core of the body warm, either by clothing or physical movement, so that complete vasoconstriction in the extremities does not occur and the blood supply is maintained. Provided that the body is willing to release the blood, it is possible to rewarm hands and feet quickly by rubbing, shaking, slapping, blowing or, most effectively, by shoving the hands into the armpits and the bare feet onto a good friend's bare stomach.

If, however, one is thoroughly cold, such tactics will ultimately fail because the body will always give priority to the warmth of its essential organs by restricting the circulation elsewhere. In severe cold, the rate of blood flow to fingers and toes may drop to just 1 per cent of its normal level during enforced inactivity. This is a statistic that I can readily believe after repeated trials while immobilised on icy belay ledges. Until one can get the whole body rewarmed by vigorous action, attempts at localised massage produce only a feeble transient effect, although this is better than none at all. Nor will the addition of extra gloves and socks greatly help this situation. Protective covering can only serve to reduce heat loss. In this case, there is minimal heat present to be preserved.

While good insulation of the extremities is not in itself enough to ensure warmth, it is no less essential. The principles are exactly the same as for one's main clothing system, but with two additional points. First, mittens are more effective insulators than gloves because they maintain the fingers in contact with each other, so reducing the surface area of the skin from which heat can escape. Secondly, it is wrong to compress the feet by the addition of extra socks in the belief that more layers mean more warmth. In fact, this merely serves to eliminate the trapped air and to raise the rate of conductive heat loss as well as preventing movement in the digits. Socks and mitts should therefore be loose-fitting.

My personal preference is to wear woollen Dachstein mitts next to the skin, with the addition of GORE-TEX fabric overmitts for extreme cold or windy conditions and in reserve a pair of thin gloves. An excellent sock combination is to wear fine nylon or polyester inners and a normal thick wool outer, on the same basis as one would wear a wool shirt over polypropylene underwear, the inner transmitting moisture away from the skin and the wool outer absorbing the flow. Thus, the inner remains dry and retains an air layer next to the skin.

The warmth of the hands is also effectively conserved by learning to execute intricate tasks while one's hands are gloved. Many mountaineers carry a pair of thin inner gloves for such operations, but the real expert can perform equally well in mittens. It is rumoured that the most prized skill of Glenmore Lodge instructors is the ability to unwrap the silver paper from a Kit-Kat bar with iced-up Dachsteins in a force 10 gale.

Finally, preventive care of the hands and feet should not be overlooked. Mistreatments at home such as overheating, wearing ill-fitting footwear and failure to wash and properly air the feet, predispose the extremities to cold injury when on the hill. While severe frost-bite is rarely suffered in Scotland, superficial frost-nip and chilblains can still cause considerable pain and permanent tissue damage.

Protection of the head deserves special attention in winter. As opposed to the hands and feet, there is a strong and copious blood flow to the scalp and vasoconstriction does not operate. A significant percentage of body heat is lost through the scalp and this rises greatly at low temperatures, having been measured as 75 per cent at −15°C from an immobile body. Furthermore, if the brain is allowed to cool by direct exposure, the onset of the light-headed state of weakened concentration is inevitably more rapid. Good headgear is therefore essential to keep general bodily warmth and mental control.

A FURTHER LOOK AT WIND CHILL

Wind chill is so much the predominant cooling agent on the hills in winter and yet is so frequently misunderstood, that it deserves a closer examination by mountaineers.

Earliest formulations of wind-chill factors, notably that of Siple and Passel (1945), were based on experimentation with rates of cooling of an exposed water surface. No account was taken of clothing insulation or windproofing and the results should therefore only be applied to exposed flesh. They give an idea of frost-bite danger to the extremities, but vastly overstate the overall rate of bodily cooling, unless, like Bell, you happen to be taking a nude dip. Unfortunately, general textbooks have failed to make this distinction, so many people have failed to realise how greatly the quoted chill indices can be reduced by proper clothing.

The more recent work of Steadman has been couched in theoretical equations of impressive complexity but precious little practical application, and for this reason alone should be treated with caution. While Steadman's formula did incorporate the insulation value of one's apparel in estimating the total heat loss from the body, it took no account of the degree of windproofing of the clothing and therefore also exaggerates the true chill effect on a well-clad climber.

Nevertheless, the Steadman model can be highly instructive when it is translated. Fig 51 gives its approximate predictions of total rate of heat loss from an average human body at an air temperature of 0°C (32°F) given three different clothing combinations and wind speeds from 0 to 64kmph (0 to 40mph).

Fig 51 RATES OF BODY-HEAT LOSS AT 0°C (32°F) AT DIFFERENT WIND SPEEDS IN CALORIES (KCALS) PER HOUR

(Derived from Steadman's 1971 Wind-chill Equation[3]. Assumes the person is walking at 4.8kmph (3mph); the heat losses in nil wind would be considerably lower if the person was stationary)

Wind Speed	Wearing Dry Undergarments	Wearing Wet Undergarments	Nude
	Vest, shirt and fibre-pile jacket TOG value $c4.0$	Vest, shirt and fibre-pile jacket TOG value $c1.3$	Nil insulation TOG value Zero
Nil 32 kmph (20 mph) 64 kmph (40 mph)	450–530 750–850 1,000–1,100	550–630 1,030–1,130 1,400–1,500	650–750 1,300–1,400 2,000–2,100

Note that the figures are given in calories and therefore equate directly with our energy intake in the form of food. Five hours of hard walking exposed to a 32kmph (20mph) wind without a windproof clothing shell may consume the body's entire daily supply of food energy (see column 1 of the table). Once depleted, the body is able to produce little further energy for progress, nor the additional heat to keep warm.

Even if one's energy reserves are limitless (ie, an endless supply of chocolate bars), a person walking at 5kmph (3mph) on level terrain will produce no more than 300–400 Kcal per hour of heat from the exertion. Yet without a windproof garment in a wind of 32kmph (20mph) the predicted rate of loss is c800 Kcal per hour, so the body's warmth would still be steadily drained unless the work rate was doubled.

A second important message from Fig 51 is that if the clothing is wetted so that its insulation drops to one third of its dry value (column 2), the chill effect is increasingly more severe as the wind

speed rises. In nil wind, the rate of heat loss is 15–20 per cent greater because of the wetting, but at 64kmph (40mph) the increase is around 40 per cent. It is easy to perceive from these figures just how rapid can be the onset of hypothermia in wet, cool and windy weather.

Fig 52 provides an alternative translation of Steadman's formula into the wind-chill equivalent temperatures. These are the lower temperatures which would produce the same rate of heat loss if the person was walking in calm conditions. For example, at 0°C (32°F) and at 64kmph (40mph), the equivalent temperature is −14.5°C (5.9°F). The graphs demonstrate that the rate of wind chilling rises slightly in colder air. This is because the initial temperature difference between skin

Fig 52 WIND-CHILL EQUIVALENT TEMPERATURES – ie, the equivalent still air temperatures to produce the same rate of cooling (*derived from Steadman's 1984 equation*)[3]

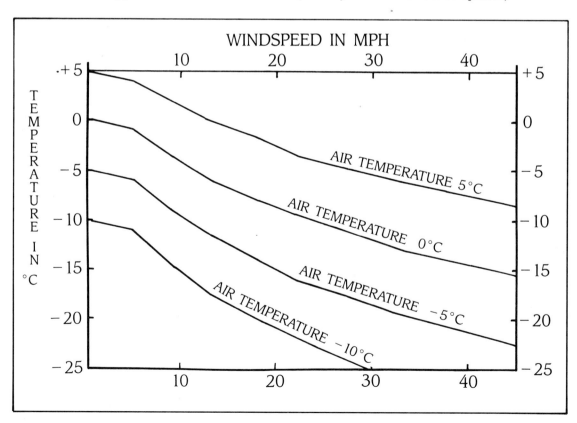

and air is greater. However, the regular use of wind-chill graphs has caused the widespread misconception that the equivalent temperature is a real air temperature. It must therefore be stressed that at an air temperature of +5°C, there is no risk whatsoever of frost-bite however hard the wind blows.

By giving a rough quantification of the frightening effect of wind chill in the absence of resistant clothing, the Steadman model emphasises the importance of the wind-proof shell. However, this does not mean that by wearing such a garment wind chill is entirely eliminated.

First, the extremities remain exposed. Secondly, the wind compresses the clothing, eliminating trapped air layers and thus accelerating the rate of conduction heat loss. The most wind-proof garment I have ever worn is a ventile jacket which, having been wetted earlier in the day, then froze during a blizzard into an armour-plated shell, which the wind could neither penetrate nor compress. The same effect is obtained with a frozen Dachstein mitten and is the one argument in favour of wearing outer garments which do absorb a certain proportion of moisture as opposed to GORE-TEX fabric which is entirely water-repellent when new. Thirdly, the wind can still enter an anorak via the sleeves, skirt and hood, unless they are tightly closed.

A moving body itself creates a chill effect because of air resistance even when there is no wind at all. This is especially significant when one is skiing. When walking into a head-wind, one's own speed should also be added to that of the wind to give the total chill effect, although in high winds the addition is negligible. More importantly, the moving body creates a 'bellows' effect within the clothing, causing an extra convective loss of heat, which becomes more pronounced in higher winds.

Nobody has yet measured the true wind-chill effect on a properly clothed person while he or she is engaged in mountaineering. Climbers can only say from experience that the winter wind places a rapid drain upon the body's heat reserves even when the best protective clothing is worn. However, the wind does not just chill; it also demands a huge extra output of energy to maintain progress. In severe combination, these two effects place mountaineers under an intense physiological stress. They must dig deep into their reserves of strength and stamina to get home and stay warm – hence the importance of proper nutrition and good fitness to produce the energy required. Both qualities are often ignored by the inexperienced mountaineer.

DIET AND FITNESS

'How does he climb
Solo and briskly
On twenty fags a day
And Scotland's good malt whisky?'

This parody of the late Tom Patey should serve to scotch the myth that an olympic regime of diet and training is essential to the enjoyment of winter mountaineering. Indeed, a liberal consumption of tobacco and alcohol might even be recommended as anaesthetising the brain to both cold and fatigue. The idea is not entirely preposterous, for the mountaineer who grimly endures hard winter days on the hills understandably develops a craving for pleasurable indulgences in the bar-room and chip shop on returning to civilisation. This psychological rebound is often necessary to muster the courage to go out and face another storm on the morrow.

However, such apparently unhealthy practices among some leading mountaineers should not obscure their underlying reserves of stamina and experience, qualities which the likes of Patey possessed in full measure, plus a limitless enthusiasm and determination with which an unwilling body could be dragged to remarkable achievements.

The relaxed and vaguely alcoholic social image of Scottish winter mountaineering is, of course, renowned. However, I would personally contend that performance, pleasure and safety on the hills are all improved if one starts the day with a clear head, clean lungs and well-rested muscles. The winter mountaineer is also wise to pay the same attention to the quality of nutrition as one would in any other endurance sport. Match your own diet against the following four criteria:

Total intake Man has a basal metabolism of 1,200–1,800 calories per day. To this minimum survival requirement must be added the energy demands of physical activity, which are of the order of 300 calories per hour of active mountaineering, plus a supplement of some 15–20 per cent to counter the extra cold of winter. Therefore, as much as 4,000 calories might be expended on an average seven-hour day on the hills.

While it is not absolutely essential to consume this amount of energy in direct sequence with its expenditure, over a period of several days the total should be fully replenished. Otherwise, the body is forced to live partly on its reserves of fat and muscle protein in order to make up the shortfall, which is a most inefficient source of energy conversion and cannot alone sustain the speeds and strengths required for mountaineering.

Therefore, a winter climbing holiday is no time to go on a diet. Indeed, within a few days the appetite becomes attuned to the body's real needs

and can be heartily indulged without fear of weight gain.

Composition If 3,500–4,000 calories is a reasonable daily target, the means of obtaining the total is largely a matter of personal preference. However, some individuals take their tastes to startling extremes. I might contrast the mountain diets of two guiding colleagues as an illustration. Mick Hardwick claims (or should I say confesses to) the gluttony of three family-sized bars of chocolate on a really hard day out, a total of over 500gm (1lb) in weight and 2,500 calories in energy of pure milk fat and glucose sugar. Health-conscious Alan Hunt, on the other hand, spurns all fats and sugars and will subsist on dried fruit and dry oatcakes, plus a high-bulk, high-fibre breakfast of porridge and endless slices of wholemeal toast. Much to my amazement, both function effectively on the hill.

Ideally, a little more balance is desirable. As Fig 53 demonstrates, each type of food plays a necessary role in bodily maintenance and energy output. Intensive sporting activity demands slight alterations in their proportions. In endurance

Fig 53 SOURCES OF ENERGY

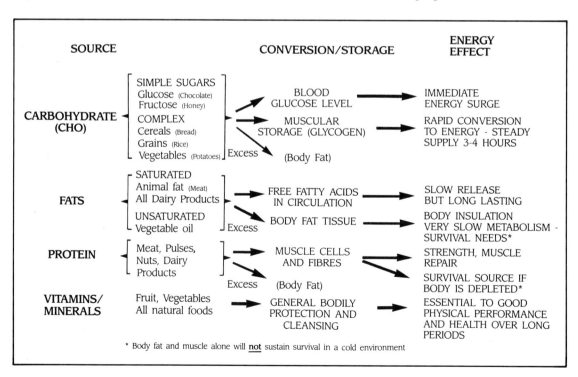

Fig 54 FOOD FOR THE HILL: SIMPLE SUGARS *v* COMPLEX CARBOHYDRATE

	SUGARS Chocolate, Mint Cake, Fudge, Jam	COMPLEX CHO Bread, Cakes, Biscuits
WEIGHT	Concentrated: 350–500 calories per 100g (100–150 per oz).	200–320 calories per 100g (60–90 per oz) – higher wastage.
DIGESTIBILITY	Easily eaten and digested except toffee/caramel when frozen.	Higher bulk – greater effort to chew and longer time to digest.
ENERGY EFFECT	Immediate energy flow is perceived.	Slower but more prolonged release.
ENERGY STORAGE	Less effective in building muscular energy stores.	Continual conversion to muscle glycogen of all excess over immediate needs.
SIDE-EFFECTS	Danger of overloading – 'rebound hypoglycaemia' – if taken in excess before hard exercise.	No significant effect on blood-sugar levels; steady energy supply without the 'highs' and 'lows' of excess sugar.
FAT UTILISATION	Excess glucose tends to reduce fat content of blood lowering long-term energy reserves.	Complex CHO retains and fixes fat in blood maintaining the longer term source of energy.
WATER BALANCE	Concentrated sugar causes water absorption and can lead to diarrhoea and dehydration.	Complex CHO stores water in muscles which is released to the bloodstream during exercise.

running, carbohydrates (CHO) are the crucial source because they provide an immediately accessible store of energy in the form of glycogen in the liver and muscles. The marathoner's best balance is around 62 per cent CHO, 25 per cent fat and 13 per cent protein.

The mountaineer's exertions, however, are thrice prolonged but at a much lower intensity, and he will therefore benefit from a 5–10 per cent higher proportion of fat, which in weight is over two times more concentrated as a source of energy but is released at a much slower rate. Fat therefore extends the CHO reserves which would otherwise be exhausted within three or four hours of hard walking. It gives a stable sustenance over a long day, is excellent protection against continual cold and reduces the risk of the sudden and dangerous exhaustion. The notorious 'bonk', which often afflicts runners and cyclists when they are depleted, cannot be risked on the winter hills. So while 'fat' has become a condemned word in modern dietary education, the traditional 'fry-up' in fact forms a perfectly acceptable basis for a

mountaineering day. Even Alan Hunt readily admits that his ability to go without fat in his food is due to his possession of an excess reserve in the subcutaneous tissues to keep him warm. Lean people undoubtedly have a greater need for a dietary supply.

Nevertheless, CHO should still constitute at least 50 per cent of the total intake. However, the exact form in which the CHO is taken is important, the simple sugars and complex grains and cereals having rather different energy effects, as are summarised in Fig 54.

A high reliance on pure glucose, otherwise known as the 'Mars bar syndrome', may have detrimental effects on the body's sugar balance when a concentrated intake is followed by heavy exercise. A sudden burst of energy may be followed by a mental and physical 'low' as the body over-reacts in its efforts to rid the system of the excess. One can only presume that the Hardwick diet works on the basis of maintaining the energy 'high' by constant eating.

Complex CHOs in the form of bread, cake,

biscuits and cereal bars are often hard to eat and digest when the body is stressed, but they form a better basis of nutrition on the hill. Sugary foods should ideally be kept in reserve for a quick top-up, and are particularly beneficial if one is exhausted near the end of the day.

My personal answer to the nutritional problem on the hill is the wholemeal honey 'buttie'. This contains a balanced diet in a single bite and was the fuel which took Eric Beard to his remarkable feats of mountain running in the 1960s. Honey is a simple CHO, but as a natural product is of better nutritional quality than highly refined, pure glucose sugars. The bread gives a basis of complex CHO and a liberal smearing of margarine the fat content as well as the moist texture necessary for ease of eating. Unlike a Mars bar, the honey sandwich will not freeze solid on the hill.

Timing Regular snacking rather than prolonged lunching is recommended on the mountains in order to give a steady supply of energy. A large lunch can also easily overload the stomach and valuable energy is expended simply in digesting the excess over the subsequent hour. It is wise to eat early in the day rather than keeping food for that sheltered summit cairn that never seems to arrive. Food is better stored in the body than in the rucksack. Snacks should also be taken before one feels desperately hungry or tired. Once the threshold of depletion is passed, it is extremely difficult to refuel and regain one's strength.

As the most immediate energy source, the CHOs should form 75 per cent of the content of hill food. The fat, protein, vitamin and mineral requirements are of a longer-term nature and are more conveniently acquired at evening meals and at breakfast.

The dietary technique of carbohydrate loading is regularly practised by endurance athletes and involves an enforced period of CHO depletion followed by two days of concentrated CHO consumption to the exclusion of other foods. The effect is to maximise the glycogen energy stores in the muscles to get an extra few minutes of high-speed energy flow during a major event. It is of little relevance to prolonged mountaineering, a depletion phase being hardly practicable if one

goes climbing every day. Climbers need a more continuous and sustained intake of food and are wiser to eat what suits than to subject themselves as guinea pigs to dietary theories. However, it is definitely worth topping up on CHO before a weekend away in the hills.

Liquid Water constitutes around 60 per cent of our total body-weight. It is essential to eat and digest, to carry nutrients through the bloodstream and to maintain the body's temperature balance. Without a sufficiency of liquid, the best-planned diet is of no avail.

As explained on p135, dehydration and over-heating are more frequently suffered in winter than is supposed. Serious physical and mental impairment is experienced with just a 5 per cent loss of body water. This equates to around 2.25 litres (4pt) and might be expended in four or five hours of sustained strenuous mountaineering if the mountaineer is wearing protective clothing. In winter, it is often impracticable to replace this volume of liquid on the hill. One might at most carry a litre (1¾pt) of liquid in the rucksack while streams are frozen or absent.

Some degree of fluid deficit is therefore inevitable, but all measures should be taken to restrict the loss. Copious mugs of tea at breakfast-time will top up the initial fluid reserves, giving perhaps as much as 0.5 litre (1pt) of surplus for later use. A generous CHO intake fixes and stores liquid in the muscles in the ratio 2.5:1 by weight of water to glycogen, which can give a reserve of over 1 litre (1¾pt) for release during prolonged exertion. Finally, clothing and walking speed should be continually adjusted to minimise sweating while adequate warmth is maintained.

The retention of water in the body requires a constant concentration of salt in the cells, and severe prolonged sweating depletes both fluid and salt reserves. If only pure water (ie, fresh snow melt) is drunk in replenishment, the body will be unable to hold the liquid and dehydration will only be relieved temporarily. Thus, salt tablets or preferably a properly balanced athletes' drink powder might be carried, although a sufficiency of salt is obtained from normal food for all but the most severe dehydration.

Fig 55 GETTING FIT FOR THE WINTER MOUNTAINS		
Activity	Physical Requirements	Training Ideas
MOUNTAIN WALKING	Low intensity but prolonged energy output; general robustness and endurance in leg muscles.	Long hill-walks in autumn (a fine season for tramping). Jogging on hilly or rough country, orienteering.
SKI-TOURING	Sustained medium intensity aerobic demands on climbs. Specific strength, resilience and flexibility in leg muscles and joints for descents.	Aerobic training: running, cycling, circuits. Roller ski-ing. Stretching and flexibility exercises (yoga).
SNOW- AND ICE-CLIMBING	Specific stamina and strength in calves, wrists and forearms. Aerobic endurance, especially on easier routes.	Specific weight-training: legs press, toe raises, pull-ups, wrist curls; high repetitions to develop stamina. Hill running for calf muscles.
MIXED CLIMBING	Variety of bodily contortions as for rock-climbing; suppleness and strength in specific muscles. Aerobic stamina less important.	Autumn rock-climbing. Strength and power in wrists, calves and arms by lower repetition weight-training plus stretching exercises. Cultivation of tolerance of cold and patience; psychological training.
General tips: Lay off training at least three days before a major trip; rest and plenty of sleep is the best immediate preparation. Don't blunt enthusiasm for the 'real' event on the mountains by overtraining.		

It is well to note that the sensation of thirst is triggered by rising salt concentrations in the cells. If both fluid and salt are equally depleted by sweating, the salt concentration will be unchanged and dehydration may develop unnoticed. Therefore, like food, it is wise to drink regularly on the hill even though one might not feel particularly thirsty. If one's urine colour turns dark yellow, it is a fairly sure sign of dehydration.

Hot drinks may be thought highly beneficial in winter. In fact, their bodily warming effect is negligible – a flask of hot soup giving only 6 calories of extra heat compared to it being served cold. However, a hot drink has a marvellous 'placebo effect' – its heat is immediately perceived and the cup is ideal for warming the hands.

There is no simple medical definition of fitness. It is a phenomenon that is highly specific to the activity being undertaken. Winter mountaineering is so highly specialised a sport that general endurance training may be of limited help. The only wholly effective physical preparation for mountain walking, climbing or skiing is actually to walk, climb and ski. Denied the opportunity for practice, any training should be designed to replicate the intended activity as closely as possible.

Of course, in a metropolitan sports centre it is hardly feasible to arrange the apparatus to hang by the wrists from two ice-axes, with icy water dripping up the sleeves, two ropes tugging at the waist and a blizzard raging all around. However, as Fig 55 suggests, there is much that can be achieved of direct benefit – for example by jogging on the hills rather than at level ground, the correct muscle groups will be developed for mountain climbing. Indeed, if one over-develops the wrong muscle groups, the effect may be to neglect the right ones, so that misguided training could actually be detrimental to performance on the hills.

If one is unable to get any prior physical preparation, it is only sensible to plan initial excursions in the hills with a high degree of prudence, until one proves one's power and potential. Three or four days' climbing is usually sufficient to gain a semblance of fitness. However, vaulting ambition and an untrained body are a dangerous couple to take on the winter mountains.

The varied components and effects of fitness (Fig 56) deserve close examination. Strength, energy-storage capacity and recovery rates in specific muscles are greatly improved, while general cardio-vascular capacity (ie, oxygen utilisation) is enhanced and, through training, the ratio of lean to fat body-mass is generally increased.

Fitness certainly reduces one's rate of energy expenditure. One can do the same journey with less food, but it is dangerous to take this idea to extremes. For example, one might increase one's potential energy reserves by training, but these cannot be realised unless the body is supplied with sufficient extra food. Only when fully charged will these reserves enable a fit mountaineer to go further, faster and for longer than his untrained counterpart. During my winter Munros round, my dietary needs increased, if anything, towards the end of the trip, despite a high fitness level.

Furthermore, the stripping off of fat tissue reduces the body's internal insulation. A lean, fit person can easily offset this loss of warmth by his own exertion, but in a winter survival situation of enforced immobility, he is placed at a disadvantage. Therefore, it might be best to be fit and fat, if such an unlikely combination could ever be achieved. Certainly, there is little harm in carrying a few extra pounds of fat on the body as an energy reserve in winter.

However, there is an enormous psychological benefit from gaining fitness: a confidence in one's ability to keep going, a knowledge that the body is capable of fighting the cold, that it has the survival reserves for an emergency, as well as a feeling of well-being and attunement to the hills. Since the winter mountains arouse our deepest excitement and admiration, they deserve to be met with a modicum of physical preparation.

Fig 56 THE JOYS OF BEING FIT	
AEROBIC EFFICIENCY	Increased capacity for oxygen uptake reduces heart rate and rate of respiration. Work rate and energy expenditure lowered. Energy conserved and sweating reduced.
MUSCULAR EFFICIENCY	'Trained' muscles: size, number and alignment of muscle fibres increased; improved blood supply. Rate of energy output reduced: energy conserved, oxygen requirements reduced; ability to sustain aerobic exercise is developed.
ENERGY RESERVES	Storage capacity of muscles expanded; body becomes more efficient in converting fats to energy. Endurance increased provided body is fully fuelled.
RECOVERY PERIOD	Body is able to restock its muscles with energy faster. Ability to climb on successive days without depletion.
TECHNIQUE	Style: neatness and efficiency of movement; the most specific aspect of fitness. Energy conserved: experience can compensate for a lack of physical fitness.

9

THE LONG DARK HOURS

Winter Overnighting: From Bothy to Bivouac

Winter's nights cannot be ignored since they occupy the greater part of the twenty-four hours and, whether by mischance or design, they will inevitably be encountered, in part or whole, by all who frequent the Scottish hills. However, they are to be enjoyed as often as they are survived. If the gathering night looms as a major hazard and challenge to the winter mountaineer that is never to be treated lightly, then its quality is equally to be appreciated whether one is crouched beside a bothy fire, roaming the moonlit tops, or pushing for the top of a hard mixed climb. So may this chapter be far more than the grim elaboration of the survival skills, but a pleasurable review of winter nights both past and present.

EARLY TRADITION

The first Scottish winter mountaineers disdained to challenge the night. The idea of deliberately forsaking the comforts and victuals of the Highland hotel in order to camp or bivouac in the hills was so immoderate as to be wholly unknown before the 1920s. While pre-dawn starts and late evening returns were normal practice, and even a sign of good form among the more ardent enthusiasts, a very clear line was drawn at the event of benightment on the tops. It became an essential and enduring code of winter conduct to take all precautions to ensure a safe return to lodgings.

Sir Hugh Munro was particularly severe in his condemnation of benightment. He recounted a navigational mishap in February 1892 on Ben Macdui when nightfall found him at the brink of the Loch Avon cliffs instead of the easy slopes of Coire Etchachan as he had intended. Having extricated himself and made a late but safe arrival at Derry Lodge, he was able to conclude that,

notwithstanding this uncharacteristic mishap, 'solitary winter climbing with proper precautions is perfectly safe . . . The one *inexcusable fault* is to allow oneself to get benighted.'[1]

This aversion to spending a night in the mountains necessitated some phenomenal treks. In March 1891, Munro based an exploration of Ben Alder Forest at Dalwhinnie. On the 22nd, he traversed the Aonach Beag ridge to its furthest point at Beinn Eibhinn, then returned to his hotel, a fourteen-hour round trip of some 48km (30 miles). The next day he fully retraced the 13km (8-mile) approach by Loch Ericht in order to traverse the neighbouring Beinn Bheoil and continue to Rannoch. Such behaviour would be regarded as totally eccentric today, when either a camp or a bothy would be used as a more accessible base.

But in March 1901 Munro finally endured the bivouac he had so strenuously sought to avoid. Descending late from Sgurr nan Each to Loch a' Bhraoin after a traverse of the Fannichs range, the way was barred by swollen torrents, forcing his companion Lawson to the admission: 'the truth is that two SMC members disgraced themselves by failing to get home on the evening they intended.'[2]

Their night was passed alternately sitting damp and despondent through the showers, then searching for a passage in the moonlit interludes. Unfortunately, the escapade also imposed an unsolicited bivouac on the carriage driver who had comes from Aultguish Inn to collect the pair, but at least their faithful attendant found shelter in the now-ruined boat-house at the Loch a' Bhraoin outlet. After some tricky river-crossings, Munro and Lawson attained their rendezvous and faced their embarrassment in the morning light.

Viewed with the perspective of the times, there was neither the equipment nor the facilities upon which nights out could be planned in winter. Camping equipment was impossibly bulky and heavy, while the open bothy system of today did not exist, many cottages which are now bothies being still inhabited by shepherds or stalkers. Most importantly, the early climbers, being largely of the professional middle-classes, had no pecuniary need to endure nights under canvas or in draughty barns. The luxury of a steaming bath, roast venison, wine and clean white sheets would surely exert the strongest attraction to us today, even at the effort of a few hours' extra walking – were it affordable.

HOWFFS, HUTS AND BOTHIES

The style and tradition of rough living in the hills was born out of necessity during the interwar years when growing numbers of working-class men sought escape from the Depression and so turned to the wild places. Without the means to afford even a tent, the 'howff' formed their cheapest and most convenient accommodation.

The 'howff' may be properly defined as a natural haunt in the hills, a cave or boulder cleft which, by fortification and cladding, can be rendered ostensibly watertight and windproof. There is no shortage of such shelters in the high cliffed corries of the Highlands. Boulders beneath the Cobbler, Ben Narnain and the Brack came to be the main bases for exploration of the Arrochar cliffs, and their habituees formed the nuclei of such famous clubs as the Creag Dhu and the Junior Mountaineering Club of Scotland (JMCS). Hard climbing, camaraderie and close communion with the mountains were symbolised by the howffs. They were used in all seasons, but particularly at New Year.

Jock Nimlin, the pre-war pioneer of many rock climbs on the Cobbler and Buachaille Etive Mor, remembered 'seeing in' 1936 under the Shelter Stone of Loch Avon without a sleeping-bag and squashed between two companions for warmth. The blowing snow had sealed all external draughts and he enjoyed an eight-hour sleep but: 'True again I have to confess that our nightcap was a peculiar mountain brew, potent as heather ale.'[3]

When its effects subsided, he recalled being awoken by the chattering of his teeth. Hard times indeed!

Another sour-dough of the hills was Ben Humble, who argued:

Mountain camping is all very well, but the inside of a tent is always the same, and once inside, there is nothing to do. Each howff is different, each has its own building problems, each its own charm, each its own memories. And there is always so much to do for howffing refinements are endless.[4]

While the established howffs in the accessible corries became much frequented, the idea of climbing up into an unknown corrie on an arctic night, without the surety that a suitable natural shelter could be found, offered an extra dimension of adventure that could scarce be ignored. On one Hogmanay, Humble and friends overnighted in the Lost Valley of Glencoe. From arrival to bedding down, they were occupied for seven hours, first in seeking a suitable site among the mass of gargantuan boulders which choke the valley lip, and then working, solely by the light of candle and fire, in installation, insulation and cooking operations. The effort expended and the fifteen-hour night which the mountaineers survived gave them a special satisfaction and a self-confidence.

The challenge and fun of winter howffing remain undiminished, and it should never be forgotten that nooks and crannies in the boulder-fields can provide vital shelter in an emergency. Nevertheless, apart from popular sites such as the Shelter Stone, the howff has largely been supplanted as a winter mountain base by purpose-built huts and bothies.

Between 1950 and 1970 several rudimentary aluminium shelters were installed at high altitudes in the Cairngorms and on Ben Nevis specifically for emergency use by mountaineers, especially in winter. Their siting was prompted by increasing public concern for mountain safety following tragedies in the Cairngorms in 1928 and 1933 and the blizzard at Corrour in December 1951 in which four perished.

Such good intentions sadly backfired. Their

Plate 35 Sanctuary in the wilderness. Culra bothy in the Ben Alder Forest with the Lancet Edge to its right (*Roger Stonebridge*)

very existence made them legitimate targets for planned stays by parties who often lacked the experience or self-reliance to survive on the tops without them, and thus the circumstances were created for the worst tragedy in Scottish mountaineering history. In a November blizzard in 1971, a school party failed to locate the Curran refuge which was sited at 1,125m (3,700ft) by Lochan Buidhe on the Cairn Lochan–Macdui plateau. Five children and a student teacher died in the ensuing open bivouac.

The Cairngorm disaster prompted removal of both the Curran and St Valery shelters from the plateaux. Those on Ben Nevis remain. In February 1979, I made a trip alone to climb on the Ben with the naive intention of staying at the hut that is marked at the head of Coire Leis. After an all-night hitch from Sheffield and a 8km (5-mile) uphill slog with a three-day pack, you can imagine my dismay to find that the hut had completely vanished under snowfields. Having sensibly arrived early in the day, there was ample time for me to transfer lodgings to the summit shelter, which is clearly marked and upraised by 2m (6½ft). It has provided vital refuge for countless benighted climbers. In the morning, despite perfect visibility, it took a diligent search to find the third Nevis hut over on Carn Dearg, another orange aluminium shell. Without a shovel, its excavation would have taken hours and to locate it in the dark or a blizzard would have been quite impossible, so for the next night I descended to the relative warmth and reliability of a one-man howff, a tight crevice under the Luncheon Stone in the Allt a' Mhulinn glen. Mountaineers are well advised to take this warning, that mountain-top shelters are never to be trusted in winter. One must always go prepared and able to camp, bivouac or snow-hole.

However, at lower levels in the glens, more commodious 'bothies' have proliferated since the war. A few in the Cairngorms such as the Hutchison or Garbh Choire huts are purpose-made, but the majority are adapted and renovated crofts, barns and shielings which were once permanent habitations. Thanks to the dedicated conversion and maintenance work of the Mountain Bothies Association, they are available for use by all mountaineers in nearly every mountain range of the Highlands and offer a facility without parallel in the Alpine countries where the system of expensive staffed huts stifles the atmosphere of adventure in the hills. Indeed, the uninitiated find their existence, free and unlocked, hard to believe. I remember the astonishment of one young novice to find that there was no resident warden to guard Shenavall through its deserted winter months. Happily, the bothies are respected by nearly all users and very rarely are cases of vandalism reported. Here is a voluntary system which largely succeeds and helps to make the Scottish mountain experience so special.

As winter accommodation, however, bothies are a mixed blessing. Continuing the tradition established by the howffs, Hogmanay sees an exodus of enthusiasts to every bothy in the Highlands, armed with wood, coal, food hampers and maybe a dram or two, their numbers such that overcrowding can become a problem. While the hills are first-footed by day, their pleasures are largely secondary to the warmth and friendship of fire-lit bothy nights.

Contrast a wet and damp midweek evening spent a month later in 1987:

Well dampened from a traverse of A' Chralaig, five of us were perched on the bank of the foaming Allt Cam-ban. With its window candlelit by friends who had already arrived from a traverse of Beinn Fhada, the bothy taunted us from the other side. Thoughts of its fire, seats and hot food dispelled any trepidation in crossing the torrent. We chose a narrow race with an intermediate island where two brave leaps would see us across, but where the rope was an essential precaution, since failure would deposit both victim and sack in a swirling plungepool! A good tip when roping up in such a predicament is to safely gauge the length of leap and space the party accordingly. Suffice to say that in this case we did not, with the result that two of our number were unceremoniously fished out of the stream like floundering porpoise.

Camban's original function as a drovers' shieling on the Loch Duich–Glen Affric route was immediately obvious on our entry. The floor of its lower level was a sea of mud, well suited to a lowing cattle herd, two rickety tables and a bench were the only furnishings, with not a stick of wood for a fire, while upstairs in the attic a leaking roof had flooded half the sleeping space.

Having shuffled through the cooking operations, our sodden boots exchanged for plastic bags as night slippers, and eaten standing to attention, there was precious little to do except shiver, and even less inclination to do it. Those lacking spirit wandered up to an early

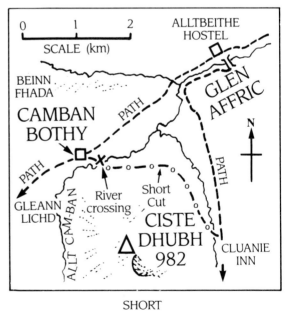

SHORT
CUT

Plate 36 'Mortifying the flesh'. High camp by the River Dee in the Cairngorms after a −15°C night (*Jim Barton*)

bed, while those with the foresight to have carried some in caroused and sang in a determined but eventually futile attempt to stave off the chill. Thanks to an unseasonably mild night temperature, most of us got some sleep despite the damp, but the dawn reveille came as no great hardship.

Admittedly, Camban would not rate highly in an 'Egon Ronay' bothy guide, but in winter, unless one sacrifices time on the hills to the efforts of carrying in extra gear and fuel, collecting and cutting wood and domestic chores, the bothies offer convenience but little comfort to the mountain traveller.

The Charles Inglis Clark Memorial Hut, sited at 670m (2,200ft) beneath the North-East Face of Ben Nevis and owned by the SMC, is the only high mountain-club hut in Scotland. With its unrivalled location and the facilities of fuel, cookers, stove, mattresses and blankets, the CIC has always been most popular in the winter season, and the exploits of its denizens, whether members, guests or gatecrashers, both on the cliffs and in the hut, have attained a legendary fame.

With materials hauled up by pony, the hut was constructed in the space of ten months, and its purpose very promptly justified. At the opening ceremony and dinner on 1 April 1929, the Rev A. E. Robertson (the first Munroist) said the grace and prayed that the hut should be a refuge in true danger. A moment later: 'the inner door of the hut was violently thrust open and two stalwart climbers lurched in, covered with snow and evidently in a state of exhaustion.'[5] They had just been avalanched 200m (250ft) down Observatory Gully!

With just eighteen bed-places, the hut has,

since the early 1970s, been overwhelmed by demand in winter. Overnight occupancy between December and April is of the order of 90–95 per cent, an approximate total of 1,700 bed-nights, all for the purpose of snow- and ice-climbing. This compares to an average occupancy of only 15–20 per cent during the summer months. In winter, it is also besieged by hundreds of would-be daytime visitors seeking shelter for sandwiches and a brew. Consequently, the hut now has to be locked or else guarded like a miniature Fort Knox with access restricted to members or those authorised by password systems.

All this is sad but inevitable given the booming numbers of winter climbers, but the solution mooted by many of building a larger second hut nearby raises the more haunting spectres of pollution, erosion and the total loss of what wilderness remains in the Allt a' Mhulinn glen. Better, surely, the labour of the daily walk up from Fort William than to defile our greatest mountain.

Indeed, the bothies themselves constitute an infringement of wilderness in the Highlands, which not even the hostilities of winter can counter. The balance between the provision of access and the integrity of the wilds is currently delicately poised. As well as its scenic detriment, any further provision of mountain accommodation could kill all incentive for the climber to learn and practise the survival skills and to know of the rich rewards which the winter camp, snow-hole or bivouac can bring.

THE HIGH CAMP

To camp in the hills in winter is rarely an act borne of necessity. On my ascent of all the Munros in the 1984–5 season, I needed to camp just once, whereas twelve nights were endured in bothies. Aesthetically, this was displeasing and dearly I would have loved the ratio to have been reversed were I not strictly bound by the principle of least effort in pursuit of my goal.

Winter camping only became a 'pastime' in the interwar years. G. B. Speirs wrote in the *SMCJ* that December camping was good for 'toughening up' purposes, yet his recollections smack of sybaritic rather than spartan pleasures. Of one pitch in Glen Keltie by Rannoch he recalled:

> . . . seldom if ever can such a dinner have been cooked in the wilds. It began with oxtail soup, then came roasted blackcock with potatoes, peas and bread sauce. The sweet was trifle, and the meal finished with port and cigars.[6]

High camping on the summits in winter required considerably greater toil, sacrifice and risk. Bill Murray and his friends were among the first with the commitment and enthusiasm to take up this particular gauntlet. So, 'in a fit of ascetic resolve' Murray with Donaldson and McCarter decided to 'sever all ties with the triumphs of 1939 civilisation in order to mortify our flesh on the icy summit of Ben Nevis.'[7]

For the 3½-hour effort of hauling 15kg (35lb) loads up to the top and the privations of their accommodation, recompense was granted in the majestic sunset, midnight and dawn views whose sight was denied to every other living mortal in the land, but which Murray bequeathed to future generations of mountain lovers in his magnificent descriptive prose:

> . . . minor hardships . . . are far outweighed by the joys of dwelling for a space on snowfields close to the sky where the dawn and sunset come like armadas in slow and solemn grace . . .[8]

However, one week previously a preparatory camp on the top of Clachlet in the Blackmount had proved less sublime. Mountain tents of the time, being made largely for use on Himalayan expeditions, were snowproof rather than rainproof. Murray and Donaldson discovered this awful truth when the moon disappeared behind a sheet of encroaching cloud and the deluge commenced.

> . . . the remainder of the night was indescribable, but anyone may sample the same experience in his own house. Let him step fully clothed into a cold bath at 2am in midwinter and recline there with a cold shower playing

overhead until 8am. He will then know like Donaldson and me, what it means to be grateful for the dawn.[9]

Even on a dry cold night, the equipment available in the 1930s could not meet the rigorous demands of the Scottish mountain summit. Warmth, ventilation and the weight carried determine the success and enjoyment of the high winter camp. Even today, with the benefit of the enormous advances in equipment design and materials, it is hard to strike a successful bargain between these three conflicting factors. Spare a thought for poor Murray and his doughty colleagues, battling away by trial and error in the days before the light-weight camping revolution and the large-scale commercial manufacture of equipment. Warmth was guaranteed then only at the price of a considerable and often insufferable extra weight and bulk of gear in the sack, while the trade-off between warmth and ventilation in a single skin tent taxed both ingenuity and patience.

The principle of an outer flysheet on a tent to provide a corridor of air-flow at a temperature intermediate between the inner compartment and the outside air had hitherto not been considered. The temperature gradient at the walls of a single skin tent was therefore so sharp as to cause atrocious condensation, a problem that was multiplied by the necessity of cooking inside the sleeping berth. The only solution then available was to increase the inside ventilation, so that, as Murray bemoaned, the choice was between remaining warm and very damp or dry and very cold. In recent years, a number of single skin GORE-TEX tents have been marketed, the fabric breathing internal vapour to the outside. Furthermore, a crucial provision in modern single-skin design is a separate bell-end for cooking which eliminates much of the vapour production and without which the vapour transmission capacity even of GORE-TEX would be exceeded.

Accepting as inevitable the evil of internal dampness, it was necessary in the 1930s to use two down sleeping-bags in order to provide the compensating warmth. The mere addition of feather-down filling is hardly an efficient answer to the insulation problem. While the thermal performance of down is unchallenged when it is dry, its insulation factor drops dramatically with increasing moisture content, two sopping-wet down bags being little more effective than one. The modern solution therefore lies in keeping the moisture at bay. Two alternative sleeping systems have emerged in the last decade:

Down and GORE-TEX: either a GORE-TEX covered down bag or a down bag with separate GORE-TEX bivouac sack, the outer repelling external moisture yet enabling a high proportion of body vapour to escape. These bags are expensive but light-weight and compact; ideal for dry, cold and short stays, but progressively less effective as humidity/wetting increase.

Fibre-pile sleeping-bags: these have a higher insulation retention when they are wet and are quickly dried, so will outperform the down and GORE-TEX bag over a long wet camp. They are cheaper, but also heavier and bulky.

Effective insulation from the ground is especially crucial to bodily comfort in winter. Bill Murray tried absorbent rubber sponge in his high camping experiments, but on discovering its exceptional hydrophilic (water-loving) quality, turned to sandwiched layers of tar and paper with more success. Others preferred to take an inflatable air-bed at the cost of another 1½kg (3lb) in the load. Thank goodness we can rely on open-cell foam-mats today, which are minimal in weight and water-resistant. In addition to the mat, I always stuff any clothing, rucksack and rope under the main body contact points, for a slowly numbing knee, hip or elbow is guaranteed to disturb the sweetest dreams.

But however good the theory, however strong the tent and sophisticated one's gear, successful winter camping remains ultimately dependent upon personal sense and organisation, particularly in siting and pitching relative to the expected winds but also in every miniscule task and refinement once inside. As products of a centrally-heated civilisation, we occasionally need to relearn the fundamentals of taking care of ourselves, and therein lies the fun in winter camping whether one is on the summit or in the glen.

Yet were we condemned to live above the 3,000ft contour throughout the Scottish winter months, we would surely not choose to camp, ever prey to the approaching storm and never released from the sound of nature's fury.

SNOW-HOLING: CONVERSION AND DECEPTION

The Lairig Ghru, 1984
In early February, Joy and I planned a trek into

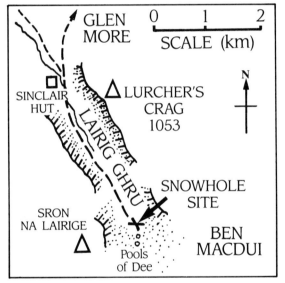

the heart of the Cairngorms with a shovel in the sacks, keen to try the survival game despite and (dare one admit such a perverse motive!) in some degree because of the recent blizzards which had created national news headlines in their unprecedented severity. The top of the Lairig Ghru and the entrance to the Garbh Choire cirque beneath Braeriach were pondered as suitably committed sites . . .

Half-doped by the non-stop drive from Sheffield, we staggered out at Glenmore camp site into the dead of a distinctly draughty night. Not a chink of moonlight leavened the blackness, and though the sky was dimly speckled with a thousand stars, not one of them gave the slightest twinkle of a friendly welcome.

For our shelter until dawn, we had brought the dubious comfort of the faded inner of an old Black's mountain tent. On such a night this mildewed and dog-eared relic did not induce sweet slumber. While the icy breeze tugged and flapped the guylines, we huddled close inside, cocooned in our bags with the hoods drawn up to pin-hole size. At dawn, the wind turned south-westerly and mounted, creeping through every vent and stitch-hole, teasing the stove flame and numbing our fingers as they hovered over the breakfast pans. Out in the soulless light of a cloud-filled sky, we shivered and fumbled through the packing routine.

Knowing that snow was on its way, we parked on the ski road at Clach Bharraig and set forth for the Chalamain gap. Four hours striking hard against the wind and through fresh drifts saw us to the Pools of Dee by 1.30, limbs already weary and spirits sufficiently dwarfed by the pervasive gloom of the day to think forthwith of our shelter. So right at the top of the grim defile of the Lairig Ghru we sought a bank of hard-packed drift and commenced to dig.

The drift we found was not just hard, but set like concrete. Never had I seen such a tough wind pack, but there again, rarely had these mountains been pummelled by such gales as those of ten days before (the 240kmph wind storm of 21 Jan 1984). The spade was useless. We had to chip our cave with our ice-axe adzes, taking turns through three long hours, and even sweating with the task until we had a hole suffice to flee the rising storm.

We blocked the door just as the darkness and first snowflakes fell. In spite of all the time and effort spent – the waste of half a mountain day, in fact – we had no cause to mourn the loss. For the next forty hours we were pinned in the hole by an incessant regime of snow and gale, supremely snug and smug in its calm security, yet able to deeply feel the elemental power of a winter storm in the high Cairngorms . . .

For in our self-imposed isolation, all worldly links were abandoned. Not for us the fleeting touch of the forces of nature that is sensed on a daytime walk in the hills. Stuck here for those

Plate 37 The wild world without. Preparing for the off outside snowholes in Coire Domhain, Cairn Gorm

Plate 38 The peaceful world within. Snowhole living on the Cairngorm plateau – 'safe from the approaching storm, and released from the sound of Nature's fury' (*Allen Fyffe*)

two long nights we came as near to being absorbed into the wild domain as modern man may dare. Each sortie outside could be pleasurably prolonged knowing that a safe nest was close at hand. Freed from the gripping fear that haunts the climber who is exposed in bivouac or camp, we lingered in the blizzard to feel its bite and sting before diving back indoors.

Only once did the cloud clear enough to allow a longer sortie, a brisk dash up the March Burn to the plateau lip and back before our boot prints were smothered. Otherwise we luxuriated – brewing, eating, reading and putting life into perspective in long unhurried dialogue. Our only chore was to clear the entrance of a growing bank of fresh drift, and our only real danger a lack of oxygen as the snow piled up.

On the third day, this brief seclusion had to end. Fuel and food were finished, yet the storm still echoed through the Ghru. With strange reluctance we left our nook and battled down the pass, heads bowed against blinding curtains of spindrift, once more plunged into the survival fight. We missed the Chalamain gap and spent an anxious hour wandering the open slopes beneath Lurcher's Crag before a dreich Glenmore emerged beneath the cloud. Its forests were mantled in a growing load of dense wet snow, through which we ploughed despairingly to reach the road.

The car was alone, its engine half-buried and choked with drifts. Yet with no help beyond our prayers, it fired on the fifth crank, and after half an hour spent digging an exit we were mobile, slithering gently down to the snow gates and onto the homeward trail.

Maoile Lunndaidh, 1986

Maoile Lunndaidh is a great bald skull of a mountain lost in the outback beyond Loch Monar. In the style of the Cairngorms, its plateau top is indented by a series of corries, of which the Fuar Tholl Mor – the big cold hole – on the north side is deep, impressive, 11km from a road head and rarely visited.

What finer an incitement to a midwinter exploration, and in the prolonged freeze of February 1986 the corrie's height and aspect suggested a good snow-hole potential.

We were four: myself supposedly the oracle on all winter matters to three student greenhorns who responded with an undoubting belief in the feasibility of our snow-hole scheme. This was a touch disarming to my own self-assurance for, after all, I was only keen to make a visit to this unknown corrie because of the very uncertainty it entailed!

The expedition did not start auspiciously.

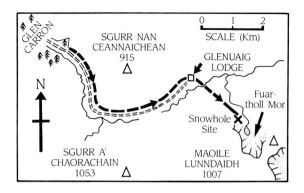

The 11km approach from Glencarron via Glenuaig Lodge was enough to reduce Dave to a state of gastric disorder. It became imperative to find our site quickly lest he weakened further. A clefted burn twists up from Glenuaig into the Fuar Tholl Mor, whose crags and recesses are wholly hidden from below. As soon as we reached the corrie lip we downed sacks and sought the first big drift in the ravine of the issuing stream. Excavations commenced at 3pm on a glorious afternoon, a sky of palest blue filling the vault above the plateau rim.

Our drift material was soft slab and yielded to the shovel like a lemon mousse. While Dave rested, we fashioned two entrances 2m apart, and tunnelled inwards. At 4.15, with the azure sky darkening at its edges, our shovels hit frozen 'spring' snow at a depth of $2\frac{1}{2}$m. This was sure warning of approaching ground. Tell-tale clumps of grass in the debris confirmed the fact, and so we were forced to dig horizontally. With only a 2m penetration, the hole would not be commodious, more of an extended coffin! Dave was now driven by the boredom and the chill to join the fray . . .

6 o'clock and the stars were winking in the heavens. A 4m 'coffin' had taken shape, its outer wall and roof a trifle thin, but still a home of sorts. Steaming with sweat and glowing with pride, the lads stood back to admire their handiwork. Meanwhile, I demonstrated the stability of our structure with a casual pat of the shovel . . .

At the first tap the roof shuddered, then buckled and silently disappeared from view. The three watching faces likewise caved in with dismay, their faith and my credibility as broken as our canopy. We were left with a giant scoop and a 1m wall of suspect strength. My mind scoured the textbook pages for an answer to the fix and Langmuir's 'semi-igloo' came to the rescue.

'We can build overlapping bricks to bridge the roof,' I announced.

We fell to, carving great pave-stones from the surface slab and piling them precariously over the void. Dave couldn't have worked harder had he walked another 11km and found a decent site! But alas, this fresh soft slab; the briquettes crumbled on each attempted overlap. The efforts first grew frenzied and then subsided as despondent weariness overcame the party.

8pm and the moon has cast a mocking glance across the corrie floor. We had a scoop, a 2m wall and a 1m hole. Huddling within, we emptied the sacks, wrestled into bivouac bags and thought of a brew, but we had counted without the breeze. From naught it rose, and to our misery it attended, spraying fine snow and smothering both stoves and matches. Dave sat hunched, hands clasped to his stomach and groaning intermittently.

'What on earth can they be thinking?' I mused. 'After all, they are paying for all this!'

A lukewarm mug was passed around as the snow piled in. There would be no hot meal and ten hours of darkness to endure . . . The 'big cold hole' indeed!

The summer shooting lodge at Glenuaig lay 3km away. The slim chance of its being unlocked was unanimously judged preferable to our probable internment up here, and the gamble paid. We staggered down under a beaming moon to find its outhouse open and, by this stage, to lie the night on a bed of deer dung was to wallow in luxury.

Next day, on the wings of sleep and food and with an extra stomach in the team, we climbed Maoile Lunndaidh and en route passed what remained of our sorry hovel, with its story-telling sets of tracks both up and down. They would have raised a smile had any others chanced this way . . .

But you known it's funny; a man who is entranced by the mountain experience can see no ill in any event. Dave caught my arm on the way down:

'Thanks for the trip, mate,' he said. 'It's good to know how things can go wrong. You learn better that way.'

Thus, while a well-sited snow-hole gains my decided preference over camping on the tops in winter, one must guard against an unquestioning reliance. Glenmore Lodge, since its inception in 1948, has used snow-holes on the Cairngorm plateau for survival training courses, using several sites selected for the consistency of their drift, even in the leanest of seasons. Students may easily be deceived by the experience that snow-holes can be made at whim in any dip or hollow in the Highlands. Might our Maoile Lunndaidh mishap firmly correct any such impression. In the West Highlands, the steepness of terrain and temperature flux are such that snow-holes are only rarely available, while even on the Grampian plateau lands, the cover is not always sufficient.

Prior knowledge obviously helps. Indeed, if I divulged the grid references of the Glenmore Lodge sites, their clustered caves might suffer an invasion of squatters that would make the tales of confrontation at the CIC hut seem tame play. In the absence of prior inspection, it is only wise to seek a site early in the day before one is committed to the long night.

The 'fully furnished' snow cave makes an excellent base for climbing or exploring, but a one-night stay hardly warrants the time and labour of excavation. By contrast, an emergency one-man 'coffin' takes less than half an hour to dig with an ice-axe alone and, despite its unfortunate appellation, is designed for self-preservation rather than consecration. The coffin is formed simply by carving a series of rectangular blocks across the surface of a drifted slope, removing the blocks and then scooping out a cavity behind. The blocks are then slid back into place over the cavity, save for the last, which is not replaced until the climber has crawled inside. However, the coffin is only wholly successful on wind-slabbed drifts where 'gravestone' blocks can be carved

Fig 57 SNOW-HOLING MEMORANDUM			
SITING		**EXCAVATION**	
SNOW TYPE	Medium density wind-pack is ideal; refrozen névé/spring snow tougher to dig; soft slab too fragile; thawing snow forewarns of internal wet or cave-in	TUNNEL	If party is large make two for speed; join in middle and block one off
DEPTH OF DRIFT	Ensure sufficient, if possible by probing	ENTRANCE	Extended walled entrance to stop drifting over
WIND DIRECTION	Windward site prevents drifting over, but most deep drifts are in the lee of prevailing wind	DIRECTION	Dig upwards if possible; debris removal easier, cold air sinks to entrance, drifting-in less likely
LOCATION	Nearby landmarks to aid location in bad visibility	**SECURITY**	
		BLOCK DOOR	Use snowbricks/rucksacks
AVALANCHE RISK	Wind-pack is often 'wind-slabbed'; risk if site is steep; check profile	TOOLS	Keep inside for digging back out
TOOLS		ROOF-MARKER	Essential; keeps out unwanted visitors if roof is thin; relocation in mist
SHOVEL	Essential; lightweight aluminium spade, detachable handle	VENTILATION	Air-shaft must be regularly opened, especially after cooking; oxygen lack
SNOW SAW	A luxury; excellent for carving blocks, more use in igloo construction	DRIFTING	Entrance cleared regularly and air-flow maintained
		COMFORT	
AVALANCHE PROBE	Another luxury, unlikely to be carried; tests for snow depth or locates hole if drifted over	ROOF	Smooth and curved to prevent drips
		FLOOR	Flat to prevent sliding; plastic groundsheets are taboo.
ACCESSORIES	Ice-axe: 'dead-man' plates as auxiliary scoops	SLEEPING	Raise 'bunks' because warm air rises

with ease. In a harder homogenous snow-pack, the simple burrow might be the more rewarding design.

NIGHTSHIFTS ON THE CLIFFS

The winter night stalks the climber with especial menace. No one venturing into the hills in winter should discount the risk of an eventual bivouac. The torch may fail and the weather turn, or an ankle twist without shelter close at hand. But on the cliffs there is no recourse, no defence or haven from the storm and scant chance to retreat or escape. If the climber is caught by the dark, he or she is at once stranded and the bivouac looms imminent. Only will and resolve will see the long night through.

With so stark the prospect of benightment and so little daylight by which to succeed, one might be sensibly expected to go prepared with stove, sleeping-bag et al, but the motto 'If you take them, you'll need to use them' holds good, so the climber takes to the mountains with more slender resources but greater speed. The big Scottish cliffs are just of that height between 200 and 400m (650 and 1,300ft) where even the hardest routes can feasibly, but with no certainty, be completed in a day. In the consequence of delay or failure has lain their adventurous appeal from Tower Ridge in 1907 to the modern Citadel.

The early 'ultramontanes' of the SMC achieved a remarkable record in avoiding the bivouac, despite tackling the long buttress routes of Nevis which today are notorious night-traps. However, most early climbing was done at Easter and past the equinox when daylight has flowered to twelve hours. Few major climbs were undertaken in the shadowed depths of the winter solstice, but on 28–29 December 1907, the first (and by no means the last) nocturnal epic was enacted on the Tower Ridge.

Charles Inglis Clark (in whose memory the Nevis hut was bequeathed), Goodeve and MacIntyre arrived at the foot of the great ridge as late as midday, in CIC's opinion: 'extremely fit after a good season's dances and other energetic amusements'.[10]

At 4pm, the three were assembled below a heavily iced Great Tower. How many climbers since have felt the deepening pit of despair in their stomachs as dusk has left them marooned at this notorious impasse? Yet few have shown the courage and tenacity of Inglis Clark and friends in forcing a passage. Unaware of the easier Eastern Traverse, they made a long and harrowing right-

ward movement to completely outflank the Tower and land in the gully section of Glover's Chimney. Not realising that the gully mouth was barred by a vertical ice-fall, their attempted descent was blocked just 30m (100ft) above easy slopes. All of Clark's prized fitness was now required as the party climbed back up, heading directly towards the plateau to the right of the gully, secured by naught but ice-axe hitches, 300m (1,000ft) of mixed ascent that today is considered grade III in standard.

At about 2am, they hauled themselves over the cornice into a calm but cloudy night, freed from the depths, but not out of trouble. Lacking a light by which to set the compass, they wandered south of the Nevis summit onto the craggy slopes of Carn Dearg and only at dawn were met in upper Glen Nevis by a scratch rescue team from the SMC. Thirty hours after departure, they re-entered Fort William's Alexandra Hotel, having completed the most devious ascent of the Tower Ridge on record.

The choice between bivouacing and pressing on in the dark is crucial to survival. Facing a sixteen-hour night without spare equipment and sixty years before the advent of helicopter rescue, Clark's party chose well, and preserved their pride at the same time. To extricate oneself successfully from a winter benightment is perhaps the mountaineer's greatest test of skill and courage. In December 1936, Mackenzie, MacAlpine, Dunn and Murray effected an equally audacious all-night retreat from the crux of Garrick's Shelf (IV) high on the Crowberry Ridge of Buachaille Etive Mor without any of the modern abseiling aids of pitons, nuts and slings. They regained the road at Coupal Bridge twenty-one hours after setting out, and in the following March Mackenzie and Murray went back to complete the first ascent.

But occasionally safe judgement decrees that there is no way out or back, and the night must be endured in icy petrifaction. The bivouac of Hamish MacInnes 3m (10ft) from achieving the first ascent of the Buachaille's Raven's Gully (V) in January 1953 was as hard and as precarious as any before or since. Leading the final hard grooves in total darkness, his rope jammed

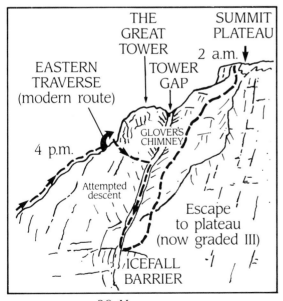

THE GREAT TOWER
SUMMIT PLATEAU
EASTERN TRAVERSE (modern route)
TOWER GAP
2 a.m.
GLOVER'S CHIMNEY
4 p.m.
Attempted descent
Escape to plateau (now graded III)
ICEFALL BARRIER

30 Hours on Ben Nevis

irreversibly. Leaving his companions Vigano and Cullen of the Creagh Dhu to the relative comfort of a bivouac in their motor-cycle suits, MacInnes, feeling that he could not survive the night in such a position, untied and soloed towards the top until a verglassed chimney barred the exit. Jammed across the cleft, he somehow did survive for eight hours clad solely in jeans, shirt and anorak until a rescue party arrived and dropped down a top rope.

Climbing bivouacs have paradoxically become more frequent in recent years. Modern mixed climbs are often so technically intricate as to demand two days. They are too hard to be climbed by night and siege tactics using fixed ropes from the cliff-base are ethically out of order in Scotland. Some bivouacs have been premeditated, with food and gear being hauled up the route, but no amount of equipment can eliminate the discomfort of a night spent in semi-suspension on a 1m (3ft) ledge. To embark on a climb knowing that a fourteen-hour bivouac is to be included requires an almost biblical zeal and faith that the route's quality will match the hardship involved. Alf Robertson and Andy Nisbet's battle on Vertigo Wall (V) on Creag an Dubh Loch in mid-December 1976 was the first and one of the few examples of a planned two-day ascent. Most leading climbers have preferred to try a bold one-day push without spare gear, knowing the score and taking the risk that a bivouac might be enforced.

The consequences have on occasion been dramatic. In a bold first-ascent attempt at New Year 1971, John Cunningham and Bill March were benighted below the crux and final pitch of Citadel (now grade VI) on Shelter Stone cliff. Having gained their high point by a series of traverses above overhanging walls, retreat was impossible. They had naught save the clothes they stood in and an uneaten lunch-pack, and then the weather turned – the wind rising to send spindrift whirling across the cliff. March recounted:

Hell, I thought, what am I doing here? I was barely sitting on a sloping ledge the size of a small tea-tray with my head between my knees 800 feet up Citadel. My teeth were chattering uncontrollably with the cold. The time was 9pm – only eleven hours to go until daylight and we had already been on the ledge three hours.

At about 2am I gazed wearily across at JC. The temperature had risen and wet snow-slides were hitting us at intervals. JC was on his knees. For one split second I thought he was praying and fear gripped me. All was lost . . .[11]

In fact, Cunningham was desperately searching relief from cramp. They weathered out the night and retreated by some hair-raising pendules and abseils in the dank chill of dawn.

Only once on the first ascent of a hard mixed climb has an all-night push been successfully achieved, when in January 1987 Sandy Allan and Andy Nisbet spent nineteen hours climbing The Rat-trap (VI) on Creag an Dubh Loch. However, given moonlight and good conditions, pure ice routes are amenable to a night ascent as their technical content is considerably more straightforward. To 'whoop' and 'shriek' up the gleaming ice of Nevis in the dead of night is for warmth and elemental thrill to be favourably compared with the dour communion of the bivouac. The great ice-climbers of the late Fifties and early Sixties were masters of the art of leaving late and somehow forcing a conclusion to their routes around the midnight hour. Smith, Haston and Wightman's nightshift in Zero in March 1960 was probably the most outrageous of these ascents, starting at 2pm with a borrowed rope and the CIC hut poker for belays on a grade V gully that had been climbed only once before. Inevitably, the climb finished in the 'wee small hours', the protagonists jubilant although slightly chastened.

Whatever the chosen style, to live through the full span of the winter mountain night completes an education in the ways of the wild. Successful survival is not an aim that stands alone, but is the means to know the hills at every hour and in their every mood, as well as to know oneself a little more closely.

10

A SEPARATE SPORT?

Scottish Winter Climbing: Its Evolution and Techniques

THE EARLY SPIRIT

Easter 1903 on the Cuillin of Skye
. . . the writer has a vivid recollection of being
spread-eagled and clinging with every available
portion of his anatomy to the ice-covered 'easy'
ridge of the Inaccessible Pinnacle, while the
level hail drove fiercely past, expecting every
moment to see his legs raised in the air, his hob-
nailers crack together once or twice like the tails
of a pennon, and then, converted along with his
three companions, like the crew of the
Hesperus, into icicles, hurled away into Coruisk
on the wings of the arctic blast. Needless to say,
we did not get up . . .
(Harold Raeburn)[1]

The climbing potential of Scotland's mountains in
winter was not recognised until the last decade of
the Victorian era. This is surprisingly late considering that English climbers had played a
dominant role in the golden era of Alpine
exploration through the middle of the nineteenth
century. Yet while English climbers were so busy
establishing the Alps as the 'playground of
Europe', they cast not so much as a single
northward glance upon the availability of snow-
and ice-mountaineering within Britain's own
shores.

However, the neglect was not a deliberate
affront. In the nineteenth century, the Highlands
were as remote to London-based members of the
English Alpine Club as the Alps themselves,
particularly in winter. It is therefore unlikely that
the existence of vast quantities of snow and ice on
British hills was even realised by climbers living
south of the Border.

Furthermore, this was the era in which mountains were being climbed for the first time in *any*
season. A winter ascent carried no additional
relevance or kudos, while in terms of scale and
immediacy of appeal, our own hills could not
compare with the giants of the Alps. Nor was
there yet a tradition of seeking difficult routes for
their own sake. Rock-climbing was in its infancy,
while mountaineers saw the summit as the all-
important goal and felt no obligation to seek out
steep cliffs unless they formed unavoidable
obstacles en route to the top, a circumstance
unknown in Scotland except on the Cuillin.

The development of snow- and ice-climbing on
home hills was therefore left for a generation who
in the first place perceived an added challenge in
the winter ascent and then sought difficulty for its
own intrinsic merit. Most importantly, it awaited
a committed band of Scottish climbers, a caucus
of local activists within which great deeds might
be stimulated and a tradition implanted.

The formation of the Scottish Mountaineering
Club (SMC) in 1889 established such a nucleus in
which these new ideas were quickly accepted and
fermented. Once the spirit was kindled, it burned
brightly and undiminished for the next twenty
years. With remarkable speed a level of technical
achievement in winter climbing was attained that
was not surpassed until the late 1930s. It was as if
the latent talent of Scots mountaineers suddenly
erupted in an attempt to make up for lost time.
Certain individuals played a key role in the new
movement: William Naismith at the outset, then
Norman Collie and later Harold Raeburn, undoubtedly the outstanding pre-1914 pioneer. A
schism within the SMC membership quickly
became apparent between the 'ultramontanes' and
the 'salvationists' – in other words, the true
climbers who revelled most in the physical diffi-

culties and the scenic mountaineers who gloried primarily in the views.

The two groupings have co-existed amicably up to the present day, although it is perhaps wrong to treat their attitudes as mutually exclusive, for it is the scenic situation that makes the physical difficulties worth their effort for most winter climbers.

The winter faces of Ben Lui, Ben Cruachan and Stob Ghabhar on Blackmount became initial testing grounds for the new mode of expression and interest quickly spread to Glencoe, Lochnagar and the icy crown of Ben Nevis itself. The good news travelled fast. By 1897 the English Alpine Club itself was holding an Easter meet in the Highlands, its interest aided to a degree by the completion of the West Highland railway to Fort William in 1894.

Even among the tiny fraternity of mountaineers, the first Scottish activists were a bold avant-garde. Not only did they go out of their way to seek the deepest chasms and steepest crags, but they also had to do it without guides – a complete departure from normal Alpine practice. In the words of a modern commentator:

> . . . there is no doubt that the pre-war ice
> climbers were regarded by the bulk of their
> contemporaries as the most Desperate and
> Dangerous Radicals – and that they achieved as
> much as they did under the circumstances was
> remarkable.[2]

What, then, were their specific achievements? The web of elegant face climbs on the north-east face of Ben Lui typified the first wave of exploration between 1890 and 1892, snow routes without complication but exposed at angles of up to 55° and descended as well as climbed by many early parties. The Central Couloir remains a classic introduction to winter mountaineering.

Then came forays into short but steeper rocky clefts where ice-draped chock-stones might be encountered. The ice-fall in the Upper North-East Couloir of Stob Ghabhar was investigated as early as 1892 and climbed direct in 1897, while the Black Shoot on Beinn Eunaich (by Cruachan) became an infamous challenge, its winter ascent

repulsing a host of suitors until December 1900. Retreats from this type of climb were often problematic, as Gibson and Robertson discovered in 1891 when they were rebuffed by a chimney cleft on Beinn a' Bhuiridh in the Cruachan range, having already surmounted a 9m (30ft) frozen waterfall: 'One man had to be let down by the rope, and the last man had to jump the thirty feet! This he did, sinking into soft snow up to his waist.'[3]

With this grounding of experience, the great ridges of Ben Nevis were tackled with astonishing élan. Between 1894 and 1896, the Tower and Castle Ridges and the Castle and North-East buttresses received their first winter ascents together with the North-East Ridge of the nearby Aonach Beag. Tower Ridge was repeated no less than five times at Easter 1896, its status quickly demoted to that of a 'trade route'. These were routes of great length, commitment and variability of condition, grade III or ocasionally grade IV by modern reckoning and still retaining their aura of difficulty in the present day. The pioneers had no hesitations in tackling steep snow-covered rock. Thus, J. H. Gibson raced up the sensationally exposed East Ridge of the Inaccessible Pinnacle at Easter 1893, clearing fresh snow off the holds as he climbed. Nor did bad weather dampen the fire, as when Raeburn attempted the pinnacle in a veritable whirlwind ten years later.

Equally, the yawning gully lines on the big cliffs were not ignored for long. Many were straightforward save for the cornice, but in March 1893 Douglas and Gibson skirmished with a climb of altogether different calibre in the north-east corrie of Lochnagar, their presumptious attempt being halted by a near vertical 60m (200ft) head-wall. The Douglas-Gibson Gully, as it became known, waited until 1950 for its first ascent by Tom Patey and 'Goggs' Leslie, and was initially regarded as Scotland's first grade V winter climb (although now demoted to grade IV). Harold Raeburn's two great gully routes were Crowberry Gully on the Buachaille Etive Mor, climbed under true winter garb in April 1909, and Green Gully on the Ben climbed in April 1906. Both are still healthy grade IIIs, even with modern equipment. These epoch-making ascents remained clouded in

Plate 39 Early pioneering – the style. Steep snow
climbing, the party moving together 5m apart on
manila hemp rope and belayed direct to the
leader's ice-axe (*A. E. Robertson/SMC collection*)

Plate 40 Early
pioneering – the gear.
Ice-axe (wood shafted
and over 1m in length),
nailed boots, manila
hemp rope, wide-
brimmed hat and other
sundry accoutrements
(*1909 SMC collection*)

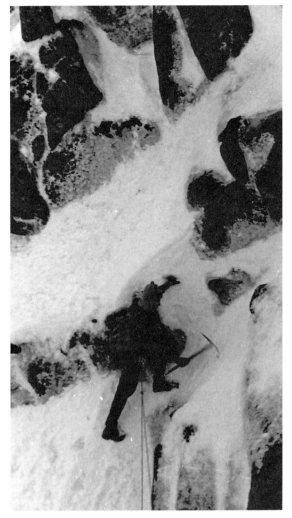

Plates 41 & 42 Stepcutting on a 1950s ascent on Lochnagar: a) with the adze (note the handhold for balance); b) with the pick, in hard watery ice. No wristloops were used for support while cutting (*Bill Brooker*)

obscurity and their records were only 'discovered' around 1970, the routes having been wrongly credited to parties in 1936 and 1937 respectively in SMC guidebooks to Glencoe and Ben Nevis.

The early pioneers were therefore formidably competent in every aspect of the winter climbing art. Furthermore, their achievements were founded wholly on personal skill and fitness, for the available equipment and rope techniques of the era were primitive in the extreme. Parties carried the same full-length ice-axes as were used for winter walking, and manila hemp rope in the length of 6 or 12m (20 or 40ft) per man plus 18m (60ft) for the leader. They wore 'hob-nailers', which were labourers' boots with clumsy wide sole welts, but adapted for climbing use by tacking 'clinker' nails to the sole edges.

Belays were effected solely by driving the axe shaft full-length into the snow and hitching rope around the head, or else by the climber bracing himself on a good rock ledge. Waist and shoulder belays were unknown prior to the 1920s. The anchorage to the mountain of these methods was tenuous in the extreme and neither the wooden ice-axe shaft nor the rope itself could withstand the strain of a long fall. The danger of shock-loading on this system was quickly appreciated. Thus, the rope was to be allowed to slip under a load, so allowing the strain to be distributed over a greater length and time. Any belays that would cause a static strain, such as sharp rock flakes, were strongly discouraged.

The principle that the dynamic capability of the rope safety-chain should be maximised still remains central to winter-climbing practice.

With so little rope, the early climbers either moved together or proceeded by short staccato pitches. The system afforded the second men a degree of security, but left the leader under no illusion as to the consequence if he slipped. Yet during the first twenty-five years of Scottish winter mountaineering, there was not a single serious accident.

The speed of early ascents was further testimony to the skill of the pioneers. Collie led the Tower Ridge in a brisk five hours and Raeburn acquitted himself on Crowberry Gully in 1909 in a mere 4 hours 20 minutes, despite a rope of three and an alarming avalanche incident. These would be respectable times for today's climber aided by crampons, two curved-picked axes and the tracks of previous parties to show the way. On step-cutting first ascents nearly a century ago, they were quite incredible.

Of course, the overall speed stemmed partially from the absence of delay in belaying operations, whereas over half the duration of modern ascents of these routes might be spent in searching and digging out solid anchors. The early practitioners had minimal security, but this was more than compensated by skill and speed. The balance between the three was struck with an amazing success, unbroken save for the Tower Ridge epic of December 1907 (see p165). Their example is too often ignored in the present era. We tend to be preoccupied with security of attachment and thus sacrifice the rhythm and style which are equally important to ultimate safety and success on the classic winter climbs.

The style of ice-climbing which developed prior to 1914 remained little altered in Scotland for the next sixty years. Dependent solely upon the nailed-boot edge and straight-picked axe, the original art was gloriously simple, but demanded excellent balance and superb precision in the wielding of the axe to cut steps. Long ice pitches additionally called for great arm and wrist stamina, but success lay in the conservation of energy through skill rather than in brute strength. Raeburn expressed it thus:

> . . . the cultivation of coconut-like biceps by any of the modern methods of muscle growing may possibly be of some use to climbers. But man, after all, is not a monkey, and the mountaineer, even though the angles approach 80°, travels mainly by his feet.[4]

Indeed, the straight-picked axe was simply not reliable for a pull on the arm when it was driven into steep ice. Thus, footsteps had to be cut in order to support the full bodyweight, with the axe shaft being used merely as a prop or strut for balance across the body. Where the angle steepened beyond the limit of foot balance, hand-holds as well as steps had to be hewn for support. This was necessary on Green Gully's first ascent where pitches of 70–80° were encountered, an angle which seems quite perpendicular when spread-eagled on an ice-sheet. The immense labour of chopping out four holds for every move at this steepness with a metre-long axe can only be realised by a personal trial. Nor did the deepening of steps serve to improve security or ease the strain, for at 70° the knees and elbows tend to interfere with balance.

The good step-cutter always thought ahead and

14 (*right*) Sticil Face (V) on Shelter Stone Crag remains one of the most respected routes of the step-cutting era – a sustained snow/ice route on a highly exposed cliff, first climbed in winter by Grassick and Nicol in December 1957 (*Rab Anderson*)

15 (*overleaf*) The crucible of Scottish winter climbing – the North East Face of Ben Nevis, with the CIC Hut on the bottom left

fashioned two or three holds above before making each move. While the arm swung and flailed the axe, the feet had to remain absolutely still and steady in their holds, the heels held horizontally to maintain the grip of the nail edges and the weight pivoting on the calf muscles which likewise were flexed in support. The sustainment of this position over long shifts was tantamount to static torture in all save the fittest.

By 1914, the hardest Scottish ice-climbs had surpassed anything that had been achieved in the Alps in terms of pure technical difficulty, while the standard of winter buttress climbing was hardly a whit less advanced. The culmination and the final act of this great era was the first winter ascent of the Observatory Ridge (III/IV) on Ben Nevis on a snowy day in April 1920 by Raeburn, Mounsey and Goggs in a startling 5¾ hours. Goggs was sufficiently enraptured by the climbing and situation to write later:

> We inhabited
> 'The palaces of Nature, whose vast walls
> Have pinnacled in clouds their snowy scalps,
> And enthroned Eternity in icy halls
> Of cold sublimity'. . .[5]

Such was the early inspiration of the Scottish winter climbers.

RETRENCHMENT AND RENAISSANCE

7.30pm, 17 March 1935, in Glover's Chimney, Ben Nevis, Graham Macphee leading the crux by diffused moonlight, George Williams belaying:

> I could now but dimly see him as he moved slowly and steadily upwards. Now and then, when in clearing holds of ice, his ice-axe struck the bare rock, I could see sparks fly out. Above the chock-stone the conditions became harder.

16 (*left*) The Cold Hole of Fuar Tholl – dank and dripping in summer, a terrifying 50m smear of vertical ice in a hard winter. Chris Watts leading on the first ascent, 10 January 1987 (*Mick Fowler*)

The entire chimney was sheeted with ice, and there was no place where the leader could take a proper rest much less to where he could bring me up. He had now run out over 30m of line, and the situation was very sensational. It was a thrilling experience watching the leader's figure dimly silhouetted against the sky as he got nearer the Tower Gap. By superb climbing he reached the Gap and announced his arrival there in no uncertain manner.[6]

This ascent, together with that of SC Gully on Stob Coire nan Lochan in 1934, re-established the vogue for winter climbing, which had lain dormant for the previous fifteen years. The lull in activity was largely due to the heavy toll of climbing talent and energy taken by World War I. It is understandable that those remaining of the older generation no longer saw any worth in hazardous pioneering after the war experience. There was also a series of mild winters in the 1920s and an absence of meteoric personalities who could inspire a new movement, Raeburn having died in 1926.

When the revival surfaced, the basic style and techniques of the pre-war period were replanted intact. A distinctive 'Scottish' tradition was thus perpetuated, and such modifications of ropework and equipment as were effected did not threaten its essential quality. The changes were individually important, however, and owed much to the innovative attitude of the group of activists who emerged within the Glasgow section of the Junior Mountaineering Club of Scotland (JMCS), led by Bill Mackenzie and Bill Murray.

First, ice-axe shafts were specially shortened in length from 100 to 84cm (40 to 33in) and slater's picks just 35cm (14in) in length were procured. Both were carried by the leader, the short pick for cutting on pure ice and the longer axe-adze for easier angled névé. In particular, the short pick greatly increased the potential scope of winter ice work. Nicks just sufficient to take the fingertips and a nailed-boot edge were cut on steep ice.

Then, rope lengths were greatly increased to 25m (80ft) per man and 45m (150ft) for the leader in order to handle long-sustained run-outs. After their all-night retreat from Garrick's Shelf on the

Buachaille (see p165), Mackenzie and Murray's parties always carried a couple of rock pitons, karabiners and slings, but only for the occasional belay or in case of retreat. Boots with narrow welts were now especially manufactured for mountaineers.

With these few changes, the existing routes were repeated with aplomb and the group went on to pioneer several new lines in Glencoe. In particular, Garrick's Shelf on the Crowberry Ridge represented a step forward in commitment and vision. They were also climbing regularly at all times during the season rather than only during the more kindly climes of late March and April when most early pioneering was achieved. However, the activities of Murray, Mackenzie and company were viewed with alarm by the rather moribund climbing establishment of the day. Twenty-five years later, Murray remembered that, while attempting new ice routes in the Thirties, he was:

> . . . damned in official letters from the JMCS for bringing Scottish climbing into disrepute – that is, by trying climbs that were not thought justifiable. Indeed, when I first produced my slater's hammer it was denounced as exhibitionism . . . Nowadays no such mistakes are made.[7]

Yet, while these modest advances were being wrought in the face of entrenched conservatism in Scotland, the Alps were experiencing a revolution in techniques, attitudes and achievement. The great ice walls of the Bernese Oberland, Pennine Alps and Mont Blanc range fell during the late 1920s and early 1930s to such illustrious exponents as Wilo Welzenbach and Armand Charlet. Then the awesome mixed north faces of the Jorasses, Matterhorn and, of course, the Eiger were tackled and conquered. For length and sustained technicality, these routes outstripped the Scottish standards. A new spirit of extremism, coupled with competitive rivalry between the national groupings in the Alps, stimulated this wave of development, but it was highly dependent on the wholesale acceptance of new equipment and techniques – rock and ice pitons for belays,

protection and direct aid, short axes and north-wall ice-hammers and, most importantly, the use of crampons.

Ten-point crampons were already in widespread use in the Alps in 1930, even by the visiting British as well as by the continentals. For speed over glacier ice and on long medium-angle snow faces, they were regarded as indispensable. Twelve-point models with two front claws were made by Grivel in 1932 and then by Stubai. They were used with crucial effect on the first ascent of the Eiger North Face by Heckmair and Vorg in 1938. On icefields of between 50 and 60° in angle, the front points allowed them literally to 'run up' the slope, relying on their axe picks for balance, thus pre-dating the so-called 'front point revolution' in Scotland by thirty years.

However, crampons were disdained in Scotland for a variety of reasons. Availability and expense was a restriction for some. It is easily forgotten that many climbers of the 1930s were sorely pressed to afford more than a rope and ice-axe, but more importantly there was an affinity for the step-cutting art, and a belief among both old and young that it was the natural foundation of winter-climbing skill. Raeburn had commented: 'an Alpine climber who starts by using crampons and employs these on every occasion will never learn to be a safe and competent mountaineer'[8] – an assertion which retains a certain relevance today. Step-cutting was regarded as a subtle craft to be applied with loving care, as Bill Murray explained:

> . . . the craft used varied accordingly to the quality of the ice: black, white, green, blue, brittle and watery, they all had their quirks, which had to be learnt until one could tell them apart at a glance and cut accordingly.[9]

Crampons could spoil the purity of that art, interfering with the communion between the climber and his medium.

However, there was also a practical assessment among the Scots that on steep ice above 60°, an angle rarely tackled in the Alps and where steps had to be cut whether the mountaineer was wearing crampons or not, crampons tended to sit awkwardly in the holds while on thinly iced rock they could not nearly match the precision of the nailed boot.

Only J. H. B. Bell of the great pre-war Scots climbers flirted seriously with the new Alpine methods. He often wore crampons and in March 1939 he made a rendezvous with Murray for an attempt on Centre Post Direct (now a good grade IV) on Creag Meagaidh 'armed with a big bagful of sawn-off brass curtain rods', their tops ringed and bottoms filed, with the intention of 'nailing' the steeper ice in the best Teutonic style. Murray, the purist, was amused at the daftness of the idea and must have harboured a genuine fear that Bell's home-made ice pitons would simply buckle under load. In the safety of posterity, we might be disappointed that bad weather prevented their test. Of all the ethical considerations, the notion of using pitons for aid on rock and ice was the most stoutly resisted among both the vanguard and the old guard before 1939.

So, these experiments apart, the Scottish tradition was little altered and thus became isolated from events abroad, its style unique and distinctive – indeed, a separate sport from Alpine climbing, no less skilled, certainly more admirable in its ethics, but undoubtedly a major step behind in the scale of its achievement.

The old practice enabled some phenomenal achievements on the classic climbs. In 1954, Len Lovat and Tom Weir in a single day climbed all three of the great Nevis ridges, up Observatory, down Tower and then up North-East Buttress, with just one axe apiece and vibram rubber soles. Even allowing for good conditions and the long daylight of late season, this feat exhibited the heights of speed and skill to which the simple methods could be brought.

However, these heights were also a ceiling. After 1945, when a new generation turned its eyes to the near-vertical buttresses and gullies that were as yet unclimbed in Scotland, the pre-war style was found wanting both in technique and security. Further compromises of tradition had to be acceded for the next advance to proceed.

Perhaps the most significant legacy of the burst of activity in the late 1930s was the publication of Bill Murray's *Mountaineering in Scotland* in 1947.

Within its pages was encapsulated all the thrill and beauty of winter climbing. The 1930s climbers had little inspiration from the great deeds of pre-1914, which were either wholly unknown at that time or else hidden in obscure journal sources, but now a fine literary tradition was created and was available for the eager consumption of the post-war generation.

1950–70: A FRUITION, THEN IMPASSE

From the new climbs section of the 1954 *SMC Journal*:

> Raven's Gully – found Very Severe and climbed by H. MacInnes (CDMC) and C. Bonington (JMCS London) on 14th February 1953.
>
> Crampons used on pitch 4, which, using two pitons, required 1½ hours. Socks used above this although crampons used on the final slopes. The chock-stone in pitch 5 was lassoed, allowing pendulum action, and saving hours of struggle as the pitch was very much iced. Two pitons used on pitch 6. The ascent took 6½ hours. 10 hours or more might easily be needed.[10]

These few clipped phrases capture all the skill, cunning and epic atmosphere of the new wave of post-war pioneering; the wearing of crampons, the acceptance of rock pitons, and in the use of socks, lassoes and pendules, the preparedness to break loose from the mould of conventional winter tactics.

Of course, the climb was Raven's Gully which, with its series of chock-stone pitches, is a notoriously unaccommodating route, and its perpetrator was Hamish MacInnes, above all others the one personality who was ever willing to stretch the bounds of convention and plough his own innovative furrow. His ethics and methods were controversial at times, but he had a significant influence in accelerating the changes in techniques that were needed to tackle the great outstanding lines on even terms.

'Raven's' was the first major grade V gully to be climbed in the west and was undoubtedly the harbinger of a stride forward in standards, but it was accompanied by a series of equally significant buttress climbs, which evinced a preparedness not just to extend the technical repertoire of winter climbing but to venture boldly onto new terrain in search of the metaphorical Grail. As Tom Patey wrote in 1960:

> All conditions were [now] regarded as climbing conditions. It merely became a question of adapting the techniques to meet the prevailing conditions – névé, powder snow, verglassed rocks, frozen vegetation etc.[11]

Scabbard Chimney and Crowberry Ridge Direct in Glencoe, and Scorpion, Mitre Ridge and Eagle Ridge in the Cairngorms were representative of the new attitude. All are still grade IV or V. Under the inspiration of Patey, Cairngorm mixed climbing was launched as a distinct brand of winter climbing that has warranted a separate

Plate 43 1960s frontpoint techniques. Setting out on the Eastern Traverse, Tower Ridge on a modern ascent. The axes are used as props, a style known as *piolet panne*. In hard snow, as here, the picks are used for support. The method gives great stability in soft snow, when the whole shafts can be sunk into the surface; or else enables balanced movement along a narrow ramp of snow

Plate 44 1960s frontpoint techniques. The *piolet ancre* or braking position, with one axe held across the body and the pick jabbed into the snow for support. A good method on névé of 50–60°

niche to the present (see Chapter 13), but over in Glencoe and on Ben Nevis it was the ice gullies which posed the obvious challenges.

Ice-climbing style saw two main developments in the 1950s. Most important was the gradual acceptance of crampons and in particular front-point models. To a degree, this was enforced by the introduction of vibram-soled boots in the 1950s and the declining availability of nailed models. However, the Aberdonian school stuck loyally to nails throughout the decade, finding them more adept for their buttress excursions yet perfectly adequate in the gullies. Others were gradually converted to the real benefits of crampons on pure snow and ice.

On medium-angled ground, crampons enabled swift continuous movement without the labour of step-cutting. Two styles of cramponnage can be identified, although in reality they have always been interchanged according to the demands of the terrain. French technique (see page 94) maximises use of the sole of the crampon, involving awkward ankle flexion but giving better grip and saving strain on the calves. When expertly applied, it is elegant and stylish, but requires a hard reliable snow surface.

The alternative German method is effectively the front-pointing technique that we know today and therefore needed the twelve-point (or 'lobster claw') crampons. The front-pointing technique is stressful on the calves, but more adaptable to the wet or loose snow which is so regularly encountered in Scotland. By kicking steps with the toes and thrusting the ice-axe shaft down into the soft snow as a prop (Plate 43), an admirable stability can be achieved, which is further improved with a second axe. Alternatively, on a harder surface, the axe can be used across the chest in the braking position with the hand over the head, thrusting the pick into the snow for balance (Plate 44).

By 1965, even Patey was converted to crampon technique for middle-grade ground, a winter traverse of the Cuillin Ridge being otherwise inconceivable and of which he wrote: 'without twelve-point crampons we would have needed to cut thousands of steps and might easily have spent the better part of a week on the climb'.[12]

On steeper ice, however, steps remained obli-gatory because of the unreliability of the straight-picked axe for traction. The idea of spiking the pick above the head for a quick pull was un-doubtedly tempting. Hamish Hamilton had tried it and peeled off at the top of one of the pitches in Crowberry Gully in 1936. It is therefore surpris-ing that the dropped or curved-pick principle was not considered as a solution to this obvious inadequacy, especially since axes were modified in other ways.

Plate 45 Modern frontpointing, or *piolet traction*. The author on Ice Gem (IV/V), Beinn Alligin. Curved or drop-picked axes required for overhead traction in steep ice. The feet are kept low, and in stable stance with the soles held horizontally for maximum toe support. Far more strenuous on the arms than *piolet panne* or *ancre* but essential on pure ice (*Steve Chadwick*)

MacInnes made an all-metal hammer-axe which became known as 'the message' as early as 1947. Fabricated from tool steel, it was a weighty but effective ice-breaker, yet the pick was straight. Other leading climbers replaced the long axe and slater's pick combination of the thirties in favour of a short 50cm (20in) axe, which was used for all cutting, plus a heavy hammer for pitonning with a short pointed hook that could be used if the axe was lost.

A more significant departure was the use of ice pitons for climbing steep ground. These were simply long metal blades 15–30cm (6–12in) in length, hammered direct into the ice and used for immediate protection or rope tension while the next steps were cut. They greatly facilitated the climbing of steeper ice, enabling two-handed cutting under tension, but were almost useless in holding a fall. The commitment of the leader on pure ice pitches therefore remained undiminished, as Joe Brown found out when an ice bulge fell away under his weight two pitches up Point Five Gully during an early attempt in January 1956. So too did everything else – ice-piton protection, belays and his belayer, Nat Allen – and en masse they tumbled some 45m (150ft) to a fortuitously soft landing at the bottom, where they were brought to a halt by their third man who was anchored at the foot of the gully. The near demise of 'the human fly' on Nevis ice remains a fond legend among Scots climbers.

Two methods of climbing steep ice during the 1950s and 1960s can be identified. Both were employed on the first ascent of Zero Gully in February 1957 by MacInnes, Patey and Nicol. This was the first of the major gullies to fall. Patey led the first four pitches in nails and thus was forced to take the fullest assistance from ice pitons on the vertical bits:

> The technique is to take tension through an ice piton placed as high as possible above the climber until the next few handholds have been cut. Then, hanging on with one hand, a higher piton is inserted and the lower one removed for further use. This is all very delicate work as any outward pull on the piton will have the maximum result.

Contrast MacInnes out in the lead on pitch five using front-pointers and the 'message'. Patey observed:

> In went the first ice piton, and with a violent heave Hamish got a crampon level where his nose had been. The only indication of his passing was a large bucket hold every six feet .

Then came a pause:

> All that was now visible of Hamish was the soles of his boots outlined against the sky – an apparent contradiction of the laws of gravity until you realised that his weight was supported by the angled points on the front of his crampons.[13]

The crampon method thus enabled holds to be cut at wider spacing and linked by a few quick 'kick-ins' of the front points with less dependence on the pitons.

The security of belaying on these new routes was improved from minimal to marginal by reinforcing the vertical axe with ice pitons and, wherever possible, by the excavation of rock-piton anchors. The direct axe belay was proved inadequate on near-vertical ground by a series of accidents, most tragically the death of three English climbers who fell out of Zero in 1958 when their wooden axe shafts broke under load. This incident stimulated MacInnes to manufacture a much stronger metal shafted axe, the first appearing in 1964.

Stronger and more supple nylon ropes replaced hemp lines after the war and on hard routes there was also a shift away from direct belays to the indirect waist belay where the belayer is tied separately to his anchors. This remains the basic method used today. However, on easier angled snow, direct belaying remained normal throughout the 1960s. Even with the new metal axe it is hard to understand the logic, especially since the use of 45m (150ft) ropes now created enormous fall potentials on the easier routes. At all costs a dynamic method of arrest was required which would minimise the residual load placed upon the axe anchors, and the use of the body belay was a patently obvious way of absorbing the initial fall energy.

However, today we have the benefit both of hindsight and technical research. Prior to 1970, climbers were largely taught by experience and their achievements cannot be properly appreciated without an awareness of the rudimentary protection techniques that were available to them. Indeed, the lack of protection was consciously accepted as part of the game.

Innovative technique was stimulated during the 1950s by regular visits of Scots climbers to the Alps where mechanised climbing methods were fast evolving and by increasing rivalry between the various groups of activists for the 'plum' lines. Thus, the strict practices of tradition were slowly levered open. However, the door was not allowed to swing beyond a certain point and the hinges stuck at the first ascent of the biggest plum of all. After countless attempts, Point Five Gully was eventually sieged into submission by Ian Clough and party over a five-day period in January 1959, fixed ropes, expansion-bolt belays and etriers all being liberally employed. The shabby style of the ascent caused a furore. The grand tradition of winter climbing in Scotland was being threatened in a competitive free-for-all.

However, Scottish climbing was spared a protracted ethical debate. A swifter and far more effective response came on the cliffs themselves in a brilliant series of ascents by Jimmy Marshall and Robin Smith of Edinburgh, Marshall reaping the fruits of a ten-year winter apprenticeship in the JMCS and Smith unleashing a tidal wave of youthful talent and enthusiasm onto the climbing scene.

In 1959, Marshall accounted for Minus Two Gully on Nevis and Smith's Gully on Creag Meagaidh, both a notch steeper than Point Five, while Smith made ascents of the Orion Face via Epsilon Chimney and the Tower Face of the Comb. Then, in superb conditions in February 1960, they combined their abilities for a devastating eight-day campaign on Nevis, during which six new routes were made, including the futuristic face climbs of Orion Face Direct and Gardyloo Buttress, plus a highly significant second ascent of

Point Five in a mere seven hours. Within two years, a new high-water mark was reached in Scottish winter climbing and the sour taste of the Point Five saga washed away.

The Marshall-Smith style struck a fair balance between modern technicality and traditional purism. Their use of crampons and pitons was not such as to devalue the essential skill of ice-axe work. Thus, the link with Murray and Raeburn was preserved, yet at a level of performance two grades higher than anything achieved before the war. Theirs was a 'real' as opposed to a 'technical' advance in achievement. Looking back, Jimmy Marshall recalls:

We were very aware that we were breaking new ground. Smith and I were leading a crusade and from our Scottish experience we felt we could climb anything on ice. Our writings were specifically aimed to incite the young mountaineers of our day to get off their butts, climb the ice-bound walls, and discover this magnificent, wild and rewarding backwater of mountaineering.[14]

So, at the dawning of the 1960s, Scottish winter climbing was indeed a lion rampant. Once again, technical standards in both pure-ice and mixed-buttress climbing had moved ahead of those practised in the Alps, yet the distinctive character and adventure of the sport had been maintained. The introduction of a specific grading system for winter routes in 1961 was a clear confirmation of the independence of the Scottish sport from other types of climbing.

The original I–V scale (Fig 58) was never intended as more than a general guide, for a route's standard could vary widely according to the conditions, and the same system had to cover gully and buttress routes of wholly different character. Yet it captured imaginations and fairly assessed the overall 'grip factor' of a winter climb, and although more recently it has been modified and extended, it has never been discarded.

When the spindrift finally settled from the flurry of activity in the late Fifties, a quiet period of consolidation was inevitable, especially with the tragic death of Smith in 1962. There was no

<table>
<tr><td colspan="2" align="center">Fig 58 THE ORIGINAL WINTER
GRADING SYSTEM
(from the 1969 SMC Climber's Guide to Ben Nevis
by J. R. Marshall)</td></tr>
<tr><td>GRADE I</td><td>Uncomplicated, average angled snow climbs, having no pitches under adequate snow conditions. These routes can on occasions present cornice difficulties, or have dangerous outruns in the event of a fall.</td></tr>
<tr><td>GRADE II</td><td>Gullies containing either individual or minor pitches; or high-angle snow with difficult cornice exits. The easier buttresses which under winter cover provide more continuous difficulty. Probably equates to the technical standard of Very Difficult.</td></tr>
<tr><td>GRADE III</td><td>Serious climbs which should only be attempted by parties experienced in winter ascents. Probably equates to the technical standard of Severe.</td></tr>
<tr><td>GRADE IV</td><td>Routes which are either of sustained difficulty or climbs of the greatest difficulty yet too short to be included under Grade V.</td></tr>
<tr><td>GRADE V</td><td>Routes of sustained difficulty which provide serious expeditions only to be climbed when conditions are favourable.</td></tr>
<tr><td>NB:</td><td>A route must be truly under snow and ice to be considered as a winter ascent.</td></tr>
</table>

and experiments with ice-daggers. However, these were not sufficient to enable a sustained advance onto the remaining unclimbed winter ground. The 'high-water mark' was also an impasse. The technical limits of the step-cutting art had been reached.

The Curtain on Ben Nevis, climbed in 1965 by Jock Knight and Dave Bathgate, although short was one notable new climb, tackling a continuously steep ice-fall out on a face – but oh, the labour involved. After two hours' cutting up the last near-vertical pitch, Bathgate complained that his left arm was 'as strong as a wet newspaper'.[15] In similar vein, the pace of development was also wilting by the late 1960s. The time was ripe for a new style of attack which could liberate the last defences of the winter cliffs to successful attack. However, when it came, the change signalled a definite and irreversible break with tradition.

NEW TOOLS, NEW ANGLES

1970: From the *Guide to Winter Climbs, Ben Nevis and Glencoe* by Ian Clough:

> The big bay above and to the right of Minus Three Gully and to the left of Observatory Ridge harbours some of the most ferocious ice climbs in Scotland. These routes brought standards of difficulty much in advance of anything previously achieved. After the passage of ten years, experts still regard them with considerable awe and they give a challenge and inspiration for the future. *Suitable only for the most expert of ice-climbers.*

In 1970, an aura of impregnability still hung over the great Nevis ice routes. They inspired a reverent fear among leading climbers and the guidebook's chilling assessment was stern warning that anyone else should stay well clear. Despite their shorter length, they were ranked as seriously as Alpine north walls in commitment and danger.

That within the next five years this aura should be completely shattered was the remarkable result of one relatively minor technical adjustment – the idea of dropping the angle of the ice-axe pick by

shortage of new climbing ability, nor was there any lack of good winter conditions. Indeed, mild seasons have rarely deterred the determined winter pioneers. Rather, the potential for new routes other than those of extreme difficulty on the mainstream cliffs had been in large part exhausted and the best energies were expended in repetitions of routes like Zero or Point Five, and the exploration of new cliffs, in particular Creag Meagaidh. The Marshall-Smith routes remained inviolate.

There were a few developments in equipment, most notably the manufacture of ice screws, which greatly improved security on steep ice, the widespread adoption of Salewa twelve-point crampons

Plate 46 The Orion amphitheatre of Ben Nevis, scene of the great advance of 1957–60. Observatory Ridge is on the right, with Zero Gully on its immediate left, Orion Face in centre and the Minus Gullies on the left-hand side

3–4cm (1–1½in) to give a better grip for a direct arm pull. In the late 1960s, Hamish MacInnes in Glencoe and John Cunningham at Glenmore Lodge training centre were independently scheming on ways to make step-cutting redundant. MacInnes's metal axes were already slightly drop-picked, but the incline was insufficient for reliable traction. Cunningham was experimenting with twin hand-daggers that could be jabbed overhead. In 1970, he and Bill March used the dagger system to make the first ascent of the Chancer, a

vertical icicle on Hell's Lum crag, but a considerable amount of artificial aid from ice screws was still required.

The real catalyst for these formative ideas came with the visit of leading climber and equipment manufacturer Yvon Chouinard from the USA in February 1970. He brought with him prototype axes and hammers with curved picks and shafts 40–50cm (15–19in) in length, which he had developed in the USA, and demonstrated their effectiveness in meetings with both Cunningham and MacInnes. With front-point crampons and two curved pick-axes with loops fitted for wrist support, it was patently clear that vertical ice could be climbed without recourse to steps or artificial aid. Immediately, Cunningham was converted to the curved-pick school, while MacInnes promptly steepened the angle on his pick to 55° to produce the alternative droop-picked 'terror-dactyl' axe, which gave a similar grip but with a jabbing action rather than the smooth swing of the curved pick. Both had their minor practical problems. 'Terrors' tended to bruise the knuckles on insertion, whereas curved picks were often difficult to extract. Within a year, 'terrors' were in commercial manufacture and Chouinard curved tools were being imported to Britain.

The subsequent upheaval in ice-climbing styles and standards has become known as the 'front-point revolution', but this is strictly a misnomer, for it was the change in axe design and the adoption of two axes that was critical. 'Front-pointing' with one straight axe had long been practised on medium angles in both the Alps and Scotland. Nor is it fair to say that the revolution originated in Scotland, given Chouinard's vital role. In reality there was vertical ice waiting to be climbed in both Scotland and North America. Several similar ideas were germinating as to how to do it and the common solution was forged by the meetings of 1970. However, Scotland undoubtedly became one of the major testing and forcing grounds for the new methods for once leading the Alpine countries in technical development.

Yet before they could be exploited to the full, there was an enormous psychological barrier to overcome. This is easily overlooked by the young generation who have been weaned on front-points. To abandon suddenly all recourse to steps and to trust one's survival to the centimetre tips of axes and crampons, required a bold nerve. As Cunningham and March wrote in 1972: 'a strong mental attitude is necessary as the apparently precarious nature of the climbing induces "psych-ing out".'[16]

Whereas a ladder of steps could usually be reversed, it proved extremely difficult to climb down vertical ice on front-points. Also, an even greater localised strain is imposed on the calf, wrist and forearm muscles. With the new method, the climber has to weigh anchor and 'go for the top', which is contrary to the more cautious traditional climbing styles.

An initial period of trial and mental adjustment was therefore understandable. The broader mass

of climbers remained intrigued but sceptical until a stunning series of fast repeats of the existing desperates by the avant-garde proved beyond doubt the potential and safety of the new style – Point Five Gully in 2¾ hours by Cunningham and March in 1971, second ascents of Orion Direct, Minus Two and Gardyloo Buttress by Mike Geddes, and then in 1973 the mind-boggling solos of both Point Five and Zero in a combined time of 3 hours by Ian Nicolson. Nicolson was attributed with the superbly laconic comment on this feat: 'you know when you're doing these big icy climbs solo you sometimes wonder what might happen if you fell off!'[17]

By 1975, there were no waverers or lingering recalcitrants. Everybody was front-pointing with two axes. The simplicity and speed of the style coupled with much improved protection methods devalued Scotland's fearsome grade V's to classic status. Indeed, the grading system was thrown into disarray. Pure ice routes became a full grade easier than their buttress equivalents, which benefited little from the new techniques. Either climbs like Point Five needed to be down-graded or else the system extended above grade V. In 1988, the debate is still continuing.

The Dundonian team of Neil Quinn and Doug Lang were the last to resist the change, less from caution than from the conviction that front-pointing was somehow cheating, but when they took 17½ hours to cut steps up Hadrian's Wall Direct in 1973, they too were persuaded that the defence of traditional ethics was no longer relevant (or productive of labour).

Thus, the floodgates were opened and the numbers of winter climbers active on ice of grade III and above vastly increased, creating the spectre of overcrowding and queuing on routes. At the same time, the new style generated a fresh wave of winter pioneering on steeper and thinner ice. The climbing of Labyrinth Direct on Creag an Dubh Loch and Minus One Gully on Ben Nevis in 1972 and 1974 respectively, signalled the final maturity of an eighty-year era of gully exploration. Both had been inspected by Marshall, but the right team had never arrived in the right con-ditions to enable an earlier step-cutting attack.

Now attention turned to the intervening faces

and the front-point style proved greatly effective on the thin ice smears of the Ben Nevis open slabs, 'terrordactyls' hooking particularly well on ice just an inch or so in thickness. Astronomy on the Orion Face climbed in 1971 with 'terrors' by MacInnes, Fyffe and Spence was the first such excursion and precursor of a series of similarly bold new climbs. Frozen waterfalls and free-standing icicles also fell within the compass of the new skill, while the drop-picked axe greatly broadened the range of mixed climbing gymnastics. Instead of the stagnation that threatened in 1969, the front-point revolution heralded a new surge of winter activism that has preserved the exploratory adventure of the sport throughout the subsequent twenty years.

HOW SEPARATE NOW?

Yet there are many who still mourn the passage of the era when Scottish ice-climbing was a style on its own, shrouded in awe and mystery.

The front-point technique was uniformly adopted worldwide, precipitating a decade of 'goulotte' climbing in the vertical couloirs of the Western Alps and giving the means to climb amazingly steep and long waterfall ice in the Canadian Rockies and Norway. In the Seventies, ice-climbing became a truly international sport. National barriers could no longer withstand the tide of popularity and competition. Continental and American climbers became regular winter habitues in Fort William. New ideas were disseminated like wildfire via the mountaineering press. Without the protection of their distinctive technical tradition, Scottish ice-climbs might be viewed as insignificant on an international scale of comparison.

It is also a valid opinion that the new style represents a retrograde step in terms of skill requirement, narrowing the range of techniques needed to climb the classic winter routes of a lower standard. Newcomers tend to vault clean over the step-cutting, cramponning and single axe skills, and begin their career by front-pointing with two axes on the easiest snow gullies. Thus, they never learn the balance and guile which marked out the climber of yore, and in conse-

quence become less resourceful as mountaineers and often ill-equipped to cope with bad conditions or retreat. It is a wise maxim that a competent winter climber should be able to climb Very Difficult rock wearing crampons and grade III ice without them, but one that is ignored by many in Scotland in favour of the fast but repetitive rhythm of front-pointing in good conditions.

So Scottish winter climbing is no longer an isolated citadel of either style or technical expertise as it was in 1960. However, it retains an enigmatic appeal to the growing numbers of British climbers who seek the winter experience, while in the most recent antics on mixed buttresses and icicles, it is still a radical force for worldwide climbing advance.

And what can never be reduced to the commonplace by technical development are the mountains themselves. The Scottish arena is unique. Its variety of climbing styles, weather, conditions and scenic grandeur has no direct compare and will always guarantee a special distinction to our winter sport. The 'icy halls of cold sublimity' remain as wildly inspiring as they did in 1920. Long may they fire the climber's dreams and deeds.

11

GULLY CLIMBING

Classic Snow and Ice – Psychology and Practice

For those people who are not satisfied until they have clawed and dragged themselves through the innermost clefts of the mountains they love, gully climbing is the ultimate indulgence. It is as near as they will ever get to dissecting the mountains' secrets and mysteries. And if this intensity of ardour extends to a wilful submission to the miseries of drip and deluge or spindrift and avalanche, then gullies are definitely the places to be.

The distinction of Scottish winter mountaineering is in large part owed to its tradition of gully climbing, and it is the gullies much more than face routes which have bred the climbing styles on pure snow and ice. Compared to the Alps, Scotland possesses relatively few unbroken expanses of snow and ice on the faces. Ben Nevis, of course, has the superb Orion Face and indeed its own *Little* Brenva, but these are exceptions to the general pattern that our winter ridge and face routes are predominantly rock-based and therefore mixed in their climbing character. Certainly, it is the gully which conjures the most vivid image of the Scottish winter scene and which exemplifies its uniqueness and perversity.

Although a streak of madness is hard to deny, the Scottish predilection is not simply a matter of determined eccentricity. The mountain geology and glacial past has created joint-line clefts at regular intervals across every cliff and corrie in the Highlands. Furthermore, as the main weaknesses on the cliffs, gullies formed the most feasible routes up faces otherwise impregnable in the early days of mountaineering, especially in winter when they are steeply banked with snow and safe from rockfall. And so, as we have seen in Chapter 10, the pioneers were inevitably drawn towards the Highlands.

Initial exploration quickly kindled a passion for the savage wildness of gully scenery and the appeal of their soaring cleaving lines has remained as powerful ever since. All the gullies' many miseries, which would otherwise repel, have been magically transmuted in the climber's mind into passing penances to be willingly paid en route to eternal redemption at the cornice crest.

ROMPING UP THE EASIER LINES

The easier grade I and II gullies have been little affected by the modern technological revolutions. The traditional style of moving together on a short rope remains the efficient approach, save for the odd ice pitch and the steeper corniced exits where belays may be demanded. Even in the latter instance, quick belay methods such as the vertical axe or boot-axe may suffice (Plate 49a & Fig 60) provided the leader feels competent and the snow is hard. These give a measure of security to second men with minimal delay, but are not adequate to hold a falling leader. So, unfettered by any equipment above rope, axes, a few slings and perhaps a couple of ice screws, parties can today enjoy the same fast-moving freedom on the easy routes as three generations have before them.

But one often hears the grade I's and II's denounced as 'snow-plods' or 'step-ladders'. It must be conceded that many of the straight, broad and open-mouthed couloirs – for instance, Number Two, Three and Four Gullies on Ben Nevis – are perhaps lacking in distinction, intrigue or even the least evocative name. And in recent years the lengthening queues on the popular cliffs have hacked the easy lines to pieces at the peak of the season, leaving them largely devoid of guile or charm. A line of bucket-holds stretching skywards gives a leadening air of inevitability to the outcome of a climb. Even worse is a passing string of parties who are using your route as their quick descent.

This admitted, there are, thankfully, countless quiet refuges spread all over the Highlands for the discerning explorer and therein a plentitude of long and twisting gully clefts whose quality mocks at those who would scorn the 'snow plod'. And with either an early start or an off-peak midweek visit, even as popular a route as Great Gully (I/II) on the Buachaille Etive Mor, may be grabbed in virgin state . . .

Plate 47 The lure of the gully line. Climbing into the jaws of Deep South Gully (I), Beinn Alligin

A gully nigh on 600m in vertical height plays the delightful trick of eliminating the toil of the day. Hardly is there a chance to grumble at the monotony of the walk-in than one is absorbed in the little ice pitches of the lower cleft. The gully line curves upwards and disappears enticingly out of view. Raven's evil slit and an ice-sheathed Slime Wall on its left tower above in foreshortened dominance of the scene and beckon a closer look. In the gully bed, the textures and angles of snow and ice alter continuously as height is gained, demanding constant care and retuning of technique. So rapt is the attention that, before you know it, the ice barrier is behind, the final bend is turned and the summit snows are yours. With the mind thus preoccupied, the body had somehow levitated without a murmur of complaint. Perched by the Buachaille's top-most cairn, there is now time in hand to contemplate a lunchtime pint at the Kingshouse or else to consider an onward traverse of the mountain's trident of tops, for the climb itself is unlikely to have taken more than three hours . . .

Glencoe has several other snaking gullies of this calibre, such as the 500m (1,600ft) North-West Gully (II) on Stob Coire nam Beith, but it is in the more remote areas that the most impressive easy lines are encountered, the massive jointing of Torridonian sandstone especially lending itself to the gouging of chasms which split the cliffs from top to toe. Try Deep South (I) and Deep North Gully (II) on Beinn Alligin as magnificent ways to reach the Horns. This pair are so sharply incised that their entrances are akin to mine-shafts and therefore hard to locate. Once inside, you climb an easy strip of snow no more than 10m (30ft) wide imprisoned by rearing side-walls which spew great torrents of ice from beneath their roofs.

Number 6 Gully (II) in Coire na Caime on Liathach, Hayfork Gully (I), The Alley (II) and Lord's Gully (II) on An Teallach likewise permit the penetration of the very innards of their respective mountains and offer a close-up appreciation of their most awesome and grotesque angles which is denied to the mountaineer who sticks solely to the crests. If they are combined with the

main ridge traverses, these routes give the complete mountaineering experience at a modest technical grade. But I'll divulge no further secrets. These grand gullies are best discovered by one's own peregrinations, and out west or up in the north many remain unrecorded, and you still may get a first ascent (or at least a second if we allow for Tom Patey's wanderings) of many fine revealing lines.

PSYCHOLOGY AND INGENUITY ON THE HARDER ROUTES

In climbing the harder gullies, the leader's psychological state and preparation remains the most vital skill. So subjective and academic a concept as 'psychology' will not find favour with the reader who wants the skills of winter climbing quantified in rules and exactitudes. Nevertheless, I shall try to explain, but first to define.

Psychology on a snow and ice route is:

Shouting 'I'm safe' from a one-step half-screw belay stance.

Evincing not a flicker of emotion as your last ice screw sings at the first hammer blow, flexes at the second and springs out of grasp at the third to tinkle merrily down the ice pitch to which you cling.

Running out 60m pitches on a 45m rope. (This requires a kindred spirit in your second.)

Taking a refreshing drink from the water-spout that gushes in your face when your axe strikes the spring-line on the ice-fall's final bulge.

Playing 'Meccano' with a broken Everest crampon 10m out from your last runner.

Laughing when the head bolt on your Chacal axe shears on the crux and leaves your pick drooping and wobbling like a drunken woodpecker.

These situations have all happened either to myself or my partners, some on several occasions.

Psychology is thus far more than the computer-like mental circuitry that controls the rock-

climber's gymnastic sequence. It is the knack of deliberate self-deception in the face of the undeniable disaster and of keeping the upper lip stiff in the face of every adversity that the winter mountains can contrive. The successful winter climber somehow steers a muddled course through these mishaps and emerges unscathed.

Robin Smith was a master of this art. He dropped or lost his ice-axe no less than three times while achieving that great week of pioneering on Ben Nevis in 1960 with Jimmy Marshall. A fourth occasion came perilously close while he was leading the crux pitch on Gardyloo Buttress: 'Then I dropped the axe. It stuck in the ice on top of an overhang 5ft below and I crept down to pick it up in a sweating terror of kicking a bit of snow on it.'

Minutes later, having just dropped an ice piton, Smith was again playing 'drum majors' with the axe: 'it started somersaulting in the air with both my arms windmilling trying to grab it and my feet scarting about in crumbly holds. Somehow all was well . . .'[1]

Disaster was thus narrowly averted for Smith was using Marshall's axe, his own resting somewhere in the vicinity of Number Four Gully where it had been left the previous day. The loss would have left just two short-hooked peg hammers between them – barely sufficient to complete a grade V first ascent.

In winter, leading is almost a separate sport from seconding. It is not exceptional for a newcomer to snow- and ice-climbing with a good degree of fitness and a sound head to master the technical skills of front-pointing and second grade V on his first week out; but to lead a grade III or IV at such an early stage requires a highly developed mental calibre that is given to few without much longer experience.

In practical terms, two facets of psychological character stand out and keeping a cool control in the lead comes foremost. On very few snow and ice routes can the leader contemplate a fall with the same equanimity as a rock-climber, even today. Protection points are too widely spaced, and when they do arrive their strength and reliability are often dubious. Even the placement of runners on steep ground is often so precarious

Plate 48 A typical Torridonian cleft. Deep North Gully (II), Beinn Alligin

and strenuous that those protection possibilities that do exist are sacrificed with a consequent build-up of the 'grip factor' as the run-out extends. An ascent of Minus One Gully (V) on the Ben with the imperturbable Dick Renshaw in 1980 impressed upon me the value of composure when one is up in front on steep ice.

Even allowing for rough weather, our climb was embarrassingly protracted for a route which has seen roped ascents in a mere 3½ hours. On our first day I led the crux, traversing out from the overhung cleft onto a glassy screen of 75–80° ice, at which I made a frenzied attack leaving my last runner far behind. 10m higher my arms wilted, calves cramped and the spindrift commenced. Suddenly I was clinging on for dear life, chipping frantically for a resting hold, then braying a screw half home before pressing on in search of some relief from the strain. And, horrifyingly, on near-vertical ground, 'pressing on' is the only possible choice if you can't stop, for it is far harder to attempt to climb down. Another 15m of shaking torment and I sagged gratefully into a scoop of snow, belayed on a couple of tied-off pegs and brought Dick up.

Now the late hour and thickening snowfall forced a retreat. Dick immediately reinforced my shoddy belay into something approaching a decent abseil anchor and down we went, all the way to Fort Bill. After five hours' sleep, we came all the way back up next day in an understandably dour mood. Dick now led the crux. His progress was not flamboyant, but oh so sure. Resting steps were chopped every 6m and screws hammered to the hilt, and he even detoured to get a rock piton runner at half-height. Not a single quiver of tension was transmitted down the rope. His protection looked so good he could have probably taken a dozen falls with impunity, but of course he didn't do that . . .

We made the top that evening, late but in as safe a manner as a hard grade V on the Ben would ever permit. The contrast of our styles on the same pitch was a model lesson to an impetuous novice as I was by comparison, and I saw how the winter alpinist prolongs his career!

(Dick Renshaw made the first winter ascent of the North Face of the Eiger with Joe Tasker in 1975.)

Along with that cool composure, the second vital quality of snow and ice psychology is an inexhaustible ingenuity, first in finding and constructing anchor points and secondly in engineering a stance and belay to the optimum efficiency for the prevailing situation. Even to the practised winter devotee, the following scenario is enacted with unfailing regularity:

At the top of the pitch you spy a likely belay spot and chop a resting stance. The available snow and ice anchors are investigated and reluctantly dismissed as inadequate, so you then attack the ice sheath covering the gully wall to your side in pursuit of some usable rock. A widening scar of bare pink rock is exhumed only to reveal a plethora of blind cracks, verglassed cracks, flaring cracks, expanding cracks behind loose blocks and sometimes no cracks at all! Having pounded your stock of nuts and pitons to near submission to little avail, the search is finally abandoned. Never mind, you can always move to a new stance; but try to go higher and there is never any spare rope left, and the ground is always too steep to allow you to climb back down. So, in the end you conveniently convince yourself that those snow anchors weren't as bad as you initially judged, and combine them with whatever crumbs of comfort the rock has offered into at best a 'scientific' and at worst a 'psychological' belay . . .

It is a small wonder that nigh on an hour can have passed in the process.

ANCHORS AND BELAYS –
REAL AND IMAGINED

It is hardly surprising that ethical restrictions on the range of allowable protection methods have never been enforced in the Scottish winter. Even with every conceivable form of modern anchor in use, the 'sporting' spirit of winter mountaineering

Plate 49b The standing-axe belay. The vertical axe is reinforced by standing on the head, and taking a waist belay with the rope running through a karabiner clipped into the hole in the axe head. In the event of a fall, the belayer feels a downward rather than an outward pull. Stronger than the boot-axe, equally quick to operate, and ideal on level ground at the top of a climb

Plate 49a The boot-axe belay, where the boot reinforces the vertical axe. It is quick to place and operate, and useful on medium-angled ground in hard snow

is admirably maintained.

There is, however, one exception. The drilled expansion bolt is strictly excluded from the permissible armoury. The two used by Ian Clough and party on the first ascent of Point Five Gully in 1959 received such censure that bolts have been effectively tabooed ever since. Certainly, to have prior knowledge of the existence of in situ belay bolts on a winter route would kill the ingenuity of the game, but any protection that is retrievable and so makes no permanent alteration to the character of a climb is freely used, from ice and snow bollards through to pitons and the most advanced camming devices (Fig 60).

In the broad gully lines, and particularly for lightly equipped parties on the easier routes, pure *snow and ice belays* are the norm. There is a lively debate between the relative merits of ice-axes and purpose-made dead-man plates for snow belaying (Fig 59). In terms of mechanical strength in a

Fig 59 ICE AXE AND DEAD-MAN BELAYS: A COMPARATIVE REVIEW

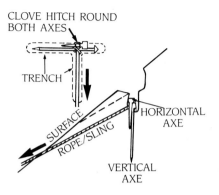

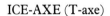

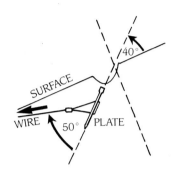

ICE-AXE (T-axe)	DEAD-MAN

Weight and Bulk

Multi-purpose use of climbing tools; no extra weight.	Heavy – 1kg (2.2lb) – for a full-size plate and unwieldy to carry.

Material Strength

Metal shafted axes essential.	Reliable; strength of snow-pack is always more critical.

Placement Time

3–5 minutes to construct a T-axe belay properly.	2–3 minutes on average.

Construction Problems

T-axe requires two axes per person; otherwise a single horizontal axe must suffice – weaker and less stable.	Two dead-men must be carried if used on every successive belay.
Correct loading point on horizontal axe is crucial to prevent pivoting (two-thirds of the way up shaft, ie at centre of surface area).	Angles of placement, plate to snow (40°) and of anchor wire to plate (50° max), are critical to the stability of the dead-man.
The belay is excavated and its placement in the T-trench is visible; greater certainty of stability.	Bedding of the plate is invisible once pulled under the surface; risk of unseen 'scooping' motion.
Vertical section of T-trench must be same depth as horizontal to prevent an upward leverage on the axes under load.	Anchor wire must be pulled straight and tight through snow-pack to avoid upward leverage on the plate.
Axes are sacrificed for the anchor, leaving the climber vulnerable until the belay is completed.	Plate often pulls several feet through snow before bedding firmly; precarious on steep ground.

Adaptability to Different Snow Types

A   Névé/Hard-pack

Highly effective – no different to dead-man.	Hard to knock in if no hammer carried.

B   Wind-slab

Secure provided horizontal axe is not placed at profile junction; the vertical axe helps avoid 'cheese-cutter' effect.	Danger that plate will pull through along the base of the slab; as the profile is not excavated this danger may not be seen.

C   Loose powder/Slush

Axes can pull through an unconsolidated pack.	Dead-man is highly effective relative to any other snow belay.

Plate 50 Hamish Burns perched on the ice bulge of No 6 Gully (II), Liathach

solid snow-pack, there is little to choose between a T-axe anchor (a horizontally embedded axe reinforced by a second vertically driven axe) and the dead-man.

The ultimate determinant is the state of the snow, but it is a decision usually made in the valley on guesswork regarding the conditions on the hill, for the dead-man is a weighty character to carry about if he is not required.

In wet thawing snow, the dead-man can be invaluable. I recall a dreich day in March 1986 when a warm front fog licked the South Post of Creag Meagaidh into a dribbling chute of slush. We had driven and walked for many hours and needed a climb. Thankfully, we had brought two dead-men and they were used on eight of the nine stances, providing the only measure of real security throughout the 350m (1,000ft) route in conditions where axe belays would not have worked.

Snow bollards always feature in practical instruction on belaying, but are rarely used in earnest, taking much time and energy to excavate. However, on abseil descents or retreats when anchors cannot be retrieved, a bollard may occasionally be vital. No time should be spared in making it big (at least 1.2m (4ft) in diameter), deeply grooved and solidly packed.

Ice bollards take even more effort to construct, but are used more frequently as belays, being dependable when sculpted properly in easy-angled ice and sparing one's stock of ice screws for the steep sections. In 1987, I encountered two superb ice bollards no more than 5m (16ft) apart on the steep pitch of No 6 Gully, Liathach (II), each made to measure a snug fit for a 2.5m (8ft) sling. A master craftsman had clearly been at work, but surely had suffered total paralysis of the arms after the half-hour of continuous chipping they must have involved. So, for those who want to preserve limited energies for the actual climbing, ice bollards are definitely among the last resorts.

Icicle threads are more convenient anchors and are regularly available in 'organ pipe' ice territory. However, their value is in large part psychological unless the icicle has a huge girth, in which event it is liable to swallow your entire stock of slings in one bite.

The performance of *ice-screw* anchors came under close scrutiny in 1984, when a horrifying photograph of a scrap-heap of three hundred

Fig 60 WINTER CLIMBING ANCHORS	
Origins in Scotland	**Modern Applications**
VERTICAL ICE-AXE Traditional; pre-1960 the universal snow belay.	Emergency belay in event of a fall when moving together. Quick belay in hard snow for bringing up seconds.
DEAD-MAN Developed in Antarctica in mid-1960s, then manufactured for UK winter use.	Rarely carried on harder ice routes but indispensable on snow climbs in thawing or unconsolidated conditions.
BURIED AXE Single horizontal and T-axe Copied the dead-man principle; used since late 1960s.	Now the standard snow belay; most common usage on exit pitches especially on level ground on top of routes.
SNOW BOLLARD Traditional.	Main use is for retreats and abseils (eg, cornice above descent gullies); too much hard work otherwise.
ICE BOLLARD Traditional.	Sometimes used on easy angled ice (saving on ice screws) and occasionally on retreats/abseils; time and effort to construct.
ICICLE THREAD Traditional.	Regularly used on organ-pipe ice; value more pyschological than tangible unless of substantial girth.
ICE PITONS Home-made by J. H. B. Bell for an attempt on Centre Post Direct (Creag Meagaidh) in 1939; used widely in 1950s.	Wholly superseded by ice screws in late 1960s; pitons tended to shatter ice when driven and have minimal lateral grip.
ICE SCREWS 'Wart-hog' Drive-in Imported from Continent in 1965; used on fourth ascent of Point Five Gully in 1965.	Still available but outmoded by the 'Snarg' which is stronger and less prone to plating/shattering the ice.
'Snarg' Drive-in First made in USA by Lowe in 1982; rapid spread worldwide.	The most popular for protection on steep ice; extruding action prevents shattering; light-weight titanium versions available.
'Tubular' Screw-in First reported by Dougal Haston in 1965; made by Salewa of Germany and imported by Tiso.	Strongest ice anchor; mostly used on main belays; design improved (tapered cores aid extrusion, four bits aid placement). *continued*

Plate 50a The loneliness of the long-distance ice pitch. South Post Direct (IV) on Creag Meagaidh. Protection notable by its absence (*Grahame Nicoll*)

Fig 60 WINTER CLIMBING ANCHORS continued	
Origins in Scotland	Modern Applications
NATURAL ROCK SPIKES/CHOCK-STONES Traditional.	Convenient and reliable but all too rare on pure snow and ice routes.
ROCK PITONS Soft steel pegs first used with ethical misgivings in 1930s but widely accepted after World War II; hard steel pegs developed and produced in USA by Chouinard in early 1960s.	Remain an essential part of the gear rack on grade III and above; selection of 6–10 usually carried, (knifeblades, king-pins, angles, leepers).
WIRED METAL NUTS/CHOCK-STONES Tapered nuts (eg, Moacs) Used in rock-climbing since late 1960s; natural spread to winter use.	Quick to place and extract; therefore used in preference to pitons if available.
Curved taper ('Rocks') Manufactured since 1978.	Have superseded simple tapered nuts, fitting irregular cracks and giving camming action.
Brass micronuts (eg, RPs) Quality and strength developed and manufactured on large scale since 1979; offset HB nuts made since 1985.	Ability to fit tiny cracks (and outward flaring in the case of HBs).
METAL CHOCK-STONES Hexentrics Simple hexagonals made c1970; offset Hexentrics (Chouinard) made since 1974.	Camming action in parallel-sided cracks.
CAMMING DEVICES ie, 'Friends' Developed for use on granite rock cracks in Yosemite, USA; manufactured since 1978; well suited to Alpine/winter climbing.	Will work in all types of flared cracks from 10–100mm (½–4in) width, but not in verglassed cracks; other trigger operated cammers made since 1984 but Friends remain the most popular.
DRILLED EXPANSION BOLTS Spread in Alpine big wall climbing in 1950s but only used in Scottish winter on first ascent of Point Five Gully in 1959 with much subsequent criticism.	Ethical taboo has persisted; adventure remains the keynote in winter climbing.

bent, twisted and snapped screws appeared in a gear-test report in *Mountain* magazine. Suddenly, the long-held confidence in all the popular models that were used on Scottish ice was questioned, particularly the Salewa spiral drive-in screw ('wart-hog'), whose use in Scotland was first reported by Brian Robertson on the fourth ascent of Point Five Gully in 1965. Since then, the wart-hog had been an essential accompaniment to the advances of the front-pointing era. Now came the news that the screw was 'bad on shock loads, its maximum load too low and subject to a high material failure rate (at as low as a 380kp load, instead of the recommended minimum of 1,000kp)'.[2]

However, the report really demonstrated how greatly manufacturing quality and minimum test standards have improved over the years. Old confidences were not being invalidated, for there was no other choice in earlier days, and more pertinently it is asking a lot of Scottish ice to absorb a 1,000kp load without shattering. Ice failure, not gear failure, has more usually been the concern in Scotland.

The report also pointed attentions towards stronger and more effective designs. The tubular drive-in screws ('snargs') have now largely displaced the wart-hog for protection on steep ground. They are stronger, but more importantly their hollow-cored design allows the displaced ice to extrude and minimises the shattering effect on hard or brittle ice which beset the placement of piton-style wart-hogs.

Tubular screw-in models were first manufactured by Salewa of Germany in the early Sixties and are stronger than the wart-hog; their strength increasing with length and tube diameter. Not requiring to be driven, they can be taken on easier routes by parties who do not carry an ice hammer. However, they have two problems: the difficulty of initial insertion and the clogging of the core with ice. Despite design improvements of tapered cores to aid extrusion and four bit heads to assist initial placement, they are slower and more awkward to place than the drive-in, and so are usually reserved for main belay anchors, with snargs being used for runners.

The effectiveness of ice screws depends most crucially on care in their placement and arrangement. Potential shock loads must be minimised, given the shattering tendency of ice. For main belays, screws are therefore best placed in pairs over ½m (1½ft) apart, and their potential loadings are equalised by crossed-sling or clove-hitch adjustment. Equally important is the choice of ice with sufficient plasticity to absorb both the tension of placement and the shock of a load, a 'blue' ice mix of uniform texture and profile being the best, and then of ensuring the optimum angle of placement at 90–100° to the downward surface of the ice.

Rock anchors enjoy a greater degree of certainty and uniformity of strength. However, the rock of gully walls and beds is notoriously unobliging in its provision of good spikes, flakes and cracks. On the faces and ridges, pressure release as the rock is exposed coupled with a steady seasonal cycle of freeze/thaw leverage, opens up the incipient joint

lines to provide more generous protection possibilities. By comparison, the gully recesses remain compacted, water-worn and unyielding.

The volcanic porphyry of Ben Nevis has a particularly mean reputation, although the pink Cairngorm granite with its profusion of blind cracks is only marginally more accommodating. Even Torridonian sandstone, which is so amiably cracked and weathered on the faces, can be black, slimy and massively compact in the clefts. The Scottish gully's only free offering of solid protection is the chance of ice-embedded boulders or wedged chock-stones across the bed, such as those which decorate Raven's Gully on the Buachaille. They shelter safe belay havens with 'bomb-proof' natural protection, but also constitute the crux obstacles on many routes.

Begrudging rock strata require the skilful placement of pitons and nuts. Pegging is a proficiency long neglected since the demise of artificial climbing in Britain, and the near-total conversion to nut protection in modern free rock-climbing. Only in the winter arena does the piton remain an essential part of the gear rack on the harder routes, yet rarely now does the climber get any prior practice in their proper placement and testing.

The advent of hand-placed tapered, hexentric and offset metal nuts in the early 1970s and the introduction of trigger-operated camming devices ('Friends') in 1979 has greatly broadened the range of rock protection. Friends in particular came as a godsend to the winter climber for they work in both downward and outward flaring cracks. However, Friends do not work in ver-glassed glass, so it is wise to take a couple of hexentrics in reserve to save possible embarrassment, but for speed and adaptability they are unchallenged and seen as indispensable by the younger generation who have never had to do without them.

Rock anchors will generally be chosen in preference to ice and snow belays, but only if they can be excavated, while on occasion cracks will be found that are so tightly glued with verglas that neither pegs nor nuts will grip or penetrate.

Once anchors are placed, all that remains – if you have any ingenuity left – is to link them in a

Plate 51 A snug belay
in Lord's Gully (II), An
Teallach. Good rock
chockstone anchor
ideally placed above the
stance by climber
David Litherland

tight equalised web of rope and slings, then position and enlarge the stance and adopt the most suitable belay method. The minimisation of potential shock loading at any point in the safety chain is the overriding requirement on most winter belays and demands the use of a dynamic belaying method together with the fullest use of the body which is positioned as a shield to the anchors so as to absorb a high proportion, if not all, of potential fall energy.

Fig 61 compares the merits of the traditional waist and modern friction-plate belay methods

Fig 61 WINTER BELAYING: A COMPARATIVE ASSESSMENT

BODY BELAY ROUND WAIST	FRICTION PLATE (eg Sticht)
Ease of Construction	
Belay tied direct to front of harness; fast and simple. Belay tied to back of harness: more awkward; an in situ sling and s/g krab on back of belt helps tying in.	Awkward with gloved hand.
Rope Handling	
No problems; rope can be paid out quickly on easy ground, therefore very suitable on easier climbs.	Greater risk of jamming when leader is moving fast on easy ground. Iced/frozen ropes will not feed.
Rope Control	
If belay is tied direct into front of harness the 'live' rope must be paid out on the same side as the belay rope/sling; if not, the belayer can be turned in to the belay under load and the live rope snatched off his back.	Once plate is clipped into harness the ropes cannot be completely lost from the belayer's grip.
Control of double ropes is difficult on intricate pitches where each rope is paid out at different rate.	Double ropes are separated on the plate; enables close independent control of each rope.
A fall places high stress on belayer; skill required.	Relatively simple to hold a fall; little strain felt.
Dynamic Capability	
Dynamic arrest is automatic because some slippage through gloved hands is inevitable; a good belayer can control the rate of slippage to create the optimum braking force.	The plate gives only minimal slippage when applied instinctively in event of a fall; therefore, shock loading on protection points and climbers is higher.
Load Impact on Belay	
Body belay shields the anchors and can absorb a high percentage of fall energy especially if belay is tied into back and if stance and positioning are solid.	With plate and belay both clipped into front of harness as is normal any load on the plate by-passes the body and is transmitted direct to the anchors.
Self-rescue Situation	
It is possible but difficult to tie off and escape from a waist belay under a hanging load.	Plate is easily locked off; escaping from the system is then simple; an assisted hoist can be rigged with the Sticht plate as the pulley point.
Summary of Applications	
Easier routes; grades I–III	Steeper intricate routes, especially mixed climbs where there is more plentiful protection.
On all snow anchors (best with back tie-in).	Never on snow belays except with back tie in to belt.
On doubtful rock/ice belay anchors.	On good rock/ice anchors.
Whenever maximum speed is essential.	
In severe conditions – iced ropes.	

with the conclusion that there is much to commend in tradition. The Sticht and other friction plates are marketed as dynamic belay devices, but in practice many climbers have concluded that they give a largely static arrest with high impact loads on protection and belay points.

Manifestly, success on snow and ice routes depends as much on 'craft and cunning' in ropework and belaying as on brazen technical prowess on front points. But more than acquiring a clinical proficiency, it is really essential to enjoy the protection game like a true sapper, to derive a

real satisfaction from unearthing and rigging a secure belay out of the least compromising terrain. Routes then become memorable almost as much for the variety and quality of their belays as for their actual climbing, and they become a great deal safer in the process.

SOLOING ON SNOW AND ICE

Soloing has emerged as a necessary antidote to the intricate manoeuvring of the roped ascent. The fetters of convention and mechanics are cast aside in exchange for warmth, speed and rhythm, for absolute freedom and a total self-reliance. In a way, soloing represents a healthy return to the style and spirit of the early pioneers.

The speed and relative ease of the front-pointing technique on good ice has accelerated the

Plate 52 The author waist belaying with two equalised rock anchors. The anchors are equalised by tying the rope tightly from each back to the harness with a figure-of-eight knot or two half hitches

vogue in the modern era, although there were some fine solo achievements prior to 1970. In particular, Dougal Haston's twenty-minute romp up Comb Gully (III/IV) on Ben Nevis when it was still a highly revered route stands as a statement of youthful defiance to traditional precepts, while Tom Patey's solo first ascent in 1969 of the girdle traverse of the entire Coire Ardair head-wall on Creag Meagaidh remains an exploit unsurpassed in its grandiose scale to the present. Immortally enshrined in climbing history as the 'crab crawl', the traverse gave 2,450m (8,000ft) of sensationally exposed grade III/IV climbing, yet was accomplished in a startling five hours. But as Patey was always quick to point out, solo climbing in those ill-protected days was no different in kind from leading. If indeed 'the leader must not fall', then why bother putting the rope on at all? While his logic was hard to refute, the practice was altogether harder to follow.

It would be an invidious task to assemble a chronology of major solo ascents on Scottish ice, for many great solos have been done on sudden impulse and never reported. Nearly all have been done 'free', in other words completely unroped. These unseen deeds are perhaps the more worthy because they are lonely acts of self-expression which have been performed less out of pride or for reputation than from an uncontainable passion for climbing and in a quest for new levels in its articulation. Yet selfless passion and selfish ego are not easily unravelled from the fierce emotional web that propels the individualist and can remain enigmatic even to the man himself.

However, when witnessed and publicised, the magnitude of some solo efforts has rocked the climbing world to its foundations. Ian Nicolson's nonchalant solos of Zero and Point Five Gullies in an hour apiece in 1973 shattered all existing conceptions regarding the impregnability of the great grade Vs and brought the front-point revolution into full maturity. The equivalent statement of technical advance and personal prowess in the 1980s came in the two days' work of Dave Cuthbertson and Graeme Livingston in April 1986. Climbing solo in tandem, the Ben's classic Vs were used merely as warm-ups to the harder modern face routes of Galactic Hitch-hiker, Slav Route, Sickle and Astral Highway.

Such feats raise standards of expectations and attainment at a stroke. The first solo ascent of a route throws aside its psychological barrier and immediately invites a wholesale attack from roped parties. Yet, caught in the rush as the floodgates open, it is easily forgotten that nearly every notable free solo in winter has taken tactical advantage of exceptional ice build-up, a hard freeze and fine weather. A day spent labouring at one's limit in more normal conditions, or fighting

and failing on a route in the worst, restores a more healthy respect for the mountain . . .

CAUGHT IN THE FIRING LINE

25 March 1979
For an hour now I hadn't been able to look up, for the spindrift was continuous. In my sack lay a hooded waterproof jacket, so tauntingly close yet maddeningly inaccessible; for I was bound to keep firm hold on my leader's ropes and paid them out inch by inch through wooden hands and stiffening wrists.

Defenceless save for an open-topped cotton anorak, I compressed my neck tight within my helmet, yet still the snow crept in, melting on collars and cuffs, then trickling icily down my spine. Shivers gripped in a rising tempo despite aching efforts to shake an arm or stamp the feet. Crammed into RD boots, whose uppers long since had worn into spongy old-age, my toes sung out a piercing chant of pain . . .

Somehow Charlie is hanging on and climbing the chimney above. The courage of his lead shames my abject prostration on this two-step stance and leaves me feeling still more wretched. Was it just two hours since that we'd ogled at a gleaming run of ice, glowed with excitement and joked with others who since had left us to our fate?

The hawsered ropes now snake more quickly through my benumbed grasp, then draw tight and tug impatiently. He must be up, and so this frigid body of mine will have to climb. First the belays – torquing and twisting at entombed screws, fumbling krabs to harness loop; then a wild propeller whirl of circling arms in a last ditch effort to warm some blood, and I'm away . . .

Forty feet are lifeless, arms blindly flailing at the ice above but the axes bounding back at every flaccid swing, body arched on submerged crampon tips which scrape in vain to find some ice and much too scared to dare to fall. Another forty feet are a stabbing torture as viscous blood forces its way back through the wrists. I feel sick with the pain and close to tears, but then the angle eases off the vertical. My head pokes out of the spindrift chute, and there is Charlie, strapped to the gully wall 9m above.

Breath returns, fingers tingle and toes still throb, yet the rest of me is deathly cold. Outside the deluge, a full-bored blizzard blasts across the North-East face, yet we'd never seen it come. And up above, down from a blur of whirling white plummets, a great cascade of cork-screwed ice – pitch 4 of 9, the crux! . . .

'We've got to get off,' I yelled in a personal plea for mercy. Charlie must have cursed the sacrifice of a heroic lead, but faced the truth that our game was up.

Two long abseils saw us down. Drenched and swaying in the first embrace of mild exposure, I gratefully staggered down to taste the rain that swept the lower glen.

Whatever the insults heaped on the infamous chute of Point Five Gully – eight ascents a day, novice chains on an introductory course, 40-minute solos and bar-room degradations to IV or even III – I'll never see it any other way than through those battered hours when it flexed its might and spat us out!

So, much of the fascination of snow- and ice-climbs is bound up in the variability of their condition. Mere numbers in the guidebook can never denote the true grade of a route as its character transforms from day to day, from month to month and from season to season. A winter climb of quality can be done on several separate occasions and enjoyed as new on each. Yet when a route is out of 'nick', it can be either dangerous or impossible.

The mechanics of production and alteration of snow and ice have been detailed in Chapter 4, but even when the mountaineer is possessed of a rigorous analysis of conditions and has selected the cliff and route to perfection, a sudden change in the weather systems can fox the best-laid plans. The day of our epic on Point Five had dawned clear, with Ben Nevis sparkling under an exceptional icing. Our painful retreat was, in fact, relatively fortunate, for several parties were caught by the blizzard at the top of their routes and met a maelstrom on the plateau.

THE FINAL IMPASSE

Whatever the conditions and weather, a troublesome exit cornice can be the bane of any gully climb from grade I to V. A prior assessment of the cornice state is not always possible when one is approaching from below. To be trapped beneath an overhanging and possibly dangerous cornice, late in the day and after a taxing climb, is not a predicament in which to appreciate its magnificent architecture. However, the cornice and its surrounds possess a strange and lonely beauty which can inspire more aesthetic reflection once it is surmounted. W. Inglis Clark remembered the scene when he was ensconced under the cornice at the top of Moonlight Gully, Ben Nevis, on its first ascent in January 1898 with particular force. Looking out across the precipices he observed that:

the grandest sight was the roof of a great crag, which, projecting like some storm window into the valley was covered with unbroken snow shining like polished silver in the moonlight.[3]

In a wind, the cornice is a place of savage wildness. The climber grapples in a whirlwind of spindrift, face and eyes caked with ice, barely in touch with gravity. As the top is breasted, axes are plunged in the summit snows and a final heave is made onto level ground to meet a scene of peaceful beauty. A tugging rope is the only link with the cauldron of fury which has just been quitted. The feeling, then, is one of the most joyous in mountaineering – a battle won, redemption gained.

The methods employed to climb cornices have been many and varied. If some slight break can be found in the lip, then a vertical trench can be dug up the head-wall, but so precarious is the climbing if the snow is unconsolidated that ladders of ice-axes have been used to give stable holds, their shafts plunged full-length at a slightly downward angle into the wall. Harold Raeburn used this means to get out of Green Gully (III/IV) on Ben Nevis on its first ascent in 1906. Such a ladder might consume a party's entire supply of axes, leaving the seconds with a tricky problem of how to follow the pitch.

Where the cornice is continuously overhanging, tunnelling is the time-honoured method, which is dangerous, strenuous, highly uncomfortable and can be protracted. Raeburn recalled the record:

> . . . of two Alpine pioneers who, on the occasion of the first ascent of Tower Gully on Nevis, actually burrowed through the great cornice at the top, taking two days to the task – the intervening night being spent at Fort William.[4]

Such extreme behaviour apart, tunnelling can take many hours and the ethics of unaided climbing are quickly abandoned if there are alternative means of assistance available, purists like Raeburn included. In 1901, he found himself extended on a cornice at the top of Gardyloo Gully:

> I had worked my hat about level with the edge when we heard the voice of an eloquent member of the SMC. A shout brought his party to the edge. I expressed a desire to shake hands with one of them, so Workman kindly extended his arm, and I was so glad to see him that I did not leave go till landed on the top.[5]

Seventy-five years later, on the adjacent Gardyloo Buttress, Alf Robertson and Andy Nisbet faced a major epic when they were trapped at nightfall under a 3m (10ft) cornice of frozen ice that could not be tunnelled. As they pondered their options, a shout came over the plateau edge offering a top rope. The unseen rescuer belayed them through-out a 90m (290ft) traverse under the roof to a point where they could abseil into the confines of Tower Gully. Once they were safely landed and untied, the rope disappeared into the darkness and their saviour has never been seen nor identified since.

If climbing the cornice has its difficulties, then the experience of J. H. B. Bell should demon-strate that attempts at its descent require even greater caution. After his ascent of the partially snowed Slav Route on Ben Nevis in 1936, he decided to jump the lip at the head of No 3 gully, no doubt expecting soft snow below. Unfortu-nately, the landing was harder than he had anticipated and he came to rest 450m (1,500ft)

lower beside the Coire na Ciste lochan, bruised but unbroken.

After fresh snowfall or wind-drifting, cornices are dangerously fragile and are likely to harbour soft wind-slabs on their scarps, conditions which put gully climbing out of bounds until settling and freeze/thaw has consolidated the mass, or indeed until the roof has collapsed. Cornice fractures have initiated some of the largest avalanches ever seen in Scotland, in power and scale coming close to the high velocity airborne snow blasts which are so feared in the Alpine ranges.

Certainly, the most impressive avalanche that I have witnessed in this country was caused by the collapse of the cornice which guarded the top of Fuar Tholl's South-East Cliff by Achnashellach at Easter 1986. As its huge white cloud mushroomed over the base of the corrie beneath, we were sufficiently moved to run for cover, despite being 200m (650ft) below the corrie's lip. The avalanche wiped the cliff-face completely clear of snow. Needless to say, we changed our climbing plans for that day and gave unspoken thanks that we hadn't set out half an hour earlier. The gully climber's problem is to know when such lethal conditions pertain and then to keep out of the chutes. Only the actual sight of such a fall can fully bring the message home.

But enough of tales of woe; their experience is often cruel but it trains the senses to know an unbounded joy when the gods turn to your side, the corrie lip is mounted, the trials of the walk-in are nearly done and your gully comes to view completely formed, shining in pristine glory and just ripe for the picking. And if there is glowing ecstasy in perfection, there is also a deeper fulfilment when, through persistence and a slice of luck, a surprise success on a climb is extracted from the most mournful thawing day when conditions seem all but lost. In the equal chance of either experience lies the eternal paradox and the enduring strength of Scottish snow- and ice-climbing.

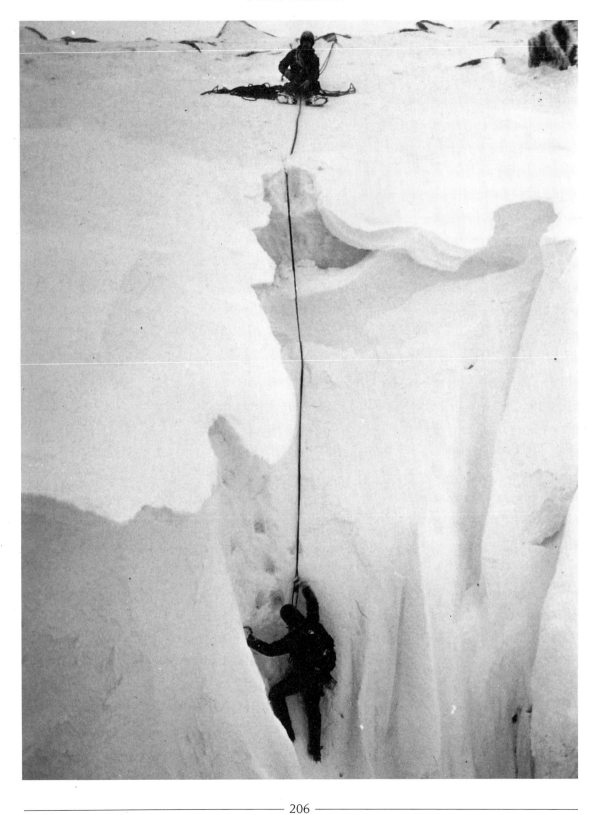

A WEST COAST BOOMER

As late as 11am on a moping mid-February day in 1987, three disheartened climbers were prowling the wet snows which filled the 'great wolf's hole', the Toll a' Mhadaidh of Beinn Alligin, scanning the encirclement of frowning cliffs for the elusive glint of frozen ice that would spark them out of indolence and into the fire of action.

Up to their left towered the Cyclopean buttresses of Tom na Gruagaich, plunging 500m into the corrie in an unmitigated sweep of banded cliff and snow-smeared terrace. There is only one vertical slice chopped out of this bewildering débâcle, a crooked corner cleft that bends out of sight into the upper cliff; over 300m of gully with a rumoured ascent some fifteen years past, and otherwise a shroud of obscurity. If only today it would harbour some ice . . .

Looking closely, its lowest steps were cloaked with a dull-grey screen; ice most certainly, but thawing through and through; ice no longer proudly gleaming but stained with the pigment of the seeping rock it masked. Yet how few gullies of this grand scale and line remain unchartered on Scotland's cliffs and what else was there to do save thrash and wallow on the easier snows?

'Let's give it a shot,' I ventured, sensing the first prickles of excitement rising up my spine.

Ray and Peter concurred without hesitation and by 12.30 we were roped at the first pitch. Five hours of light for at least 300m looked a tall order, but there again we could always play the honourable retreat.

The first innocuous pitch; step right up, axes brandished ready for a half-minute rout, and suddenly you are clinging to 8m of vertical and protectionless slush. I squirmed and bridged to its upper lip, then eased into a mantelshelf,

Plate 53 The notorious exit cornice of Douglas-Gibson Gully (IV), Lochnagar. Note the drooping lips of soft slab on either side of the exit trench (*Andrew Nisbet*)

teetering in air-borne equilibrium for an agonising second before collapsing onto the snows above.

A second sandstone tier came all too soon and was one step harder, although at least it proffered a runner for courage. A body wedge in a bulging crack gained precious feet, but as my axe scraped and pecked over the top the skin of ice peeled off. With a desperate wriggle and two knees plonked on the soaking rock beneath, I exited – prayer-like both in thoughts and stance.

Pitch three offered a choice of lines, but all wept slushy tears today. I opted right onto a tapering ramp, bridging up on diminishing nicks in the ice, cajoled a blade peg into a hairline crack, then cleared holds in the underlying rock for the final moves; hard, but much more neat and controlled.

A fourth step proved short but sweetly beguiling. A thicker curtain of ice tempted a wholesale pull on the axes, but quickly collapsed on investigation, so instead I climbed the spongy tufts of moss beneath.

Ray and Peter followed the remains of each pitch with brisk gusto, but already two and a half hours had been squeezed from our grasp, and the gully's rightward kink was not yet reached. Nor could we now view the 'honourable retreat' so smugly. Four abseils would exact stiff dues in anchor pegs and 'friends', and with 150m of ground hard-won, the thought of descent met with increasing reluctance. So boldness spurred us on, yearning for the slightest frost, and anxious for the upward view that would spell our fate.

Three long easy rope-lengths turned the corner, taking us into the very heart of the cliff, now clutched in a commitment to see the issue through. Easy level ledges snaked temptingly off left and right from every pitch, leading across the giddy exposures of the bounding faces but ending nowhere. It was up at all costs. Up in a steepening corner groove of the same wet ice, up to a barrier pitch of a height ungauged, down which a candle of white ice flickered dimly in the gathering gloom, then up out of sight into cloud and hopefully the top.

Counting every minute, we sped on as fast as

the soggy ice allowed. Belays were made good and sound with pegs and nuts, but this left no time to search protection. Our urgency imparted a rising thrill to the climbing that was perfectly matched by the outward scene. Framed between the tilting gully walls, the black and yawning gash of Sgurr Mhor and the white abyss of the Toll a' Mhadaidh formed a savage back-drop for the final showdown.

A weaving 40m pitch was climbed on nought but faith, balance and the odd tuft of frozen grass to gain the candle's base. Our crux now reared a goodly 15m in height with a plumb vertical start that would be insurmountable unless the ice improved. Darkness was but minutes away and an all-night vigil looming large as Ray and Peter hurried to my tiny two-peg stance.

With crampons poised just inches above their heads, I gingerly swung onto the column, and for the first time both picks and points bit into a thick and solid pack of ice. Swiftly levering myself over the vertical, I then scampered up to a bottleneck exit. With a wide straddle and a blind pull right onto magnificent frozen snow, the pitch was climbed, and above me a thin pale runnel of névé led direct to the cornice and a coal-black sky.

Gasps of relief and beams of torchlight filtered from the depths when I shouted down the good news. Dinner would be better late than never, for it was past seven when we pulled over onto the level summit snows to feel a teasing pinch of frost in the soft night breeze. The string of orange lights round Gairloch Bay twinkled a merry greeting away to the north, but the mountain world was already dark and deep in slumber.

Subsequent enquiries established the gully's name as West Coast Boomer, 'boomer' being a Glaswegian term for a thing of excellence. We could not disagree for it had granted the greatest of 'moping' winter days that could possibly be wished.

(The gully will be grade III/IV in more favourable frozen conditions. Our ascent was likely the third, although the identity of its original perpetrators remains uncertain.)

17 (*right*) Teetering on watery ice. The author on the first ascent of Ice Gem (IV/V), a fine 160m icefall tucked away in the Toll a' Mhadaidh of Beinn Alligin (*Steve Chadwick*)

12

ICICLE ANTICS

Modern Ice-fall Climbing

FIRST STEPS TO SALVATION

Even standing on crampon tips on the top of the pedestal, I was only just able to reach the thicker ice at full stretch. A curtain of icicles hung down to knee level, but their effect was merely decorative. With a few exploratory kicks from the crampons, they disintegrated en masse, clattering 3m down onto the surface slick of bone-hard ice that formed my landing site should I make a false move. Behind the curtain lay a smooth and fiercely overhung wall of rock with not a vestige of a hold for a crampon point.

A second knife-blade was persuaded a centimetre or so into the crack on my right. I contemplated using them for aid, but even in unison they would scarcely have held my body-weight, still less a fall. Prudence dictated retreat.

'I'm coming down,' I called to Steve, but the very moment the words were out, a final surge of vain-glorious hope welled inside me; ambition demanding one last fling and clouding the reason for better or worse . . .

One last time I stretched up, mittened right hand squeezed among the icicle stumps holding my body in, left leg dangling free and right foot precariously lodged on the pedestal top. Surely it was a forlorn gesture. I blindly swung my axe up and left . . .

18 (*left*) The poise and grandeur of winter buttress climbing – Western Rib (II), Coire an-t Sneachda (*Andrew Nisbet*)

'Clunk' – the reassuring sound of metal teeth biting on yielding ice. A good placement? Well, maybe, but this was no time to ponder; it was all or nothing. I unclenched my jammed right hand and my 10 stones plus swung out onto the axe. It held. One deep breath and then I muscled up, crampons scrattling against the rock in search of support until the elbow locked and I could hold myself steady for a precious moment. I grabbed the shaft of the hammer axe and swung it hard and fast a foot above. The moment was gone. No chance to swing again. Trusting what I had, I pulled up and yanked the first axe out. The move was repeated . . . once . . . twice, and then on the third heave I jerked my knee up to my chin and kicked my toes onto the lip of the ice.

Crouching like a spider on a sloping glassy mantel barely 30cm wide, lungs heaving, heart pounding and one leg still dangling over the void, I was embarked. The only problem now was to actually climb the ice, which hung with Damoclean intent fully 40m above my head.

A minor smear of ice tucked away in one of Liathach's secret recesses, trivial by comparison to the grandiose scale of the whole mountain, just one of the many struts of its magnificent winter architecture, and yet to the ice-climber it is a shining jewel of rare and ephemeral beauty. The ice-falls and icicles which can develop over the steepest cliffs and watercourses in a hard season have given a new impetus to exploratory winter climbing in the last decade. Those who dare to tackle their smooth and glassy verticalities may be guaranteed a genuine adventure where calculated risk must be pushed to its very limits.

THE MODERN ICE SCENE

Climbing steep open ice demands guts, but is equally dependent upon modern techniques and hardware. Prior to the front-point revolution, there had been only a handful of excursions onto icicles and ice-falls, Smith's Route (Gardyloo Buttress) and The Curtain on Ben Nevis being the most notable in Scotland. These were not only major achievements of the step-cutting style, but also significant pointers to future developments.

Only when front-pointing was firmly established and the era of classic gully exploration was completed did a wholesale movement towards the ice-falls begin. What would have been murderously strenuous and frighteningly precarious in the step-cutting era now became merely hard and gripping, fully justifiable to the longer necks of the climbing fraternity. As Fig 62 shows, the shift out of the gullies split into several directions.

Low-level waterfalls are highly popular when frozen during prolonged frosts. The Steall Falls in Glen Nevis and Oui Oui on Creag Dubh, Newtonmore, provide excellent training in grade III ice-craft, but many more challenging frozen plunges have been attacked since the mid-1970s. Enthusiasm for these climbs is in no small part due to the absence of the mind-numbing walk-in which is obligatory for the higher ice routes. 'Five minutes from the road' is a guidebook phrase to inspire any leg-worn winter climber.

But the waterfalls also have an aesthetic appeal. Nobody could fail to be moved as they round a bend in the road at the sudden sight of a thin white line of ice cascading down the hillside, even though one might not have the slightest intention of trying to climb it. Waterfall climbing (of a non-aquatic variety) is, of course, confined to exceptionally cold winters and is the more highly sought for its rarity value. 1986 offered the required freeze-up, and Britain's highest fall, the triple-tiered, 200m (600ft) spout of the Eas a'Coul Alumn by Kylesku in the far North-West was conquered by Andy Cunningham and Andy Nisbet. Many of these falls have been tackled when an appreciable volume of water is still flowing down the back of the ice. I've heard rumour that an ill-timed attempt on the Falls of

Plate 54 The author contemplates the road to Salvation, a short but patently vicious grade V/VI icicle on the south side of Liathach (*Steve Chadwick*)

Glomach in 1987 failed after a few feet with the fallen leader submerged under the ice covering the plunge pool at the bottom. Luckily, he was fished to safety by his second man. The lowest of Scotland's low-level ice-falls was found on the side of Edinburgh Castle in January 1987. Although only grade III in standard, the route's name 'Breach of the Peace' suggests that the ascent was not without outside interference.

The waterfalls will doubtless continue to provide an esoteric amusement, but the main thrust of ice-climbing advance has more appro-

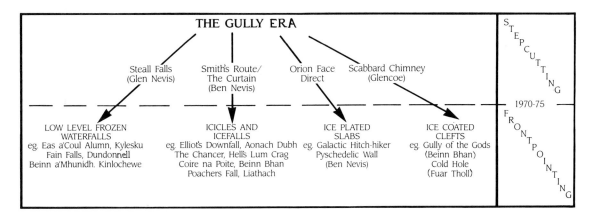

Fig 62 THE SHIFT FROM THE GULLIES: MODERN ICE DEVELOPMENT

priately been on the high mountain cliffs where good conditions can be expected for at least a couple of weeks in each season.

Pure ice-falls and icicles may be encountered in every major winter arena and occasionally in new locations where ice-climbing potential had hardly been suspected prior to 1970. For instance, in the Southern Highlands, Coire Diamh on the north-west side of Beinn Udlaidh above Glen Orchy yielded over a dozen grade IV and V ice-falls to the 1970s front-pointers, yet had no winter climbs of any grade recorded prior to 1969.

The Cairngorms are not renowned for pure ice-climbing, yet they still possess an iceman's paradise in Hell's Lum Crag. Facing south-east, it usually develops fine runs of ice on its slabs and overlaps early in the season with the assistance of a daily sunshine and freeze cycle. Indeed, the icicle epoch was really initiated on Hell's Lum when Cunningham and March climbed The Chancer in 1970. This ascent turned eyes long blinkered by gully walls towards similar free-standing monsters all over Scotland. In the eastern Gorms, Creag an Dubh Loch has, on rare occasion, sported superb ice-falls, the line of Goliath (V/VI) being the most notable so far climbed.

Of course, Ben Nevis has its icy spouts, chiefly on and around the Carn Dearg cliffs. The Curtain is the model of an ice-fall climb – accessible, relatively short and safe from objective danger, but awesomely smooth and demanding of technique. As it lies back sufficiently to give an easy grade IV with modern tools, it is undoubtedly Scotland's most hacked and hackneyed piece of ice. Other nearby ice-falls such as the Heidbanger icicle on Central Trident Buttress (grade V), Gemini (V) and Shield Direct on the left side of Waterfall Gully are less often on display and are intended for the admiration rather than the consumption of the majority, being longer, thinner and 10° steeper.

However, it is in the North-West Highlands where the most impressive ice features have been found, thanks to the angular geology of the Torridonian sandstone and quartzite massifs. The gaunt savage peaks towering over their moorland plinths pour streams of water ice out from their joint-line springs and over their banded cliffs – but only when the proportioning of water supply with successive melt/freeze cycles is engineered with the most opportune precision.

In Applecross, Beinn Bhan's nest of great corries harbours in the words of Hamish MacInnes, 'some of the finest ice-climbing in Europe'. The colossal 300m (1,000ft) back-wall of the central amphitheatre, Coire na Poite, exhibits perhaps the largest expanse of icicles in Scotland and was one of the first new places to be investigated with 'terror' axes and front-point crampons in the early Seventies.

From here northwards to the remotest outpost of Creag Urbhard on Foinaven, a rich harvest of stupendous icicle climbs has been reaped over the last decade. Some are pure ice from bottom to top such as the Poacher's Fall (V) on Coire Dubh Mor, Liathach, but on others the ice runs out on hostile ground and icicle antics must be combined with hard mixed climbing to succeed, Tholl Gate (V/VI) on Fuar Tholl being a fine example of this intimidating genre.

There are, of course, a few 'plums' yet to be picked, for example the Third Waterfall on Creag Urbhard, of which Andy Nisbet pronounced: 'were it to be climbed direct it would be by far the most impressive ice-climb in Britain'.

To have publicised such a prize is somewhat out of the character of North-West pioneering where those who have made the exploratory effort generally keep such hard-won secrets close to their chests. One must presume that Andy is confident that the route will not form more than once in a lifetime, or else that the 240km (150-mile) drive north of Inverness plus the 13km (8-mile) walk that is necessitated every time one suspects it might have formed, will be an effective deterrent to the most ardent suitors.

The two other modern styles of ice-climb are more localised in availability. *Thin ice-plating* over wide expanses of slabby cliff is created by heavy riming rather than an overhead drainage source. As explained in Chapter 4 (p80), it is a phenomenon largely confined to the upper reaches of the Nevis cliffs, where the smooth slabby rock strata and humid climatic conditions are especially predisposed to surface icing. While the routes made on these iced rocks since the mid-1970s are uniformly bold in character, their technical difficulty varies greatly with the thickness of ice. The angle of the routes is not especially steep, being typically in the 65–75° range. A liberal coating (ie, 8cm (3in) or more) gives good secure placements and then the actual climbing may be straightforward.

However, in leaner conditions, one dares not swing the axes or crampons with vigour, for they will strike the underlying rock and cause the ice to 'dinner plate' alarmingly. Instead, one must teeter upwards, hooking the last-most notches of the axe-picks into the surface and kicking the crampon tips with the most gentle precision. Progress is not just precarious and agonisingly strenuous, but one proceeds in the imminent fear that the ice

may disappear altogether, leaving the appalling prospect of reversing a pitch.

Whatever their technical difficulty, these routes are notoriously ill-protected. Rarely is the ice thick enough to allow the insertion of ice screws, but conversely, it is usually too well-bonded to allow the rocks below to be excavated. Even if one can expose some rock, any cracks are likely to be glued with verglas and will therefore be useless.

Yet, despite these obvious discouragements, a network of routes has been established across the Minus Buttresses, the upper Orion Face, the Hadrians and Psychedelic Walls and Gardyloo Buttress. They require a steady head and control and fully warrant the respect they are paid by today's young climbers. The Orion Face Direct was an early precursor of the style, taking iced rocks on its crucial pitches above the Basin, but now it is names like Journey into Space, Galactic Hitch-hiker, Pointless and Albatross which fire the dreams of the ambitious.

Thin ice-plating is, of course, encountered on occasion in other areas, usually as part of a climb that is mixed in character, but only on the Ben does it form the full substance of long sustained routes.

The iced cleft is tentatively offered as the fourth mode of modern ice-craft. Strictly, this is an extension of the final phase of gully exploration to the north-west, but only an optimist would describe an ice-lined overhanging chimney of Torridonian sandstone as a gully. Coire an Fhamair on Beinn Bhan boasts the two finest such routes so far climbed which are aptly entitled Gully of the Gods and The Great Overhanging Gully. Both require contortionist bridging tactics in total contrast to the neater footwork of normal front-pointing and doubtless can be guaranteed to stretch both the mind and hamstrings. The impressive dyke lines on the Black Cuillin appear to offer potential for similarly awesome winter routes. However, the run-off of rainfall from the gabbro rock is so rapid that the gradual seepage of groundwater needed for reliable ice formation is rarely achieved. The rare combination of heavy snowfall followed by a slow melt and refreezing is alternatively required. The chances of suitable conditions are therefore even slimmer than those on the north-west mainland, but they remain as a hope for the next Ice Age.

STEELING THE NERVES –
GEAR, GRADES AND ETHICS

Recent ice activities have been abetted by continual improvements in tools and hardware:

Boots Vertical ice particularly requires rigidity in the boot soles which must act as a platform for the levered support of the body's whole weight on front-points. The introduction of plastic boots around 1981 was therefore particularly appropriate. Their moulded shell construction offers a more lasting stability and better ankle support than the plate-stiffened leather models used previously, which tended to warp and soften with use. Some ice-climbers still prefer the closer fit of a leather boot, but the majority go for the greater support and warmth of plastic.

Crampons The stability of the 'foot platform' also demands a crampon of maximum rigidity. Salewa Chouinard and Camp 'Footfangs' were the original rigid models. After fifteen years they remain popular, but there are now a host of alternatives. Clip-on cable bindings are now used regularly as attachments on plastic boots. Not only are they quick and efficient, but they have been proven to offer a reliably tight fit. No margin of movement can be allowed between crampon and boot when climbing on steep ice.

Axes and hammers Prior to 1978, climbers had a choice between droop-picked ('terrors') and curved pick-axes. Many people compromised and carried one of each, but this was an awkward marriage since their actions are so different, one hand jabbing, the other one swinging. Happily, Simond combined the two shapes and produced the 'banana' picked Chacal axe in 1979. Every major manufacturer quickly followed suit with their own versions, and now there is a wide range of axes on the market with interchangeable picks, adzes and hammerheads. The new generation of axes has eliminated the problems, yet enjoined the advantages of curved and drooped picks. The new

axes can be swung on the thick ice or jabbed and hooked on the thin. Most advantageously, they give good firm penetration without the same tendency to shatter the surface as curved tools. Shaft lengths vary between 45 and 55cm (18 and 22in) according to personal preference.

Most serious ice climbers will periodically sharpen their ice picks and crampon front points in order to improve penetration, although such practice inevitably diminishes the life of the gear. Worn down and blunt tools can ideally be retired from ice climbing and used on mixed routes. It is essential that wristloops are fitted to the exact length of the axe shafts with wrist knots or slides to prevent them pulling through a gloved hand. Even the strongest of muscle would not get far on vertical ice on front-points without the support of secure wristloops, so spare a thought for the climbers of the step-cutting era, when all cutting was done without a loop.

While the improvement of tools raises no ethical qualms, the style of climbing new ice routes is now subject to searching scrutiny by journal editors and magazine reporters. Tensioning, resting and even aiding on embedded axes or ice screws were previously all admissible sins. However, with the superb quality of gear and the dwindling stock of unclimbed lines in the 1980s, it quite rightly became important to achieve a 'clean' ascent, with any deviations from the ideal being honestly reported.

The greatest difficulty of making an unaided front-point ascent lies not in the actual climbing, but in placing protection. It is technically feasible to free-climb long sections of sheer or even gently overhanging ice, but how on earth does a leader stop to place his much-needed ice screws on such ground?

In theory, one has three options, but the third is reserved only for the strongest of will and muscle:

1. Don't stop, do without protection and go for the top on a mixture of ability and adrenalin.
2. Clip a sling from harness to ice-axe for rest and support while hammering the screw. This is the unethical option, but is ostensibly safe, provided one is sure that the embedded

axe-pick will support the body's full weight. Catastrophe results if it does not.

3 Insert the screw while hanging solely by the wrist from the axe. Two hands are needed for the initial placement, one to hold the screw and the other to hammer, and the problem can be solved only by sliding the wrist-loop up to the elbow of the axe arm. So precarious and urgent is this operation that one is often forced to accept a half-driven or badly angled screw, but if the boldness for option 1 is lacked, then it is the only choice for the purist.

Whatever the option chosen, the placement of protection is undoubtedly the most difficult and hair-raising operation on vertical ground. It is therefore essential to stop and place good protection wherever the angle eases. With a resting footstep and a semblance of balance, the operation is infinitely easier and, with good gear, one is more readily prepared to stick one's neck out on the steep stuff above.

My own way out of the ethical tangle is to clip a loose sling from harness to axe if I am forced to stop on vertical ground. I take no tension on the sling, but use it as back-up protection in case I lose balance while placing the screw. Not even my second would probably notice if I did take tension. Responsibility for ethical practice on ice lies with the individual's conscience, as it ultimately should.

However, the whole problem of protecting vertical ice may be rapidly alleviated if the potential performance of new titanium screws with wide cores and four bits is realised, for they can be inserted solely with one hand if the ice is of a consistent texture.

Since the typical icicle climb is relatively short but technically vicious, it ill-fits the traditional winter-grading system in which grade V was only accorded to routes of great difficulty which were over 150m (500ft) in length. Yet these modern routes are fully two grades harder in pure technical severity than any of the classic grade Vs of the step-cutting era. 30m (100ft) of the Shield Direct is worth ten ascents of Point Five. Length can no longer always be the deciding criterion and

Plate 55 The 250m plunge of Poacher's Fall (V) in Coire Dubh Mor, Liathach. First climbed by Richard MacHardy and Andy Nisbet in 1978, it is now established as one of Scotland's finest icefall routes

this requirement has been rescinded in recent years.

Some of the old gullies which have become significantly easier with front-pointing have been slightly down-graded. For instance, Zero is now generally agreed to be IV/V and Green Gully III/IV depending on conditions, but these modifications are insufficient to restore consistency. Either more wholesale demotions or the expansion of the

Plate 56 The author on the crux pitch of Umbrella Fall, a 'modern' grade IV of comparable quality to the neighbouring Poacher's Fall. Note the three ice-screw protection points in the 20m vertical section, all placed strenuously but ethically!

system is required to eliminate the ridiculous inconsistencies between 'modern' Vs and 'traditional' Vs. While grade VI is now officially acknowledged in mixed climbing and likely to be expanded further, the grade has not yet been clearly sanctioned on pure ice. Instead, it is creeping insidiously into usage but at different rates between areas and various groups of climbers. For instance, the split grade V/VI is now cautiously offered for new desperates. In 1988 the system is something of a mess and we may hope that it is fully resolved over the next five years. Until then, climbers should beware the grading of modern ice. Get some advice from the local experts or, better still, form your own opinion when your neck is leaning back over the vertical and examining the route.

A CAUTIONARY TALE

The grading of a feature that may exist only for one week every two years is, of course, in large part a hypothetical matter. Even when formed,

the thickness and shape of ice-falls may vary widely from year to year and this alters the difficulties that are encountered to an even greater degree than those on the traditional gullies.

The factors governing icicle development have been discussed in Chapter 4, but it is well to remember that those rare periods when they do exist must come to an end some time.

The craggy flanks of the Three Sisters of Glencoe develop a myriad of ice-falls during a good season, but undoubtedly the most famous is the 30m (100ft) icicle barring the entrance to No 5 Gully on the West Face of Aonach Dubh, which became known as Elliott's Downfall. When formed, it hangs free of the rock for nearly 15m (50ft) and offered a tantalising challenge until Dave 'Cubby' Cuthbertson made the first ascent in February 1979.

Towards that season's end when the winter's freeze was slowly waning at lower levels, the icicle still winked down at passing travellers. Wisely or not, three rather hung-over climbers, Pete Thexton, John Given and Phil Swainson, in

Plate 57 Modern ice tools. (L to R) the curved-pick Charlet-Moser hammer, drop-picked Terrordactyl, and their hybrid the banana-picked Chacal.

search of a short but exciting day, decided that it would bear a repetition.

Thexton took the lead, leaving his companions standing in a drip of cold melt-water in the cave below. His progress was steady and sure, but he was unhappy with the ice-screw protection and moved left at 12m (40ft) into a small grotto where he placed a tied-off piton as a back-up runner.

His second, Given, watched him move baçk onto the ice just 5m (16ft) away from success when there was a resounding 'Bang!'

I dived into the cave. A pillar of ice is in the sky settling for a shattered brittle second on its fang into the slope, like a factory chimney might just before it tilts out and thunders down.

Plate 58a, b The collapse of Elliot's Downfall (V) Aonach Dubh, Glencoe, March 1979. A hair's-breadth escape for climber Pete Thexton, and exciting entertainment for photographer Phil Swainson

When he opened his eyes again, the ice was gone, but Thexton was still there clinging to his 'terrors' 15m (50ft) up, inches above the fracture line: 'the fracture had sprung from the tip of Pete's right axe, run down beside him and curved back under his feet'.[1]

Thexton's ice screws had pulled out of the tumbling ice, yet somehow he had stayed on. It was a truly miraculous escape. Unable to help,

Swainson took the opportunity to capture Thexton's horrific position on film (Plate 58). Now his seconds could see the volume of water that had been draining behind the ice and that the whole tonnage of the icicle had been hung from a sheet of ice just 20cm (8in) thick. Their leader meanwhile put his heart in his mouth and abseiled off the piton that had probably saved his life.

Icicles are fragile beasts, at all times to be treated gently, but strictly to be admired from a safe distance when a thaw sets in.

THE CLOWN PRINCE OF SCOTTISH ICE
A PROFILE OF MICK FOWLER

Up on my local cliffs on the south-east corrie of Fuar Tholl, there lies an obscure but remarkable box cleft cut out of the sandstone. Its enclosing walls are absolutely sheer for over 50m (160ft) and in a hard winter they dribble streams of watery ice. Simon Jenkins and I had spied the ice forming and building in the hidden recess on two visits to the corrie with course parties over the New Year holiday. When our week's work was done, we planned a quick raid to snaffle the ice run down the cleft's left wall. So short and accessible a route would nicely suit our Saturday off. We could even have a good lie-in, drive the 11km (7 miles) up the glen and then take a leisured pace.

At 9.30 we drew up to the parking lay-by at Achnashellach. A dark-blue Ford saloon was already parked and a cursory glance inside as I shouldered my pack revealed sleeping-bags strewn across the seats and, more disturbingly, a North London garage sticker. I was stung to the quick.

'I don't believe it. He's here!' I exclaimed.

The walk up to the corrie was leadened by a depressing sense of inevitability. I knew at once that the secret cleft was no longer my personal property.

Sure enough, we found tracks at the snow-line which staggered upwards in a series of tortuous zig-zags. They were definitely the steps of car-worn sleep-starved travellers. Up they wound into the corrie and disappeared into the jaws of the cleft. There was naught we could do but follow, for we had set our minds on the route.

Drawing near, I spied a spidery figure spread-eagled 20m (65ft) up our line of ice. The constant tapping and jabbing of axe-picks echoed down. This chatter was broken now and again by a louder crash and tinkle as some ice plated off, to be followed by gutteral grunts and muttering. Protection was notable by its absence, the angle being close to vertical, and the ice already thin and fast disintegrating under the attack.

It was unmistakably Mick Fowler in fullest flow. We introduced ourselves to his partner Chris Watts and watched his progress, controlled and sure yet patently irreversible. Nearly 30m (100ft) out from the last runner, the angle eased and he took a belay. No longer self-engrossed, he now noticed our presence. A cheery Cockney voice floated down:

'Oh, dear! So it's you, Martin. How are you doing, old boy?'

It was hard to be annoyed. There was a boyish charm and enthusiasm in that greeting that beckoned forgiveness. In any case, there was no cause for complaint. We had been fairly 'pipped at the post', but our embarrassment was considerable for our rivals had driven close on 1,000km (700 miles) further in order to beat us. Mick and I must have been the only two people in Britain aware of this obscure streak of ice. Our timing was quite immaculate.

We made a second ascent of the route that day while Mick and Chris went on to climb a rather more fearful ice-smear up the back-wall of the cleft – the Cold Hole (grade V, but beware).

Never again have I rested easy during my explorations in the North-West Highlands. The ghost of Fowler stalks my steps wherever I go. The sight of a car parked at a remote road head is sure to bring me out in a cold sweat. Midweek climbing is the only cure, for then I know that he is safely lodged behind an office desk in the metropolis and I can climb safe from the threat of a sudden swoop.

Fowler's activities in the Scottish winter have acquired a legendary fame. Somehow, on a weekend-time budget, he can drive up from London and pinch plum ice routes from under the noses of both natives and local residents and still get back to work for 8am on Monday morning. Scots climbers are understandably dismayed but

Plate 59 The second ascent of Pipped at the Post (V), Fuar Tholl; Simon Jenkins climbing. Photo taken by a victorious Mick Fowler, 10 January 1987

modern rock-gymnasts. However, the stereotyped style and tactics of modern crag-climbing were of limited appeal. To a man whose mind was imbued with a spirit of commitment and adventure as well as a sense of the outrageous, there was a much wider world to explore. Thus he turned his energies to sea cliffs of the loosest variety, and of course to ice.

After a brief apprenticeship of one week and two weekends in 1978, he coupled ability and boldness to make a fine series of new routes in Wales in the exceptional February of 1979. A visit to Scotland with Tony (Victor) Saunders followed in March and the result was Shield Direct, the awesome line-up the right side of Carn Dearg Buttress on the Ben. The ascent was an eye-opener:

Realisation that such a good line was not climbed on the most popular cliff really made me wake up to the potential of Scotland. We graded it V and were very confused when it was reported as VI in the journals and guides as neither of us ever said this.

Local opinions were obviously sufficiently impressed at the sight of the route that they made it first grade VI in the country without having set a foot on it. The second ascent was not made until 1986: Mick still maintains it is a 'good' grade V.

In his grading as in his whole approach to climbing, Mick is a traditionalist. His only concession to purism is that he will on occasion clip in to his axes while placing protection on vertical ice. For him, grade V represents the pinnacle of achievement of the step-cutting era, and he believes it should retain its cachet, grade VI being reserved for those routes which in difficulty and boldness go beyond the feats of Patey, Smith and Marshall.

I look on routes like Astronomy and Smith's Gully as grade Vs. The likes of Zero and Orion Direct which were mega-Vs when first climbed have now become much easier due to front-pointing, and this should be recognised by their being downgraded to IV. I don't understand the reluctance to do so.

undoubtedly impressed. Prior to his arrival on the scene, they had a virtual monopoly of winter pioneering – a game where local knowledge and constant availability seemed crucial. Yet the list of Fowler's first ascents in Fig 63 comprises a substantial proportion of the hardest and best icy lines climbed in the last decade and many are as yet unrepeated. So how does he do it?

A considerable natural talent is undoubted. In 1977 Mick was frantically rock-climbing at the highest standard throughout Britain, creating and repeating routes that still attract respect from

Those who consider Point Five a standard grade V will therefore be somewhat perplexed by Mick's own grade Vs.

To achieve such a marvellous string of routes over the last ten years has required exploratory enthusiasm and dogged persistence. The North-West Highlands satisfy Mick's exploratory instincts to perfection, offering natural ice lines in a wild remote setting, which must be climbed on sight (ie, without any prior inspection). The highly technical mixed climbing of known summer rock routes currently in vogue in the Cairngorms is less to his taste. It is the lure of the wholly unknown and the appeal of 'the line' that counts.

Persistence has been essential. Mick is sometimes suspected of holding some divine communication upon which to predict good conditions, but, like the rest of us, he simply watches the forecast on television and hopes. The long drive north therefore often ends:

At 4.30am slumped across car seats with a force 10 gale and lashing sleet outside rocking us

Fig 63 NOTABLE FOWLER RAIDS ON SCOTTISH ICE			
Route	Grade	Partners	Date
THE SHIELD DIRECT Carn Dearg Buttress, Ben Nevis Graded VI in the Nevis guide; not repeated until 1986	V	Tony Saunders (alt leads)	15.3.79
SHEET WHITENING Coire na Feola, Beinn Bhan First foray into the North-West.	IV	S. Fenwick, M. Lynden (alt leads)	31.12.81
THE FLY Coire Ardair, Creag Meagaidh First complete ascent without siege tactics	V	Tony Saunders (alt leads)	19.2.83
MR SOFTEE North Face Aonach Dubh, Glencoe Steep pure ice; Saunders forgot axes so Fowler led	V	Tony Saunders	20.2.83
GULLY OF THE GODS Coire Fhamhair, Beinn Bhan A line first eyed by Patey and Bonington in 1969	V	S. Fenwick	3.4.83
THOLL GATE SE Cliff, Fuar Tholl	V/VI	Phil Butler (alt leads)	16.3.84
GREAT OVERHANGING GULLY Coire Fhamhair, Beinn Bhan Described as 'extremely steep'; an impressive weekend's work	V/VI	Phil Butler (alt leads)	17.3.84
UMBRELLA FALL Coire Dubh Mor, Liathach Rapidly becoming a classic ice-fall route along with neighbouring Poacher's Fall.	IV	Phil Butler (alt leads)	1.4.84
FUHRER SE Cliff, Fuar Tholl	V	Chris Watts (alt leads)	15.2.86

erratically to sleep, the enthusiasm levels distinctly low.

In successive attempts on his 1988 route on Aonach Dubh's North Face, his team drove 4,800km (3,000 miles) and survived several car rotations on an icy Loch Lomond road plus a 200m (600ft) fall in an avalanche on the ramp beneath the climb. Prior to the last bid even Fowler was becoming despondent: 'on calculation, we had so far achieved half an inch of climbing for every mile driven – not up to the usual standard at all.'

The final attempt was not without its excitements – Fowler locked outside the Kingshouse Hotel at 4.30am with partner Watts sleeping soundly inside, the unfortunate failure of Watts to remember his crampons necessitating a two-hour detour back to the hotel, then forcing the route in worsening weather, knowing that their driver was leaving for London at 8pm prompt. No wonder it is one of Mick's few grade VIs.

For Icicle Factory in Coir' a'Mhadaidh, Skye, he was tipped off by his father who was holidaying in Scotland and whom he had persuaded to go

Fig 63 NOTABLE FOWLER RAIDS ON SCOTTISH ICE			
Route	Grade	Partners	Date
BODY FREEZE Coire Ghranda, Beinn Dearg	IV	Chris Watts (alt leads)	22.2.86
SOUTH GULLY Coire a'Mhadaidh, Black Cuillin	III/IV	Tony Saunders (solo together)	1.3.86
ICICLE FACTORY Coire a'Mhadaidh, Black Cuillin Skye's hardest icicle climb	V	Tony Saunders (alt leads)	1.3.86
THE BLACK HOLE Orion Face, Ben Nevis	V	Tony Saunders (alt leads)	5.4.86
PIPPED AT THE POST SE Cliff, Fuar Tholl	V	Chris Watts (alt leads)	10.1.87
COLD HOLE SE Cliff, Fuar Tholl Beat the author by one hour to the first route despite a 600-mile longer drive.	V	Chris Watts (alt leads)	10.1.87
TEST DEPARTMENT Coire Dubh Mor, Liathach	V	Chris Watts	11.1.87

UPPER GIRDLE
Coire Mhic Fearchair, Beinn Eighe
Climbed in two sections; 800m (2,620ft) total length;
  a rare but effective excursion into mixed climbing
	V/VI	Chris Watts (1st section), Tony
		  Saunders (2nd)
			21.2/14.3.87

WEST CENTRAL GULLY Coire Mhic Fearchair, Beinn Eighe First direct exit	VI	Mike Morrison	5.4.87
AGAINST ALL ODDS N Face Aonach Dubh, Glencoe Finally climbed on third visit	VI	Chris Watts	14.2.88
N.B.: Several other first ascents of grade III, IV and V are excluded.			

walking in the Cuillin the previous day. The phone call reporting copious ice came to Mick's home in London at 6pm Friday and by 8am Saturday he and Victor were walking into the corrie. Enthusiasm like that deserves rewards.

West Central Gully on the Triple Buttress, Beinn Eighe is with little doubt the hardest gully climb in Britain and was graded VI by Mick after a harrowing first ascent in April 1987. The final 80m (260ft) head-wall is vertical or gently overhanging throughout. Close to the top, Mick ran out of steam in the most inopportune position and his means of extrication shows the depths of ingenuity that the hardened ice-climber must display to ensure self-preservation. Protection was a single knife-blade piton a considerable way below:

A high axe placement over a bulge is good, but all strength is gone. That weak drained feeling comes over me, legs dangling beneath an icicle fringe, axe firmly planted above it. I try and pull up to clip my harness into the axe . . . can't do it . . . no strength. I hang limply from the wrist-loop. It is time for the last resort. My axes have long safety cords attached to the straps of my ten-year-old rucksack. Wriggling my hand out of the wrist-loop, I cross arms to keep my rucksack in place, and lower onto the straps. The stitching strains nastily, but holds. Heart in mouth, I take a rest . . .

A second attempt brought the most slender of successes – all good character-building stuff as Mick would have us believe.

Mick does no training for his winter climbing. The midweeks are understandably spent recovering. However, the proximity of the chalk cliffs of Dover has played a major role in training the Londoners to the highest standards of performance on ice, the soft rock being climbed with axes, crampons and ice screws for protection and belays. Only the Scottish cold is absent. After one abortive weekend in Torridon, Mick even found better ice conditions in the middle of his own city. This was the big freeze of January 1987 and St Pancras Station's wall had developed a magnificent spout of ice from a broken drain. With his second belayed to a parking meter, the icicle was duly climbed, but protracted negotiations with British Rail police followed.

Partner quality is another key to Fowler's success. Although Mick is the prime motivator, he has a team of equal ability who will lead through on all routes. Victor Saunders and Chris Watts are regular partners, while Phil Butler can, on occasion, produce a scintillating lead. Such was the disintegrating crux pitch of Tholl Gate, which even Mick had regarded with some suspicion.

Mick has no particular affectation with gear as do so many modern climbers. Between 1979 and 1986 he used the same pair of crampons on all routes – a set of 'bent tin' Salewa Classics. His simple style and approach draw their inspiration from the great ice-climbers of the 1950s. He has particular admiration for Tom Patey and Robin Smith, and himself is a modern example of the adventurous spirit which has pervaded the development of Scottish winter climbing since the days of Naismith and Raeburn. In an era when regimentation, technical intricacy, and ethical wrangles are spreading insidiously into the winter scene, Fowler brings a refreshing breeze, showing us that, above all, climbing is still fun.

At the age of 32, Mick is still single and there is no sign of the flame dying. He maintains his 'other life' as manager of an Inland Revenue tax collection office with remarkable aplomb, and is amassing a fine record of climbs in foreign parts during his summer vacations.

But those who think that Mick has mopped up the last remaining challenges on Scottish ice need not fear. He sees endless possibilities ahead and comments: 'I'll get even older and shrivel up before it is all dealt with.'

13

THE MIXED PERSPECTIVE

Mixed Buttress and Face Climbing
by ANDREW NISBET

DEFINING THE STYLES

Happiness is Hoar Frost
Black Spout Buttress (Grade III), Lochnagar

The third grovelling mantelshelf brought me standing to attention on a sloping ledge, with my nose pressed into the hoar frost and an imminent awareness of unstable equilibrium. The upward solution was a similar ledge at waist level and to the right, but the absence of hand-holds in my present position seemed to prevent any movement without toppling off. 3m below was the large belay ledge, which was

3m too far despite the information from Alf that our mate had fallen from that very move the week before, landed on the sharp rock immediately beneath and not hurt himself.

This was the crux of Black Spout Buttress, one of the Lochnagar's classic grade IIIs, and Alf and I were in our first season of winter climbing. When unable to move either up or back down, the stuck position in between comes to feel increasingly reassuring. Then a movement is found to be possible after all. Scraping of hoar revealed a tiny side-pull, just sufficient for clawed fingers inside Dachstein

Plate 60 The Tough-Brown Face of Lochnagar, scene of recent mixed climbing advances with grade VI routes such as Nymph, Tough Guy, Trail of Tears and Diedre of the Sorrows (*Andrew Nisbet*)

mitts, and giving just enough balance to swing a crampon up and force a strained leg to lift my weight onto the ledge. It was a move of total commitment for my limited experience, but was backed by a lack of alternatives and a deep-down faith that as long as we didn't give up we were bound to succeed.

Traditional mixed sport; climbing rock and frozen turf under deep powder and hoar frost, and swimming-cum-grovelling over short desperate walls – it's hard to imagine that a 6m Moderate pitch could provide such an 'interesting' problem in winter.

Skating on Thin Ice
Goliath (Grade V/VI), Creag an Dubh Loch

What am I doing out here, shuffling across this thinly iced slab in the middle of Creag an Dubh Loch's south-east Gully Wall with 122m of cold air below my crampon points? Is this insanity? The ice is too thin for axe placements, so one false move and I'll be hurtling through space to an unknown collision below, and even this assumes that my runners, a tied-off knife-blade and a wart-hog in a turf sod 9m away, will hold.

This was faith carried to the extreme. We were so close to the top of Goliath but even in these 'once a decade' conditions the ice had run out. When the sensible options (like retreat) have been ruled out, all that are left are the silly ones, and traversing across this dwindling unprotected slab towards nowhere was beginning to feel particularly silly. Total concentration and control was required now. Every kick of the crampons needed the precise force – too hard and the ice would shatter, too soft and the points might not penetrate. A momentary dropping of the heels or rotation of the foot and I would be flying. Each step was taking minutes but the prospect of reversing was as appalling as the blind corner ahead.

And then I saw it, winking at me through the clear ice, a perfect crack destined to hold a perfect peg, and offering a hand-rail of deep placements leading round that corner to unexpectedly easy ground, and success on one of Scotland's last great problems.

Torque like a Demon
Nymph (Grade VI), Lochnagar

Lay-backing off an axe in the main corner and leaning excruciatingly out left beyond its arête, I could just reach the crack in the base of a subsidiary corner. The problem was to make the transfer, but the crack would only admit one tooth of an axe, the pull was directly outwards, and at full stretch I could get no leverage. Not surprisingly after the 12m of axe lay-backing below, my strength was failing and it was now or never. As I transferred my weight to the other axe, it suddenly slipped out and I swung back into the main corner dangling on the rope.

So it was back to square one, front points balanced on a ripple in the blank slab that was the only foot-hold on the entire pitch. It's fortunate how a small fall can sometimes relax you and generate more commitment. If only I could get some torque on that terrible placement, it might just hold. This time my mind was focused, the transfer was more dynamic, and the one tooth of the axe was somehow holding. The next move had to be statically controlled for any outward pull would rip out the axe. Straining and stretching, crampon points flat against the slab, I reached into the wider part of the crack, ramming a pick in up to the hilt. Then, with a mad lay-backing rush, I sunk my axes into the reassuring turf of the belay ledge.

'Nice lead, Colin.'

Thank goodness I was only seconding!

In recent times, every winter climbing style that isn't dependent on thick ice has tended to be lumped together and labelled as 'mixed'. The term 'mixed' originates from Alpine climbing where it refers to a mixture of rock and ice, often broken rocks cemented together by ice as on the North Face of the Matterhorn, and usually climbed with bare hands and crampons. Two features of Scottish conditions complicate this simple definition: hoar frost (rime) and frozen turf.

Hoar frost (see p41) can plaster the faces and gives Scottish winter crags that wonderful pure

Plate 61 Hat askew and legs akimbo – the expression says it all. Brian Sprunt extended on thin ice and soon to fall during the second ascent of Epitome (VI), Lochnagar in 1980; a route requiring a combination of mixed and bold ice climbing techniques (*Andrew Nisbet*)

white appearance. It is probably the most unique feature of Scottish mixed climbing. A group of widely-travelled French guides visiting in 1979 said that the only time they had come across vaguely similar conditions was in Patagonia (South America). Although colloquially described as hoar frost, the correct name is rime (or rime ice) since it is formed from the water droplets in mist, true hoar being formed by the deposition of water vapour onto a pre-existing snow surface in cold, still conditions. Being a form of ice rather than snow, heavy riming causes the underlying rock to become verglassed. Therefore, the use of bare hands is somewhere between the ineffectual and impossible and attempts to brush off the hoar only serve to make the surface icier.

Many of Scotland's mountain crags, and particularly those of granite and schist, are heavily vegetated with only limited areas of steep clean rock. When frozen, the moss or turf acts as a form of reinforced ice, providing placements often as reliable as the best névé. Many buttress climbs are almost entirely reliant on turf for progress and, even at the highest grades, turf often provides the key holds. This sort of climbing is sometimes referred to as 'tufting'.

So, not only is 'Scottish mixed' a different style to 'Alpine mixed', but the word itself is sometimes

Plate 62 The traditional Cairngorm mixed climbing style – one axe and tricouni nailed boots. Mike Taylor leading on the first ascent of Eagle Buttress (III/IV), Lochnagar, in 1956 (*Bill Brooker*)

a misnomer, since certain Scottish mixed climbs involve the same style of moves all the way up. However, the term has survived despite its inadequacy, not least because it can be taken in a derogatory sense (ie, mixed versus pure) by those without the initiative to leave the ice gullies. But, as an aficionado of mixed climbing, I aim to convince you otherwise.

Mixed climbing can be divided into three sub-categories:

1 Traditional rock- and turf-climbing.
2 Thin ice smears or semi-consolidated snow.

3 Torquing: crack-climbing using twisted axes as hand-holds.

Each is graphically illustrated by the introductory essays, but they are not always so easily separated. There are inevitable overlaps due to conditions (eg, ice forming in unusual places) or personal preference (gloved rock-climbing versus axe torquing).

The second is typical of Ben Nevis's thinly iced slabs. It differs radically from the others because you are climbing on the ice surface as opposed to the underlying rock and difficulty is dependent largely on the quantity and quality of the ice present.

Nos 1 and 3 above overlap considerably, but it is convenient to distinguish them to highlight the latest torquing techniques that have brought harder rock-climbs into the domain of winter climbing. Using the traditional gloved-hand techniques, it was very unusual to see summer Very Severes receive true winter ascents despite the surge in rock-climbing standards. Now a considerable number of Hard Very Severes in the Cairngorms have been climbed under powder and even the odd Extremely Severe (E1 or E2) has gone with co-operative rock features and a lot of effort. The torquing style has remained something of an obscure cult. It takes a certain nerve to abandon gloved-hand techniques and trust to the twisted pick of the ice-axe instead. Many have remained sceptical that torquing in the underlying rock cracks constitutes winter climbing at all.

This mistrust of both the effectiveness and ethics of the mixed techniques has dissuaded many people from trying the climbs. The majority prefer the easy gratification of steep ice, and indeed the euphoria of the front-pointing style on ice has yet to wear off.

The aversion will probably continue as long as Ben Nevis remains our most popular winter-climbing venue. The Ben has plenty of ice but is a mixed climber's nightmare, offering little turf, scant and shallow cracks which do not permit torquing, and poor protection.

THE MIXED APPEAL

The number of mountaineers climbing regularly in other areas is gradually growing and with it an awakening to the real qualities and advantages which mixed climbing has to offer over pure snow and ice. These are, namely, a greater reliability of suitable conditions, logistical intrigue, technical interest and unfailing variety, the regular availability of good protection, safety from avalanches and a thankful escape from the crowds which throng the classic ice gullies – in sum, the allowance to push to one's physical and technical limit (be it grade II or VI). By good planning and organisation, one can maintain a high degree of control over the most precarious or potentially hostile situation rather than being subjected to the random risk and uncertainty of pure snow and ice.

One of the pleasures of winter climbing is to sit with the guidebooks after work (or for the very keen during work) and plan the following weekend's routes. With ice-climbing a high proportion of fantasy and eventual frustration are usually involved because the particular ice route may form into condition for only a couple of weeks a year and certainly not, say, on this mild day in early December. However, since the sole requirements for mixed routes are frozen turf and a good sprinkling of snow or hoar frost, then classic climbs of all grades are in condition for at least three-quarters of the time between January and March, and frequently in November, December and April, too.

This gives the opportunity to choose the route in advance and then to plan and execute the logistical decisions to allow the maximum chance of success. This is in pleasurable contrast to the 'Let's go up and see what's in condition and see if we've time to try it' approach necessitated on fickle ice routes. To arrive at the foot of the route in a suitable mental and physical condition, early enough in the day and with the right equipment is often half the battle won and leaves the rest to personal skill. This to me is true mountaineering.

The logistical demands of a mixed climbing expedition are themselves fascinating. For example, take a weekend trip to Braeriach:

What is the weather forecast, the walking conditions and the likely condition of your route? When to pack, when to shop; is the car ready to leave immediately after work? Are the roads clear, do you approach from Braemar or Aviemore, on skis or foot, over or around the Cairngorm plateau? Do you stop at the Sinclair Hut, or Corrour, or press on to the wee corrie bothy? What do you wear walking in; how much gear can you afford to carry, one rope or two, half or full rack; do you cook meals or just brews, or not at all? Can you find the bothy? When do you get up in the morning to balance maximum rest with enough daylight for the route? Do you have petrol for the journey home? Will your boss let you fall asleep at work?

The variety of technical moves between different mixed climbs or even on a single route is really extraordinary. Any of the rock-climbing contortions may be required – jamming, lay-backing, mantelshelving, chimneying. Then add in the winter peculiarities of thrutching, squirming, wriggling, grovelling, crawling, scratching, scraping, chipping, chopping, and all the torquing and hooking moves, the number depending on the ingenuity of the climber and the design of his axes. Not surprisingly, with all these to choose from, it can take ten minutes to work out each difficult move on a route.

Saying this, of course, admits to the disadvantage that mixed climbing is highly time-consuming. Seconds have to be either patient, hardy and immune to the cold or else wear plenty of clothing. Practising disco manoeuvres on belay stances can be quite warming – the noisier the better to drop hints to a slow leader. Many climbs are a battle with limited daylight, but in itself this gives an added challenge and excitement to the mixed sport.

Because in mixed climbing one is relying largely on the underlying rock for progress, the protection is usually reassuring. One can forget the scary experience of belaying on axes and screws in rotten ice. As long as the leader is willing to hang around in awkward positions and clear the snow from the cracks, then normally the protection is available. This is important because it allows one to try moves of a highly experimental nature without great risk of injury, which in a remote Cairngorm corrie could be very serious indeed.

Mixed climbing can also be the salvation of the man who lacks the specific strength and power-to-weight ratio needed for hard rock-climbing. However determined you are to pull up on a small hold on a rock climb, if you haven't got the finger strength, then you can't do it. In winter, though, because you have a big hold for each hand all the time (the wrist-loop on your axe shaft), you can hang on a bit longer, clear some more snow away, try a different axe move or try a different line, and

eventually upward progress will be made. Determination, persistence and a dose of optimism will ultimately wear down most mixed climbs.

With regard to mixed climbing, you could try the following psychology:

If it takes you two hours for the first 15m, then they must be the crux of the route. If the protection is below your feet, then there must be a good crack in the uncleared snow just above. If it's just got dark and you have two pitches left, then they'll just take a little bit longer than in daylight. If the only gear you've got left is two knife-blade pegs, then you'll find two knife-blade cracks at the stance.

Such positive philosophy can be highly dangerous on other types of climb, but on the mixed it will regularly succeed. You may frequently have a 'pseudo-epic' – ie, an extended adventure where the party remains just in control of the situation – but rarely a 'genuine-epic' where the party is out of control and at the mercy of fate. On almost all Scottish mixed climbs you can push as hard as you dare, yet at any time decide to call a halt and a series of abseils will take you quickly down. Multiple abseils down unknown ground by torchlight can be daunting, but once done a few times they become routine, although the mental demands of safe abseiling are considerable and can never be lapsed.

So, mixed climbing yields to a committed approach, good planning, early starts and the willpower not to be deterred by minor setbacks nor the need to expend a lot more time and energy than expected. Every route, and possibly every pitch, will involve moments when success seems within easy reach, and others when the top seems light years away. These have to be rationalised or even ignored. The reward for all these trials is surely a deeper and more lasting satisfaction than the sudden adrenalin rush offered by pure ice-climbing.

A BRIEF CAIRNGORM HISTORY

The progress of Cairngorm mixed climbing has been erratic, with only a small number of pioneers, and a see-saw competition with ice-climbing. A spirit of exploration has been a continuous driving force since World War II, but the emphasis between mixed and ice has shifted according to whichever type of new route was most accessible with the available techniques of the day.

The 1950s were a golden age for mixed climbing, the Aberdonian school of 'tricouni tricksters' led by Tom Patey creating superb buttress routes in nearly every corrie in the Gorms. Patey, Brooker, Grassick, Nicol and their colleagues, without any past tradition on which to build, quickly attained a startlingly high standard on snowed-up rock, for which their preferred tricouni footwear was ideally suited. Scorpion on Carn Etchachan was climbed as early as December 1952, and history has accorded it as Scotland's first grade V. Eagle Ridge (V), the 'queen' of Lochnagar's ridges, followed in 1953, while Sticil Face (V) in 1957 made a bold winter strike onto the open faces of Shelter Stone Crag. The standards set by these climbs were not surpassed until the late 1970s.

The Aberdonian dominance was broken in 1958 when a raiding Edinburgh party led by a cramponned Jimmy Marshall climbed Parallel Gully B (V) on Lochnagar. This ascent heralded the widespread adoption of crampons, opening up the ice-climbing possibilities, and so causing a swing away from mixed climbing, for which crampons were initially found most ill-suited. Around 1970 there were signs of a mixed revival, but this was quickly extinguished by the front-pointing revolution.

Now steeper, thinner and more watery ice-lines were accessible and, with the whole climbing world enchanted by the speed and efficiency of the new style, mixed climbing again took a back seat. However, throughout this ice-climbing era, the classic mixed routes had maintained some popularity and, with the number of new ice-lines in the Cairngorms relatively limited by its climate, attention inevitably turned once again to the buttresses.

Yet it took a few years for climbers to realise

Fig 64 THAT WEIGHED-DOWN FEELING: HARDWARE FOR MIXED CLIMBING

Recommended racks for a party of two.
It will be noted that considerable affluence as well as ability is needed to tackle the harder modern routes.
These selections are necessarily generalised. Particular types of route may require more or less of each item. They assume that the party is climbing close to its limit of ability and therefore needs whatever protection is available.

Grade	Wired Nuts ('Rocks')	Large Hexentric Chocks	'Friends'	Pitons	Slings	Ice Screws	Karabiners
II–III/IV	1 set from sizes 1–9	Sizes 7–9	Useful but not essential	4–6 of assorted size	3 long (2.5m) 2 short (1m) 3 extensions	1–2 drive-ins (wart-hog) (for turf)	10–16
IV–IV/V	1 set from sizes 1–9	Optional	3 or 4 of sizes between 1 and 3	6–8 of assorted size	2 long 3 short 6 extensions 3 tie-offs	1 drive-in	15–25
V–VI	1 full set plus some extra	Optional (in case cracks are glazed and won't take Friends)	Full set of 5 from size 1 to 3	8–10 of assorted size including leepers and blades	2 long 3 short 8 extensions 4 tie-offs	Rarely of use on very hard routes	18–35

Extensions: short slings for extending runners
Tie-offs: short thin tape (10–12mm width) for tying off pitons

Plate 63 Modern mixed climbing in Glencoe. Rab Anderson leading on the improbable line of Neanderthal (VI), Lost Valley Buttress, during the first ascent in 1986 (*Grahame Nicoll*)

that front-pointing worked efficiently on steep vegetated rock and that at last the standards of the Fifties could be overtaken. The scavenging of all possible new routes soon pushed exploration onto steeper, cleaner and harder rock-climbs. Citadel (VI, summer VS) and The Needle (VI+, summer EI) on Shelter Stone typify the excellent routes climbed in winter during the last decade. Creag an Dubh Loch's giant slabs and overlaps and the fierce Tough-Brown Face on Lochnagar were also targets for the new advance. Crack-climbing with two axes was a logical extension of climbing vegetated cracks by more traditional means. In the Eighties, the novelty of axe torquing has maintained the interest.

Another feature of climbing in the Eighties is an increased spirit of competition, fuelled by the news columns of magazines hungry for new route information. This competition has led to training and a fitter, stronger band of climbers as well as the near extinction of 'easy' new routes, even in the most remote corries. Since most ice streaks that form even occasionally in the Cairngorms have now been climbed, it seems that future new route activity must be pushed onto harder and harder mixed climbs.

EQUIPMENT

In mixed, as in all forms of winter climbing, the ability of the climber is more important than the gear used. This is especially true on the lower-grade mixed climbs where you use your hands a great deal and anything spiky on the feet will suffice. Furthermore, on harder routes the ideal equipment varies considerably with the particular type of climbing encountered. However, there are some modifications of equipment which will pay dividends on all types of mixed routes:

Crampons Shorter front-points are used than in pure ice-climbing in order to reduce the considerable strain on leg muscles when standing on small rock-holds. Vertical second points (as on the traditional Salewa Classic and Everest models) are important. The forward incline on the second points of many models designed for pure snow and ice prevents the crampons from lodging securely on small holds and makes them very clumsy for intricate climbing. Point sharpness does not matter as it does on ice unless thin glaze or verglas is expected. Even if a crampon is sharp at the start of a mixed route, it certainly won't be by the end. Some mountaineers advocate hinged crampons for mixed climbing on the grounds of their extra flexibility to withstand abuse from rocky ground. However, I have always worn a rigid model because of their added support when precariously poised on front-points. In short, the pair of blunt worn crampons you have retired from ice-climbing will probably do fine on all types of mixed ground, save possibly for thin ice.

Esoteric footwear Mixed climbing has always been a shade eccentric in its practice. This is one of its attractions and footwear is no exception. The original success of tricounis in the 1950s encouraged a series of experiments to combine the design advantages of nails and crampons – hence the appearance of 'trampons', which were home-made strap-on tricouni plates, designed by Norman Keir and worn by him on the first winter ascent of Red Guard (V) on Carn Etchachan in 1977. I used them on several routes on the upper tier of Carn Etchachan in 1981–2, and the winter ascent of The Needle (VI) on Shelter Stone Cliff in 1985. The experiment has been discontinued because, although slightly better on some moves (eg, rounded holds and bridging), and slightly worse on others (eg, tiny nicks, horizontal cracks), they are disastrous if you find yourself stranded on thin ice and are ineffectual on turf.

Axes Banana picks are best for all grades of climbing. The extra reach from a longer axe (55cm/22in) can be useful, but it is more tiring to swing than a 50cm (20in) axe. A long axe and a short hammer make a good compromise, but my personal preference is for two 55cm (22in) tools. Wrist-loops should be fairly tight-fitting, either knotted or tightened by a rubber slider, so that axes can be left safely dangling from the wrists on rock moves. Although an advantage to have sharp axes, it is impracticable since they blunt so quickly on rocky mixed ground and regular sharpening will quickly wear the picks out. Personally, I never sharpen my mixed-climbing equipment.

Gloves These should be as thin as your circulation will allow. With thinner gloves, it is less tiring to grip the axes, 'hand on rock' moves are easier, and manipulation of hardwear is simplified. I use thin rubberised gloves (working gloves) for leading hard pitches, when the high effort and grip factor keep the circulation going, and Dachstein mitts for seconding, belaying and easier leads. Some people use ski-gloves, which offer good grip and hand protection, but are surprisingly cold when wet. On lower angled climbs where more loose snow is found, thin gloves are not practicable and Dachstein mitts are more suitable. Climbers with poor circulation will need to wear mitts, unfortunately to their disadvantage, on all routes.

Other items Wear plenty of clothing. However, avoid overtrousers if possible because they limit leg movement and make knee moves slippery. In fine, calm weather, one can advantageously avoid wearing a cagoule on the route. Sweaters or pile jackets offer more friction for wedging and chimney moves, but ultimately keeping warm is the prime concern, and it is easy to underestimate clothing needs when you first arrive at a cliff, hot and steaming after the walk in. On hard or constricted climbs, all spares and kit can be stowed in one rucksack, which is carried by the second, leaving the leader unencumbered and free to climb to the limit.

THE ART OF TORQUING

When climbing at above the grade III level, I find the rock holds too small to be of general use in gloved hands. While individual styles vary, I also believe it a mistake to rely on the hands too much because as you progress up the grades the inventive use of axes becomes increasingly necessary. If axe skills have not been developed, then a plateau of achievement will be reached. In particular, one should make an early start on learning the trick of torquing. Despite being a modern vogue among the avant-garde of winter climbing, torquing is by no means new. Prior to World War I, Geoffrey Winthrop-Young had observed:

One or two guides in the Alps have perfected a remarkable trick. When a vertical or sloping crack in a slab gets too small even to admit a finger, and all other holds are lacking, they force the point of the pick into the crack above their heads, and give a slight outward and upward twist to the shaft with the wrist, so that the point of the pick and its square edges are jammed slantwise and upwards in the crack. Holding the shaft rigid in this position, they then raise their weight by sheer strength inside the bent arm which holds the shaft, at the same time using whatever friction-holds they can find for their feet to help them. A second's cat-like clinging of the feet and of their free hand to the rock gives them just time to thrust the pick further up the crack and twist it firmly in again.[1]

Modern torquing is just as Winthrop-Young described it, except that, with an axe in each hand, the process is considerably less dynamic. One simply leap-frogs the axes alternately up the crack. In general, the narrower and deeper the crack, the more secure the placement. The exact technique depends on the design of your axe and hammer, but nearly every width of crack can be covered:

1 Hairline (under 4mm): Batter the pick into the crack or slot it in above a constriction and use it for a direct downward pull. This does not involve the twisting action of true torquing.
2 Thin (4–15mm): Torque on the inserted pick maintaining a constant sideways pull to hold it in place.
3 Finger (15–30mm): Jam the pick further in, including the head-retaining bolts or weights, and torque, albeit more precariously. This facility depends on an appropriate axe design (Simond Chacals work well).
4 Finger to hand (30–40mm): Slot in the hammer head and pull down to a narrowing or else torque on the inserted hammer head. The success of either ploy depends on the shape of the head, tapered for slotting, square for torquing.
5 Wrist to clenched hand (40–70mm): Use the axe adze, slotting or torquing. A straight adze will work in thinner cracks.
6 Off-width (greater than fist width): As in rock-climbing, this is by far the most awkward width. Improvise (eg, with a pick to adze wedge) or abseil off.

If dependent on torquing, the precise line of the modern mixed route will often seek the best cracks rather than the equivalent summer line which may follow flat rock-holds. The Cairngorms are particularly accommodating in the provision of thin cracks. These are often too thin or outward flared to be of use in summer, but are ideal for torquing.

Plate-steel axe picks are much more flexible (springy) then forged picks such as the Chacal, and offer more bite and security in blind cracks. However, they also bend if battered too hard against blank rock or twisted very violently, but slightly bent picks can be straightened in a vice without ill-effects. I have worn down at least twenty picks of several different makes over the

Fig 65 COMPARISON OF MIXED AND ICE-CLIMBING GRADES

(With typical examples of recommended quality and an approximate horizontal equivalence of modern difficulty)

CLASSIC ICE (Step-cutting First Ascents)		MODERN ICE (Front-pointing First Ascents)		MIXED CLIMBING	
Grade	Examples	Grade	Examples	Grade	Examples
I	No 3 Gully, Ben Nevis			I	Ledge Route, Ben Nevis
II	Gardyloo Gully, Ben Nevis			II	Central Buttress, Lochnagar
III	Crowberry Gully, *Buachaille* Etive Mor			II/III	Castle Ridge, Ben Nevis
III/IV	Green Gully, Ben Nevis			III	Shadow Buttress A, Lochnagar
IV	No 6 Gully, *Aonach* Dubh – Glencoe / The Pumpkin, Creag Meagaidh			III, III/IV	Observatory Ridge, Ben Nevis / East Buttress Ordinary, Beinn Eighe
V	Point Five Gully, Ben Nevis / Minus Two Gully, Ben Nevis	IV	Cascade, Stag Rocks / Umbrella Fall, Liathach	IV, IV/V	Route Major, Carn Etchachan / Savage Slit, *Coire* an Lochain
		V	Minus One Gully, Ben Nevis / Labyrinth Direct, *Creag* an Dubh Loch	V	Eagle Ridge, Lochnagar / Red Guard, Carn Etchachan
		V/VI	Tholl Gate, Fuar Tholl	V/VI	The Link, Lochnagar
		VI	West Central Gully, Beinn Eighe	VI / VI+	Trail of Tears, Lochnagar / The Needle, Shelter Stone

last ten years, yet only broken one.

While experimenting with these techniques, one must expect to fall off occasionally, but they all require cracks and the protection should be good – provided that you remember to put it in. Once mastered and taken to its full potential, torquing opens up an exhilarating new world of hard mixed gymnastics.

GRADES, ETHICS AND CONDITIONS

Because of the widening gap in style between mixed and pure ice-climbing, the grading of mixed climbing has become increasingly distinct over recent years. Furthermore, the traditional mixed routes such as Eagle Ridge have been less affected by front-point technique than the classic ice gullies and thus have retained their difficulty. The grading of modern mixed routes has also tended to be conservative, with the result that the climber used to the classic snow/ice routes will inevitably have greater difficulty on a mixed climb of equivalent grade. Fig 65 gives an approximate comparison between the grades of classic ice routes, modern ice routes and mixed climbs, but it is wrong to infer an exact equivalence, for ice and mixed climbs are quite different in the modern day.

The apparent stiffness of mixed grades has deterred many people from trying the routes. Indeed, it might be said that the present confusion of the grading system suits the Scottish climbing establishment, maintaining the spirit of adventure in our sport, and thwarting the visiting Sassenach climbers. To many, its very eccentricity is part of its charm, like the 'Scottish VS' rock-climbing grade that persisted for so many years.

Might the following explanation help to redress the balance and give a proper guide to the different mixed grades in current usage:

Grades I and II The traditional grades for the classic ridge scrambles such as the Aonach Eagach, these are consistent and clear in their usage.

Grade III The standard grade for the classic ridge climbs, Tower Ridge being the benchmark of the type, ie, Moderate to Difficult rock-climbs rather than scrambles under snow, involving sustained pitches and steep moves where commitment of weight to axes is necessary. They can be much harder under deep soft snow.

Grade III/IV An intermediate grade, often long sustained routes but not sufficiently technical for grade IV.

Grade IV This wide grade represents a psychological jump. Many will quickly reach the III/IV standard but to climb IV requires a commitment to the sport. Most mixed IVs are harder than the classic grade V ice gullies, involving technical moves in an exposed position, climbing onto open steep ground and placing protection in strenuous positions. The shorter the route the more technical is the climbing.

Grade IV/V Such a route usually contains a short, very hard section, normally well protected but requiring modern techniques such as torquing. Often the route itself will be short. Beware that some climbs of this genre are still graded IV.

Grade V Usually Vs are long and sustained, needing modern techniques and a high standard of fitness, plus an element of planning (ie, first light start, finish in darkness, a large rack of gear). The leader will not generally carry a sack. The routes may, however, be well protected.

Grade V/VI The boundary between V and VI is still unclear, so this is a 'hedger's' grade.

Grade VI Only a few of these routes have been led on sight at the first attempt. To have a good chance of success, all conditions must be right, meaning snow, weather and personal preparation together with precise planning.

Conditions are of key importance to all climbers. Choosing a route in good condition can make or break the day. Ethics, on the other hand, are a subject of great debate among first ascensionists and their rivals, but should be only of incidental interest to other climbers who will (quite reasonably) do their best to climb the route in good style, and if this fails will either abseil off or cheat a little to get up. Conditions and ethics overlap in that a sufficient amount of snow has to be determined to justify a 'winter' ascent (as against a rock-climb).

Mixed ascents are often attempted when the ice-climbs are out of condition, usually because of unconsolidated snow, which unfortunately means that less than ideal conditions can be expected, although the routes may still be safely climbable. When, then, is there too much snow? Below grade III, the climbing is usually in balance and, while a little slower in deep snow, may well be no harder. At grade III to IV, climbs are not sufficiently steep for fresh snow to fall off, and both holds and protection cracks will be choked, requiring patient clearing. Moves from walls onto snow-banked ledges become particularly taxing in deep soft snow, and in such conditions it is well to drop a grade from your usual standard. Steeper routes of IV and V are less susceptible to snow accumulation, and their difficulty can be unchanged even after a major blizzard, but this is dependent on the temperature and wind direction during the fall. Even when a cliff is plastered white, it does not necessarily mean poor conditions, for the covering might be of thin hoar frost rather than loose snow.

When is there too little snow? The subjective answer is 'when the route no longer feels like a winter ascent'. This sounds a vague and evasive answer, but in fact, the 'winter' ambience is quickly sensed when you are actually climbing. However, the more specific and widely accepted definition is that a route is in winter condition when it is easier to climb with axes and crampons than with boots and bare hands, which effectively means that all pitches of a climb must have substantial snow or hoar frost on them.

Dubious ethical practices on a mixed ascent are many and varied:

Bivouacing on the route.
Climbing the route first in summer.
Abseil inspection in summer.
Seconds jumaring to save time and energy.
Lowering on the ropes after a fall or failure (yo-yoing).
Clipping into embedded axes for a rest.
Clipping into protection for a rest.
Standing in slings on embedded axes.
Traditional aid moves.
Pre-placing protection/belays in summer.
Sieging (either fixing ropes or abseiling into previous high point).

Opinions vary on the relative merits of an 'on-sight' ascent with the odd rest or aid point, and an all-free ascent of a route thoroughly reconnoitred the previous summer. Sieged ascents are not generally acknowledged in Scotland. Routes should be done in a single push to be credited.

MIXED CLIMBING IN DIFFERENT AREAS OF SCOTLAND

Granite: Cairngorms, Arran

Granite is very suited to mixed climbing. Ledges and lower angled sections are heavily vegetated, as is steeper ground on north-facing crags. The vegetation is usually based on soil, which gives deep and reliable axe placements. Granite joints weather into horizontal and vertical cracks, which offer good protection and torquing possibilities on steep ground. Many of the routes are in remote corries, requiring a prior overnight stay (often in a bothy), have had few ascents, and require more general mountaineering skills than climbs elsewhere.

Andesite: Ben Nevis – Stob Coire nan Lochan, Glencoe

The same rock exhibits quite different formations in the two venues. Ben Nevis's faces are slabby, clean and frequently crackless, and so highly unco-operative to mixed techniques. Of course, the Ben has the magnificent classic ridges – Castle, Tower, Observatory and North-East Buttress – and these routes give many their first taste of mixed climbing. Some of the face routes become mixed in style if the ice is thin or absent (eg, Route 2 on Carn Dearg Buttress). A notable recent ascent which is genuinely mixed in character is Centurion, the summer Hard VS crack-line which splits the Carn Dearg Buttress. This was climbed as far as its junction with Route 2, which was then used to finish, at grade VI, in February 1986.

By contrast, the andesite of Stob Coire nan Lochan is columnar in structure, well cracked and vegetated on its ledges, sporting soaring groove lines of magnetic appeal, and offering sensationally steep winter climbing. Central Grooves and Unicorn (grade VI) are two of Scotland's finest modern mixed routes.

Rhyolite: Glencoe – eg, Buachaille Etive Mor; Gabbro: Skye

Although clean and poorly cracked, and thus frequently unhelpful to the mixed climber, the rock of the Buachaille Etive Mor has yielded several hard routes, Guerdon Grooves (VI) on the impressive Slime Wall being the most notable strike of recent years. The Buachaille also has several classic easy routes to satisfy the mountaineering instinct, most notably Curved Ridge and North Buttress. The great chimney lines on the North Face of the Aonach Dubh are now coming into their winter maturity. Dank, dark and slimy, this forbidding cliff satisfies the modern mixed climber's tastes to perfection.

The potential of Skye has been little explored,

but there is an obvious want of vegetation on the clean gabbro, and a lack of reliable conditions.

Schist: Beinn an Dothaidh, Ladhar Bheinn, Creag Meagaidh, Fannichs

Many crags in the Central Western and Southern Highlands are schist, which tends to be very heavily vegetated, thus offering much scope for mixed climbing, particularly in the middle and lower grades. The climbing can be rather repetitive (turf, turf and more turf), but there are dozens of schist crags to be explored on quiet mountains away from the regular winter-climbing trail. However, on Creag Meagaidh, the buttresses lack distinction compared to the famous ice-lines.

Torridonian Sandstone: Beinn Bhan, Fuar Tholl, Liathach, An Teallach

Sandstone forms extremely steep tiers split by horizontal terraces which are generously vegetated. The rock is alternately blank and compact, and cracked and blocky. Mixed routes are variable in quality. Some are spoilt by their blatant escapability along the terraces, or else are imbalanced in standard with short vicious pitches through the tiers linking long meandering sections on the ledges. However, there are many good turfy lines on the easier buttresses and some excellent harder routes are being found where continuous lines are offered, the 450m (1,500ft) Die Riesenwand on the Coire an Fhamair headwall, Beinn Bhan (V) epitomising the bewildering exposure and devious route-finding of the best sandstone routes.

Quartzite: Beinn Eighe

Quartzite is very steep and blocky, with plentiful square-cut foot-holds and often good cracks, but little vegetation (or ice). There is good climbing in the higher grades. The Triple Buttress of Coire Mhic Fhearchair is the most Alpine of Scottish cliffs, its three great prows being among the finest Scottish mixed routes, particularly the grade V Central Buttress. Harder routes are now being established on the intervening walls.

A FINAL NOTE FOR POSTERITY

I conclude this chapter with heavy eyes and an aching back, still in an advanced state of physical destruction, although it is now four days since an epic climb on Shelter Stone Crag with Andy Cunningham. So I'm in no need of reminding of the commitment and effort of top-level mixed climbing, nor of a prediction for the future of this branch of winter mountain sport. In 1961 Jimmy Marshall prophesied the winter routes of tomorrow: 'they will be rock-climbs under hellish conditions'.[2]

It was a comment made with considerable foresight, for nearly thirty years later it still holds true. And if, as I suspect, the big unclimbed lines in the Cairngorms all involve pitch after pitch like those on Postern Direct, then I wish the next generation all good luck. Their effort will be great but the rewards immense:

Reaching out from under the roof I can lodge my hammer between two loose stones wedged across a vertical 15cm corner crack, which soars up unremittingly for 9m. With axe hooked over my hammer head, these two stones must take my whole weight . . . Andy ducks as the stones rip out and hurtle past his stance, then holds me as I too hurtle into space. I dangle from the runners. We just can't fail here 250m up the Shelter Stone Cliff in a raging blizzard and just 20m from the top. So I switch on tunnel vision, and once more launch out . . .

But equally, the classic routes established over the last decades will be there to offer challenge, pleasure and variety at every standard of mixed climbing to both beginner and expert, and the Scottish weather can with surprising regularity smile kindly as we climb in the high Cairngorms.

could be practised on the prepared pistes and then transferred to the more demanding off-piste conditions, albeit with some loss of style on the way. The graceful telemark was a rarity, the Alpine techniques of snow plough and stem christiana the norm, with the exciting parallel the preserve of the experts.

Then came the arrival of what could be termed the Nordic package deal. Boots, skis and sticks for use with Nordic techniques were offered at bargain prices and advertised as 'instant' skiing. Waxing, hitherto a troublesome esoteric chore with traces of the occult, no longer was necessary. The fish-scale ski base that helped the ski grip when climbing yet hardly affected the amateur's downhill performance was widely marketed. 'Slide one way, stick the other, and away you go,' was the message. Nordic as an alternative form of skiing was seized upon much as the alternative life-style and diet. It had the air of being different, a sort of home-grown simplistic style. It also encompassed a regard for the environment that has put Nordic skiers firmly in the conservationist ranks.

This renewed interest stimulated advancement of the true Nordic techniques, which now have an important position in the Scottish skiing world at both recreational and competition levels. The cheap primitive package deals that created a wide following, yet did the skills of the sport no real good, are a thing of the past. Equipment has been adapted and modified to cope with the variance of Scottish conditions, and in particular to meet the growing desire to ski the high tops and plateaux. Meanwhile, Alpine-style touring has seen a steady growth in popularity and improvement of gear and techniques, together with a more radical diversion into steep gully skiing.

The basic 'lean on the pole' technique of Zdarsky's day has now passed. The skills of skiing, be it Alpine or Nordic, that are favoured are now very refined, as is the equipment used by both schools. Each camp has its adherents, each has its place in the Scottish winter wilderness, and either could prove Raeburn's early doubts on the suitability of Scotland's hills for ski-touring to be wrong.   AH

MODERN NORDIC GEAR

Skis

The large temperature fluctuations around zero

Plate 64 Nordic gear, showing the contrast between lightweight low-level/racing kit (top) and mountain touring equipment (bottom); in particular the vibram-soled mountain boot, 3-pin binding and metal-edged ski (*Helen Charlton*)

which we experience in Scotland dictate a steel-edged ski. Scotland admittedly can be a skier's nightmare, with rapid periods of thaw followed by refreezing, not to mention the effects of wind. Skis without steel edges are difficult to handle in these icy or crusted snow conditions.

Because Nordic skis tend to be narrower than Alpine skis, the bearing surface area is reduced – which is why they are usually used in longer lengths than Alpine skis. As a rule of thumb, for Nordic mountain-touring, you need a ski which is about 20–5cm (8–10in) taller than you. If you are very heavily built, then you will need a longer ski in order to bear your weight. Even if you are fairly small, don't forget to take the weight of your pack into account.

Typical Nordic mountain-touring skis have widths of around 65, 55 and 60mm (2½, 2 and 2¼in) at tip, waist and tail, making them considerably lighter than Alpine skis and giving about

Fig 66 NORDIC FLEX AND CAMBER

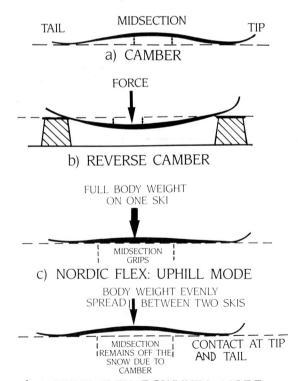

TAIL **MIDSECTION** **TIP**

a) CAMBER

FORCE

b) REVERSE CAMBER

FULL BODY WEIGHT
ON ONE SKI

MIDSECTION
GRIPS

c) NORDIC FLEX: UPHILL MODE

BODY WEIGHT EVENLY
SPREAD BETWEEN TWO SKIS

MIDSECTION
REMAINS OFF THE
SNOW DUE TO
CAMBER

CONTACT AT TIP
AND TAIL

d) NORDIC FLEX: DOWNHILL MODE

10mm (½in) of side cut in the waisted mid-section. The side cut produces an arc along the edge of the ski and interacts with the ski flex to give the ski its turning properties.

Ski flex needs to be thought of in relation to the *camber* (Fig 66) of Nordic skis. If you lie a Nordic ski on the ground, you will see that the mid-section is up in the air. This denotes the camber of the ski. When you are skiing, you will flatten out the camber with your weight. The degree to which you can do this will depend on the flex, or stiffness, of the skis.

When turning, you want not only to be able to flatten the ski, but actually to force it into *reverse camber* (ie, with the tips raised above the mid-section). The more flexible the ski, the easier it is to pressure it into reverse camber. When a ski is on its edge and pressed down, it assumes an arced curve, formed by the interaction of the side cut and the reverse camber. It is this arced curve which allows you to turn easily. All *you* have to do is to get the ski onto its edge; get the camber into reverse and the ski does the rest. The ski makes a carved turn.

If the skis do not have side cut, or if you do not edge them properly, or if they are so stiff that you cannot get them into reverse camber, then the skis will not carve. They will still turn, but they will skid round. This will be a combination of side-slipping with rotation of the skis. In poor snow conditions, you will tend to fall down if you are skidding, for your skis will wash out sideways. You are more likely to remain in control if you carve your turns.

The ability to carve your turns is the reason why you must make sure that a ski for mountain touring has got about 10mm (½in) of side cut and that it will go into reverse camber for you. You should test the flex of the ski by setting the tail of the ski firmly on the floor and grabbing the tip

19 (*right*) Lost in the gothic architecture of Beinn Eighe's Triple Buttress. Victor Saunders edging round an awkward step on the first winter ascent of the Upper Girdle Traverse (Their line of steps can be seen on the snow terrace behind) (*Mick Fowler*)

with one hand. Use the other hand to push the ski in the middle. You should be able to flatten the ski and then push it through into reverse camber. If the skis flex into a smooth arc, then this ski will turn for you.

The wider the ski, the better it will cope in 'crud' (sticky wet snow) and crust. This would be true of powder, too. Wider skis are also stronger, which may be worth considering for longer, more serious tours, but the beauty of Nordic skiing is the lightness of the equipment and, of course, the wider the ski the heavier it is.

A unique and essential feature of Nordic skis is that they can be flattened when your weight is all on one foot, so that the mid-section grips when you are skiing uphill, yet have sufficient camber that the mid-section remains off the ground when your weight is distributed evenly between the skis, as when sliding downhill in a 'schuss'. They have what is known as *Nordic flex* (Fig 66). Therefore, a Nordic flex ski can have its mid-section fish-scaled or waxed for uphill grip without impairing downhill glide. This avoids the need for heavy drag-producing skins on moderate hills and enables continuous travel on undulating ground.

By contrast, skis with *Alpine flex* are more easily pressed together, the whole base flattening as one, so that, in downhill mode, the entire length of the sole is in contact with the snow. Grip waxing or fish-scaling would therefore make downhill performance slow and 'snatchy'. As a result, Alpine touring ski bases must be kept smooth, and thus require adhesive skins for climbing.

However, the stiff centre section of a Nordic flex ski tends to make a flat spot in the ski when you make downhill turns. So a ski with Alpine flex will give better turning properties. There are some Alpine flex Nordic skis on the market which are usually termed *telemark skis*, but unfortu-nately are rather more expensive than the Nordic flex Nordic skis.

On steeper hills, a waxed or fish-scale base on a Nordic flex ski will not provide enough grip to climb, so the stiff centre section is no longer of effect, and one must use climbing skins, or else make endless zig-zag manoeuvres. It is therefore recommended that, when touring in mountainous terrain, skins are carried with Nordic skis.

Bindings

The binding system which will satisfy all the needs of Scottish touring is the 75mm (3in) Rottefella Super Telemark. This is a traditional three-pin 75mm (3in) Nordic Norm binding with a flat steel bail and a serrated boot-gripping strip, which runs from the binding body about half-way to the heel plate, which is also serrated.

Boots

Boots should match the robustness of the skis. They should have reinforced 75mm (3in) Nordic Norm pinholes and be warm and waterproof with leather uppers and vibram soles. Good Nordic mountain-touring boots will have the same features as a good mountaineering boot. Additionally, the soles should have good lateral stiffness for control in turning and should have a heel groove for use with cable bindings. Gaiters are as essential as in general mountaineering. Also, the best modern boots have quick-drying linings, suich as Cambrelle, which are a real boon in Scotland.

Poles

Strong but light aluminium poles with large robust baskets are essential. More and more Nordic tourers are turning to adjustable models, some of which even convert into avalanche probes. Pole length should be about 10cm (4in) longer than for Alpine skiing. They should fit just under the armpit with the tip on the ground.

20 (*left*) The soaring line of Central Grooves (VI), one of the magnificent hard mixed routes on Stob Coire nan Lochan, Glencoe. Murray Hamilton leading the second pitch (*Rab Anderson*)

FISH-SCALE AND WAXED SKIS COMPARED

A never-ending argument rages among Nordic skiers over the merits and demerits of waxable skis

Fig 67 A WAXING CHART FOR THE FULL RANGE OF NORDIC SKI WAXES

HARD WAX TYPE	Temperature	Wax Consistency	Snow Type
Polar	−18°C (0°F)	Hard	Fresh and fine granular
Special green			Fresh and old granular
Green	−10°C (14°F)		Fresh and old snow
Extra green			Fresh and fine grained
Special blue			Fresh and fine grained
Blue	−5°C (23°F)		Fine grained older
Extra blue			Fine grained older
Special purple	0°C (32°F)		Variable wet dry
Purple			Variable wet dry
Extra purple			Falling and new
Special red			Falling and new
Red			Slightly wet
Extra red			Wet or new melted by sun
Yellow	+5°C (41°F)	Soft	Moist wet new
KLISTER			
Green	Very cold	Hard	Ice
Blue	−5°C (23°F)		Ice
Purple	Around 0°C (32°F)		Damp, corn (spring) snow
Special red	0°C to + 2°C (32°F–35.6°F)		Wet, corn (spring) snow
Red	Above 0°C (32°F)		Wet snow
Silver	Above 0°C (32°F)		Wet, dirty snow
Yellow	+14°C (57°F)	Soft	Wet, new snow

for Nordic touring compared to the waxless fish-scale type.

On sustained steep ground, there is no problem. Whatever the type of ski, Nordic mountain tourers should use climbing skins to go up and have the full length of their skis glide-waxed for the descents. No grip-wax is necessary.

However, on ridges, plateaux and undulating terrain, the snow may vary from fine dry powder, to wind-slab, to solid ice, to wet crud and crust, and all can be encountered in the course of a day. The selection of a suitable wax to handle these sudden variations is almost impossible and the convenience of a waxless ski is an advantage.

Three main types of waxless base are suitable for mountain-touring skis: hair strip (mohair); pattern (fish-scale) and composite material (mica based). In general, the fish-scale base has wider application and suits most purposes, except very dry snow and ice. The fish-scale patterns are either cut out of, or raised up from, the base, to look like roof tiles, fish-scales or grooves. There is a common misconception that fish-scale skis require no preparation, but to keep the skis turning well on descent, the bases should be sprayed regularly with a proprietary fish-scale base spray, and the smooth tip and tail sections should be prepared regularly with glide-wax.

However, unless the camber of the skis is very finely tuned to the skier, there will be friction from the fish-scale pattern on descents which will make the skis slow. Slow skis can be exhausting and dispiriting and they are considerably more difficult to turn. Furthermore, it must be remembered that the pattern will wear gradually, reducing uphill grip and diminishing the useful life of the ski compared to a waxable model.

Using waxable skis gives you a wider range of options. Most simply, you can glide-wax the full length of your waxable skis ready for the downhills and skin up all the major inclines, heaving up on your arms on any short uphills once you have taken off your skins.

A refinement on this which will cope with most Scottish conditions is to use skins for the major climbing sections and prepare the bases of your waxable skis to make them 'waxless'. To do this, you should glide-wax the tip and tail section leaving the mid-section from the heel plate to about 15cm (6in) in front of the three pins free of wax. Take some fine sandpaper to this mid-section and rub it lightly round and round in a circular motion. This will produce a do-it-yourself grip effect ('microschuppe'), which will work very well in a variety of snow conditions.

You may, however, wish to venture into grip-waxing the mid-section. Sophisticated waxing is finely controlled by snow temperatures (see Fig 67), but is rarely effective in variable Scottish conditions. To simplify matters, most waxing companies produce a basic two-wax system, one for above freezing-point and one for below. These waxes come in blocks or in tubs and should be crayoned on thinly to the mid-section, then rubbed in with a cork. If the wax does not grip, put it on a little longer and a little thicker. Use these waxes for new snow or snow that has not altered since falling.

Klister wax is used for old snow which has changed. In Scotland this would usually mean that it has melted and refrozen. Klister comes in tubes like toothpaste and should be smeared on the mid-section carefully and then be spread out thinly using the spreader provided with the tube.

So, all you need for simple waxing in Scotland is a two-wax system, a tube of universal klister, a can of wax-removing liquid with some old rags and two corks. You should clean your ski bases at the end of each day of Scottish skiing, as they will probably be stuck up with pieces of heather and grit.

Many skiers will suggest to you that it is wisest to get fish-scale skis for your first pair of touring skis and keep an eye on your friends with waxable skis. Then, when it comes to buying your second pair, you will know straightaway whether or not waxing seems a good idea for the type of routes that you have enjoyed.

NORDIC TECHNIQUES

It is foolhardy to think that just because you have walked in an area, you will be able to ski the same ground when it is covered in snow. All hill-touring, be it Alpine or Nordic, is an athletic and skilful pursuit. Anyone wanting to Nordic ski in Scotland's winter mountains must first serve an apprenticeship on the lower slopes by tackling Nordic light touring in the forests and on prepared tracks, and preferably by going to a recognised Nordic ski school for a series of lessons with qualified instructors.

If you are used to downhill Alpine skiing, you will have to modify your techniques on a number of fronts in order to enjoy Nordic touring. First, when Nordic skiing, there is nothing holding down your heels. On your downhill skis you will be able to make big forward and backward movements and be held securely by your boots and bindings. The same movement on Nordic skis is likely to end as a head-plant or flying buttocks arrest. So you have to work to maintain your balance, which requires leg strength and skill.

It is important to adopt a low, stable stance to overcome this balance problem. The hands should be held low and forward; the ankles and knees should be flexed and the skis kept at hip-width apart. This wide, stable stance can be further refined by skiing with one foot slightly advanced of the other (as in the traverse position). This will give a firm platform from which to absorb the vagaries of snow and terrain. By keeping your speed under control and using this stable stance, you need not lose your balance.

Many downhill skiers think that because their heels are not clamped down, they will not be able to make turning movements, but with the right gear there need be no problem. The boot will be held firmly by the three-pin binding and the lateral stiffness of the boot means that it will not twist or slip off the plate. So, it is possible to execute any manoeuvre in the downhill skier's

repertoire, with the added advantage of being able to perform the famous loose-heeled turn – *the telemark*.

However, because of the stability problem, a Nordic skier does not have the leeway for recovering from errors that downhill equipment affords, so your technique cannot be sloppy. Secondly, if your skis have Nordic flex, you will have to make more vigorous movements to get the skis into reverse camber for turning than you would with an Alpine flex ski. So this means that your edging and weighting has to be that bit more precise than on downhill skis. You will find skiing easier if you make pronounced weight shifts in order to execute a turning movement on Nordic flex skis. The easiest way to do this is literally to step from one ski to the other in exaggerated movements.

For safe and enjoyable descents, all the skier needs to be able to do is to ski a traverse in a shallow line, with an exaggerated low stance, then change direction to take up a new traverse. When the snow conditions are bad, this direction change is best made by stepping up the hill and coming to a halt. You should then perform an outward-facing *kick turn*. In slightly better snow, a *stem turn* can be used. From your traverse position, raise up and stem out your uphill ski, rolling your uphill ankle inwards at the same time. Transfer all your weight onto this stemmed-out ski and throw your upper body-weight straight down the slope at the same time. This should get the stemmed-out ski into reverse camber, so that it will carve round, bringing the unweighted ski around with it onto the new traverse. The stem turn should be performed at low or moderate speeds.

Another useful turn for poor snow is the *jump turn*. It can be used in very heavy snow, in sastrugi (wind ridges), in breakable crust and in narrow channels where width of snow-cover is limited. Start from the traverse and plant your downhill pole at your side, with a slight lowering of the hips. This acts as the trigger for the turn. Then explode upwards, out of your boots, lifting both your skis off the snow and turning them when they are in the air. Land lightly in your new traverse position, rolling your ankles up the slope and flexing your knees as you land.

Many skiers will prefer just to step or jump onto one ski, as this is less athletic. This is the telemark turn and is where Nordic gear comes into its own. From your traverse position, plant your downhill pole at your side, as before, then literally step your uphill ski straight down the fall-line. Immediately pick up your other ski to avoid remaining in an awkward right angle, bringing it nearly parallel to the other ski, with considerable weight on it. Now, sink down low, with your ankles rolled up the slope. This should have brought you into the classic telemark position (Plate 66) with the ski which you stepped round in the lead.

Armed with a sound traverse position and the kick turn, the stem turn, the jump turn and the step telemark, the Nordic skier will be able to negotiate almost any snow at almost any angle – given the patience and practice to master the manoeuvres. As all these turns require a radical weight shift, any skier used to skiing on groomed pistes may find them rather difficult at first on hill country.

Uphill techniques for the mountain tourer are a matter of personal strength and body build. It is worth practising the uphill kick turn, so that you can execute a zig-zag ascent fluidly without losing rhythm and wasting energy. On flats and gentle uphills, the easiest way to progress is to skate from one ski to the other, making a complete weight transfer at each stride and planting your poles for extra thrust. Use your arms in whatever way seems natural to you. When you get tired of skating, just stand and punt along with both your poles. If you bend over at the waist as you punt, this will stretch your back muscles, which may get rather tired on a long day out with a heavy pack. If you do manage to keep your balance and use a complete weight transfer in your skate, you will be amazed how you eat up the miles. It is a technique which is definitely worth practising.

Plate 65 The Nordic stance (*Sylvia Dowse*)

Plate 66 Helen Charlton demonstrating the telemark turn (*Maggie Worth*)

Plate 67 Skating uphill on Nordic skis (*Helen Charlton*)

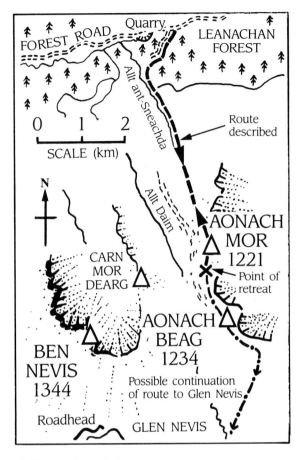

Map labels: FOREST ROAD, Quarry, LEANACHAN FOREST, Allt ant-Sneachda, Route described, 0 1 2, SCALE (km), N, Allt Daim, AONACH MOR 1221, Point of retreat, CARN MOR DEARG, AONACH BEAG 1234, BEN NEVIS 1344, Possible continuation of route to Glen Nevis, Roadhead, GLEN NEVIS

A Day on Aonach Mor

Threats to develop Aonach Mor as a downhill ski area make it seem important to ski this, and its neighbouring peak of Aonach Beag, while they are still the winter preserve of the committed ski-tourer. The prevailing wind suggests a northern starting point from Leanachan Forest. The snow-line is disappointingly high at about 600m, and the cloud hovers menacingly. A few weak blue patches come and go in the greyness above. The prospects do not seem encouraging.

We park the van just beyond the limestone works in Leanachan Forest. Our skis strapped onto the sides of our rucksacks, we stride up through the forest paths and onto the moorland by the Allt an t-Sneachda. Following up the burn, we reach the first threads of snow. It is beautiful, firm snow, the sort of stuff you dream about having for your April trips in Norway.

Yet here we are in Scotland . . . I can't believe our luck!

We have a steady climb of over 600m onto the summit of Aonach Mor. At first there are one or two bits of grass-skiing, but eventually we reach continuous snow, gaining height easily on our skins.

Each of us ascends in a private world at a personal pace, but higher up we unite, for the cloud base has dropped suddenly and we can only see for about 20m. We stop and work out a strategy. The shoulder of Aonach Mor is flat where we are, yet drops steeply to the east, and even more steeply to the west into the Allt Daim valley. Memories of a trip just a few weeks earlier are still fresh. Then some cliffs 'appeared sooner' than they should have done; so now we play safe. Sylvia skis ahead on a bearing until reaching the limit of sight, when the rest of us leap-frog up to her.

Progress is frustratingly slow. We seem to be getting nowhere. Surely we should be on the summit of Aonach Mor by now? Yes – we are dropping down. Or are we? It is eerie. We can see nothing, hear nothing. We cannot tell what the gradient is. Where is the fall-line? We take off our skins. Our skis now seem to have minds of their own.

We must be to the south of Aonach Mor summit. Another pow-wow. We have got plenty of time to go on to Aonach Beag, but what's the point? We will make slow progress. The cloud will prevent us from skiing the downhill stretches except in tiny short legs. No swooping descents for today.

What a tragedy – for the snow is perfect. Nothing needs to be said. We turn and retrace our steps. I am out in the front now; going at a snail's pace in an enormous plough in readiness to stop at any sudden danger.

Then there is a whoop of delight from behind me. I turn. The cloud has soared and the colours are so vivid that I cannot believe that they are real. Brilliant sunshine pierces through. We dash to our left to marvel at the sight of 'The Ben' wreathed in a swirling, ever-changing pattern of cloud. Shafts of brilliant light dance over its top. We gaze across the cliffs of the western flank of Aonach Mor. We look far into the distance over Corpach and Loch Eil and then out over the hills of Lochaber to the north and east.

What a panorama, and not another person is to be seen apart from ourselves. A moderate wind, beautiful snow, temperature just below zero. What more could you want? Only a full day of it, rather than a few hours!

I am getting cold lingering over the views, so we must get going. But shall we go up again and on to Aonach Beag, with the risk that the cloud could drop; or shall we continue homewards?

The prospect of an instant perfect run of 500m down off Aonach Mor is too much of a lure. If the cloud drops again, we could miss it, and besides we need to get out of the wind. We are off, each skiing as fast as we dare. The snow is so good that parallels are no problem, even with our heavy day-sacks.

This is exhilarating stuff. Eventually, we drop out of the wind and the snow softens to a perfect consistency for telemark practice. We have still got a good hour of skiing time left. So we telemark down and skate back up a huge empty hillside until our legs are burning and we call it a day. No matter that our intended route was abandoned on grounds of safety, for ultimately the weather and snow were kind. We get back to the van pleasantly tired and contented, and we have even had the chance to improve our technique.   HC

ALPINE EQUIPMENT

It is perfectly possible to make simple tours using ordinary downhill ski equipment and this method may be used to introduce beginners to touring or to get away from the crowds on a piste skiing day. Before you do this, however, normal precautions dictated by mountaineering experience should be taken and the outing treated as any other hill expedition.

On a fine windless day, when the snow surface is soft, downhill skis and boots may be sufficient. The uphill sections can be walked with the skis carried across a shoulder or strapped to a rucksack and normal hill-walking boots can be used to reach the snow-line if it is far. But if there is névé or ice about, crampons and axe will be needed, and if visibility is anything but perfect, then it is best left to another day.

Plate 68 Alpine touring gear – boots, heel lift bindings and harcheisen (*Alan Hunt*)

To go on to fully explore the Alpine ski-mountaineering experience, a considerable amount of additional specialist equipment will be needed. At prices in force in the winter of 1988, a set of Alpine ski-mountaineering equipment would cost in the region of £400 to put together, so unless you have unlimited funds, it is worth making sure you get the right equipment at the outset.

Boots

I put these first above all the other items because if you get it right, life is good, but get it wrong and life will be hell. Most well-known ski-boot manufacturers offer special designed ski-mountaineering boots, but unfortunately the full range and choice is not readily available in the UK. The best time to see a decent range is during the April/May touring season in the larger Alpine centres. If you are unable to purchase your boots abroad, it is a good idea before buying to have a look at the current range used for touring courses at Glenmore Lodge centre.

The boots will at best be a compromise between a downhill boot and an ordinary mountain boot. I prefer a boot that offers stiffness and support for skiing rather than sacrificing these points for walking comfort. The modern construction of a plastic shell and separate inner boot allows almost complete freedom from constriction when they are unclipped for walking, yet can provide excellent support when adjusted to the downhill mode. A broad foot can be a problem because plastic boots do not stretch, yet feet expand when warm, so allow for this when choosing your size. The boot should have a vibram-type sole and be sufficiently broad to allow edging when crossing steep slopes on foot, something the narrow parallel sole of a normal ski boot does not allow.

A recent development of interest is the fitting of full-width vibram soles to normal downhill ski boots. The Salomon rear-entry boot seems to be particularly suited to this and it could be a modification that lends itself to other types of downhill boots. Do ensure that the ski anti-friction plate on the bindings still operates if you have this boot adaptation.

Skis

Conventional downhill skis can be used effectively for touring and some people prefer this option because of the better performance on descent. A moderately stiff downhill ski, such as a *giant slalom* (GS) type, will give good control on icy ground, yet be sufficiently responsive in varied snow conditions. It can also be used to full advantage for recreational downhill skiing.

However, mountain touring often involves skiing ground that has rocks lurking below the snow ready to tear at the plastic running surface of the skis. Added to this is the desire to get as far down the mountain as possible on skis with the inevitable linking of snow patches to cross heather and rock-strewn ground. This will play havoc with the sleek racing-type base of a good piste ski. Also, downhill skis are designed to perform at their best at a given length in relation to a skier's weight, usually in the region of 190–210cm (75–82in), but in the off-piste conditions common to touring, with many varieties of snow and the need to make kick turns on steep slopes, a long ski can be a disadvantage.

An alternative is to use a so-called 'mid' length or *compact* ski designed for mid-ability downhill skiers. These tend to be shorter for a given weight and easier to turn in varied snow, but not so good on icy ground and slower and less stable on straight runs.

The *specialist mountain-touring* skis that are available today tend towards offering the downhill performance of GS piste skis on a somewhat shorter length, ie 175–195cm (69–77in). They will have a tough running surface that sacrifices gliding properties for durability on the rocks and a bright reflective colour incorporated to assist in locating them if they are buried. Metal or carbon fibre will be used in the construction to ensure strength and lightness. A broken ski on a long tour can be more than an inconvenience. A notched tail and a single perforation at each end to assist in the fitting of skins or making an emergency stretcher are now common.

Bindings

The modern ski-mountaineering binding is highly sophisticated, robust in construction and incor-

Plate 69 Changing mode: stripping skins off Alpine touring skis ready for the descent (*Alan Hunt*)

porates a modern safety-release system when in the uphill or downhill mode. The practical points to consider are:

1 The availability of basic spares – buy them when you first acquire the bindings and carry them with you on the hill.
2 Can you get in and out of them reasonably easily with a rucksack and using gloved hands?
3 Is the change of mode from uphill to downhill easily operated?
4 They must have strong safety straps with an equally strong attachment point to the ski. 'Ski stoppers' are for the piste only. A lost ski when touring cannot be contemplated.
5 They should allow for the ready fitting of harcheisen (ski crampons). These are essential on hard névé for ascending anything but the easiest gradients.
6 They should not freeze up and thus prevent a smooth change of mode.
7 Although not essential, an incorporated step device that keeps the heel raised for climbing steep slopes can be useful.

Simple binding maintenance at home may save endless trouble on the hill. Check the fixing screws regularly and apply a thread sealant if they are working loose. Also check the proper operation of the release system, adjusting and lubricating as necessary.

Sticks

You will see all sorts of sticks in use on the hills: sophisticated telescopic models, extra long for greater support when climbing, extra large baskets for greater support in soft snow, shafts tacky taped below the grip to allow for a varied hand position, even extra hand-loops to compensate on a traverse. Practice will help you decide which to adopt, but all sticks must be strong and the metal type are normally to be preferred.

Skins

Brushed-nylon skins are essential for uphill travel. Make sure they are the same width as your skis. Skins come in different lengths, so cut them down if they are too long – 2cm (¾in) shorter than the ski at the tail is about right – and round the corners off at the tails to help them to stay in place. Some have adjustable tensioning straps to keep the skin in place, but more commonly they are of the 'stick-on' variety. I have used the adhesive type for many years without any problems by taking the following precautions:

1 Well-glued skins are similar to the old fly-papers that used to hang up at ceiling level.

They collect all sorts of bits and pieces, and every effort should be made to keep them as clean as possible by scraping off this and any snow with a knife before storing them away, the tails and tips being folded to the middle.

2 When on a tour, keep the skins in a warm place on your body and they will stick more readily when the time comes to use them.

3 Clean and dry the ski base thoroughly before applying the skins. A strip of old towel is good for this. Press the skin down hard from tip to tail, being particularly thorough at the tail. If you do have trouble here, a piece of cycle inner tube or first-aid plaster will stop the problem until you can effect a proper cure.

4 Dry the skins at the end of the tour as soon as you can, preferably off the skis and folded as before, and scrape off all the bits of glue, etc that have been left on your ski sole and would otherwise spoil your downhill glide.

5 Reglue the skins periodically when they start to lose their stick, but do this well before you next wish to use them. Special replacement glue is available for this purpose. Apply it sparingly but thoroughly in a warm atmosphere, paying careful attention to the tail of the skin.

To get maximum life from the skins, avoid skinning over rocks and fit harcheisen in good time on icy surfaces.

Repair Kit
This need only be a 'get-you-home' type kit. Pliers, wire, a spare basket and sticky tape should do the trick, with the addition of epoxy glue and a screwdriver for multi-day trips.

ALPINE TECHNIQUES

We had carried the skis up to the Monadh Liath plateau, north of Laggan. The sunny south-facing slopes had many thawed brown patches, linked by névé and icy strips at this early hour. It was to be a taster of ski mountaineering on a fine spring day. We had walking boots on our feet, plastic ski boots in the sacks and skis strapped under the lid. Skiing and mountaineering experience in the party ranged widely. Some of us had piste skied a fair bit, some not so much, but all could manage a fairly controlled snow plough turn. Some of us had fifty-plus Munros behind us in winter plus a spread of ice-climbs. Others had no more than a dozen plus a bit of ice-axe braking practice and had seldom used crampons in anger.

On the tops the surface was in perfect condition, an inch or two of fresh snow that had come down overnight on a firm consolidated base with only occasional deeper drift areas and icy patches. I congratulated myself on the choice of situation and was equally pleased on our luck with such good weather for this introduction to the sport. The undulating summit plateau meant we could travel with minimum skill, absorbing to the full the splendid isolation of this area and the emotive views it affords of the deer forests of Ben Alder, Drumochter and Gaick against the southern sky.

I had chosen a sheltered shallow gully bowl for our final descent, in the prevailing lee of a spur fingering out from the plateau. With a northerly aspect it should hold snow far down and, with luck, we might be able to ski to the road. And, as a final bonus to the day, it looked as though the snow was virgin and we would be able to make our own tracks, a satisfying and egotistic off-piste skiing experience. For the less able, there was plenty of space for long easy angled traverses with linked kick turns.

We set off. The first plunging falls were accompanied by shrieks of laughter as the stucco figures clawed their way out of the deep drifts and mantelshelved back onto the raft of their skis. They continued an increasingly fragmented, exhausting and demoralising progress valleywards. The better skiers managed a fair degree of control, but it was all so different from skiing the piste. The rucksack weight upset the delicate mid-balance position and further exacerbated the problem of regaining a position of attack on the skis after a fall. The varied snow texture meant that one ski would suddenly diverge from the intended path. The snake-like powder tracks we had dreamt of began to seem elusive as their precursor. The inexorable cycle of defeat began earlier for the less able skiers. Confidence declined and fatigue increased in ratio to expertise. Anger, frustration and bad language replaced the earlier good-humoured shrieks.

The better skiers made it all the way and were able to look back to see their tracks interspersed with the rambling trails and excavations of the others, who arrived in depressed relief glad to be down but far from happy. The natural mountaineers had long since returned to their preferred mode of travel, shouldered their skis and begun the leg-sucking wade through the drifts. I went back to the drawing-board to go over the plans.

'One must recognise mistakes and poor judgement in order to profit by them or one is doomed to repeat them in the future,' Rob Taylor wrote after a harrowing mountaineering accident in Kilimanjaro, when he narrowly escaped with his life. Luckily, we too escaped without any serious consequences, but it could have been so different and we did profit from the experience:

1 Strong mountaineers do not necessarily make good ski mountaineers. Skiing ability is usually more important and is the key to pleasurable progress down the hill.
2 Mountaineering judgement and criteria are not necessarily the same in the ski-mountaineering context. Who would choose to walk down the drift-filled lee valley which we had skied?
3 Skiing off the piste with a rucksack in variable snow is more demanding than on similar angled groomed slopes and requires practice to raise the skill level. Different snow requires different techniques (see Fig 68), and experience will help dictate the best method, whether it be extra edge on ice or 'traverse, kick turn, traverse' in breaking crust.

On this occasion, as by far the most experienced skier in the group, I should have skied an easy line

Fig 68 ALPINE DOWNHILL TOURING TECHNIQUES	
Technical Manoeuvre	Applications
Side-slipping – no turns.	Safest way of losing height on steep slopes.
Traverse with side-slip – kick turn – traverse.	The reliable 'get you home' technique; kick turns best done from a platform facing uphill with partner support below if in difficulty.
Traverse with snow-plough or stem turn.	Snow-plough turns are very tiring in deep snow but enable good control of speed; easier if whole party uses the same tracks.
Linked snow-ploughs in the fall-line.	A good technique for narrow-descents, but not on steep terrain; of some help in deep snow; readily leads on to parallel technique.
Linked parallel turns in the fall-line.	Best technique for deep snow; less effort and good control ensured; once mastered, a delight to execute especially in powder.
Edge-to-edge short swing turns.	For steep and/or narrow slopes; athletic; practice needed to maintain rhythm and control.
Jump turns.	For crust or heavy wet snow; very tiring.
Descending with skins on.	For bad visibility; enables a straight downhill course to be held; danger of pitching head-first over tips due to the drag.

for the others to follow, with the less able skiers bringing up the rear. The track would have been almost pisted by the time they travelled it and much easier to handle.

If you are a 'rough and ready' skier you may still enjoy ski-mountaineering, but your energy output and your safety margins will inevitably be more critical than those of the more able. Therefore, practice is important. Ski on the piste with your touring gear on, improving your technique, then ski off-piste in safe areas in a wide variety of snow conditions. Practise those kick turns on steep slopes with a safe run-out where a fall is not likely to be followed by a big slide. By constantly varying the challenge, you will add breadth to your experience. Cruising the piste will not do that, no more than will 'making do' with brute strength but precious little style.

No matter how strong you are, no matter how stylish on the piste, the real test of Scottish touring comes when you are faced with breaking crust, knee-deep heavy 'porridge', iron-hard névé with sastrugi (wind-packed ribs), or a slope that will mean ice-axe braking if you fail to make that kick turn. Of course, you can always take your skis off and, if in doubt, this is what you should do, but competence is the source of real satisfaction and it only comes with diligent practice.   AH

Nordic or Alpine?

THE ALPINE VIEW
Alan Hunt

The debate over which discipline is more effective for Scottish mountain conditions has been going on since the days of Raeburn and Rickmers, and it is not for one person to come down in favour of either. My personal preference is for Alpine skis and techniques for mountainous terrain with occasional tours on Nordic skis if conditions are optimum, by which I mean no ice and no really steep slopes.

I have had some fine outdoor experiences on Nordic skis, touring the peripheral Monadh Liath from bothy to bothy, travelling lonely, stalking access roads by moonlight or gliding through the silent forest after a deep fresh fall when service roads are blocked. I have also seen reasonably able Alpine skiers reduced to tears of frustration at their inability to cope with the differing techniques called for by Nordic skis.

It is my opinion that the level of skill required to cope with the broad range of conditions encountered on a Scottish mountain ski-tour is greater when Nordic equipment is used. Once mastered, however, the Nordic option does mean faster travel because of the lighter equipment and kick and glide uphill technique, and in late season when it comes to carrying your skis to and from the snow-line, the Nordic option is a runaway winner. However, when you meet those icy patches that need the rigid platform afforded by Alpine skis and plastic boots, I know where my choice lies.

THE NORDIC RESPONSE
Helen Charlton

Nordic technique is undoubtedly more precise, but, having said that, many people who dabble in Nordic skiing with a cheap off-the-shelf equipment package do not experience just what is possible on the best quality gear. If you spend the same money on Nordic skis and boots as you would on equivalent Alpine equipment, many of the apparent difficulties presented by Nordic technique will disappear. Modern kit even has the appropriate torsional strength to handle icy conditions.

Also, few skiers spend enough time on practising technique. Alpine-trained skiers cannot expect just to put on Nordic skis and achieve instant success. Much of the problem in changing style is psychological rather than real. Newcomers find their handling characteristics unusual so they 'freeze'. I recommend the visualisation technique in such cases. See yourself skiing well, as if you were back on Alpine gear, and will yourself to match that imagined performance.

With top-quality equipment and intensive practice, the Nordic style can handle nearly all Scottish routes, while the lightness and comfort of Nordic gear wins every day for me over the heavier Alpine kit for the wilderness touring typical of the Highlands.

Ultimately, the choice lies with the individual, and the multitude of factors that influence the decision certainly upholds that statement of Dr Winger over eighty years ago.

15

ON SKI IN SCOTLAND'S HILLS

Safe Travel and Great Deeds
by ALAN HUNT

ROUTE PLANNING AND NAVIGATION ON SKIS

All winter mountaineers at some stage in their adventures will be forced to descend from the summits by the light of a head-torch and will have to terminate a journey because of adverse weather conditions, be it a thaw, bad ground conditions, falling snow or strong winds. Few can say with hand on heart that they have never made the wrong decision when faced with such a predicament on the high tops.

The consequences of forced changes of plan on a ski-tour can be especially serious. Further, the skier has a greater complexity of factors to consider before an outing than the general mountaineer. The interplay between weather and snow conditions crucially affects the speed and feasibility of ski travel and requires the most careful attention by tourers when route-planning.

Skiing Close to the Wind: Two Experiences

'Ring as soon as you get back,' said the cryptic note on the seat of my car and, almost as an afterthought, 'Dog jumped out when I opened the door.'

The two small red reflections in the torchlight told me that she had as always, come back to wait my return, curled up, twitching tail over nose on the lee side of a rear wheel. Twelve hours previously we had made an early start from the Cairn Gorm ski-ground car park in clear frosty conditions on a practice run for the Alpine High Level Route, our objective later in the month. Cairn Gorm, Ben Macdui, The Angel's Peak via its North-East spur, Braeriach and back through the Chalamain Gap (see Fig 69, p262). The snow had been mainly good throughout, crisp on the ski edges with a few nasty ice patches to test angulation and control in a side-slip. The grade II ice on the waterfall approach to Angel's Ridge added interest to a fine route onto the lonely arctic-like plateau to the west of the Lairig Ghru.

We learned a lot – how to crampon on high-angled ice in ski-mountaineering boots, which proved as good as ordinary boots, perhaps even better being more rigid; how to carry skis strapped on each side of our sacks, not too high so that the tips caught when bending forward, not too low so that the tails dragged, a fine arbitration that is hard to get right. Most of all, we learned the need for steady uninterrupted progress to complete such a long round trip.

We had descended from Sron na Lairige towards the Sinclair Hut in rapidly failing evening light, our sense of direction helped by the brightening glow from the hut window as the customary occupants snuggled into the rodent-infested comfort of that seedy shelter.

The term defensive skiing is a perfect description of our progress. You cannot attack rapidly descending névé in the dark, nor miss a turn, fail to hold an edge, or lose a traverse line. Beyond the limit of our vision lay cornices, cliffs, drop-offs to unseen depths. We snow-ploughed gently downwards.

Crossing the rocky chaos of the Chalamain Gap by the light of our head-torches we sensed the car park and relaxation; time for a bite or two of those flattened, wool-specked emergency chocolate bars we had carried all winter and never used. A final skating traverse with the snow patches glowing fluorescent in the moonlight to show us the way, brought us back to those small red reflections and the by now thrashing tail.

Friends were concerned at our late return. Skiing in the dark? At Loch Morlich phone-box we made the obligatory phone call before carrying on to the house to feed the dog and rehydrate ourselves. 'What went wrong?' they said as we burst in, still complete in our hill gear.

Well, what did go wrong? Fortunately, nothing; we had returned in the dark, later than anticipated, just as other winter mountaineers do all over the Scottish Highlands. We had torches, there was a good moon and a favourable weather forecast. We had, however, been 'skiing close to the wind' in terms of the margins of safety. Any one of a host of possible mishaps could have left us with our backs to the wall, even fighting for survival with the harsh, unforgiving elements.

Some years later, I had to terminate a similar tour below Braeriach summit as storm-force winds arrived earlier than predicted:

We side-slipped and slithered into the depths of Gleann Einich, down the only safe slope our spindrift-confused navigation could locate. Exposed skin was agonised by the shot blast of driven ice, and from our knees downwards a tormented mass of whirling snow and ice particles concealed boots and skis from view. The down-draught impelled us valleywards, ski edges grating over rocks and ice patches, and with the sudden snatch of a soft drift threatening to pitchpole us into oblivion.

With relief, we finally reached the comparative shelter of the glen and began the long, easy angled glide to the main road, hoping the thinning snow-cover would hold all the way. It was past midnight when aching limbs and rock-scratched skis delivered us to the Coylumbridge phone-box; cars were in the ski-ground car park, the access road now closed by drifted snow. We took a taxi to the police station at Aviemore in order to allay any worries about the isolated cars and their missing occupants, and hopefully find a floor to sleep

on, even the comfort of a police cell! We finished up stretched out in the railway station waiting-room, shivering until dawn. I got my car back three days later choked with wind-blown snow that now dripped in the thaw.

These two incidents well illustrate some of the complications that the ski-tourer may have to face on a winter-mountain outing. Route-planning strategy prior to a trip and decision-making on the hill must take several factors into account:

1 The length of a touring day is difficult to assess, and only experience will indicate the range of time that a trip might take. In good snow, a fit skier may achieve a steady 6kmph (about 4mph) on Nordic gear and 5kmph (3mph) on the heavier Alpine kit over level ground, plus for either technique a climbing rate of 10 minutes per 100m (300ft) of vertical ascent. A steep 300m (1,000ft) descent might take no more than 10 minutes, and gentle inclines can be cruised at 8–12kmph (5–7½mph). All this changes if the snow becomes patchy or difficult, and once visibility is reduced in any way, be it by nightfall, spindrift, falling snow, or mist, the skier's speed of travel falls far more dramatically than that of the walker. Furthermore, the skier has to make extra stops to change or adjust gear. A single accurate prediction of trip duration is therefore impracticable.

2 Safe escape routes must take easy terrain on skis. Escapes are often considerably longer in distance for the skier than the climber and may be inconvenient in terms of transport arrangements, thus greatly extending the finish to an outing. Consider this when advising others of a return time. Furthermore, an early decision to escape in deteriorating conditions is especially critical to the tourer, allowing swift downhill travel on skis while good visibility lasts.

3 Sudden weather changes place the ski tourer at greater risk, partly due to 1 and 2 above, but also because the skier is more likely to be caught committed in remote country due to

his ability to travel faster and further when the going is good. The tourer must therefore be highly discriminating in interpreting the predicted timing of weather changes, for the forecast is at best an approximation.

4 Bad visibility coupled with a featureless snow-cover dramatically impairs balance and orientation on skis. Relative momentum with the ground cannot be sensed, and prior judgement of slope is, of course, impossible. For descents in mist, a good idea is to keep the skins on to ensure control of speed and maintenance of direction.

5 Strong winds, especially if gusty, disturb skiing balance and control, as well as playing havoc with the snow-cover on the tops.

6 Slope angles need careful interpretation by skiers when formulating a route plan. A range from 10° to 30° in slope angles is of little significance to the foot traveller, but for the skier 10° is an easy glide, while 30° is a steep serious slope, certainly equivalent to a 'black' piste run and requiring favourable snow coupled with expertise. It is, therefore, critical when plotting a route to check that all slope angles are safely within one's margins of ability.

Angles can be calculated from contour spacing. On the OS 1:50,000 Landranger maps, the approximate conversions from the spacings between the thick 50m contours are:

> 2mm spacing = 27°;
> 4mm spacing = 14°;
> 6mm spacing = 9½°;
> 8mm spacing = 7°.

For comparative reference, the White Lady piste run on Cairn Gorm averages 21° and a grade I snow gully is around 45°.

7 Snow conditions may change as suddenly as the weather. For instance, thawing spring snow can turn into bone-hard névé within an hour of the onset of a sharp frost. Ski-edge control becomes difficult and what would earlier have been a harmless slip may now commence a bone-rattling plunge valleywards.

Ski conditions are difficult to predict from the valley bottom. The scouring effect of wind action and the glint of icy patches are usually obvious, but other unfavourable conditions may not be revealed until they are underfoot and you are committed on a tour. Such is breaking crust, the *bête noire* of all tourers, which can be encountered on descents without any prior warning. Frustrating and slowing, bad crust is too exhausting for anything other than easy-angled traverses linked by kick turns.

The chances of powder-snow skiing are much more likely early in the season when cold weather prevails and the melt-freeze cycle can sometimes hold off for several days after a fresh fall, if the wind does not blow it away in the interim. Spring snow at the end of March and throughout April can be a coarse-grained delight to ski tourers, but remember that early in the day it may well be frozen hard and far from pleasant.

8 The extent of snow-cover plays a dominant role in the tourer's choice of route. One can expect a lower snow-line on slopes with a northerly aspect, with gullies, burns and stream beds holding the deeper drifts and offering possibilities of a continuous final descent by a series of linked probes right down to the valley floor. Especially in spring, this decision may save a long walk through the heather at the end of the day, while enabling a pleasant morning ascent on the barer southern slopes with the sun-softened névé surface giving optimum grip to the skins.

9 Avalanches are a particular hazard to skiers, who typically seek the medium-angled open slopes where wind-slabs commonly accumulate. Travelling at much greater speed than the walker, the skier can quickly get onto dangerous ground without being aware of the change. It is also wise to be aware of the ease with which ski tracks can cause a break in the tension area at the top of a convex slope in wind-slab conditions. Consequently, tourers should be well versed in the assessment of avalanche risk.

When forced to descend or traverse a suspect slope, the mountaineer should take several precautions to minimise the risk:

a) Ski slowly and carefully under control. Descend by diagonal traverses linked by easy turns. Undue vibration, as for instance might be caused by a fall, can trigger the slope.

b) Ski well away from convexities at slope tops or on shallow gully side-walls, which are zones of tension in an unstable snow-pack.

c) Descend one at a time across the danger area.

d) Remove your hands from the ski-pole loops ready to cast them away if you find yourself engulfed. However, it is probably wise to keep binding safety straps tied. The last thing you want to see is your ski sliding away down the fall-line of an unstable slope in the event of a slip, although there is a risk of being injured by flailing skis if an avalanche occurs.

e) If the worst happens, the old wives' tale of skiing down and away from an avalanche should be disregarded. All this is likely to achieve is a burial in the deepest part of the debris cone. It is far better to try to ski across and off a moving wind-slab, although probably it will be to no avail.

f) Avalanche transceivers are obligatory for touring in the Alps and should be considered for Scotland, their expense notwithstanding. In the event of an accident, immediate help in searching cannot be relied upon as is often the case on popular Alpine tours. Therefore, the party should all be well practised in the use of the devices to make an effective search in the event of a burial. The recognised frequency for transceivers is now 457kHz throughout Europe.

10 Navigation on skis is far more difficult than on foot because it is impossible to judge the distance travelled when one's speed is so variable. The use of an altimeter is therefore recommended. With the substitution of an altimeter in place of the walker's timing estimates and pacing counts, the tourer can still keep an adequate control over his progress. With altitude as one's means of ground reference instead of distance, the detailed plan of route may be quite different from that of the walker, particularly in the technique of contouring on skis.

Compass work is difficult when one is moving on skis because both hands are holding the poles. It is therefore useful to carry the compass strapped to the wrist for ease of reading.

Where there are steep slopes or corniced edges in the vicinity, it may be wise in a white-out to ski with the party roped together to avoid involuntary descents. There can be few more nerve-racking situations than being out in front on skis in white-out conditions, and the security of a rope can alleviate the mental stress. The line of the rope will also assist the person at the rear to monitor the direction of travel of the leader. In a total white-out, a reversion to foot travel should be considered as the safest option, but bear in mind that walking in deep loose snow will be far slower and more exhausting.

11 The style of skiing also plays a major role in one's choice of route. Alpine ski-touring is mainly a downhill business and a tour that involves long and distinct ups and downs is preferable to a high plateau circuit, whereas the latter outing is more suited to the kick and glide Nordic style when really fast travel is possible over undulating terrain without the complication of constantly removing and applying skins at every break of slope.

The particular idiosyncrasy and great joy of ski touring is the ability to cover much longer distances over the winter hills than is possible by walking, and despite all the hazards and pitfalls discussed above, one can and should be more ambitious in the length of a route planned on skis.

Plate 70 Approaching Cairn Gorm summit in misty conditions, the first stage of the Four Tops tour (*Alan Hunt*)

A ROUTE TO SAVOUR:
THE CAIRNGORM FOUR TOPS

Let us now put all these variables into practical use with a look at Scotland's most famous and arguably its finest ski-tour. The traverse of Cairn Gorm, Ben Macdui, Cairn Toul and Braeriach, the four 4,000ft (1,220m) tops, is a very long outing, but it has a circular route and can be abbreviated at several places, while it takes the skier over some of the most remote terrain and reliable snow-cover that the Highlands can offer.

Once Cairn Gorm's northern corries are left behind, encounters with other travellers will be brief and, after the Lairig Ghru is crossed, you are likely to enjoy near-total solitude until the Sinclair Hut is reached. Because of its remoteness, the difficulties of navigation on the plateaux and its exposure to the elements, the tour should be attempted only in settled weather that is likely to last throughout the round.

Although the slopes are never excessively steep, a high level of competence is required to avoid unnecessary energy expenditure. A tired skier on the Braeriach plateau is a long way from home by any route.

The guidebook time for this tour is 12–15 hours. This can be derived by personal calculation for each section using the suggested rates of travel for Alpine techniques given in 1 above. The results are shown in Fig 69. Taking the chair-lift to the Ptarmigan Restaurant for section A, a total skiing time of about 9 hours is obtained, and if an additional 10 minutes per hour of travel is added for rests and gear adjustments, a total time of 10½–11 hours results.

If the chair-lift system is not used – as is worthwhile if you make a pre-dawn start more than 2 hours before its opening time – a further 1½ hours will be added to make 12 in total. Then, if the skiing conditions are not optimal, the tour could easily stretch to the 15 hours guidebook limit.

Clearly, there are insufficient daylight hours for this length of outing until very late in March and thereafter a lack of snow-cover may necessitate slower foot travel on the lower ground. Only the fit skier favoured by conditions will make the

Fig 69 THE CAIRNGORM FOUR TOPS TOUR (OS 1:50,000, sheet no 36). Length: 32km (20 miles); ascent: 2,100m (6,890ft)

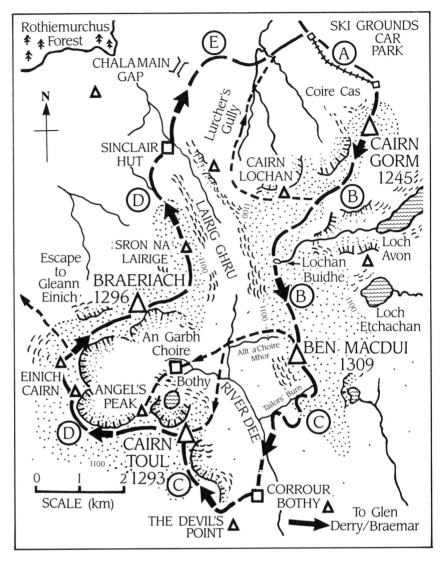

Route Times in Good Conditions	Time (hrs)	
Ⓐ CAR PARK – CAIRN GORM	¾–2	(depending on your ethics)
Ⓑ CAIRN GORM – BEN MACDUI	2	
Ⓒ BEN MACDUI – CAIRN TOUL	2½	(add 1 hour for Angel's
Ⓓ CAIRN TOUL – SINCLAIR HUT	2½	Ridge)
Ⓔ SINCLAIR HUT – CAR PARK	1½	
Extra for stops	1½	
TOTAL	10¾–12	

Alternative/Escape Routes shown by short dashed lines.

round without a pre-dawn start or twilight finish.

If time is pressing, section B on its own can make a fine day tour, especially for the Nordic enthusiast, taking in the tops of the northern corries rim and returning from Ben Macdui down the spur to the west of Cairn Lochan, with a fine run down to Lurcher's Gully to finish. A time of 5–6 hours should suffice for this. Skiers intent on the complete round will probably contour south of the northern corrie tops to save time.

Section C provides the finest descent of the tour down the Tailors' Burn from Macdui summit, a drop of 600m (2,000ft) to the River Dee, but this slope has a reputation for being avalanche prone, so a careful prior assessment of the snow's state should be made before a final commitment. Furthermore, once the descent is made, there are no convenient homeward escape routes. Escape to the north through the Lairig Ghru defile is long and very prone to strong winds due to funnelling in the pass. Otherwise, one is forced to descend to Braemar, which is 110km (70 miles) by road from your start. It is a prospect to weigh most carefully before pressing on from Macdui in worsening weather.

An alternative descent from Macdui is the Allt a'Choire Mhoir, which is slightly steeper but leads straight across to Coire an t-Sabhail, which provides a good direct approach to Cairn Toul summit provided there is no cornice at the exit. The normal ascent route is to follow the summer path route west from Corrour Bothy. Either way involves a foot section on the final steepenings.

The most challenging way onto the Cairn Toul plateau is to follow the route as taken by myself in the introductory account, going up to the Garbh Choire Bothy, then climbing the ice-fall (with axe and crampons) to reach the North-East Ridge of Angel's Peak, which gives a route of true Alpine character to the summit. Although never very difficult, the ascent requires winter climbing experience, particularly if it is to be tackled unroped (as it should for speed).

Section D is the most rewarding part of the journey as you cross the undulating plateau from Cairn Toul to Braeriach summit. This is as near to true arctic terrain as one will encounter in Britain, and its wilderness atmosphere should be savoured

to the full. It is also the most committed section of the journey. There is no easy way back into the Lairig Ghru until the Sinclair Hut is reached, and the only escape route leads down into Gleann Einich and a 12km (7½ mile) ski or walk back to the main road at Coylumbridge, undoubtedly an 'emergency exit' only.

After the exhilarating descent from Braeriach to the Sinclair Hut, the correct route back to the car park is straightforward, and it can be negotiated by torchlight if necessary. However, this is still inhospitable country and people have been overcome by storms here so close to safety. So aim to finish in daylight and enjoy contouring round from the Chalamain Gap back to the car park. The downhill skiers will have long since gone home.

A REGIONAL REVIEW OF TOURING POTENTIAL

The aspirant ski-mountaineer has a mouth-watering choice of hill country in Scotland for touring. Given unlimited time, the observant opportunist can take advantage of snow and weather conditions to make fine ski-tours almost anywhere in the Highlands. Unfortunately, most people have to plan their time off some way in advance or else are confined to weekend trips, so it is advantageous to know the areas that offer the most reliable conditions, when these are most likely to be found and the most representative routes in each.

Most tours lend themselves readily to either Alpine or Nordic techniques. The steepness of the topography on occasion suggests the more suitable mode, although the determining factor will often be the technical skiing ability of the tourer and the quality of his or her equipment. Ice-axe and crampons should normally be carried by all members of the party for mountain-touring, although they may be seldom used.

The period from early February through to mid-April gives the most reliable snow-cover. The later you go, the more likely are foot sections because of the receding snow-line and the dreaded breaking crust is more frequently encountered, but the early spring can offer glorious sun-tanning conditions, while the longer days allow for ex-

Plate 71 Touring in the Southern Highlands; on Ben Chonzie (*Bill Brooker*)

tended tours or else a greater margin of error.

Earlier in the season, the snow-line will be lower, but skiing conditions are more variable, from iron-hard névé through to powder, with frequent wind-slab forming after winter storms. Days are also shorter, the onset of blizzards more likely and minor access roads may be impassable. However, when it is good, a February tour can be an absolute joy with deep snow-cover and start-lingly clear atmospheric conditions. Prior to February, touring opportunities are dependent on the chance of major individual snowstorms, for a good snow base rarely develops early in the winter.

The Eastern and Central Highlands and the Cairngorms offer the most reliable snow-cover, the touring season lasting sometimes into May on the higher plateaux. Further west, the thawing maritime air can work with the efficiency of a giant blow-lamp at times and strip the cover from slopes and summits exposed to its hot breath in a few days, added to which the more rugged terrain of the western and northern mountain blocks holds less snow and requires a thicker cover for good skiing. Favourable touring conditions are, therefore, a matter of good fortune.

SOUTHERN HIGHLANDS

The central and eastern portions of this district provide the most reliable touring, particularly the Ben Lawers range, and are accessible for day excursions from the central belt of Scotland. For the more distant visitor, an early to mid-season visit is to be preferred to catch the best snow-cover. Good Nordic terrain is to be found on the Glen Lyon group hills to the south of Loch Rannoch, of which the Carn Mairg circuit (Fig 70) is a fine example and gives the collector of Munros four relatively easy ticks.

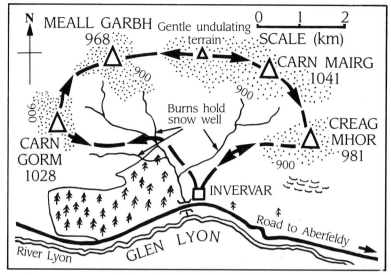

Fig 70 THE CARN MAIRG GROUP, GLEN LYON (OS 1:50000, sheet no 51) A medium-length round tour over the rolling hill country typical of the Glen Lyon and Breadalbane districts of the Southern Highlands. The route is easily escapable to the south and can be done in either direction. Length: 17km (10½ miles); ascent: 1,300m (4,250ft)

CENTRAL HIGHLANDS

This is a reliable snow-holding area, particularly on the high ground between Ben Nevis and Drumochter. One existing ski area, the White Corries of Glencoe, and another proposed at Aonach Mor will tempt the sinful, while the more ethical can use the services of British Rail to gain access to the remote Ben Alder Forest at Corrour. Away from the Black Mount, the hills fringing Glencoe are too steep for good touring. The Aonachs, Grey Corries and Ben Alder ranges tend to favour Alpine techniques, but the round of Creag Meagaidh (Fig 71) and the hills immediately west of Drumochter can provide some of the best Nordic mountain-tours.

THE CAIRNGORMS AND GRAMPIANS

Excellent snow-holding capabilities, together with generally colder and finer weather than further west, plus convenient road access at The Cairnwell and Cairn Gorm ski grounds give the high plateaux of the Cairngorms and the Grampians the greatest touring potential in Scotland. However, large tracts are as remote, if not more, than any other part of the Highlands. This is a serious mountain block and its challenge to the committed tourer can be awe-inspiring. Major expeditions require high levels of competence in both mountaineering and skiing skills.

Because of the generally rounded nature of the terrain and the long distances involved, most of

Fig 71 THE CIRCUIT OF COIRE ARDAIR, CREAG MEAGAIDH (OS 1:50000, sheet nos 34 or 42). A magnificent tour in the heart of the Central Highlands, with easy skiing on the tops and a fine final descent off Sron a'Choire. Not easily escapable: The Window offers the only exit south from the summit area but is not easy to find; mountaineering competence important. Length: 18km (11 miles); ascent: 1,150m (3,750ft)

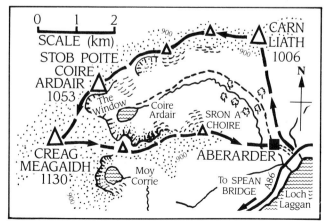

Plate 72 Descent from Ben Chonzie (*Bill Brooker*)

the touring is very suitable to Nordic techniques, but escape routes or alternative exits may need the ability to ski steep terrain.

Apart from the major challenge of the Four Tops, there are some excellent long traverses possible further east, for instance from The Cairnwell to Glen Muick over Lochnagar, a superb long Nordic day. At the other end of the scale are the excellent and convenient tours of the Glen Feshie hills and the flat tops of Gaick and Atholl to the east of Drumochter and the main A9.

THE WESTERN HIGHLANDS

Although the Western Highlands potentially offers many fine and remote tours, the difficult access, higher rainfall and limited snow-holding capacity naturally deters skiers. However, in full winter garb, the area offers the true wilderness experience which is becoming so elusive a delight in our shrinking world.

The most reliable conditions are to be found from Glen Affric north up to Achnasheen, but if snow lies low on the hills the minor access roads may be difficult. Glen Cannich and Glen Strathfarrar probe into this area and can provide access to fine Alpine touring mountains. There are several opportunities for bothying trips in this area. Indeed, to reach the heart of the Monar Forest hills an overnight stay is usually essential. If conditions are right, this could be a ski-touring experience hard to better anywhere in the Highlands.

The Sgurr na Lapaich group (Fig 72) offers a challenging round, yet is possible in one long day from the Cannich roadhead. It is best suited to Alpine techniques and can be started alternatively from Glen Strathfarrar, where the north-facing slopes will hold more snow in the late season.

THE NORTHERN HIGHLANDS

As with the west, the Northern Highlands sees few tourers, yet in Central and Easter Ross, snow holding is excellent and quick access is afforded by the upgraded A832 and A835 roads. The Fannichs and the Beinn Dearg ranges can give fine outings, best suited to the Alpine tourer, with the latter offering extended multi-day bothy-based possibilities over to Seana Bhraigh and Gleann Beag. Further east, Ben Wyvis, a target for future ski developments, offers an excellent day tour for either Nordic or Alpine techniques.

An excellently illustrated and detailed guide to the individual tours throughout the Highlands is now available. Entitled *Ski Mountaineering in Scotland*, it was produced by the SMC in 1987.

EXTREME SKIING: THE CHALLENGE OF THE GULLIES

'I'll just try a turn,' he said and jumped into space. I was left trying to extend the collapsible ski poles borrowed from Glenmore Lodge store, suddenly alone and gripped. We had just soloed up Aladdin's Mirror, a grade I climb in Coire an t-Sneachda, our skis strapped to our sacks, ski boots and crampons on our feet. We planned to ski back down again and by climbing up the route we could check out the snow and pick our line. It had been a sudden decision at the end of a week working at the Lodge. Here was the excitement we required after six days spent observing others at fever pitch, or at least so Ian reckoned:

'The snow's in great nick,' he had said, 'soft pack on a firm base; just what we need to give us a buzz.'

So that is how I came to be stood at the top of this slippery 45° slope to doom, with borrowed skis and boots and these ridiculous poles that varied in length from 2 to 6 feet but wouldn't lock in one place. As many of you will know the Mirror takes a zig-zag line with a long exposed traverse to join the easier Aladdin's Couloir at the top. Now if I followed Mark and Ian along the Mirror, the potential for a rapid slide down the Mirror ice-fall or even an airborne descent of the grade IV Aladdin's Buttress were all too real. Suppose the stupid sticks collapsed on me as I launched into one of my turns! 'To hell with that!' I muttered, and took the slip road down the Couloir, still steepish, but a straight run with a long and hopefully forgiving run out if I lost control of the situation.

We regrouped back at the top, and it was then that I made the second wrong decision of the day.

'The Couloir in Coire an Lochain was in good condition the other day,' I said in the enthusiasm of the moment, wholly forgetting that then I had walked down its firm névé in 12-

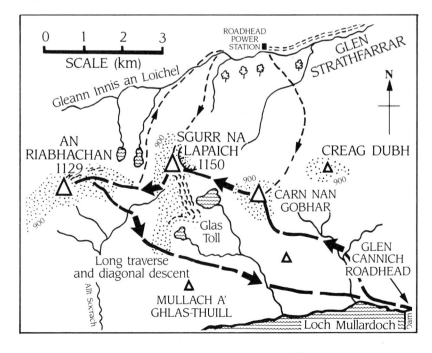

Fig 72 THE CANNICH HILLS, SGURR NA LAPAICH GROUP (OS 1:50,000, sheet no 25). A challenging tour of the Western Highlands after heavy snowfall. The southern approach from Glen Cannich is preferable when the snow-line is low and involves a steep foot climb to the top of Sgurr na Lapaich. The Strathfarrar approach holds more snow in late season, but road access is restricted. Length: 19km (11¾ miles); ascent: 1,500m (4,900ft)

Plate 73 Steep ski-ing in the Coire an t-Sneachda gullies (*Martin Burrows-Smith*)

gully broadened out and the snow improved – my nerves jangling and heart on full pump. Ian fared no better, and we held our edges watching Mark high above, poking the snow with his downhill stick, winding himself up for the commitment. The turn was followed by an exclamation of fear, anger and disgust. Out came his axe, and he cut a large platform, took the skis off, then sensibly and determinedly cramponned down the iron-hard névé.

I took off on a long descending traverse back to the ski grounds, musing on the mixed fortunes of a day's steep skiing, but pleased to still be bodily intact.

Now both these couloirs have often been skied. Harry Jamieson, at one time a Cairngorm ski instructor, had done them way back in the mid-1970s at the same time as Saudan and Vallencant were raising eyebrows with their extreme Alpine descents. Coire an t-Sneachda can be easily reached from the Cairn Gorm pistes and occasionally downhill skiers wander over. Herein lies the risk. There has been at least one accident to a piste skier attempting one of these gullies. Gully skiing must be accepted for what it is – highly dangerous. A slip will at best mean a long slide and a big fright. At worst, well it is only wise to know the score. To assess the suitability of a gully for a ski descent requires the sound judgement born of countless hours of ski-mountaineering experience and of course to make a descent in good style requires a high level of skiing ability.

Some may well doubt the sanity and point of skiing steep and confined ground in an exposed and serious situation and not infrequently I have shared similar feelings myself. However, speaking personally, the challenge has become addictive and I'm constantly searching for the perfect ski descent hopefully completed in good style and control.[1]

So wrote Martin Burrows-Smith, leading exponent of the art. Extreme skiing would seem to be much akin to solo climbing in terms of its dependence on the adrenalin rush. It can hook some people while terrifying the majority.

point crampons. But I was determined to restore my 'bottle' after baulking at the Mirror, and set off, by-passing the cornice and stamping a platform on the strip of wind-pack that covered one edge of the broad but otherwise icy gully. It felt just a touch steeper on bendy piste skis than when I had confidently strolled down it some days before, all 12 points biting the surface, but I plucked up courage and made that all-important first turn.

Suddenly the wind-pack narrowed to something less than the 200cm of my skis, and their edges were barely holding on the now icy surface. My temporary surge of 'bottle' vanished instantly, and I side-slipped until the

But Martin is no fool and he is certainly Scotland's most experienced skier of steep ground. He, too, has moments of doubt. Of Forked Gully on Stob Coire nan Lochan, Glencoe, he commented: 'A lot of side-slipping required. Disappointing and worrying.' He is also possessed of the mountaineer's vital survival instinct: 'Ice and fear prevented the link from the summit of Sgurr Fiona into Lord's Gully on An Teallach.' Confidence is all important when one is faced with that first committing turn, but it must be the confidence of experience and not bravado.

For the aspirant skier of steep slopes, a brief list of some suitable gullies and slopes in the northern corries of Cairn Gorm might give a taste of the heart-pounding excitement the activity can offer. Of course, snow assessment is absolutely critical, preferably gained first by climbing the gully, and the experienced ski-mountaineer will ideally look for firm wind-pack (although not slab) or coarse-grained spring snow. Equally important is the tight adjustment of ski bindings, for they must not release in mid-flight, together with a proven ability to side-slip out of trouble.

Coire an t-Sneachda

The Goat Track: Steepest at top; lots of space, so room for error in soft snow.

Point Five Gully (between Goat Track and Fiacaill Buttress): Steeper than the Goat Track, with the feel of a real gully descent.

Aladdin's Couloir: Best to start at the col where joined by the Mirror; steepest at the narrows; a good first grade I descent.

Man other gullies hereabouts have been skied, but they are all more serious propositions because of cornices, narrows and steeper sections.

Coire an Lochain

The Corrie Side-walls: The slopes between Fiacaill Ridge and the main climbing cliff, and the scarp at the opposite side above the lochan. Sometimes a small cornice develops and rock

Plate 74 Lord's Gully, An Teallach, skied by Martin Burrows-Smith from the junction

patches outcrop on the slope. Beware of convexity in the middle.

The Couloir: Straightforward steep skiing in good snow.

Once these relatively straightforward descents have been accomplished, one can move on to more remote Cairngorm gullies, for instance Diagonal Gully on Stag Rocks and Castle Gates Gully on Shelter Stone Crag. These can be incorporated into a ski-tour and offer thrilling highlights in a long mountaineering day.

Outside the Cairngorms massif, there are abundant possibilities for steep skiing in grade I gullies, but many involve a lengthy approach. Provided there are no great cornice problems or encounters with ascending mountaineers on foot, Scotland's potential for fine exciting descents is literally endless.

If this all sounds rather daunting and inappropriate, there is no compulsion to try the game. Just sit back and let Martin Burrows-Smith take you down Lord's Gully, the great forked cleft splitting the pinnacles on An Teallach:

> A quick coffee, some chocolate, then awkwardly on with the skis, trying to ignore the 300m of couloir ghosting down to the loch. Tighten the sack, grip the poles, warm up the legs, adjust to the 2m of metal edge on the feet; then . . . don't delay . . . Go!

> A few bouncing jumping side steps, getting into a rhythm for the first turn. Total commitment, double-pole plant for stability and launch into the fall line. Upper body quiet, skis turn in mid-air, pulse racing . . . I'd underdone the turn. An instinctive twist of the skis across the line of travel and they bite . . . great, the form was there. I could relax and enjoy it. The slope was steep, perhaps 50°, but the snow's smooth texture more than compensated. One turn at a time down the ridge into the narrows. It was tight. A short hop avoided a lump of ice; then I could cruise, linking turns down the lower section with a long orgasmic, diagonal schuss into the brightness on the far side of the coire . . .

> The relief that I was still in one piece was tinged with the usual sadness that it was all over. A long fast run back to the car remained – GS turns, drop-offs and schusses unwound in a care-free cruise to the jungle of trees by the road.[2]

GREAT DEEDS ON SKI: LONG-DISTANCE TOURS

The Easter meet of the SMC in 1913 when the Cairngorms massif was crossed three times ranks as an early landmark in Scottish ski-touring achievement. Thereafter, for forty years little was recorded of note. Competition downhill skiing provided an outlet for the record-breaking mentality, while ski-mountaineering spirits of the day such as Willie Speirs were content to plough their own lonely furrow and simply enjoy the hills.

In January 1953, Speyside was enjoying heavy snowfalls with temperatures down to $-8°C$ (17.6°F). Conditions on the hills were ideal for ski-touring and before daybreak one morning Norman Clark set off from Glenmore to make the first traverse of the Cairngorm Four Tops. His route was anti-clockwise, first traversing Braeriach and Cairn Toul, then swooping back into the Lairig by Soldier's Corrie (Coire an t-Saighdeir). What a superb final descent it must have been off Cairn Gorm back to Glenmore without the inelegant teeming confusion of the modern pistes, which were not established until the early 1960s.

In April 1962, Adam Watson junior, the great naturalist and current advocate for the protection of the fragile Cairngorm environment, added the summits of Ben Avon and Beinn a'Bhuird to cover the Cairngorm Six Tops in a 16-hour day starting from Invercauld by Braemar and finishing in Glen Derry, a total distance of 61km (38 miles) with 2,650m (8,700ft) of climbing. He used fairly primitive Nordic equipment, and his main sustenance was six tins of fruit, all of which were, of course, carried in his sack in addition to clothing and sleeping-bag. Most remarkably, this great feat was done on a pure impulse occasioned by good snow and weather. Adam Watson had done no skiing at all over the previous six weeks. Twenty years later, he looked back to that wonderful day and commented pertinently:

> The weather can be too settled . . . A breeze does wonders for the body and the snow, and even a fairly strong wind drifting the snow can be good as long as it's not in your face most of the time.

> Equipment is relatively unimportant . . . What is the best equipment is a topic for endless argument. But whatever equipment makes you feel better will be less tiring for psychological reasons. And on a long day it's how your mind feels that is crucial . . .

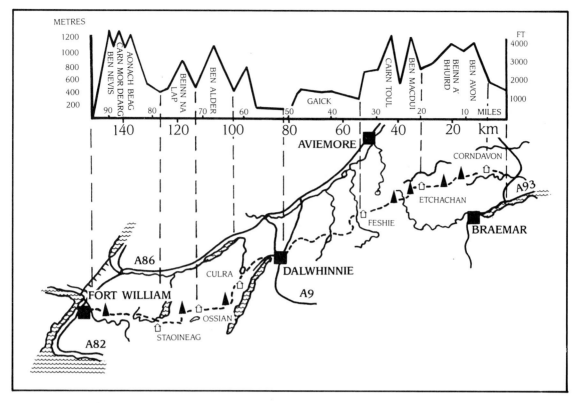

I could have taken less time by not taking photographs, looking at views and wild life, and talking to people . . .[3]

In February 1986, the Six Tops were completed in a round trip of 63km (39 miles) plus 3,750m (12,300ft) of ascent from the Cairn Gorm ski grounds by Blyth Wright and Roger Wild in 23hr 25min. They used Nordic gear. So complete was the snow-cover that they wore skis all the way.

Blyth Wright was also involved in a marathon 80km (50 mile) coast-to-coast crossing on Nordic skis in 1982, starting from Shiel Bridge in the west to Beauly on the east coast, accomplished along with Sam Crymble, Keith Geddes and Tim Walker. However, this was essentially a low-level crossing. They left at 7am and travelled by way of the Lichd-Affric watershed to Cannich, reaching Beauly at around midnight.

These efforts using Nordic techniques served to illustrate the speed of travel with lightweight equipment, but it was Alpine techniques that were used on the more demanding terrain of the

Fig 73 THE SCOTTISH HIGH LEVEL ROUTE, 26 February to 5 March 1978, by David Grieve and Mike Taylor (Sandy Cousins and Derek Pyper to Dalwhinnie). (Original drawing by Sandy Cousins)

'Scottish Haute Route'. The concept of a high-level route across the Highlands linking the Cairngorms and Ben Nevis had been germinating for many years, and various attempts were made. This was to be Scotland's answer to famous Alpine Haute Route from Chamonix to Zermatt. It was first travelled in seven days starting on 26 February 1978 by David Grieve and Mike Taylor. Their route of 160km (100 miles) began on Deeside at Crathie and is shown by the dotted line on Fig 73.

The serious nature of this trip and the variance of Scottish touring conditions is well illustrated by David Grieve's account:

The conditions experienced on this section

(Glen Feshie to Dalwhinnie) were arguably the most dangerous we encountered. The chilling effect of gale and rain must not be underestimated. Once wet, stops to rest and eat became inadequate because of rapid chilling. The tendency to press on quickly in order to keep warm increased fatigue and exhaustion/exposure was perhaps already taking effect.[4]

And later in Lochaber . . . 'the slope leading over the Carn Mor Dearg col was unskiable . . . in fact, it was quite poisonous with soft new snow lying on old, and numerous patches of green ice.'

Conversely, there were pleasant and rewarding moments, for example on their first night at Corndavon Lodge bothy: 'Abundant firewood was to hand and a fine steak supper was shortly washed down by a bottle of claret in front of a roaring fire,' as well as some great skiing:

On the summit (Beinn na Lap) the cold was very severe with considerable spindrift. Westward, the Mamores and our ultimate goal of Nevis looked magnificent. Conditions for the descent were the best yet – soft powder on a frozen base, extending right down to the Loch Treig railway line . . .

The descent from Nevis in the grey light of evening was a fitting climax to the trip. 500m of perfect powder snow followed by a further 400m of variable packed snow, frozen crust and Easter snow.

But like so many Scottish finishes, 'The final mud slide to the Youth Hostel in Glen Nevis was accomplished by torchlight.'

But it is V. A. Firsoff in his seminal work *On Ski in the Cairngorms* who takes us back to the atmosphere of earlier touring and who draws on the natural environment of the Cairngorms to enrich his encounters:

It was calm on the Great Moss, the air just stirring at the edge of the snows, which were much more patchy than usual at this time of year, so that I had to choose my way carefully to avoid uncovered ribs. Mossy cyptel and club mosses were preening themselves in the warm sun. Golden plovers were invisibly voicing the solitude of the melting snows to the pale sky, and some small birds, which may have been snow buntings, darted along the obtuse crest in the direction of Meall Dubhag.

Having crossed the snowless tops of Carn Ban Mor, I started down at a fairly good speed towards Loch nan Cnapan. Ptarmigan, all paired off, the cocks speckled with black, but the hens still pure white, fluttered up at my passage like huge butterflies.

The burns were rumbling ominously underfoot, with here and there a dark 'pocket' gaping open or a miniature crevasse marking the danger zone. On the way back, the snow actually collapsed under me and landed me in a narrow chest of moss-grown rocks some 3m deep with swirling water rushing furiously underneath. Not without difficulty did I lever myself up on my arms, and my hands were shaking when I had re-emerged on the surface.[5]

Mountaineering, and that includes travel on skis, should give time to take photographs, to talk to people and to look at the views and the wildlife. If we don't notice the mosses, the small birds and the smell of the sun-dried grass between the thawing snow patches, we will be missing an essential aspect of the mountain experience. And if in our haste to break records we miss the scars left by our own and others' intrusions into the wilderness, we will find ourselves sliding into the dark gaping crevasse of indifference.

The great beauty of being on ski in the mountains is the accentuated experience created by combining the thrill of a gliding descent with the rewards of physical effort. Break records by all means, but as Adam Watson said: 'The best days on the hill are the ones you snatch unexpectedly without much planning.'

CONCLUSION

A Winter on the Hills – Part II

This winter flies by without pausing to take breath and give a single respite of cold settled weather. As surely as night follows day, the blizzards have given way to rainstorms and thaw. The hills have been plastered white, then blasted bare a dozen times, and February has almost passed, leaving naught but fond memories of the fortnight of frost in early December that now seems so long ago. It is proving a season where only dogged persistence pays rewards, snatching the windows of good weather, plugging away in the bad and buoying the spirit with thoughts of a better March. But occasionally, from the throes of the turmoil and struggle, a mountain day of precious perfection is fashioned . . .

24 February: On the Plateau

The wind and snow were insistent, driving head-on at 60–80kmph (50mph) – blizzard conditions at night on the top of Cairn Gorm. Who might envy Ian and I, battling through the deepening drifts on the long slow climb out of Coire Raibert, eyes fixed on the compass needle, out of food, low on energy and with safety on the other side of the hill? How, then, can I explain that in so seemingly grim a predicament, our consuming emotion was exhilaration.

Firstly, make no mistake, despite the cold vile night, we were glowing with the heat of the fight, armour-shielded against the wind in hooded jackets and double mittens. Feeling snug and well insulated, the raw power of a storm on the plateau can be savoured to the full.

Then there was the thrill of uncertainty. Were our bearing and timing correct? Could we be veering down the slope? Would we hit that crucial cairn that sits atop the Fiacaill a'Choire Chais and signals safe return? Success, and even survival, depended solely on our own skill and resource. Our reserves were low, but we had a margin of control. Could we use it?

Add to this the keen satisfaction of a great winter climb, wrested against the odds and now close to successful conclusion. The pleasure can sustain an empty stomach far into the night and gives new strength to wearied limbs. Here was one day out of the many which are plagued by mishap or written off by the weather, where we had played our hand and won every trick.

Guessing the state of the snow and ice on Carn Etchachan, finding our way to the Shelter Stone in a near white-out, then locating the base of the climb on our first sortie and discovering great conditions – from the start we seemed to have the day under control and the gods on our side. Then we had enjoyed a fine and taxing climb. There was the hilarity of wedging self and rucksack through the bottleneck chockstone of an ice-lined chimney, the precise sequence of ice-axe placements to surmount the exit bulge, the joyous romp up névé ramps and ledges, a tense 10m scratching up a bare rock corner and the exploratory wanderings up the final grooves before a sudden ending.

Then had come our only moments of doubt. Which way back – round the plateau or down to Loch Avon and up over the top? Light was short and the snow showers were merging into blizzard, so the decision was crucial. We wavered and suddenly felt vulnerable. Stumbling by chance round to the head of Castlegates Gully, we took the option offered and went down it to the loch. Confidence was immediately regained by action. We had sped along the lochside and then outwitted the dangerous wind-slabs fast building on Raibert's open slopes by a weaving climb up the rocks on its left.

And that is how we came to be here – on the plateau in the thick of a storm, but immensely happy. Although we had seen virtually nothing

since leaving the car at 7am, we still sensed a rare and lasting oneness with the mountains. The winter experience stretches far beyond the visual plane.

And this ne'er-to-be-forgotten day was capped by marvellous good fortune, for suddenly a great white pile shone on the torchlight. We had hit the cairn! Forty minutes later, the key was turning in the car door and we could dare contemplate hot brews of tea and well-earned rest.

Mid-March and a weather-window levers open; but don't rush and leap. Give the snow a day to settle and a night to harden, sort the gear, plan the route and, when the mind and body are fully tuned, cross the fingers and go . . .

14 March: The Cuillin Crest

Glen Brittle on a placid frosted morn gives quiet sanctuary from the rush of modern life. The sea stretches lazily out to Rhum and Canna and its waves lap softly up the shingle beach. Smoke drifts aimlessly from the cottage chimneys, the adjoining fields are bleached to palest green and bared of summer's gaudy encampments, while the eternal Cuillin rise razor-sharp into the steel-blue sky. The glen exudes a timeless peace, but can give no rest to the mountaineer who, seeing the ridge all clear and snow-capped, feels a dream within close grasp. The vision of a never-ending fairy crest of iron-hard snow has spurred plans and speeded a long journey. Now on arrival, the vision is almost tangible.

But one can never be sure until the ridge is

breasted. Useless powder-snow deceitfully masking the rocks and the tempered coat of névé so desired – they look much alike from the valley floor. Would I be lucky today?

The screes of Gars Bheinn's south-west flank exact stiff penance at any time of year. Today, under an inch of the dreaded powder-snow, they almost broke my spirit. It is a glorious moment when the toil is done and you gratefully collapse onto the summit crest. The depths of Coruisk and Scavaig are suddenly disclosed, the serrated edge of Blaven bristles beyond. Ahead, the Main Ridge twists and vaults over a clutch of castellated peaks towards the northern sentinel of Gillean. Liquid light from a hazy sun softened the impact this morning, but still I gulped with the excitement of the scene.

However, the snow had not yet declared its

Plates 75 & 76 The Cuillin Ridge arrayed in winter garb from Sgurr Dubh Mor. The main skyline peaks are (L to R) Sgurr Dearg (Inaccessible Pinnacle), Sgurr na Banachdich, Sgurr a'Ghreadaidh, Sgurr a'Mhadaidh, Bruach na Frithe, Am Basteir, Sgurr nan Gillean

true intent. Thin powder predominated on the first easy sections, but on the climb to Sgurr nan Eag, I found my feet rebounding off a solid pack beneath the surface fluff. Hopes fluttered briefly, and on the ensuing descent all doubts were dispelled. All those loose ramps and boulder-fields which tax one's patience in summer were wholly buried by clean smooth névé, hardened by a weekend's frost into a magnificent climbing surface. It was immediately essential to wear crampons and

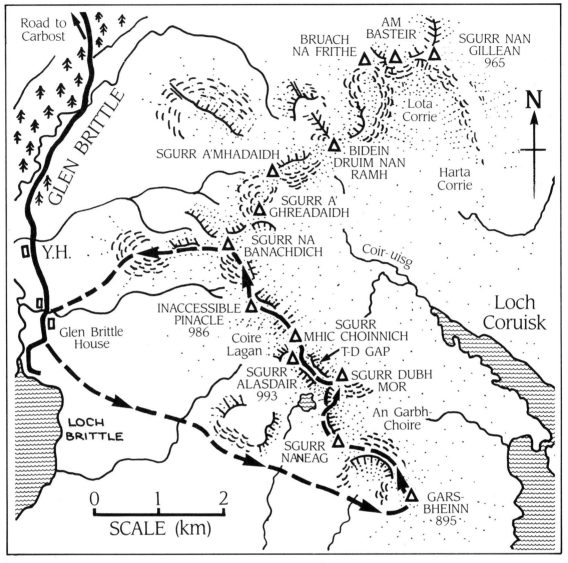

thereon I could progress with security and precision of footwork.

For me, a Cuillin traverse is incomplete without a detour to the outlier Munro of Sgurr Dubh Mor, and I cramponned tracks across the fields of snow hanging above An Garbh Choire to gain the peak. In soft midday sunshine, the snow gleamed brightly, but the heat was insufficient to melt the surface. Safe, crisp conditions; cold calm weather; my zig-zag tracks weaving behind into infinity, and a pristine ridge reaching ahead – for an hour I revelled in unsullied joy.

21 (*right, above*) The magic ridge. The central Cuillin fired by the sunrise viewed over the water from Loch Carron. (L to R) Sgurr Alasdair, Sgurr Mhic Choinnich, Inaccessible Pinnacle (Sgurr Dearg), Sgurr na Banachdich (*Clarrie Pashley*)

22 (*right*) Extreme skiing. Martin Burrows-Smith 'at it' in the gullies of Coire an-t Sneachda, Cairn Gorm (*Richard Mansfield*)

23 (*overleaf*) On the northern Cuillin Ridge at dawn, January 1982. Sgurr a' Fionn Choire (left) and Am Basteir (right) (*Bob Barton*)

However, the Thearlaich–Dubh Gap gives the rudest shock to the buoyant northward traverser, and doubly so in winter. Its notorious chimney was choked in powder and complicated by the odd smear of verglas. It delayed me for a tense strenuous hour before I could recoil the rope and continue in carefree style. With arrival at Alasdair, at 993m, the crowning peak of the Cuillin, the famous circuit of Coire Lagan, is joined. The corrie lochan was half-frozen and the remainder shot through with a turquoise glint. The encircling peaks reared like Alpine giants in their winter raiment. Thearlaich's nearby slabby crest lay under an unbroken sheath of snow, Mhic Choinnich's square chisel head stood bold and black behind, and the Inaccessible Pinnacle rose with equine grace on the far side of the amphitheatre.

The snow held good. Thearlaich's tricky descent and the spiralling gangway of Collie's Ledge were firm and sure, but I sensed I was tired climbing up the ramps beneath the Pinnacle. Ankles ached with the continuous flexing and knees burned with the non-stop crampon rhythm. As my strength flagged, so too the weather grew languid. The sun dissolved behind an advancing wall of cloud. The hills of Harris on the western horizon were swallowed up and then the peaks of Rhum shrouded from view. The wind was still light, but the Cuillin were not to be spared.

The Pinnacle was happily in easy condition. A thin drape of powder could be quickly brushed off the knobbled holds of the East Ridge, and no ice lurked beneath, only the firm dry rock of summer. Up and down inside thirty minutes, I pushed on to Banachdich. Here a light snowfall commenced.

It was 4pm and both my fatigue and the weather demanded a halt. I'd failed on the *integrale*, but could descend secure in the knowledge of having snatched an appreciable slice of Britain's greatest ridge in wonderful winter conditions. If half the Cuillin Ridge was this good, then I tremble to think of the thrill of completing the full winter traverse.

But first I lingered and watched the reality disappear. The saw-toothed ridge, so sharp and icy earlier in the day, first faded in the encroaching haze, then vanished without trace as the clouds drew in their chilling veils. The window had closed and once again the winter Cuillin were spirited away to the realms of mystery.

17 March: The Final Descent

Within an hour, the western sky had fired to a flaming brilliance, then burnt down to a steady amber glow. The table-top Applecross Hills now etched a coal-black silhouette against the sun's fading embers. At the instant the last pink rays vanished from the tips of the Torridon peaks, the night frost stole in and crisped the snow.

Yet, as we four stood in mute admiration by the cairn on Fuar Tholl, a subtle difference in the air was sensed. A January sunset brings a sudden bite of sterile cold that scours all life from the day. Its beauty is intense but final; but tonight, though the air was chill and pure, life somehow lingered in the afterglow.

When we descended the shadowed corrie, the answer was made clear. A myriad of burns tinkled down and trickled out from under melting snow-beds and a film of dust raised by the daytime sun still hung over the heather moor. A balmy breeze wafted up the slopes from the glen, bearing the rich scent of pinewood and the happy sound of birdsong.

No longer does winter stand alone in icy supremacy, but is intertwined with the warming stems of the coming spring. Here at the equinox and for a few brief weeks on either side, the seasons make a glorious bond. The

24 (*left, above*) Making tracks through the Lairig Ghru on a ski backpacking expedition, with the Devil's Point directly ahead and the upper slopes of Cairn Toul to the right (*Jim Barton*)

25 (*below*) December sunset from the summit of Fuar Tholl, looking down Loch Carron and over to Skye

Plate 77 Moments of
utter peace and solitude
– sunset at the top of
the climb

purity of winter is retained on high, but in the glens the air vibrates with the life and hope of nature reborn.

So rare an evening at a stormy season's end gives time to pause and reflect on the past months in the hills – their trials and glories, our mistakes and good fortunes, and the frustrations and successes. And whether our chosen course is to ski the rolling high-tops or the steep couloirs, climb gully or buttress on the ice-bound cliffs, or merely to take a leisured stroll above the snow-line, a night of such peace fuses our many aspirations to a common cause.

The spirit of adventure, the freedom of the wilds and the thrill of action – they all spring from the spell cast by the hills. In so many different ways, we each seek to know the beauty of Scotland's winter mountains, and yet, for all our striving, their secrets remain elusive.

We entered the dark forest, crunched along the pebbled stalking track, then strode down the lane through the groves of pines under a starlit shaft of sky. On the valley road sequins of frost already glistened on the tarmac. With strange reluctance, we climbed into the car and stowed away our dreams for another year.

APPENDICES

Plate 78 Ben Nevis, 'wreathed in a swirling
ever-changing pattern of cloud', as seen
from Aonach Mor (*Helen Charlton*)

I

SCOTLAND'S WINTER MOUNTAINS

A Historical Review

Although there were isolated explorations earlier in the nineteenth century, Scottish winter mountaineering was only truly established as a recreational and adventure pursuit with the formation of the Scottish Mountaineering Club in 1889. Thus the sport is now a century old, and it is timely to review its progress and development.

There is a rich and exciting catalogue of achievements, events and epics contained within this one-hundred-year span. However, the chronology here presented must, through lack of space, be selective in its content. The definitive history of the winter game – and one hopes it is soon written – would fill a large volume in itself. So only the major ascents and most influential developments are here picked out and set against their natural backcloth of weather and conditions. It is inevitable that in a subjective selection, many great climbs and tours are excluded from the list, and for these sins of omission, I apologise in advance.

Key to categories:

NAT Major natural events (weather, snowfall, conditions).

GEN Events common to all aspects of winter mountaineering, and points of general interest.

SKI Ski-touring.

CLI Important snow, ice and mixed climbs.

1812	GEN	12 November: Col Hawker climbs Ben Lomond and is obliged to cut steps with a knife on the icy snow of the final slopes; the first recorded piece of winter mountaineering.
1870	CLI	No 3 Gully of Coire na Ciste (1), Ben Nevis, climbed under snow; the first known ascent of a graded snow climb.
1883	GEN	Ben Nevis summit observatory commences operation.
1884	GEN	Ben More, Crianlarich, climbed by William Naismith in March using an alpenstock. The inadequacy of alpenstocks on hard snow was soon realised, and they were replaced by ice-axes for winter use in the 1890s.
1887	GEN	Cairngorm Club formed; growing recreational interest in summer hill-walking, soon to spread to winter mountaineering; other local clubs, such as the Dundee Ramblers, also sprang up at this time.
1889	GEN	Scottish Mountaineering Club formed under the initiative of Naismith. One of its avowed aims at inception was the encouragement of winter ascents. At the first annual dinner, the President, Prof G. G. Ramsay, admitted that in mountain pioneering the Scots had lagged behind members of the English Alpine Club, who had achieved so much in the Alps over the previous thirty years
	GEN	First recorded winter ascent in the Cuillin of Skye, Bruach na Frithe climbed by Swan.
1890	GEN	The first volume of the *SMC Journal* appears with articles by Hugh Munro and A. I. McConnochie strongly encouraging winter-mountain expeditions. The *Journal*'s 'Notes and Climbs' section provides a record and inspiration for the new and growing winter activism – eg, Munro's 110km (70-mile) three-day round in the Eastern Grampians in January 1890.

1891	GEN	New Year's Day: A. I. McConnochie crosses the Cairngorms from Coylumbridge to Braemar via Braeriach and Cairn Toul in thirteen hours.
1891	GEN	Munro's Tables published, giving a major impetus to Scottish mountain exploration.
1891	CLI	Explorations of gullies and snow faces in the Southern Highlands – notably Ben Lui and the Cruachan group.
1892	SKI	Naismith writes enthusiastically on Scotland's ski-ing potential in the *SMCJ*.
1893	GEN	'Snowcraft in Scotland' by Naismith appears in the *SMCJ*, the first instructional treatise on the Scottish winter sport, which was dubbed by Naismith 'one of the noblest forms of recreation'.
1893	CLI	Inaccessible Pinnacle, Skye, climbed by J. H. Gibson in April with snow on the rocks; other semi-winter climbs made on the Cuillin.
1894	NAT	Activism thwarted by 'dreary months of rain' in the early winter, but redeemed by late snows.
1894	CLI	29 March: First winter ascent of Tower Ridge (III), Ben Nevis, by Collie, Collier and Solly in a remarkable five hours – a major landmark and still Scotland's most famous winter climb.
1894	CLI	Several climbs recorded on the Buachaille Etive Mor at Easter – eg, Great Gully (II).
1895	GEN	Extension of West Highland Railway to Fort William opens potential for further exploration of Ben Nevis and Lochaber. First SMC Easter meet to be held at Fort William.
1895	CLI	Castle Ridge (II), Ben Nevis (Collie, Naismith, Thomson, Travers) and NE Ridge (II), Aonach Beag (Maclay, Naismith, Thomson) climbed – classic mountaineering routes.
1896	NAT	First recorded avalanche incident on a Scottish climb during attempt on Centre Post, Creag Meagaidh – cornice collapse in thaw conditions; a narrow escape for Douglas, Raeburn and Tough.
1896	GEN	Highly favourable snow and weather conditions at Easter. Tower Ridge repeated five times during SMC Fort William meet.
1896	CLI	3 April: NE Buttress (III/IV), Ben Nevis; first winter ascent in seven hours by Naismith and party.

1897	CLI	Two notable gully climbs: the Upper Couloir (II), Stob Ghabhar, giving A. E. Maylard and party a genuine ice pitch, and Gardyloo Gully (II), Ben Nevis, (Hastings and Haskett-Smith).
1900	GEN	Easter mountaineering on the Torridon Hills – six-man ascent of Northern Pinnacles (II) and Main Ridge of Liathach in wintry conditions.
1902	NAT	Wind-slab avalanche witnessed on Ben More, Crianlarich, and its cause correctly diagnosed as 'superimposed dry snow' on a wind-swept ice-slope.
1903	GEN	Further semi-winter exploration of the Cuillin during SMC Easter meet – eg, the Dubhs Ridge and T-D Gap.
1904	SKI	Skiing in Scotland given impetus by W. R. Rickmers in an illustrated *SMCJ* article.
1904	CLI	North Trident Buttress (IV), Ben Nevis (Maclay, Raeburn, C. Walker and H. Walker), Central Trident Gully (III), Ben Nevis, (Raeburn, W. and Mrs Inglis-Clark) – Harold Raeburn now the leading winter activist.
1905	SKI	Raeburn is sceptical of Scotland's ski-touring potential in his article 'Scottish Snow', and discusses the Norwegian langlauf technique.
1906	CLI	April Green Gully (III/IV), Ben Nevis, climbed by Raeburn and Phildius – the hardest pre-1914 ice-gully; 'two of the pitches were what is usually known as perpendicular' (HR). Although recorded, this ascent was not established and acknowledged by guidebook writers until *c*1970.
1907	GEN	28–9 December: Protracted all-night epic on Tower Ridge (Goodeve, C. Inglis-Clark, McIntyre) – the first of many. The party extricated themselves from the cliffs by courageous climbing on uncharted ground, reaching the summit at 2am.
1907	CLI	Central Buttress (III), Stob Coire nan Lochan, Glencoe, climbed by Raeburn, Ling, Glover and W. InglisClark.
1907	SKI	Scottish Ski Club founded.
1909	CLI	Easter: Crowberry Gully (III), Buachaille Etive Mor, climbed by Raeburn, Brigg and Tucker in 4½ hours – another ascent that was not acknowledged until *c*1970; now the epitome of Scottish winter-gully climbing.
1910	GEN	First of a series of mild, wet and snowless winters which retarded winter pioneering.

1913	SKI	Great trans-Cairngorms tours achieved during SMC Easter meet at Aviemore – contrary to Raeburn's view, a potential for ski-touring on the high tops is fully realised.
1914–18	GEN	World War I imposes a near-complete interruption on mountaineering activism and extinguishes the enthusiasm for bolder pioneering – a legacy which continued for the subsequent twenty years, during which recreation and enjoyment replaced exploration and adventure as the criteria of winter mountaineering.
1920	GEN	*Mountaineering Art* by Harold Raeburn published; the first textbook to devote a substantial portion of its content to the Scottish winter sport.
	CLI	April: The last of the great Nevis ridges falls in winter; Observatory Ridge (III/IV) climbed by Raeburn, F. Goggs and W. Mounsey – Raeburn's last major Scottish winter ascent, and the sole winter advance during the 1920s.
1925	GEN	Junior Mountaineering Club of Scotland (JMCS) formed, providing a channel for youthful climbing energies, which bore fruit in winter during the 1930s.
1929	GEN	1 April: Charles Inglis-Clark Memorial Hut (CIC) on Ben Nevis opened; the ideal base for future winter pioneering on the mountain.
1932	SKI	Scottish Ski Club hut erected on the slopes of Ben Lawers.
1933	GEN	January: Tragedy on Cairn Gorm: Ferrier and Mackenzie, both young and ill-equipped, perish in storm. The incident was one of the first winter fatalities and attracted much general publicity, which cast doubt on the sense and purpose of winter mountaineering.
1934	CLI	March: SC Gully (III), Stob Coire nan Lochan, Glencoe, climbed by P. Baird, E. Leslie and H. Fynes-Clinton, a Cambridge University party.
1935	CLI	17 March: Glover's Chimney (III), Ben Nevis, climbed by G. Macphee, G. Williams and D. Henderson. This climb, together with SC Gully, heralded a renaissance in Scottish winter climbing that was cut short by World War II.
1936	CLI	Despite Macphee's lament in the *SMCJ* that 'Munrovitis' was sapping the SMC's younger talents and energies, this was a year of new activism and equipment modifications – longer ropes 36m (120ft) per man, and short slater's picks for step-cutting.

	CLI	April: Semi-winter ascent of Slav Route/ Zero Gully by J. H. B. Bell and C. Allen gives clear evidence of new enthusiasm to explore intimidating winter terrain. Willingness to climb through the winter season; Crowberry Gully repeated in February. All-night retreat from Garrick's Shelf on the Buachaille in December by Dunn, MacAlpine, Mackenzie and Murray emphasises the seriousness of climbing in the darkest month.
1937	CLI	March: Garrick's Shelf (IV), Buachaille Etive Mor, climbed by W. Mackenzie and W. H. Murray – probably the hardest pre-war ascent on ice.
1938	CLI	Comb Gully (III/IV), Ben Nevis, climbed by F. Stangle, R. Morsley and P. Small.
1939–45	SKI	While the war interrupted serious mountaineering activity, skis were used extensively on the Scottish hills for armed services mountain training.
1945–7	GEN	RAF Mountain Rescue service commenced, to be continued after the war in service of mountaineering accidents. Rescue equipment now in place in major climbing centres. Local men carrying out rescue work on an *ad hoc* basis. Donald Duff, surgeon at Fort William's Belford Hospital, developing rescue equipment and techniques. Henceforth winter mountaineers in distress could take comfort that an organised rescue effort would be mounted.
	GEN	Flood of ex-WD equipment available to mountaineers. Nylon ropes and vibram-soled boots appear in the UK, together with pitons and karabiners. Improved gear lays a foundation for an advance in winter climbing over the next decade.
1947	GEN	*Mountaineering in Scotland* by W. H. Murray published – a literary landmark which provided a historical tradition for the inspiration of future winter mountaineers.
1950	GEN	*A Progress in Mountaineering* by J. H. B. Bell gives an instructional update to Raeburn on Scottish winter climbing.
	CLI	29 January: Giant's Head Chimney (IV), Lochnagar, by W. Brooker and J. Morgan. 28 December: Douglas-Gibson Gully (IV), Lochnagar, by T. Patey and G. Leslie (Patey was 18 years old). A new advance begins in the Cairngorms.

1951	NAT	1950/1 is the snowiest winter of the century to date at high altitudes; snow lies for 102 days at Dalwhinnie (300m).
	GEN	30 December: The Corrour tragedy – four perish in a severe blizzard en route from Corrour to Ben Alder Cottage.
	SKI	Scotland's first ski-tow is operated at Glen Shee, beginning the progressive divorce of downhill skiing from mountain-touring.
	CLI	Zero Gully, Ben Nevis, spectacularly repulses H. Nicol and A. Rawlinson, who fell from the last pitch to the foot of the climb; both survived.
1952	GEN	Three avalanche fatalities in Cairn Gorm's northern corries; two died on Nevis in the following year. These accidents created a new awareness of Scotland's avalanche hazard, especially the windslab.
	CLI	6 December: Scorpion (V), Cairn Etchachan, climbed by Patey, M. Taylor, G. Nicol and K. Grassick – a bold ascent on a major face, Scotland's first grade V. Remarkably, Patey forgot to bring gloves for the climb, yet the party somehow won through.
1953	SKI	January: Norman Clark makes the first continuous traverse of the Cairngorm 4,000ft summits in a one-day round trip from Glen More.
	CLI	14 February: Raven's Gully (V), Buachaille Etive Mor, gets its first winter ascent from Hamish MacInnes, and a young Chris Bonington, after several epic attempts by MacInnes and members of the Creagh Dhu Club, Glencoe's first grade V. Crampons worn by MacInnes, and soon to be generally adopted in preference to nails on steep ice. 25 January: Eagle Ridge (V), the queen of Lochnagar's winter routes, and the epitome of the 1950s tricounied mixed-climbing technique, yields in an astounding 4½ hours to Patey, Brooker and Taylor. 2 April: Mitre Ridge (V), Beinn a'Bhuird: another classic buttress route climbed by Patey and Brooker.
1956	GEN	Winter climbing courses run by the Mountaineering Association in Glencoe, the first practical instructional training in the winter skills.
	CLI	4 March: Parallel Buttress (V), Lochnagar, climbed by Patey, J. Smith and Brooker in severe conditions of high wind and blown powder. 25 January: The great Joe Brown is violently rejected by Point Five Gully, falling 45m to the foot of the route when the ice gave way. Point Five and Zero Gullies now the prime objectives for several competing teams.
1957	CLI	18 February: First winter ascent of Zero Gully (V), Ben Nevis, by MacInnes, Patey and G. Nicol in five hours, MacInnes using frontpoint crampons and ice pitons placed for protection and tension. 27 December: Sticil Face (V) on Shelter Stone Crag climbed by Ken Grassick and Graeme Nicol, an impressive face route snatched from Patey – one of the hardest 1950s routes and still respected.
1958	CLI	22 February: Parallel Gully B (V), Lochnagar, climbed by the Edinburgh raiding party of Jimmy Marshall and Graham Tiso; a major ice-line solved in crampons, and a significant pointer to the coming surge of ice pioneering by the Edinburgh-based group.
	CLI	Tragedy in Zero Gully: three English climbers killed when wooden axe broke under load in a fall. MacInnes stimulated to produce metal shafted axes by this accident, which forcibly demonstrated the lack of security on the new steep ice-routes. Waist belays now the norm, and rock piton anchors used whenever available in preference to direct axe belays.
1959	CLI	A golden year in winter pioneering. Point Five Gully (V) was sieged into submission over five days in January by Ian Clough and party but more significant ascents in purist style were: Orion Face/Epsilon Chimney (V), Ben Nevis, by Robin Smith and R. Holt. Minus Two Gully (V), Ben Nevis, by Marshall, J. Stenhouse and Dougal Haston. Tower Face of the Comb (V), Ben Nevis, by Smith and Holt. Smith's Gully (V), Creag Meagaidh, by Marshall and Tiso. Aladdin's Buttress (IV), Coire an t-Sneachda, Cairn Gorm – boldly soloed by Tom Patey.
1960	GEN	In the early 1960s, Glenmore Lodge began winter survival and skills training courses largely under the initiative of Eric Langmuir, setting a standard of excellence that has been maintained to the present and has greatly improved the knowledge and safety of the winterclimbing fraternity.
	CLI	February: Jimmy Marshall and Robin Smith repeat Point Five Gully in good style and climb six new routes, including Orion Face Direct (V) and Gardyloo Buttress (V), in an eight-day campaign on Ben Nevis. This was the pinnacle of achievement of the step-cutting era, and their routes cast an aura of difficulty which was not dispelled until the adoption of front-pointing in the 1970s.

1961	SKI	Cairn Gorm chair-lift opened and downhill ski-ing developed in Coire Cas. The ski access road also opened up the Northern Cairngorms, giving quick access to ski-tourers and winter climbers that has rarely been spurned, despite ethical misgivings.
	CLI	Winter grading system (I–V) introduced in Malcolm Smith's Cairngorm Guides.
1962	SKI	April: Adam Watson skis the Cairngorm Six Tops (ie, those tops over 4,000ft, plus Ben Avon and Beinn a'Bhuird), starting from Invercauld and finishing at Derry Lodge, in sixteen hours. Wooden Nordic skis used.
1964–5	GEN	Hamish MacInnes markets short metal-shafted ice-axes and hammers. Salewa ice-screws and front-point crampons imported and used for the first time in Scotland.
1964	GEN	Avalanche accident on Beinn a'Bhuird: one victim, Robert Burnett, found alive after twenty-two hours' burial – one of the longest survival times under snow debris recorded anywhere and certainly the longest in Scotland.
1965	GEN	31 January–1 February: Cuillin Main Ridge is traversed for the first time in winter by Patey, MacInnes, B. Robertson and D. Crabb – north to south with one bivouac – closely followed by Tiso and J. Moriarty. Thus the greatest mountaineering expedition in the British Isles was established after many conjectures and attempts.
	GEN	Search and Rescue Dogs Association (SARDA) formed under the initiative of Hamish MacInnes. The use of dogs enabled much greater speed and efficiency in avalanche rescue.
	CLI	Two notable first winter ascents on iced slabs: The Curtain (originally V, now IV), Ben Nevis, by D. Bathgate and J. Knight, and Djibangi (IV/V) on Creagan a'Choire Etchachan, Cairngorms, by J. MacArtney and W. Barclay. Explorations in the Northern Highlands (Fannichs, Beinn Dearg) by members of the Corriemulzie Club.
	SKI	On Ski in the Cairngorms by V. A. Firsoff published – the first commentary and guide to ski-touring in the area.

1969	CLI	Excellent conditions and a highly productive winter. Forays in the Northern Highlands by Patey produce classic routes such as March Hare's Gully (III/IV), Beinn Bhan. Over twenty-five middle-grade new routes produced by Glencoe Winter School of Mountaineering parties largely led by MacInnes and Clough. Patey soloes the 2,450m (8,000ft) Crab Crawl across the cliffs of Coire Ardair, Creag Meagaidh, at III/IV. Deadmen snow-anchors manufactured and widely adopted in Scotland.
	CLI	Winter climbs guide, Ben Nevis and Glencoe, by Ian Clough published. Mountain magazine begins regular reporting of winterclimbing developments.
1970	GEN	The 'frontpoint revolution' is initiated by Chouinard's visit to Scotland and his discussions with MacInnes and John Cunningham; MacInnes produced the droppicked Terrordactyl axes and Cunningham adopted the curved-pick style.
	CLI	Patey, Clough and Jim McArtney – three of the greatest winter pioneers – killed in separate accidents. Cunningham and Bill March demonstrate the potential of frontpoint methods with their icicle climb, The Chancer (IV/V) on Hell's Lum Crag, although their ascent was partially aided.
	SKI	Scottish Mountains on Ski by Malcolm Slesser, a touring guidebook, published.
1971	GEN	November: 'The Cairngorm Tragedy': five children and one teacher perish in a blizzard after failing to locate the Lochan Buidhe refuge on the Macdui–Cairn Lochan plateau – the worst winter tragedy to the present. Sparked an intensive debate on training methods and the hazards of high-mountain shelters.
	CLI	Astronomy (V), Ben Nevis, climbed by A. Fyffe, K. Spence and MacInnes using 'terrors' – a hard open-face route. Repeats of the 1950s routes using front-point techniques, including an ascent of Point Five in less than three hours by Cunningham and March. The new style proves its worth and lays the seeds for a new wave of pioneering.
1972	CLI	11 March: Labyrinth Direct (V), Creag an Dubh Loch, front-pointed by James Bolton without runners or wrist-loops from a belay of axes and useless ice-screws – Scotland's hardest and boldest ice-route at that date.

1973	SKI	Harry Jamieson, a local ski instructor, skies several grade I gullies in the Northern Cairngorms, including Aladdin's Couloir.
	CLI	Ian Nicolson soloes Zero and Point Five Gullies in a combined time of three hours – a myth-shattering feat which opened these and comparable routes to wholesale attack from front-pointers.
1974	CLI	February: Minus One Gully (V), the last of Nevis's unclimbed gully lines falls to Ken Crocket and Colin Stead.
1977	GEN	Cairngorm Automatic Weather Station commences operation – a new source for winter weather data and forecasting.
1978	GEN	Equipment advances – banana-picked Chacal axes appear and further facilitate the ascent of steep ice; GORE-TEX material greatly improves the performance of shell garments in winter.
	SKI	The Scottish 'Haute Route' – a continuous traverse from Ben Avon to Ben Nevis of 160km (99 miles) established by Mike Taylor and David Grieve using Alpine techniques in seven days starting 26 February.
	CLI	Major developments in the North-West and on Ben Nevis, and a renewed interest in Cairngorm mixed climbing. Poacher's Fall (V), Liathach (Andrew Nisbet and Richard MacHardy), and Central Buttress (V), Beinn Eighe (first complete ascent by Alex MacIntyre and Alan Rouse), demonstrate the North-West's ice- and mixed-climbing potential respectively.

Several major thin-ice face routes climbed on Ben Nevis, notably Galactic Hitch-hiker (V) (Mike Geddes and Con Higgins), Pointless (V) (Gordon Smith and Nick Banks), Psychedelic Wall (V) (Arthur Paul and Norrie Muir), and Route 2 on Carn Dearg Buttress (V) (Geddes and Rouse).

1979	NAT	An abnormally cold, snowy and prolonged winter in which the lowest temperatures for two hundred years were recorded in many places in Northern Europe.
	CLI	Sustained activity in all areas. Significant routes included:

27 January: Link Face (V/VI), Lochnagar, by John Anderson and Andy Nisbet – a venture into the technical unknown, VS summer ground – and harbinger of 1980s grade VI mixed climbing.
February: Elliot's Downfall (V), Aonach Dubh, Glencoe, led by Dave 'Cubby' Cuthbertson with one rest point – a short vicious icicle and a longstanding problem.
15 March: Shield Direct, Ben Nevis, by Mick Fowler and Victor Saunders, a staggering line that prompted its unilateral declaration as Scotland's first grade VI by the usually conservative *SMC Journal*, Fowler's first Scottish winter coup – he still maintains the grade is only 'good V'.

1980	CLI	Another memorable season with several major advances, notably:

26–7 January: Die Riesenwand (V) Beinn Bhan, by Andy Nisbet and Brian Sprunt, tackling the stupendous 400m head-wall of Coire an Fhamair. Climbed with a bivouac.
5–6 January: Postern (VI), Shelter Stone Crag, climbed free with a bivouac by Murray Hamilton, Kenny Spence and Alan Taylor.
23 February: Citadel (VI), Shelter Stone Crag, by Hamilton and Spence – the first complete ascent with one aid point after many epic attempts and partial successes. A touchstone of modern mixed climbing.
16 January: Goliath (V/VI), Creag an Dubh Loch, by Neil Morrison and Andy Nisbet; a summer HVS climbed mainly on thin ice – bold and exposed; one point of aid.
8 March: Epitome (VI) Lochnagar – a short desperate route led by visiting Polish climber Jan Fijalkowski with rests on axes, showing the high standards of mixed/ice-climbing attained in other countries since the front-pointing revolution. No longer could Scots claim a monopoly of winter expertise.

1981	CLI	Updated winter climbs guide to Ben Nevis and Glencoe by Ed Grindley makes a liberal and perhaps over-generous use of grade VI. Cairngorms winter climbs guide by John Cunningham and Allen Fyffe published.
1982	NAT	Exceptional cold spell in early January. Braemar registers Britain's equal lowest recorded temperature of −27.2°C (−16.9°F).
	GEN	15 February: A 'black day' for avalanches; four separate accidents, three on Ben Nevis and one on Creag Meagaidh, with three fatalities, demonstrating the coincidence of deadly conditions across the country when snow and weather so favour.

	SKI	The Lurcher's Gully affair ends with rejection of the planning application to extend Cairn Gorm's ski area westwards – a temporary victory for conservationists over the growing downhill-ski interests.
	SKI	13 January: A Glenmore Lodge team of Sam Crymble, Keith Geddes, Tim Walker and Blyth Wright ski coasttocoast from Loch Duich to Beauly on Nordic gear – c100km/62 miles in seventeen hours.
1983	CLI	3 April: Gully of the Gods (V), Beinn Bhan – the great cleft cleaving the Coire an Fhamair headwall climbed by Fowler and Fenwick.
		20 February: Fly Direct (V), Creag Meagaidh's major outstanding line, gets a clean ascent from Fowler and Saunders.
		February: Central Grooves (VI), Stob Coire nan Lochan, climbed after several attempts by Kenny Spence and John Mackenzie.
1984	NAT	21 January: The day of the 'great storm', a blizzard unmatched in severity in modern times.
		Cairn Gorm's anemometer unfortunately malfunctioned when the wind speed was rising above 160kmph (100mph). Hundreds of skiers, climbers and travellers trapped, and five lives were lost in the Cairngorms. Remarkably, a new grade V route was climbed by Rick Allen and Brian Sprunt during the storm – Raven's Edge on Buachaille Etive Mor.
	CLI	28 January: Guerdon Grooves (VI), Buachaille Etive Mor, climbed by Cuthbertson and Paul – hard and serious, HVS in summer.
		16–17 March: Fowler and Butler pick two Torridonian plums – Tholl Gate (V/VI) on Fuar Tholl, and Great Overhanging Gully (V/VI) on Beinn Bhan.
1985	GEN	Martin Moran ascends all the Munros within the calendar winter season taking 83 days for the 277 summits which involved 126,000m (415,000ft) of climbing. Motorised support and transport between the mountains used. Helped by a particularly dry and cold winter.
	SKI	Martin Burrows-Smith skis down Hell's Lum in the Cairngorms, a grade II/III winter climb, and one of the hardest 'extreme' descents yet achieved.
	CLI	A lean year with one major exception: Colin MacLean and Andy Nisbet's ascent of The Needle on Shelter Stone Crag, E1 in summer, grade VI+ in winter; climbed over two days, 13–14 February.

1986	NAT	Britain's highest-ever recorded wind speed, a gust of 275kmph (171mph), registered by the Cairn Gorm AWS at 00.30 on 20 March.
	CLI	A remarkable year, giving superb conditions in all areas and at all levels – over one hundred new winter routes produced between November and the end of April including:
		21 February: Eas Coul Aulinn, Britain's highest waterfall ascended at IV/V by Andy Cunningham and Andy Nisbet.
		30 March: Dierdre of the Sorrows (VI+) on Lochnagar by Doug Dinwoodie with Nisbet, probably the hardest mixed route yet achieved, E2 5c in summer. The crux pitch only yielded after eleven hours of effort spread over three attempts.
		8–9 February: Centurion, Carn Dearg Buttress's great central corner line, Ben Nevis, climbed as far as Route 2 with a bivouac by Mackenzie and Spence at grade VI.
		April: A soloing tour de force on Ben Nevis by Dave Cuthbertson and Grahame Livingston, climbing in tandem on two separate days – several of the harder modern routes included, and a testimony to the skill of modern climbers as well as the effectiveness of ice-climbing tools.
1987	NAT	12–17 January: A big freeze-up, during which the Cairn Gorm AWS registered its lowest temperature, −16.5°C (2.3°F), in ten years of recordings.
	SKI	*Ski Mountaineering in Scotland*, edited by D. Bennett and W. Wallace, published – an updated touring guide produced in response to the growing popularity of the sport both in the Nordic and Alpine camps.
	CLI	Despite more variable conditions, another good year for new routes. Several fine ice and mixed lines added in the North-West, notably Fowler's West Central Gully (VI) on Beinn Eighe, climbed as late as 11 April.
		Grade VII claimed for a new route on Lochnagar, Torquing Corpse, climbed by Grahame Livingston and M. Lawrence in January, after several attempts and a top-rope rescue. Undoubtedly extremely hard and serious, but the required tactics raise the future spectre of 'engineered' winter climbing in contrast to the truly adventurous spirit of pioneering to date.
1988	NAT	The warmest winter in a decade of Cairn Gorm weather readings. The next Ice Age is delayed at least for one more year.

GLOSSARY

Gaelic Names
To help the reader's geographical understanding of the Scottish mountains, translations of the most commonly occurring topographical names are given below: With this list, nearly all of the Scottish mountain names in the text can be understood.

ALLT	Stream, burn
AONACH	Mountain ridge, hill, moor
BAN	White, light-coloured
BEAG	Small
BEALACH	Pass
BEINN/BHEINN (BEN)	Mountain
BIDEAN/BIDEIN	Peak, summit
BINNEIN	Pointed peak
BUIDHE	Yellow
CAORANN/ CHAORAINN	Rowan tree
CARN/CAIRN	Heap of stones, cairn-shaped hill
CLACH	Stone
COILLE	Wood
COIRE/CHOIRE	Corrie, glaciated valley bowl
CREAG	Rock, crag
CRUACH	Stack-shaped hill
DEARG	Red
DUBH	Black
EAS	Waterfall
FIONN	White, pale-coloured
GABHAR/ GHABHAR	Goat
GARBH	Rough
GEAL	White
GLAS/GHLAS	Grey, grey-green
GORM	Blue, (of grass) green
LAIRIG	Pass
LIATH	Grey, bluish-grey
LOCHAN	Small lake
MAM	Large rounded hill
MAOL	Bald, bare
MEADHOIN/ MHEADHOIN	Middle
MEALL	Rounded hill
MONADH	Moor, hill-range
MOR/MHOR (MORE)	Big
MULLACH	Summit, top
ODHAR/ ODHAIR	Fawnish brown
RIABHACH (RIACH)	Brindled, greyish
RUADH	Red, red-brown
SAIL	Rounded hill
SGURR/SGORR	Rocky hill or peak
SPIDEAN	Peak, summit
SRON	Jutting ridge
STAC/STUC	Steep conical hill
STOB	Pointed hill
TARSUINN	Transverse, cross
TOLL	Hole, hollow
TOM	Small rounded hill
UISGE	Water

Technical terms
Nearly all technical terminology is explained in the text, but some general climbing terms require translation for the benefit of non-climbers:

Abseil
Method of descent on a cliff face by sliding down a doubled rope anchored above, using a friction device attached to the climber's harness. The ropes are then retrieved by pulling on one end. Used in event of retreat or escape.

Anchor
The climber's means of attachment to the cliff, whether by sling, inserted chockstone, piton or ice screw.

Belay
Encompasses the climber's anchorage, the attachment of rope to the anchors, and the method by which the rope is paid out to or taken in from those who are in process of climbing.

Crux
Hardest section of a climb.

Karabiner
Metal snaplink for clipping the rope into anchors.

Pitch
Individual stage of a climb between belay points. Normal pitch length is between 20 and 45 metres.

Piton
Metal blade or peg hammered into cracks in the rock as an anchor.

Runner
Anchor placed by the leader while climbing, and clipped into the rope with a karabiner to provide a running belay.

Stance
Ledge occupied by a climber while belaying.

III

BIBLIOGRAPHY AND REFERENCES

READING LIST

Apart from the specific books detailed below, the *Scottish Mountaineering Club's Journal*, and its *District* and *Climbing Guides* form essential reading for any devotee of the Scottish mountains. Indeed, the Journals have provided a comprehensive and authoritative history of a century of winter mountaineering in Scotland. The growth of a Scottish winter tradition owes much to its records, and it is to be hoped that the SMCJ retains its role by carrying the history onwards into the next century.

The sources listed devote either the whole or a significant part of their content to matters directly relevant to Scottish winter mountaineering. Most are currently available in print, but important older works are given for completeness, and so that enthusiasts can seek them out in their local library vaults.

CLIMATE, WEATHER, SNOW AND AVALANCHE

Barton, R. & Wright, B., *A Chance in a Million?* (Scottish Mountaineering Trust, 1985) The definitive textbook on the Scottish avalanche phenomenon; clearly written with many case studies.

Daffern, Tony, *Avalanche Safety for Skiers and Climbers* (Diadem, 1983) Well illustrated with some Scottish examples.

Fraser, C., *Avalanches and Snow Safety* (John Murray, 1978) Clear coverage of the technical ground, but wholly Alpine in its applications.

Kilgour, W. T., *Twenty Years on Ben Nevis* (A. Gardner, 1905 (reprinted Anglesey Books, 1985)) An entertaining history of the Ben Nevis observatory.

Lamb, H. H., *Climate History and the Modern World* (Methuen, 1982) Gives a global view of climatic change, and its natural and human consequences.

Langmuir, E., *Mountaincraft and Leadership* (MLTB/Scottish Sports Council, 1984) Contains chapters on British mountain weather and avalanches.

Pedgeley, D. E., *Elementary Meteorology* (HMSO, 1978) A standard textbook for those who want to make a serious study.

—. —, *Mountain Weather* (Cicerone Press, 1979) Well illustrated paperback covering all mountain weather topics.

Perla, R. & Martinelli, M. jnr, *Avalanche Handbook* (US Dept of Agric Forest Service, 1976) A more detailed textbook than *A Chance in a Million?* and global in scope, but well explained and illustrated.

Seligman, G., *Snow Structures and Ski Fields* (MacMillan, London, 1936) A classic exposition on snow in all its wonderful forms; beautifully written; now slightly outdated and out of print but worth seeking in the libraries.

Sissons, J. B., *The Evolution of Scotland's Scenery* (Oliver and Boyd, 1967) A definitive textbook of Scotland's geomorphology, and particularly its glacial heritage.

WINTER MOUNTAINEERING
Textbooks

Barry, J., *Snow and Ice Climbing* (Crowood Press, 1987) Entertainingly written textbook, British based.

Bell, J. H. B., *A Progress in Mountaineering* (Oliver and Boyd, 1950; reprinted in paperback with introductory biographical essay by Hamish Brown as *Bell's Scottish Climbs* – Gollancz, 1988) Partly instructional, partly inspirational; gives the flavour of winter climbing in the 1930s and 40s.

Chouinard, Y., *Climbing Ice* (Sierra Club Books, 1978) A lavishly illustrated textbook on ice-climbing worldwide, but with good Scottish coverage; influential when first published as it covered the front point revolution.

Cliff, P., *Mountain Navigation* (Bookmag, 1978 (revised 1986)) Clear and concise coverage of the navigation skills.

Hunter, R., *Winter Skills* (Constable, 1982) Introductory textbook to winter mountaincraft and survival skills.

Langmuir, E., *Mountaincraft and Leadership* (MLTB/Scottish Sports Council, 1984) Covers the Winter Mountain Leadership Certificate syllabus; written by former principal of Glenmore Lodge; the standard text for general mountaineering.

MacInnes, H., *International Mountain Rescue Handbook* (Constable, 1972 (revised edition 1983)) Highly technical, but useful for the serious winter climber since it draws strongly on the author's Scottish experience.

March, W., *Modern Snow and Ice Techniques* (Cicerone, 1973 (revised 1984)) Concise paperback textbook; for many years the only text covering modern winter climbing techniques.

Raeburn, H., *Mountaineering Art* (T. Fisher Unwin, 1920) Textbook by Scotland's greatest early pioneer; out of print but worth seeking for its fascinating insight into the techniques and equipment of the day.

Narratives

Alcock, D., Barry, J., Wilson, K., *Cold Climbs* (Diadem, 1983) Compilation of essays and illustrations of Britain's classic winter climbs; some excellent writing, first ascent accounts and fine photos; essential reading for the budding winter climber.

Borthwick, A., *Always a Little Further* (Faber, 1939 (reprinted Diadem, 1983)) A gem of a book, capturing the hardship and spirit of 1930s Scottish climbing; chapters on howffing and an epic ice-climb on Stob Ghabhar.

Crocket, K. V., *Ben Nevis* (Scottish Mountaineering Trust, 1986) The definitive history of climbing on the Ben; excellently researched and written; traces the winter story of Britain's greatest snow and ice arena.

Moran, M. E., *The Munros in Winter* (David & Charles, 1986) The account of the first completion of all the Munros within a single calendar winter season, with much general information on the mountains in winter.

Murray, W. H., *Mountaineering in Scotland* (J. M. Dent, 1947)

—. —, *Undiscovered Scotland* (J. M. Dent, 1951) Compilation volume published by Diadem, 1979. These two books, especially the former, are still acknowledged as containing the finest essays on Scottish winter mountaineering ever written; highly influential when first published; they continue to inspire the modern generation.

Patey, T. W., *One Man's Mountains* (Gollancz, 1971 (now in paperback)) A collection of Patey's essays; classic accounts of Scorpion, Zero Gully, the Cuillin Traverse and Creag Meagaidh Crab Crawl, plus historical reviews of climbing in the 1950s; highly satirical and entertaining.

SELECTIVE GUIDEBOOKS

NB: The SMC's area climbing guides cover more fully the winter routes in each region.

Fyffe, A., *Cairngorms Winter Climbs* (Cicerone Press, 1987) Updated version of original guide by John Cunningham; covers Cairngorms, Lochnagar and Creag Meagaidh.

Grindley, E., *Winter Climbs on Ben Nevis and Glencoe* (Cicerone Press, 1981) Updated version of Ian Clough's original guide; controversial and now largely discredited introduction of grade VI routes on the Ben.

MacInnes, H., *Scottish Winter Climbs* (Constable, 1982) A high proportion of Scotland's winter climbs crammed into one volume with a huge number of black and white photographs – highly useful for both the novice, and the experienced climber who wants to explore new cliffs and areas.

CLOTHING, DIET, FITNESS

Langmuir, E. *Mountaincraft and Leadership (ibid)* Sections on hypothermia and windchill.
Ottaway, P. B. and Hargin, K., *Food for Sport* (Resource Publications, 1985) An informative handbook, in paperback, of sports nutrition.
Wilkerson, J. A., *et al, Hypothermia, Frostbite and other Cold Injuries* (The Mountaineers, 1986) Gory pictures of frostbite, but good coverage of clothing and hypothermia.

SKI-TOURING AND MOUNTAINEERING

Bennett, D. and Wallace, W., *Ski Mountaineering in Scotland* (Scottish Mountaineering Trust, 1987) Guidebook to all the major Scottish ski tours; superb photographs.

Cliff, P., *Ski Mountaineering* (Unwin Hyman London, 1987) Excellent, well-illustrated manual to Alpine ski-touring.
Field, P. and Walker, T., *Cross-country Skiing* (Crowood Press, 1987) Instructional textbook to the Nordic style from beginner to advanced level.
Firsoff, V. A., *On Ski in the Cairngorms* (W. & R. Chambers, 1965) A classic account of Scottish hill-touring, but not currently in print.
Gillette, N., *Cross-country skiing* (Diadem, 1979) Although based on American experience, this gives a thorough and highly entertaining instruction in Nordic ski-touring.
Godlington, D., ed, *Ski Technique and Instructional Manual*, Books I and II, (British Association of Ski Instructors, revised 1984)
Sheridan, G., *Tales of a Cross-country Skier* (Oxford University Press, 1988) Anecdotal accounts of Nordic tours worldwide; some Scottish interest and very entertaining.

REFERENCES

CHAPTER 1

1 'Lament for the Highland Glaciers', *SMCJ*, Vol 28, no 158, 1967.
2 Sissons, J. B., *The Evolution of Scotland's Scenery* (Oliver and Boyd, 1967).
3 Lamb, H. H., *Climate History and the Modern World* (Methuen, 1982).
4 Munro, H. T., *SMCJ* Vol 1, No 1 (1890) p20.
5 Manley, G., *SMCJ* Vol 30, No 163 (1972) p14.
6 Gillon, S. A., *SMCJ* Vol 8, No 47 (1905) p233.
7 Thom, A. S. in Parnell, B.K. Aonach Mor, a planning report on the prospect of winter sport development, Department of Planning, Glasgow School of Art.
8 Buchan, A. *et al*, trans Royal Society of Edinburgh, No 43 (1905).
9 Manley, G., 'The Mountain Snows of Britain's Weather' 26 pp192–200 (1971).
10 Manley, G., 1972, *ibid*.

CHAPTER 2

1 'Twenty Years on Ben Nevis', W. T. Kilgour (1905), reprinted Anglesey Books, 1985, pp82–4.
2 Begg, J. S., *SMCJ*, Vol 33, No 175 (1984), p49.
3 Baird, P. D., *CCJ*, Vol 17, No 91 (1957), p148.
4 Brown. W., *SMCJ*, Vol 2, No 2 (1892), pp59–60.
5 Douglas, W., *SMCJ*, Vol 2, No 2 (1892), p73.
6 Inglis Clark, W., *SMCJ*, Vol 16, No 95 (1923), p266.
7 Broadhead, D. J., *SMCJ*, Vol 33, No 176 (1985), pp170–2.
8 Kilgour, W. T. (1905) *ibid*.
9 Perla, R. and Martinelli, M. jnr, *Avalanche Handbook* (US Department of Agric Forest Service (1976)).

CHAPTER 4

1 Seligman, G., *Snow Structures and Ski Fields* (Macmillan, London, 1936).
2 Naismith, W., *SMCJ*, Vol 2, No 4 (1893), p166.
3 Ramsay, Prof G. G., *SMCJ*, Vol 4, No 20 (1896), p77.
4 Macphee, G. G. *SMCJ*, Vol 21, No 122 (1936) p91.
5 Naismith, W., *SMCJ*, Vol 1, No 2 (1890), p57.
6 Patey, T. W., *SMCJ*, Vol 27, No 153 (1962), p282.

CHAPTER 5

1 SMC District Guide. The Southern Highlands (1949 edition), p45.
2 *SMCJ*, Vol 1, No 3, pp126–7.
3 Munro, H. T., *SMCJ*, Vol 1, No 1 (1890), p21.
4 Almond, H. H., *SMCJ*, Vol 2, No 5 (1893), p236.
5 McConnochie, A. I., *SMCJ*, Vol 1, No 1 (1890), p12.
6 Raeburn, H., *Mountaineering Art* (Unwin, 1920), p154.
7 Raeburn, H., *SMCJ*, Vol 8, No 48 (1905), p291.

CHAPTER 7

1 Naismith, W., *SMCJ*, Vol 1, No 5 (1891), p217.
2 Geddes, M., *Cold Climbs* (Diadem, 1983), p132.
3 Bonington, C. J. S., *The Next Horizon* (Gollancz, 1973), pp108–9.

CHAPTER 8

1 Bell, J. H. B., *A Progress in Mountaineering* (Oliver & Boyd, 1950).
2 Borthwick, A., *Always a Little Further* (Faber, 1939; reprinted Diadem, 1983), p149.
3 From Dixon, J. C. and Prior, M. J., 'Wind-chill indices – a review', *The Meteorological Magazine*, Vol 116, No 1374 (Jan 1987).

CHAPTER 9

1 Munro, H. T., *SMCJ*, Vol 2, No 2 (1892), p50.
2 Lawson, H. G. S., *SMCJ*, Vol 6, No 35 (1901), p154.
3 Nimlin, J. B., *SMCJ*, Vol 24, No 139 (1948), p6.
4 Humble, B. H., *SMCJ*, Vol 25, No 143 (1952), p18.
5 Inglis-Clark, W., *SMCJ*, Vol 18, No 108 (1929), pp333–4.
6 Speirs, G. R., *SMCJ*, Vol 19, No 109 (1930), p12.
7 Murray, W. H. *Mountaineering in Scotland* (J. M. Dent, 1947; reprinted Diadem, 1979), p168.
8 Murray, W. H., *ibid* (J. M. Dent, 1947; reprinted Diadem, 1979), p180.
9 Murray, W. H., *ibid* (J. M. Dent, 1947; reprinted Diadem, 1979), p186.
10 Inglis-Clark, C., *SMCJ*, Vol 10, No 56 (1908), p74.
11 March, W., *SMCJ*, Vol 29, No 162 (1971), pp364–8.

CHAPTER 10

1 Raeburn, H., *SMCJ*, Vol 9, No 50 (1906), p60.
2 Campbell, R. N., *SMCJ*, Vol 30, No 163 (1972), p48.
3 Robertson, R. A., *SMCJ*, Vol 1, No 5 (1891), p238.
4 Raeburn, H., *SMCJ*, Vol 8, No 48 (1905), pp297–8.
5 Goggs, F. S., *SMCJ*, Vol 15, No 90 (1920), p316.
6 Williams, G. C., *SMCJ*, Vol 20, No 120 (1935), p396.
7 Murray, W. H., *SMCJ*, Vol 28, No 155 (1964) p2.
8 Raeburn, H., *Mountaineering Art* (Unwin, 1920), p160.
9 Murray, W. H., *SMCJ*, Vol 30, No 166 (1975), p321.
10 *SMCJ*, Vol 25, No 145 (1954), p240.
11 Patey, T. W., *One Man's Mountains* (Gollancz, 1971), p40.

12 Patey, T. W., *ibid*, p86.
13 Patey, T. W., *ibid*, p35.
14 Marshall, J. R., in personal correspondence (1988).
15 Bathgate, D., *SMCJ*, Vol 28, No 156 (1965), p110.
16 Cunningham, J. & March, W., *Alpine Journal* (1972), p79.
17 *SMCJ*, Vol 30, No 164 (1973), p186.

CHAPTER 11

1 Smith, R., *SMCJ*, Vol 28, No 155 (1964), pp29–30.
2 *Mountain*, No 94, Dec/Jan 1983–4, pp46–7.
3 Inglis-Clark, W., *SMCJ*, Vol 5, No 26 (1898), p50.
4 Raeburn, H., *SMCJ*, Vol 8, No 48 (1905), p291.
5 Raeburn, H., *SMCJ*, Vol 6, No 36 (1901), p252.

CHAPTER 12

1 Given, J., 'Peter and the Icicle', *Mountain* No 71 (1980), pp22–3.

CHAPTER 13

1 Winthrop-Young, G., *Mountain Craft* (Methuen, 1920).
2 Marshall, J. R., *SMCJ*, Vol 27, No 152 (1961).

CHAPTER 14

1 From Simpson, M., *'Skisters'. The Story of Scottish Skiing* (Landmark Press, 1982), p30.
2 Naismith, W., *SMCJ*, Vol 2, No 2 (1892).
3 Raeburn, H., *SMCJ*, Vol 8, No 48 (1905).
4 From Simpson, M. *ibid*, p30.

CHAPTER 15

1 Burrows-Smith, M., *SMCJ*, Vol 33, No 177 (1986), p301.
2 Burrows-Smith, M., 'Cruising the Corries' *Climber* (February 1988).
3 Watson, A., *SMCJ*, Vol 32, No 174 (1983), p388.
4 Grieve, D., *SMCJ*, Vol 31, No 169 (1978), pp227–36.
5 Firsoff, V. A., *On Ski in the Cairngorms* (W. & R. Chambers, 1965), p85.

IV

WINTER WEATHER ON A MOUNTAIN-TOP

The Cairn Gorm Data *by Jim Barton*

THE SUMMIT WEATHER STATION

Conventional weather stations cannot work reliably in the severe icing and strong winds of a mountain winter. The station on Cairn Gorm summit was purpose-built by Heriot-Watt University Physics Department in 1977 as a research project to aid mountain forecasting and climate study. Its design is a radical departure from normal because the instruments remain sealed in a heated enclosure for most of the time and are exposed automatically for a three-minute period every half hour. Power to heat and run the station is supplied from mains electricity in the mountain-rescue radio relay hut on which the station is mounted.

The instruments measure air temperature, wind mean (a 2½-minute average) and maximum gust (over 3 seconds) and wind direction. These observations may seem rather limited, but we can infer useful information on air-mass type, passage of fronts, gustiness and local wind-speed effects. Other variables such as rainfall or snowfall are difficult to measure reliably in a windy environment, and require continuously exposed instruments. The readings are broadcast by radio telemetry and received by the Meteorological Office in Aviemore, the Chairlift Company at the ski area, and by Heriot-Watt University in Edinburgh. The station regularly runs for six weeks without attention, and overall reliability has been better than 90 per cent in recent winters.

PRESENTATION OF THE STATISTICS

Presented here are tabulated statistics for the winter months, November to March, beginning in 1978–9. It must be appreciated that the observations are specific to Cairn Gorm summit (1,245m/ 4,084ft) and that some of the details will not apply to other mountain areas. Nevertheless, the year-to-year values may be used to build up a picture of the Scottish mountain climate based on a series of objective readings of wind and temperature.

A full winter represents a sequence of over 7,000 observations (48 per day for 5 months), which must be reduced to a manageable size for further discussion. The temperature statistics listed in Table 1 and plotted in Fig 74 are the extremes (lowest and highest), the lowest and highest daily averages and the mean value taken over the whole winter, November to March. The wind statistics are given in Fig 75 and Fig 77, this time as an overall mean followed by the highest values averaged over times from one month to the three-second gust.

TEMPERATURE

Winter mean temperatures are consistently below freezing, the average from 1978–9 to 1987–8 being −2.8°C (27°F) and the individual winters covering a range from −1.8 to −3.9°C. A value for 1983–4 is not given as there was insufficient data for a representative average that winter. For comparison, the same five-month winter average for the Ben Nevis summit temperature during 1884–1903 was −3.8°C (25.1°F).

Every winter, at least some time in the five months, temperatures have risen well above freezing, at least to +6°C (43°F) and in some cases to above +10°C (50°F). This is a consequence of

Fig 74 CAIRN GORM SUMMIT: WINTER TEMPERATURES (°C/°F)

Winter	Lowest Minimum	Coldest Day	Winter Mean	Warmest Day	Highest Maximum
1978–9	−15.3 (4.4)	−13.9 (6.9)	−3.5 (25.7)	+6.5 (43.7)	+10.8 (51.4)
1979–80	−11.4 (11.4)	−10.1 (13.8)	−3.5 (25.7)	+6.8 (44.2)	+9.3 (48.7)
1980–1	−11.4 (11.4)	−7.4 (18.6)	−1.9 (28.5)	+8.1 (46.5)	+10.5 (50.9)
1981–2	−12.6 (9.3)	−9.8 (14.3)	−2.2 (28.0)	+5.5 (41.9)	+7.5 (45.5)
1982–3	−11.7 (10.9)	−9.8 (14.3)	−2.3 (27.8)	+3.8 (38.8)	+7.2 (44.9)
1983–4	−9.9 (14.1)	−8.6 (16.5)	—	+6.9 (44.4)	+10.2 (50.3)
1984–5	−12.0 (10.4)	−11.0 (12.2)	−2.9 (26.7)	+4.8 (40.6)	+7.5 (45.5)
1985–6	−12.0 (10.4)	−10.2 (13.6)	−3.9 (24.9)	+4.3 (39.7)	+6.6 (43.8)
1986–7	−16.5 (2.3)	−15.9 (3.3)	−3.6 (25.5)	+3.0 (37.4)	+6.6 (43.8)
1987–8*	−9.6 (14.7)	−8.3 (17.0)	−1.8 (28.7)	+9.7 (49.4)	+12.6 (54.6)

NB No mean is given for 1983–4 as only 30 per cent is available.

* To 6 March 1988

Britain's maritime climate, where warm air-masses can move in from the south-west. Mild westerly weather was a feature of the 1987–8 winter, the warmest in the series so far.

The winter of 1985–6 (27 January to 3 March) was coldest on average, with a spell of thirty-six days below freezing, with extensive snow-cover and good ski-touring conditions at the end of February. By contrast, the very cold spell in January 1987 was short-lived, but a record minimum of −16.5°C (2.3°F) and daily average of −15.9°C (3.3°F) occurred on the 12th, in cold easterly winds bringing in polar continental air. Within a week, temperatures had risen as the weather pattern changed and milder air returned. It is interesting to note that the lowest temperature recorded on Ben Nevis summit, −17.4°C (0°F) in January 1894, occurred in similar easterly winds.

WIND

Wind is the most dramatic feature of the Cairn Gorm climate. The Cairn Gorm wind statistics are given in Figs 75 and 77. The winter average from

Fig 75 CAIRN GORM SUMMIT: WINTER WIND SPEEDS (kmph/mph)

Winter	Winter Mean	Highest Month	Highest Day	Highest 2½ Min	Highest Gust
1978–9	—	—	—	169 (105)	238 (148)
1979–80	50 (31)	56 (35)	93 (58)	142 (88)	177 (110)
1980–1	61 (38)	72 (45)	113 (70)	148 (92)	203 (126)
1981–2	58 (36)	67 (40)	109 (68)	170 (106)	195 (121)
1982–3	63 (39)	88 (55)	135 (84)	201 (125)	227 (141)
1983–4	—	—	—	207 (129)	235 (146)
1984–5	55 (34)	63 (39)	129 (80)	167 (104)	203 (126)
1985–6	55 (34)	66 (41)	125 (78)	185 (115)	275 (171)
1986–7	58 (36)	69 (43)	145 (90)	185 (115)	207 (129)
1987–8*	53 (33)	67 (42)	101 (63)	159 (99)	191 (119)

NB Statistics for 1978–9 and 1983–4 are limited by lack of data.

* To 6 March 1988

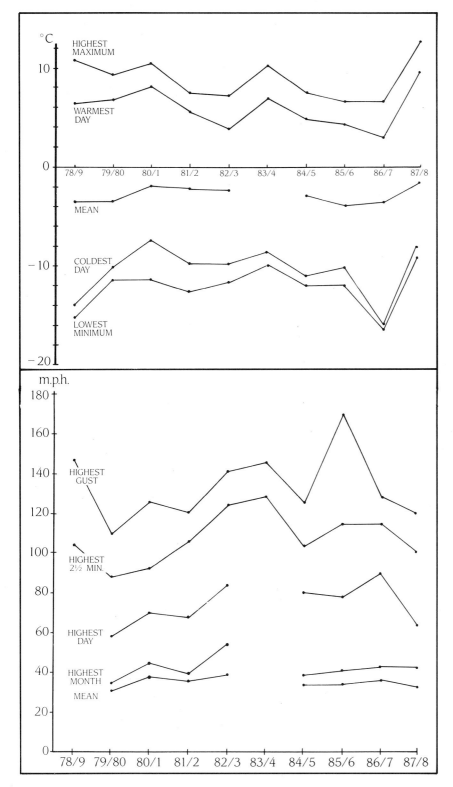

**Fig 76 Cairn Gorm
summit temperatures:
the winters of 1978–9
to 1987–8**

**Fig 77 Cairn Gorm
summit wind speeds:
the winters of 1978–9
to 1987–8**

1979–80 to 1987–8 is 56kmph (35mph), which can be compared with Ben Nevis summit (1895–1904) at 27kmph (17mph), and with an exposed coastal site, Tiree (1970–84), at 33kmph (21mph). The low figure for Ben Nevis is a result of the Ben's summit shape, as the 550m (1,800ft) cliffs of the North-East face tend to deflect winds up and over the summit, except for south-easterlies. The measured wind-speed at the old observatory was therefore diminished by such local topographical effects. Cairn Gorm being a fairly rounded summit does not show this effect. Caution must always be exercised in comparing observations from different places.

Strong winds require a large pressure gradient across the weather map and this usually occurs either in westerlies, with a low to the north-west, or in south-easterlies if pressure is high over Scandinavia and low to the south-west of Britain. The prevalence of winter gales can be emphasised by examining the number of days for which at least one 2½-minute wind observation exceeded 62kmph (39mph) (gale force 8). On average, there are about 100 such days on Cairn Gorm in the 151-day period from November to March. The comparable figure for Tiree is 25 days. The windiest month so far is January 1983 with a remarkable 88kmph (55mph) average in a series of westerly gales. The wind dropped below 40kmph (25mph) (force 6) for only a few hours in the month and gale force occurred on all 31 days. However, February 1983 became much calmer after a stormy start, and an anti-cyclonic spell lasting 11 days followed – crisp winter weather which is such a bonus when it arrives.

Fig 75 includes some spectacular gust values, and the maxima well exceed 161kmph (100mph) every winter. Because the station samples only two 2½-minute periods every hour, the recorded values are clearly not necessarily the true maximum for the hour as would be obtained by a continuously exposed instrument. In general, the gusts are about 25 per cent higher than the corresponding 2½-minute means, but higher gusts occur in turbulent winds.

The highest gust to date of 275kmph (171mph) was observed at 0049 GMT on 20 March 1986, direction 168°, temperature −5.4°C (22.2°F), preceded by a gust of 278kmph (137mph) half an hour earlier.

V

METEOROLOGY

Theory and Terms *by Jim Barton*

To study winter mountain weather, the first requirement is a sound background in general meteorology, which can be put to good use in understanding weather maps, in getting the best out of forecasts and in interpreting our own experience on the hills. This appendix introduces these background ideas and concepts in non-mathematical terms. For further information consult the Bibliography and cultivate the habit of daily weather observation, however casual.

THE ATMOSPHERIC SKIN

On the large scale, the atmosphere is surprisingly thin: compared to the globe, it is about as thick as the skin of an apple. The weather systems that affect us directly are confined to the lowest layer or troposphere in which the air is well stirred up. By contrast, the air in the next layer, the stratosphere, experiences little overall vertical motion. Therefore, the weather activity within the troposphere will be discussed here.

Fig 78 Idealised cross-section through the northern hemisphere

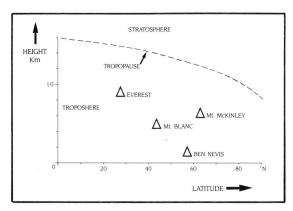

Fig 78 shows an idealised cross-section of the lower atmosphere with the tropopause (the boundary between the troposphere and the stratosphere) at a height of 16km (10 miles) over the equator, decreasing to about 8km (5 miles) over the poles. Some well-known peaks are also shown in terms of latitude and height: all the world's mountains lie within the troposphere.

Weather systems clearly represent energy. Where does this energy originate? The earth's surface receives more energy from sunlight in the equatorial regions than in high latitudes and this imbalance is particularly marked in winter. The atmospheric skin reponds by exporting heat from the tropics towards the arctic regions and weather systems are the result. Given warm air to the south and cold air to the north (a northern hemisphere view-point), a zone of lukewarm air in the middle latitudes might be expected, but in practice the division between air-masses is quite distinct (see Air-masses and Fronts, below).

ISOBARS: DRAWING AIR-PRESSURE MAPS

There is a strong connection between the type of weather and both the barometer reading, ie, air pressure, and its change over a short time (1–3 hours), the pressure tendency. This connection suggests that air pressure may be a useful variable in constructing a weather map, and this is indeed so. Pressure is the weight of air in a vertical column of unit area cross-section above the point of interest. Air pressure is measured in units of millibars. The average sea-level pressure is always around 1,000mb. Variations of a few per cent above or below occur, depending on the thickness of the air above and its density, which is the amount of air in a given volume. Cold air is denser than warm air, so a cold part of the atmosphere will exert a higher pressure at the surface than the same depth of warm air.

Air pressure over a region at any given time can be represented by plotting barometer readings on a map of the area (Fig 79). Then the pattern of air pressure is revealed by drawing lines, known as isobars, which are contours of equal air pressure, just as contour lines on a conventional map reveal the shape of the land surface. This is a simple example of a surface chart, in which the pressure readings are those on a hypothetical sea-level surface. Because air pressure falls with height (see page 305), barometer readings from weather stations are corrected to sea level before being plotted on the chart.

Fig 79 shows a series of closed isobars defining a low-pressure area, a familiar feature on British weather maps. The isobars are drawn at the conventional 4mb interval. If such a low moves across the country, the barometer at any one place would show pressure falling at first, and then rising as the low moves away. The surface chart, or synoptic chart, therefore displays an overall view of the weather at any one instant.

ISOBARS AND WIND

The presence of several isobars implies the existence of a pressure gradient or change of surface pressure over a horizontal distance. Air at higher pressure experiences a net force, tending to move it towards lower pressure. In other words, unequal pressure gives rise to wind, but because of the intervention of a second force (caused by the earth's rotation), winds on the large scale blow not directly from high to low pressure, but along the isobars. In the low of Fig 79, the corresponding winds would circulate anticlockwise around the low centre. One can calculate the wind speed expected from a given pressure gradient. For example, a gradient of 2mb pressure change over 100km (62 miles) distance gives a wind speed of about 48kmph (30mph). This calculated geostrophic wind relates to wind 500m (1,600ft) or so above ground level in freely moving air away from obstructions near the surface.

This relationship between pressure patterns and winds is very important in interpreting weather maps. Deep lows with large pressure gradients (isobars closely spaced), mean strong winds. Conversely, surface charts with few isobars mean calm weather.

AIR-MASSES AND FRONTS

The contrast between cold polar air and warm tropical air brings in another important idea: that of air-masses. These are regions of air of large horizontal extent, perhaps 2,000km (1,200 miles) or more across, in which the air properties such as temperature and humidity are fairly uniform and characteristic of the source region of the air-mass. For example, continental air-masses are less humid than maritime air-masses that originate over the oceans. Polar continental air is cold and dry, tropical maritime air is warm and moist.

The boundary between two air-masses is known as a front, by analogy with the line of battle between two opposing armies. The frontal zone may be quite sharp in relation to the size of the air-masses – about 100km (60 miles) wide. Looking at the earth as a whole, the cold-to-warm air

Fig 79 Barometer readings at selected sites (marked ○) and corresponding isobars drawn at 4mb intervals

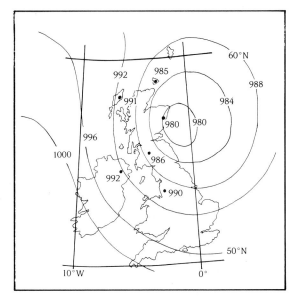

Fig 80 Warm and cold fronts on the weather map

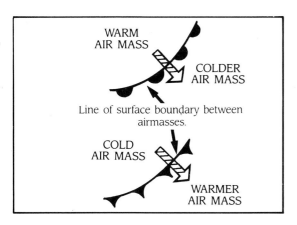

Fig 81 Vertical cross-section (X–X) across warm and cold fronts

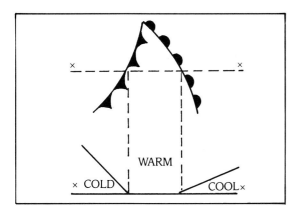

Fig 82 Life cycle of a typical depression:
a) Polar front
b) Wave formation
c) Deepening depression
d) Mature stage occlusion
e) Depression now filling

transition in mid-latitudes is often sharply defined as the polar front, lying roughly east/west across the Atlantic. If a warm air-mass is moving into cold, a warm front results, while a cold front is the boundary of an advancing cold air-mass. Fronts have their own symbols on the surface chart (see Fig 80) and the symbols are always placed on the side towards which the front is advancing.

Vertical cross-sections of warm and cold fronts are shown in Fig 81. In both cases the frontal surface is sloping at a shallow angle in such a way that the cold air undercuts the warm air. Warm frontal surfaces slope at about 1 in 150, cold frontal surfaces are steeper at 1 in 60.

WEATHER SYSTEMS: DEPRESSIONS OR LOWS

Despite the apparently random patterns of isobars and fronts on surface charts for the British Isles, there is a kind of order in the chaos and particular weather systems appear so often that we must pay them due attention.

The frontal depression is one type of low-pressure area. This begins as a small kink or wave on the polar front (Fig 82a), representing a slight northward extension of the warm air-mass into territory previously held by the cold air. The warm-cold temperature contrast means that heat energy is available to allow the frontal wave to grow in size and for the associated low to deepen, as in the sequence of Fig 82. The wedge-shaped area of warm air is the warm sector, lying between warm and cold fronts. As the low deepens, the depression develops, evolving a new type of front known as an occluded front, in which the warm sector is raised clear of the surface. Eventually, the low begins to fill and to lose its identity as a weather system. This life cycle might take four to

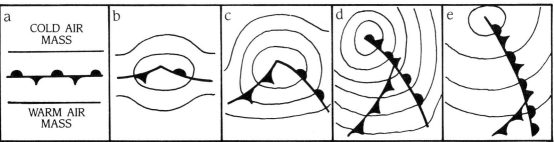

five days, during which the depression could travel several thousand kilometres. Frontal depressions commonly form off the eastern seaboard of the USA, travel eastwards and reach Britain in various stages of their development, which is a major reason for the variable nature of our weather.

It is important to grasp that a low is not simply a large whirlpool of air moving bodily – the speed of the moving low-pressure structure is not the same as the speed of the winds blowing within it. A very slow-moving but deep low could bring stormforce winds. Air moves into a depression circulation and out again at a higher level. The depression is a complicated three-dimensional wave caused by the warm and cold air mixing process on a large scale.

Depressions are far from abstractions of meteorological theory – they bring vigorous weather. Air is moving upwards in the frontal regions and this upward motion leads to cooling and formation of clouds over a large area, usually giving rain or snow as the front passes. Precipitation areas for a typical low are indicated in Fig 83. The air behind the cold front is likely to generate cumulus clouds, with rain or snow showers.

Depressions need not necessarily be formed by the warm and cold front process. In winter, polar lows are non-frontal depressions sometimes forming in the air-stream behind the cold front of a conventional low by heating of the cold air over a relatively warm sea, and give rise to rain or snow showers. Fig 84a shows a polar low west of Scotland.

Another non-frontal feature which can give cloud, rain or snow is the trough of low pressure, as shown in Fig 84b often occurring to the south of a frontal depression.

WEATHER SYSTEMS: ANTICYCLONES OR HIGHS

As their name suggests, high-pressure areas, or anticyclones, are the meteorological opposite of the low (Fig 84c). Fronts are not usually associated with highs nor are they necessary for their formation. Air has a clockwise motion around a high and is generally slowly sinking or subsiding, leading to an overall warming and therefore

Fig 83 Precipitation areas in a mature depression

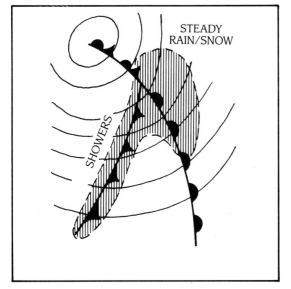

Fig 84 Types of pressure system:
a) A polar low (P) in a cold northerly air-stream
b) A trough of low pressure
c) High pressure or anticyclone over Britain
d) A ridge of high pressure

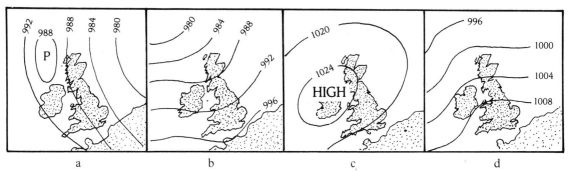

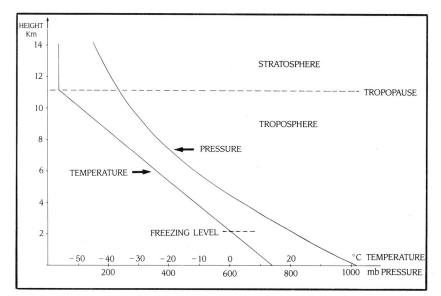

Fig 85 Pressure and temperature in the 'standard atmosphere'

dissipation of cloud. So highs can bring clear skies and sunshine with little wind near their central areas. Complications can arise if fog forms near the ground, a common occurrence in autumn anticyclones. Very large and persistent highs can become established in such a way that the advancing depressions are steered around them away from their normal tracks, a situation known as blocking. Highs tend to be anchored over continental land-masses such as Russia, particularly during winter.

A ridge of high pressure (Fig 84d) is analogous to the trough of low pressure. Ridges are often found between lows, giving a short respite from wet weather until the next front arrives.

THE ATMOSPHERE IN THE VERTICAL

The surface chart shows the atmosphere in the horizontal. Obviously, mountaineers are interested in weather changes in the vertical dimension also.

Pressure falls with height, because if there is less atmosphere above, it exerts less weight. Change of pressure with height is not linear but follows an exponential curve. Fig 85 shows this curve for the 'standard atmosphere' in which the surface pressure is deemed to be 1,013mb and temperature +15°C (59°F). In this example, pressure falls initially at the rate of 8.3m (27ft) per

mb. Pressure at 1,000m (3,280ft) is close to 900mb, just over 10 per cent down on its surface value.

Temperature is the second feature of Fig 85, which shows that it falls linearly with height as far as the tropopause. This is approximately true in practice and is caused by air that is rising, experiencing lower pressure. Equilibrium demands that the air expands, which leads to cooling. Conversely, air that has been caused to sink experiences compression and warming. The rate of fall of temperature with height is called the lapse rate, and is 6.5°C per kilometre in the standard atmosphere, a value close to the average actually observed. It follows from such a lapse rate that there must be some height at which air temperature equals freezing point, 0°C (32°F) ie, the freezing level. In Fig 85 the freezing level is at 2,300m (7,500ft); if sea-level temperatures were 6°C (43°F) then freezing level would be at around 1,000m (3,000ft). This is clearly important in assessing snow level and snow condition.

A further property, known as stability, is also related to temperature and height. A localised parcel of air will cool if it is forced to rise. The lapse rate prevailing in the surrounding air-mass dictates whether or not this air will continue rising, like a balloon, or will sink back down. The first case is an unstable atmosphere, where the parcel remains warmer than the surrounding air, with positive buoyancy tending to keep the air bubbling upwards once it starts rising. The opposite extreme is a stable atmosphere, with air in layers, such that the parcel meets a layer of air warmer than itself and therefore subsides. Stability has a strong influence on the formation and growth of clouds. Extremely stable air often occurs during anticyclones, producing valley temperature inversions, which may reveal themselves as layers of haze, valley fog or a low-level cloud 'sea', above which the hill-tops rise into clear and slightly warmer air.

WATER:
VAPOUR, CLOUDS AND PRECIPITATION

Water vapour is a term that sometimes causes confusion: water in the atmosphere occurs in all three forms as solid, liquid and gas. Water vapour is the latter – a dry, invisible gas, the amount being expressed in millibars as its share in the atmospheric pressure. Fig 86 shows water-vapour pressure at different temperatures. The curve is the maximum pressure allowable, as adding more water vapour causes condensation to take place and liquid water begins to appear in droplet form. At this point, the water vapour is saturated and the curve's value is saturated vapour pressure (SVP). Air containing less water vapour than SVP (eg, point A in Fig 86) would reach SVP if it were cooled (to point B), where condensation would occur. Relative humidity is the actual vapour pressure in the air as a percentage of the SVP at that temperature, so saturation means 100 per cent RH. To take an example, tropical maritime air, warm and humid, at +15°C (59°F) and 80 per cent RH contains 8.5g of water (as vapour) per kilogram of air. If this were cooled to +5°C (41°F), then saturation would be reached: +5°C (41°F) and 100 per cent RH corresponds to 5.4g water, so the excess, 3.1g, would appear in liquid-droplet form as condensation.

Here we have a strong clue to cloud formation: unless the air is completely dry, there must be a condensation level at which SVP is reached and excess water appears either as liquid-cloud droplets or ice crystals. Forecasters can use the RH and lapse rate observations for a given air mass to

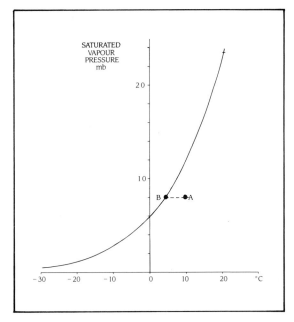

Fig 86 Water vapour pressure at different temperatures. Cooling a sample of vapour from A to B would reduce condenstion

estimate condensation level and hence cloud base.

Cloud droplets are tiny – around $\frac{1}{100}$mm across. Especially in such small volumes, water has the surprising property of remaining liquid well below freezing point. It is not until −40°C (−40°F) is reached that all such supercooled droplets become ice particles. Clouds encountered on Scottish winter mountains are often in the range 0° to −10°C (32–14°F), in which the droplets are supercooled liquid. On impact with any solid object, the droplets freeze and build up an icy crystalline deposit to windward known as rime.

Cloud heights can be classified as low (height of base 0–2,000m/0–6,500ft), medium (2,000–6,000m/6,500–20,000ft) or high (6,000–12,000m/20,000–40,000ft). All of these types are seen in the clouds associated with a frontal depression. Firstly, upper-level cirrus gives warning of the approaching warm front, especially when it thickens and changes to medium-level alto-stratus, through which a 'watery sun' might still shine palely. The widespread lifting of the warm air-mass produces an unbroken sheet of grey

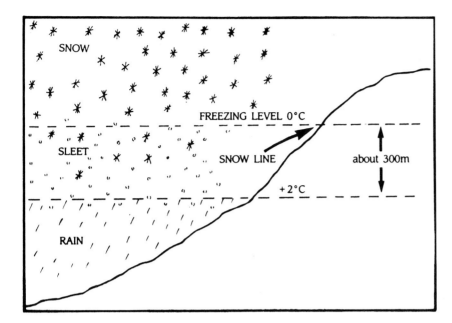

Fig 87 Cross-section of snow falling below freezing level

stratus at low level, with cloud base below the hill-tops. Thinning cloud and a lifting of its base might occur in the warm sector. As the cold front passes, the change in air mass tends to lead to unstable air, which is easily triggered off into large cumulus or shower clouds, giving locally heavy falls of rain, hail or snow with bright intervals between. This classic sequence of clouds, wind and weather associated with a frontal depression is very common in westerly weather, usually taking one to three days to unfold, depending on the speed of movement of the fronts.

Precipitation describes drizzle, rain, hail, sleet and snow. It is not usually seen from shallow clouds, requiring a reasonable depth of cloud in which to grow. In winter over Britain, condensed water in clouds produces snow-flakes above freezing level by the Bergeron process, in which ice crystals grow at the expense of supercooled water.

Once the flakes are large enough, they fall through the cloud and begin to melt as they pass below the freezing level, forming raindrops once the temperature is around 2°C (35°F) (Fig 87). Thus, the familiar sequence of rain, sleet then snow occurs when a hill is climbed on a wet day in winter. Rainfall is enhanced in mountainous areas as the air that has been forced to rise over the hills cools and produces local cloud.

To sum up, the weather map, if it is read properly, is as valuable as the ordinary map. If the right questions are asked the forecaster can be met half way and our own on-the-spot judgement can be used. Weather type, air-mass, fronts, wind, stability, cloud, freezing level – all these elements are linked together and it is always a fascinating exercise to assess what weather awaits us up on the hill.

VI
APPENDIX
Contacts and Addresses

Association of British Mountain Guides (ABMG)
The Secretary, Daneville House, William Street, Penrith, Cumbria
Office/Bureau: 061 274 3264
Training and assessment of qualified mountain Guides – internationally recognised. Private instruction and guiding in winter mountaineering on an individual or group course basis.
Individual guides who regularly run Scottish winter programmes are:

> Geoff Arkless, 3 Marion Terrace, Deiniolen, Gwynedd LL55 3HT
> Alan Kimber, 15 Annat View, Corpach, Fort William, Argyll
> Martin Moran Mountaineering, Park Cottage, Achintee, Strathcarron, Ross-shire
> Paul Moores, Tigh Phuirt, Glencoe, Argyll
> Mick Tighe (Nevis Guides), Bohuntin, Roybridge, Inverness-shire

British Association of Ski Instructors (BASI)
Grampian Road, Aviemore, Inverness-shire
Training and assessment courses for ski instructors in both the Alpine and Nordic skills.

British Mountaineering Council
Crawford House, Precinct Centre, Booth Street East, Manchester M13 9RZ
Unifying body for all climbing clubs in England and Wales. The BMC runs Scottish winter climbing courses based in Glencoe.

Glenmore Lodge – The National Outdoor Training Centre
Nr Aviemore, Inverness-shire
Courses in all aspects of winter mountaineering and ski-touring.

Highland Guides
Inverdruie, Aviemore, Inverness-shire
Courses in Nordic skiing; privately run.

Junior Mountaineering Club of Scotland (JMCS)
Edinburgh section: c/o 134 Golfdrum Street, Dunfermline, Fife
Glasgow section: c/o 9 Ilay Court, Bearsden, Glasgow
Other sections based in Perth, Lochaber and London; traditionally, the club for young novice mountaineers to join as a means of gaining experience and progressing to SMC membership.

Mountaineering Council of Scotland (MCS)
The Secretary, 58 Victoria Park Drive North, Glasgow G14 9NW
Co-ordinating body for all Scottish climbing clubs.

Scottish Mountaineering Club (SMC)
The Secretary, 22 Bonaly Terrace, Edinburgh EH13 0EL
Scotland's senior climbing club; now a century old.

Scottish Mountain Leader Training Board (SMLTB)
1 St Colme Street, Edinburgh EH3 6AA
Administration of Winter Mountain Leadership and Mountaineering Instructor's certificates – training and assessment courses for experienced mountaineers which are run at Glenmore Lodge.

Scottish National Ski Council
18 Ainslie Place, Edinburgh EH3 6AU
National governing body for skiing in Scotland; initial contact for skiing clubs and courses.

INDEXES